Admin911: SMS

ROD **TRENT**

Osborne/**McGraw-Hill**

Berkeley New York St. Louis San Francisco
Auckland Bogotá Hamburg London Madrid
Mexico City Milan Montreal New Delhi Panama City
Paris São Paulo Singapore Sydney
Tokyo Toronto

Osborne/**McGraw-Hill**
2600 Tenth Street
Berkeley, California 94710
U.S.A.

For information on translations or book distributors outside the U.S.A., or to arrange bulk purchase discounts for sales promotions, premiums, or fund-raisers, please contact Osborne/**McGraw-Hill** at the above address.

Admin911: SMS

234567890 DOC DOC 0198765432

ISBN 0-07-213022-9

Publisher
Brandon A. Nordin

Vice President & Associate Publisher
Scott Rogers

Acquisitions Editor
Michael Sprague

Project Editor
Monika Faltiss

Acquisitions Coordinator
Timothy Madrid

Technical Editor
David Baur

Copy Editor
Marcia Baker
Dennis Weaver

Proofreader
Mike McGee

Indexer
Claire Splan

Computer Designer
Elizabeth Jang
Lauren McCarthy

Illustrator
Michael Mueller

Series Design
Gary Corrigan

Cover Design
Joe Heiner
Kathy Heiner

This book was composed with Corel VENTURA™ Publisher.

Acknowledgments

I want to extend a big thanks to the following individuals at Osborne/McGraw-Hill for making this book possible: Project Editor, Monika Faltiss; Acquisitions Coordinator, Timothy Madrid; and Copy Editors, Marcia Baker and Dennis Weaver. But, a special point of gratitude goes to the Acquisitions Editor, Michael Sprague, whose power of perception may, indeed, be beyond that of mortal men. Thanks, Michael!

The Admin911 series would not be possible without the vision, direction, and experience of Kathy Ivens. I hope that more people have the good fortune of working with Kathy. Kathy, I *really* appreciate your insight and knowledge. I have learned more through this experience, than all the nights I have spent watching Steve and Terri Irwin wrestle those 'crocs.'

And, of course, I could never leave out the illustrious technical editor, David Baur. David has the job of kings. You can scribble on my pages anytime.

**I would like to dedicate this book, and all my good fortunes,
to my family: Eric, Rachel, and Alex; but most of all, to my beautiful wife, Megan,
without whom nothing is possible.
To all those die-hard SWYNK fans, I give you this book. Go easy on the emails!!!!**

About the Author

Rod Trent writes technical articles, scripts, and utilities on Microsoft Systems Management Server (SMS) for SWYNK.com (http://www.swynk.com/trent), where he is the managing editor over the SMS section. He is also the managing editor for MyCEDevice.com and MyPocketPC.com. Rod is the author of several books and whitepapers on Systems Management, most notably, Microsoft SMS Installer from McGraw-Hill. He has served in various capacities during his thirteen years in the computing industry and has settled on Systems Management as his area of expertise. Rod writes from the Cincinnati, OH area where he lives with his wife and 3 kids.

Contents

Chapter 1

Primary and Secondary Site Server Installation

The Microsoft Systems Management Server 2.0 server installation is straightforward as long as your system meets the prerequisites. Just insert the SMS 2.0 CD and follow the prompts. You do need to address a few items before installation, however, to avoid problems during the configuration processes. Site configuration is the key part of enabling SMS 2.0 in your organization and your time is best spent concentrating on the configuration, instead of troubleshooting installation issues.

Installation Requirements

The requirements for SMS 2.0 are specific. Missing even one of the required components can cause the installation to fail.

Server Operating System

Depending on the SMS Service Pack you have, you can install SMS 2.0 on Windows NT 4 or Windows 2000.

SMS 2.0 SP 2 (your best choice), installs on Windows 2000 server and takes advantage of Active Directory. This combination is the best option because of the stellar stability and performance level of Windows 2000, as well as the advances in SMS 2.0 SP 2.

CODE BLUE

Even with SP 2 applied, SMS doesn't yet support nesting of multiple *Organization Units* (*OUs*). Windows 2000 allows OUs to be contained within other OUs all the way down through the Active Directory tree. Although SMS 2.0 SP 2 allows interoperability with Windows 2000, it only works within the first and second OUs.

SMS 2.0, up to SP 1, requires Windows NT 4.0 with SP 4a with the Y2K patches. SP 6a for Windows NT 4.0 is recommended, however, because it includes all the fixes for the operating system and all the Y2K patches.

Avoid Windows NT 4.0 SP 5, which has an issue with *Windows Management Instrumentation* (*WMI*) when installing SMS 2.0. The following error message displays:

Setup cannot compile MOF file *drive*:\SMS\Bin*Platform*\Sms_schm.mof. Do you want to continue?

Then, each MOF in succession displays an error message and cannot be compiled. Even though the post-installation message indicates SMS was installed successfully, the SMS site displays a question mark in the SMS Administrator console because the installation actually didn't complete. If you experience this error message, you can recover by following these steps:

1. Retrieve the Wbemdsk.exe file from the SMS SP1 CD and place it into the <SMS_root>\Bin\<platform> directory, overwriting the existing file.
2. Also, place the same retrieved Wbemdsk.exe file into the <SMS_root>\Inboxes\Clicomp.src\Wbem\<platform> directory.
3. Retrieve the Compver.ini file from the SMS SP1 CD and place it into the <SMS_root>\Inboxes\Clicomp.src\Wbem directory.
4. Install the WMI server components from the SMS 2.0 SP 1 CD. Use the following command line: *Wbemdsk.exe /s /server.*
5. Every MOF file that failed to compile must be compiled manually using the Mofcomp.exe utility found in the WINNT\SYSTEM32\Wbem directory. From the \Wbem directory, run the following commands (where *x* is a mapped drive letter to the SMS Site server).
6. Mofcomp x:\<SMS_root>\Bin\<Platform>\sms_schm.mof
7. Mofcomp x:\<SMS_root>\Bin\<Platform>\smsprov.mof
8. Mofcomp x:\<SMS_root>\Bin\<Platform>\cmprov.mof
9. Mofcomp x:\<SMS_root>\Bin\<Platform>\cpprov.mof
10. Mofcomp x:\<SMS_root>\Bin\<Platform>\pollprov.mof
11. Mofcomp x:\<SMS_root>\Bin\<Platform>\netdisc.mof
12. Remove the failed connection in the SMS Administrator console by right-clicking it and choosing delete.
13. Restore the entry in the SMS Administrator console by right-clicking the SMS Server node, pointing to All Tasks, and clicking Connect to Site Database. Finish the wizard after choosing to "Reconnect to the site database for this site server."
14. Restart the computer.

SQL Server

SMS 2.0 requires SQL Server 6.5 with SP 5, or SQL Server 7.0. The recommended setup is SQL Server 7.0 with SP 2. SQL Server 7.0 provides much in the way of performance gains, as well as automated processes to increase the database size dynamically if needed.

If SQL Server is already installed on the server on which you are performing the installation, the SMS installation can create the database and log devices for you. If SQL Server sits on another server across the network, you need to create the database and log devices manually.

If at all possible, you should install SMS and SQL Server on the same server. SMS 2.0 offers a better mechanism for providing real-time data reporting. To provide this, the SMS 2.0 services are in constant contact with the SQL Server database. If the database sits across the network, you are adding the network connection capacity into the performance calculations.

CODE BLUE

Technically, SMS 2.0 requires SQL Server 6.5 with SP 4, not 5, but SP4 is known to cause general protection faults in the SMS system unless you take these special steps to troubleshoot a known problem:

Find sqlcrt60.dll, on the SMS 2.0 CD in the \SQLSetup\SQLhotfix\i386 or \SQLSetup\SQLhotfix\alpha directory. Copy the file to the \Mssql\Binn directory on the server that has SQL Server installed.

Internet Explorer

Microsoft Internet Explorer 4.01 with SP 1 must be installed on the SMS server. SMS 2.0 uses Internet Explorer to perform its help functions.

MDAC

Microsoft Data Access Components (*MDAC*) is a key Microsoft technology that enables *Universal Data Access* (*UDA*). Applications can be deployed over the Web or a LAN using these components, which allow the application to integrate information easily from a variety of sources. The components include *Microsoft ActiveX Data Objects* (*ADO*), *OLE DB*, and *Open Database Connectivity* (*ODBC*). For more information on MDAC, visit: http://www.microsoft.com/data/.

NTFS File System

SMS must be installed on a NTFS partition. *File allocation table* (*FAT*) partitions provide no NT security and have less performance gains for volumes over 1GB. SMS uses the security of NTFS to secure access to SMS directories and shares.

Site Planning

Once SMS 2.0 is installed in a production environment, making changes is difficult to impossible. Therefore, a well-planned installation can help you avoid issues after the site is up and running.

Three-Letter Site Code

The three-letter SMS site code is the identification code for the SMS site. This code is used when the different sites in the SMS hierarchy communicate. The three-letter SMS site code is also used to determine the server that receives the role of senior SMS site. The senior site is based on a specific numbering scheme using numeric and alphanumeric characters:

- **A-Z** The alphanumeric characters are ordered so *A* is the lowest designation while *Z* is the highest. Alphanumeric characters take precedence over numeric characters.
- **0-9** For numeric characters, 0 would be a lower designation than 9.

Using this character scheme, a site code of 999 is the senior site over 000, AAA is the senior site over 999, and ZZZ is the senior site over AAA. When two SMS sites have exactly the same three-letter SMS site code, they would both act as the senior site. When planning the SMS hierarchy keep the site codes, between sites, distinct.

Site Name

The *Site Name* is a descriptive title for the SMS site. When viewing the different sites in the SMS Administrator (Microsoft Management console with the SMS Snap-in), this descriptive name makes it easier to reference the particular site. Some companies use a site name that describes the geographical location or the physical location of the server.

Site Domain

SMS must be installed into a Windows 2000/NT domain. SMS 2.0 doesn't need to sit on a PDC or BDC, as it did in SMS 1.2, but careful planning of the domain is a must. If your SMS hierarchy is going to encompass multiple domains, you must establish the proper domain trusts. The only reason to think about placing SMS on a PDC is to ease the burden of account management and synchronization.

SMS Service Account

The *SMS Service Account* is the account commonly used for communicating with the SMS services, as well as with the other SMS sites. If you choose the defaults during installation, SMS names this account *SMSService*. For better security within your SMS hierarchy, you should modify the default name to fit your organization. Some of the services that use the *SMSService* account are:

- SMS Executive Service
- SMS Site Component Manager
- SMS Site Backup
- SMS SQL Monitor
- Crystal Info Services
- SMS Client Configuration Manager

The SMS Service account password should be a secure password. The SMS service account must be granted Domain Admin rights to the Windows 2000/NT domain and the *Logon as a Service* right in which it's installed.

Number of SMS Clients

During installation, you are asked for the number of clients that will be inventoried by SMS. Calculate this number by including servers, client computers, and network hardware, such as routers and switches. Then add sufficient numbers to cover growth.

If this is a Primary SMS site, this number includes all the clients assigned to the current site, plus all the clients in child sites. SMS uses this number to create the SQL device and the log files.

Number of Administrator Consoles

To complete the creation and configuration of the SQL database, SMS needs to know how many Administrator Consoles are going to connect to this site. SMS gives each Administrator console five connections to the SQL database.

Components

Which components does your site require? You definitely need the client inventory, but does your organization need the License Metering component or the Crystal Info snap-in?

License Metering requires an additional SQL database, and generally needs an additional server for better performance. The *Crystal Info snap-in* is intended for sites with 500 or less clients in inventory because of the performance issues between Crystal Info and an active site.

CODE BLUE

To work around the performance issues surrounding 500-client limitation, you can install a SMS Primary site dedicated to Crystal Reports. The site acts as a repository for the reported information and offloads some of the Site Server processing activity. A site dedicated to Crystal Reports will dramatically improve connection performance because it doesn't need to fight against the other SMS components, such as software distribution and Intersite communication. The additional SMS primary site also serves as a redundant link for the SMS site, allowing a better option for disaster recovery.

Server Configuration

One of the most critical planning components is the consideration of the size and power of the server. Inadequate disk space, RAM, and processor speed and quantity can keep the installation from being successful later. You also need to plan for growth in your organization. In addition, consider the eventuality that SMS problems will arise and, the more hardware available, the less amount of downtime you will experience.

NOTE: It takes a long time to recover from a failed SMS site. Microsoft will soon release a new Online Backup and Recovery Expert Wizard to ease the time and burden of restoring a broken site.

Server RAM

The SMS 2.0 minimum RAM requirement is 64MB, with 128MB recommended. While this may be adequate for small deployments, 256MB or better is a more realistic number. Adding more RAM to the SMS server definitely improves performance. For every 64MB added, you will see an additional 35 percent gain in performance. RAM is an inexpensive upgrade that definitely makes a difference.

CODE BLUE

By default, SQL 7.0 tries to use as much RAM as is installed in the server. When no free RAM is available, the server can lock up. When adding additional RAM, configure SQL so that it uses no more than 70 to 80 percent of the total installed RAM count.

Disk Storage and I/O

The disk storage requirement for SMS is 1GB, but 6GB is a far more realistic number. The SQL Server installation alone (without the database creation) is a little over 250MB.

Both SMS and SQL Server run disk-intensive processes, so a fast storage system is required. Disk storage is the most costly of all the server upgrades, but can provide substantial performance gains if the right hardware *RAID* (*redundant array of independent disks*) system is selected.

NOTE: Software RAID, though a cheaper solution, is not recommended.

By default, SMS creates a 50MB database and a 20MB transaction log. In larger sites, the database requirement can quickly balloon beyond the initial settings. You can use the following formula to determine your database requirements:

7.4MB + ($x \times$ 70K) = database size requirement

(x is the number of inventoried clients in your site)

For example, based on 2000 clients:

7.4MB + (2000 × 70KB) = 147.4MB

If the SMS server also serves as a distribution server for software applications and advertisements, consider increasing the size of the total storage.

For example, a full distribution of MS Office 2000 is over 500MB. SMS receives the package instructions from the application's source, compresses the package at the server, and then decompresses the package on the distribution point. If the SMS server is configured as a distribution point, not only does this 500MB package sit on the server's drives, but so does the compressed version during the package creation. Each package distributed will use three times the size of the package at one point in the process. This 500MB package needs to use at least 1,500MB of storage!

Processor

SMS 2.0 requires at least a 133 MHz processor, while SQL Server requires a 166 MHz processor. When planning the SMS site, including at least a dual-processor system makes sense. Adding more processors to the SMS server gives the computer the capability to process more instructions simultaneously.

As the SMS site is in the planning stage, remember, the number of processors should also relate to the total user count. Sites with over 400 users should consider using a dual-processor system, while sites with several thousand users should consider a quad-processor system.

Growth Considerations

When you are planning the server that houses the SMS site and services, you should plan for growth and also for hardware that remains in place for at least two years. When the next version of SMS becomes available, the server's minimum requirements will change. Putting money into a server that can outlast the next version of SMS can save money later.

The following minimum hardware recommendations are based on the minimum SMS site configuration: one Discovery Data Record per week, one Management Information File per week, one Software Inventory Complete File per week, and five Status Verification Files per week. More stringent configurations require more hardware power.

- Up to 500 inventoried clients: Pentium 166 MHz, single disk drive, 128MB of RAM
- Up to 5,000 inventoried clients: Pentium Pro 200 MHz, three disk drives, 192MB of RAM
- Up to 20,000 inventoried clients: Pentium II 300 MHz, five disk drives in RAID, 256MB of RAM
- Up to 50,000 inventoried clients: Quad Pentium II XEON 450 MHz, eight disk drives in RAID, 512MB of RAM
- Up to 100,000 inventoried clients: Quad Pentium II XEON 450 MHz, twelve disk drives in RAID, 1GB of RAM
- Secondary Site Server: Pentium 166 MHz, one disk drive (concentrate on disk space for storing package distributions), 128MB of RAM

Server Optimization

You may have the best equipment money can buy, but if it isn't properly configured, SMS can be slow and seemingly unresponsive. There are several pieces to server optimization: disk, processor, RAM, and video. Because the product is SMS, you sometimes forget it sits on a Windows NT/2000 operating system. Using specific Windows NT/2000 optimization techniques increases the performance of SMS.

First, make sure no hardware incompatibility issues exist. Check the Windows Hardware Compatibility Guide to see if your particular hardware is listed. A wise practice is to check this guide prior to purchasing equipment for the SMS deployment. The Windows Hardware Compatibility List can be found at http://www.microsoft.com/hcl/default.asp. The list is provided by the Microsoft Windows Hardware Quality Labs (http://www.microsoft.com/hwtest/default.asp). The Web site uses a searchable form, allowing verification on all Windows products and hardware manufacturers.

Disk Optimization

Disk optimization is key to providing optimum performance for SMS. The SMS services retrieve and write client inventory files, create and compress software distributions, perform maintenance routines, record status information, and store information. Following these standard disk guidelines can greatly improve performance for your SMS installation.

- Install each application (SMS, Windows NT/2000, SQL Server) on its own disk or disk array.
- Create the SQL Server log devices and data devices on their own physical disks (if the default installation is selected, SMS gives you the option to do this).
- Bus-mastered SCSI disks, which include a processor chip on the controller, decrease the demand on the CPU.
- To avoid disk channel congestion, only use three to four drives on each channel.
- Choose the proper cluster size for the volume. The volume cluster size is evenly divisible by the average file size (rounded to the nearest kilobyte). This cluster size minimizes disk I/O transaction overhead and wasted disk space. You can determine the average file size by running CHKDSK on the volume, and then divide the total kilobytes of disk use by the number of files. Windows NT tries to configure the cluster size for you, based on the values in Table 1-1.
- Add more RAM. Windows NT/2000 is memory hungry. If there isn't enough RAM to complete operations, the operating system uses disk space.

Volume Size	Default Cluster Size in Kilobytes
0–512	0.5 (512 bytes)
513–1024	1
1025–2048	2
2049 or higher	4

Table 1-1. Windows NT Default Cluster Sizes on NTFS Volumes

- Use some form of hardware RAID (software RAID provides less performance than hardware RAID). RAID is a series of disks configured into one volume, which provides better performance. RAID also provides redundancy and fault tolerance in some implementations.
- Stay away from compressed NTFS volumes. While the compression feature on Windows NT/2000 doesn't tax the system severely, it does cause CPU use to go up from 8 to 10 percent when the files are accessed.

Using Windows Counters to Check the Disk

You can use Windows NT/2000 disk performance counters to determine whether you might run into a problem with a disk.

Windows NT/2000 disk performance counters aren't enabled by default. They must be enabled before you can retrieve specific disk performance information. To enable the disk performance counters, enter **diskperf –y** at a command prompt, and then reboot the system. To turn off the disk performance counters, enter **diskperf –n** at the command prompt, and then reboot the system.

Determining Disk Bottlenecks

Use the following counters to determine whether (and where) you may have disk bottlenecks

- **PhysicalDisk\ % Disk Time and % Idle Time %** *Disk Time* is the percentage of elapsed time the selected disk drive is busy servicing read or write requests. *% Idle Time* reports the percentage of time during the sample interval the disk was idle.
- **PhysicalDisk\ Disk Reads/sec and Disk Writes/sec** *Disk Reads/sec* is the rate of read operations on the disk. *Disk Writes/sec* is the rate of write operations on the disk.

- **PhysicalDisk\ Avg. Disk Queue Length** *Avg. Disk Queue Length* is the average numbers of both read and write requests queued for the selected disk during the sample interval.
- **LogicalDisk\ % Free Space** *%Free Space* is the total free hard disk space available.

Determining Paging File Performance

Use the following counters to check the performance of the paging file:

- **Paging File\%Usage** *Paging File\%Usage* is the amount of the Page File instance in use, given in percentage.
- **Paging File\%Usage Peak** *Paging File\%Usage Peak* is the peak usage of the Page File instance, given in percentage.

TIP: A SQL Server 7.0 utility exists that can place stress on the disk subsystem for testing. You can download it from: ftp://ftp.cyf-kr.edu.pl/pub/mirror/Microsoft/SoftLib/mslfiles/sql70iostress.exe

Network Optimization

When planning a SMS site, remember, the Site Server receives a lot of network requests. These requests come from the client computers, child sites, secondary sites, network components, and so forth. Everything that interacts with the SMS system makes requests of the SMS server. Even if you haven't implemented 100MB connections in your organization, you should consider it for the SMS server.

NICS

Many new server configurations include *network interface cards* (*NICs*) that offer dual ports. They can be configured as a redundant link if one port goes down, or the dual ports can be bound to provide twice the network performance.

For those sites where SMS uses a SQL Server across the network, a fast NIC is recommended. To provide better real-time access to data, SMS 2.0 contacts its SQL Server database about every six seconds. Unless the database is sitting on the same server as SMS (recommended) a considerable amount of constant network traffic occurs between the two computers.

Another instance where a fast NIC is desirable is when you use the SMS site server as a CAP and Logon server. It is recommended these functions be pushed to other servers but, if these functions must reside on the SMS site server, be sure to take into account the additional network requests the server will experience.

Domain Accounts

The installation of SMS creates a number of Windows NT/2000 domain accounts. When these accounts are propagated throughout the Windows NT/2000 domain hierarchy, you can see an increase of network bandwidth. The following accounts are created:

- **SMS Client Network Connection Account** The SMS Client Network Connection Account is created by the SMS installation. One account per site is created.
- **SMS Server Network Connection Account** One SMS Server Network Connection Account is created per site.
- **SMS Remote Service Account** Two accounts are created per *Client Access Point* (*CAP*).
- **SMSCliToknAcct& Account** One SMSCliToknAcct& Account is created per domain, regardless of the number of sites installed within that domain.
- **SMS&_<*Domain_Controller_Name*> Account** One SMS&_<Domain_Controller_Name> Account is created for each domain controller in the enumerated domain.

You can use the calculations in Table 1-2 to determine how many accounts are going to be created.

Account	Calculation
SMS Client Network Connection account	1 *x* <number of sites in domain>
SMS Server Network Connection account	1 *x* <number of sites>
SMS Remote Service account	2 *x* <number of CAPs per site>
SMSCliToknAcct& account	1 *x* <number of domains>
SMS&_<DC_Name> account	1 *x* <number of DCs in the enumerated domain>

Table 1-2. Calculations to Determine How Many Operating System Accounts Are Created During Installation

Bandwidth and Speed

Later on, after the site is set up and configured, you can limit the sender availability and the amount of bandwidth consumed by SMS. SMS uses *senders* (shown in Table 1-3) to distribute the myriad of files that pass through the hierarchy. If your network is connected using different speed lines, consider separating these into sites. Place the faster connections in one site and the slower connected locations in their own sites.

NOTE: You must carefully plan the SMS site hierarchy using the metrics of your *wide area network* (*WAN*)/*local area network* (*LAN*) environment. Secondary sites should be placed across slow WAN links.

Sender	Description
Standard Sender	The default sender that sends to other sites via a LAN or WAN connection.
Asynchronous RAS Sender	Uses *Remote Access Service* (*RAS*) to send to other sites over an asynchronous line. The Windows NT/2000 RAS service must be installed on the site server.
ISDN RAS Sender	Uses RAS to send to other sites over an ISDN line. The Windows NT/2000 RAS service must be installed on the site server.
X25 RAS Sender	Uses RAS to send to other sites over a X.25 line. The Windows NT/2000 RAS service must be installed on the site server.
RAS over SNA Sender	Uses RAS to send to other sites over a SNA link. The Windows NT/2000 RAS service must be installed on the site server.
Courier Sender	Used for copying packages to removal media for distribution to remote sites (the SMS sneaker-net sender).

Table 1-3. Sender Types

Determining Network Bottlenecks

You can use Windows NT/2000 performance counters for determining network bottlenecks.

- **Network Interface\ Bytes Total/sec, Bytes Sent/sec, and Bytes Received/sec** *Bytes Total/sec* is the rate at which bytes are sent and received on the interface, including framing characters. *Bytes Sent/sec* is the rate at which bytes are sent on the interface, including framing characters. *Bytes Received/sec* is the rate at which bytes are received on the interface, including framing characters.
- ***Protocol_layer_object*\ Segments Received/sec, Segments Sent/sec, Frames Sent/sec, and Frames Received/sec** *Segments Received/sec* is the rate at which segments are received, including those received in error. This count includes segments received on currently established connections. *Segments Sent/sec* is the rate at which segments are sent, including those on current connections, but excluding those containing only retransmitted bytes. *Frames Sent/sec* is the rate at which data frames are sent by the computer. This counter only counts the frames (packets) that carry data. *Frames Received/sec* is the rate at which data frames are received by the computer. This counter only counts the frames (packets) that carry data.
- **Server\ Bytes Total/sec, Bytes Received/sec, and Bytes Transmitted (Sent)/sec** Bytes Total/sec, Bytes Received/sec, and Bytes Transmitted/sec provide the number of bytes the server has sent to and received from the network. This value provides an overall indication of how busy the server is.
- **Network Segment\ % Network Utilization** *%Network Utilization* provides the overall bandwidth against the network interface.

Processor Optimization

SQL Server fully uses multiprocessor computers. If you want more processing power for SMS, consider purchasing a server configuration that includes dual or quad processors. Remember, adding more processors to a computer doesn't increase the actual speed of the computer; it only adds more processing capacity. If a system is under a heavy load, such as a large SMS site may be, the computer seems to be able to process faster because it can process more items at once.

Reducing Processor Demands

Installing a bus-mastered SCSI controller can take some processing demand off the CPU(s). The *bus-mastered controller* provides processing power for the hard disk I/O, allowing the

CPU(s) to concentrate on the SMS services and processes. Processor performance is second only to hard disk I/O congestion problems. If the processing power is inadequate and the CPU(s) become overloaded, everything screeches to a crawl.

Always use the computer manufacturer's multiprocessor support drivers. These come in the form of the vendor's *hardware abstraction layer* (*HAL*). This HAL is developed around both the operating system and the specific equipment.

NetWare Considerations

If you have a number of NetWare servers in your organization, you should definitely plan for a multiple processor system. The *Gateway Services for NetWare* (*GSNW*) uses both the network interface (IPX/SPX) and the processor. Microsoft recommends installing the Novell 32-bit client on Microsoft SMS servers when connecting to NetWare server configured as CAPS and Logon Points. The Novell 32-bit client is an intensive client, causing undue stress on the processor. Rather than planning the full migration of your NetWare servers, give the SMS server more power through multiple processors. Note, Microsoft recommends the Novell IntranetWare client version 4.5 or later.

Determining Processor Bottlenecks

You can use Windows NT/2000 performance counters for determining processor bottlenecks.

- **Processor\ Interrupts/sec** *Interrupts/sec* is the average number of hardware interrupts the processor is receiving and servicing in each second. It doesn't include DPCs, which are counted separately. This value is an indirect indicator of the activity of devices that generate interrupts, such as the system clock, the mouse, disk drivers, data communication lines, network interface cards, and other peripheral devices. These devices normally interrupt the processor when they have completed a task or require attention. Normal thread execution is suspended during interrupts. Most system clocks interrupt the processor every ten milliseconds, creating a background of interrupt activity. This counter displays the difference between the values observed in the last two samples, divided by the duration of the sample interval.
- **Processor\ % Processor Time** *% processor time* is the percentage of time the processor is executing a non-Idle thread. This counter was designed as a primary indicator of processor activity. It is calculated by measuring the time the processor spends executing the thread of the Idle process in each sample interval, and subtracting that value from 100 percent. (Each processor has an Idle thread that consumes cycles when no other threads are ready to run.) It can be viewed as the

percentage of the sample interval spent doing useful work. This counter displays the average percentage of busy time observed during the sample interval. %Processor Time is calculated by monitoring the time the service was inactive, and then subtracting that value from 100 percent.

- **Process(*process*)\ % Processor Time** % processor time of the specific process is the percentage of elapsed time all the threads of this process used the processor to execute instructions. An *instruction* is the basic unit of execution in a computer, a *thread* is the object that executes instructions, and a *process* is the object created when a program is run. Code executed to handle some hardware interrupts and trap conditions are included in this count. On multiprocessor machines, the maximum value of the counter is 100 percent times the number of processors.
- **System\ Processor Queue Length** *Processor Queue Length* is the number of threads in the processor queue. A single queue exists for processor time even on computers with multiple processors. Unlike the disk counters, this counter counts ready threads only, not threads that are running. A sustained processor queue of greater than two threads generally indicates processor congestion. This counter displays the last observed value only; it isn't an average.

RAM Optimization

Random access memory (RAM) is the key to improving Windows NT/2000 performance. The more RAM available to the operating system, the better the server performs when processing data. More RAM means Windows NT/2000 can swap information in and out of RAM, instead of increasing the demand on the disk subsystem.

Optimizing the Paging File

To achieve the greatest performance from the installed RAM, you must correctly configure the operating system's page file. The Windows NT/2000 paging file is an area (or multiple areas) of hard disk set aside to receive information from RAM. The paging area is a temporary storage place for queued information that is held until information in RAM is processed and enough space is cleared. When RAM is limited, the system spends almost as much time writing to the page file as it does reading from it. To check the paging file size:

- In Windows 2000, go to the Advanced tab of the System Properties dialog box and click Performance Options.
- In Windows NT 4, go to the Performance tab of the Systems Properties dialog box.

You can modify these parameters for optimum performance (click Change). To improve performance further, the paging file can be placed on a drive separate from the operating system files. You could go as far as to put the paging file on a separate physical drive of its own. Operating system files are constantly being accessed. When the paging file sits on the same drive, the system must process system files and paging files on the same disk. This can cause system performance problems and it can also fragment the drive over time. Putting the paging file on its own physical disk also enables you to delete and re-create the paging file quickly if it becomes fragmented or corrupt.

NOTE: Although placing the paging file on a separate drive gives major performance gains, one caveat exists with this procedure: when the paging file resides on a separate drive from the operating system, the Windows 2000/NT Dump capability is disabled. When Dump is enabled and the computer blue screens (the term blue screen is an industry term that describes a critical computer error that exhibits itself in the form of an actual *blue screen*), the entire contents of information in RAM are saved to a .DMP file in the %WINDIR% directory. This file can be used to troubleshoot the reason for the system crash.

Another excellent optimization tip when configuring the paging file is to set both the minimum and maximum sizes to the same value (use the listed maximum value). Both Windows NT and Windows 2000 dynamically increase the paging file size based on the minimum and maximum values. Setting both of these values to the maximum size turns off the paging file's dynamic size adjustment. The downside to this is the paging file size never changes and the maximum amount of disk space is always used, but this keeps one operating system process out of the mix when attempting to obtain as much performance as possible.

Windows NT/2000 calculates the default maximum page file by taking RAM + 11MB. If disk space isn't an issue, for better performance you should consider increasing the paging file to 150 percent of physical RAM size. This provides a higher ceiling should the paging file experience heavy use.

Determining Memory Bottlenecks

You can use Windows NT/2000 performance counters for determining memory bottlenecks.

- **Memory\ Available Bytes** *Available Bytes* is the amount of physical memory—in bytes—available to processes running on the computer. It is calculated by adding together the space on the Zeroed, Free, and Standby memory lists. *Free memory* is ready for use. *Zeroed memory* is pages of memory filled with zeros to prevent later processes from seeing data used by a previous process. *Standby memory* is memory removed from a process's working set (its physical memory) on route to disk, but still available to be recalled. This counter displays the last observed value only; it isn't an average.

- **Memory\ Pages/sec** *Pages/sec* is the number of pages per second read from or written to disk to resolve hard page faults. (Hard page faults occur when a process requires code or data that isn't in its working set or elsewhere in physical memory, and must be retrieved from disk). This counter was designed as a primary indicator of the kinds of faults that cause system-wide delays. It is the sum of Memory: Pages Input/sec and Memory: Pages Output/sec, and is counted in numbers of pages, so it can be compared to other counts of pages, such as Memory: Page Faults/sec, without conversion. This counter includes pages retrieved to satisfy faults in the file system cache (usually requested by applications) noncached mapped memory files. It displays the difference between the values observed in the last two samples, divided by the duration of the sample interval.
- **Paging File\%Usage** Paging File\%Usage is the amount of the Page File instance in use in percentage.
- **Paging File\%Usage Peak** Paging File\%Usage Peak is the peak usage of the Page File instance in percentage.

Optimizing Video

The *video subsystem* is a frequently overlooked component of server performance. Always use the latest video driver from the manufacturer. The vendor releases updates to fix bugs, improve performance, or add functionality. Even though the driver may support high resolutions, try to keep the video configuration to a minimum. The optimum configuration for the best video performance would be an adequate screen size (800 × 600, 1024 × 768, and so forth) and 256 colors. Setting the video configuration to higher colors can cause additional CPU stress. If you intend to run the SMS Administrator console on the server, the video must be configured for 800 × 600, with 256 colors.

Stay away from CPU intensive screen savers. The best rule to follow for idle server screens is to lock the screen and use the standard Computer Locked screen saver. This provides both security for the server and less stress on the CPU. The openGL screen savers included with Windows NT/2000 take a large amount of CPU time.

A Checklist for Component Configuration

You can use the information in Table 1-4 as a checklist for yourself as you complete the planning for your SMS installation.

	Processor Speed	Processor Capacity (multiple CPUs)	RAM	NIC Speed	Disk Speed	Disk Size
SMS Site Server with SQL Server	✓	✓	✓	✓	✓	✓
SMS Site Server w/out SQL Server	✓	✓	✓	✓		
SMS Child Site Server with SQL Server	✓	✓	✓	✓	✓	✓
SMS Child Site Server w/out SQL Server	✓	✓	✓	✓		
SMS Secondary Site Server				✓	✓	✓
Software Metering Server	✓	✓	✓	✓	✓	✓
SQL Server		✓	✓		✓	✓
Logon Point				✓		
Client Access Point			✓	✓		✓

Table 1-4. Critical Components per SMS Server Type

SMS Specific Performance Tools

You have several tools available to make sure your SMS system performs well.

SMS Console Load Simulation Tool

The *SMS Console Load Simulation Tool* (UILoad.exe) is a utility that can simulate the server load multiple SMS Administrator consoles that would be generated on the SMS site. UILoad.exe is included on the CD of the *Microsoft Systems Management Server 2.0 Resource Guide*. UILoad.exe can run on any computer that has Windows NT 4.0 or Windows 2000, with the WMI service installed. There are versions for both i386 and Alpha processors. Running UILoad.exe displays the screen shown in the following illustration, offering the following input options:

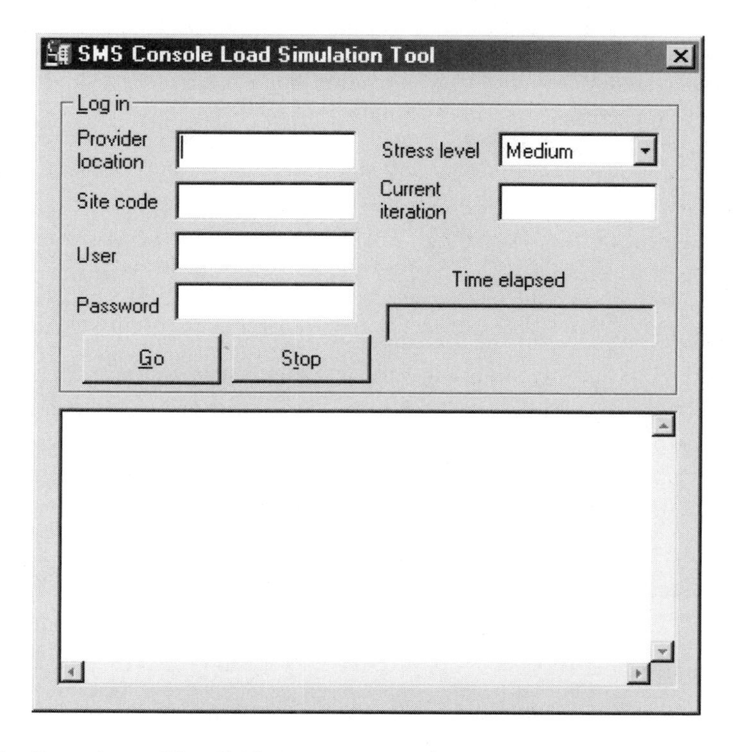

- **Provider Location** The SMS site server machine name.
- **Sitecode** The three-letter site code of the SMS site.
- **User** The login user account name. This account name must have sufficient rights to query the SMS site server. This account needs sufficient WBEM rights, as well as the proper Windows NT permissions. The SMS Service account is a good account to use.
- **Password** The password for the specified user login account name.
- **Stress Level** The Stress Level sets the number of SMS Administrator consoles that will stress the SMS site server, as follows:
  - **Low** Simulates up to ten simultaneous SMS Administrator consoles.
  - **Medium** Simulates 10 to 20 simultaneous SMS Administrator consoles.
  - **High** Simulates 25 to 50 simultaneous SMS Administrator consoles.

When you enter the information and click GO, UILoad.exe connects to the specified SMS server and starts the load simulation. The bottom window scrolls information as the utility progresses.

You can run the test as long as you need to retrieve the load information. The Current Iteration line displays the number of times the simulation has run, and the Time Elapsed line tracks the simulation period.

SMS Object Generator Tool

The *SMS Object Generator Tool* (SMSObgn.exe) is on the CD of the *Microsoft Systems Management Server 2.0 Resource Guide*. SMS 2.0 services process files for every component of the SMS system. These files are referred to as objects of the SMS system. SMSObgen.exe can generate these objects to test the load signature on the current system. This tool is specifically designed to help size hardware and to determine if the current LAN/WAN capacity is capable of providing optimum performance for the SMS system. It's a great tool to use during the SMS pilot process to help plan the SMS infrastructure and to establish capacity standards across the company. As shown in the following illustration, SMSObgn.exe can generate the following objects:

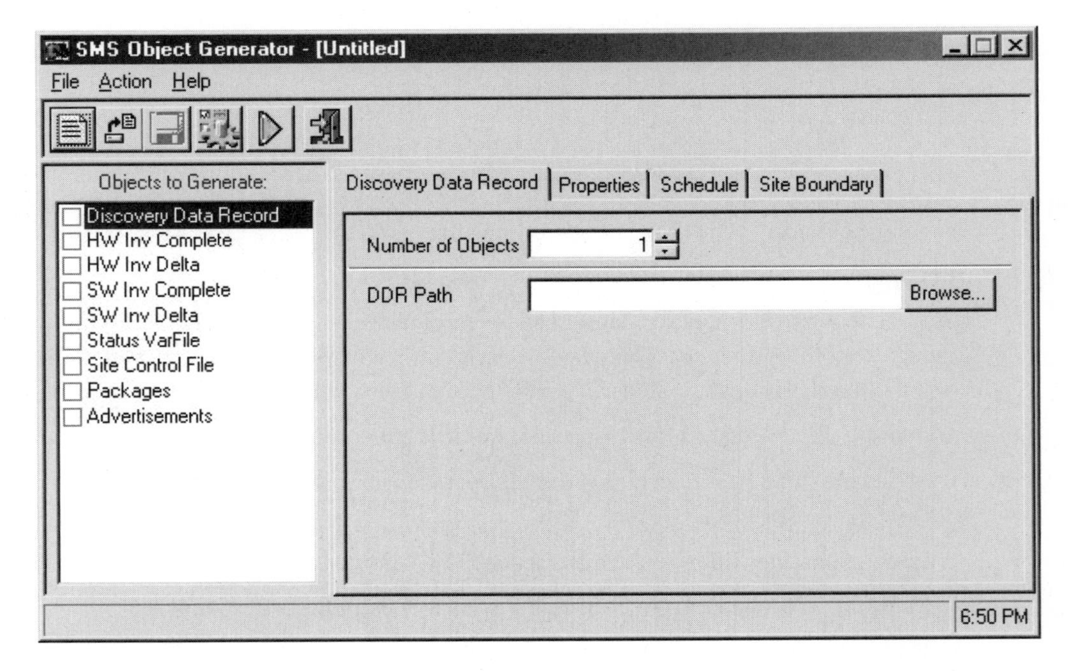

- **Discovery Data Record (DDR)** The file used by the SMS system to report discovery data to the SMS database.

- **Hardware Inventory Complete** The file (.hic extension) created when the hardware inventory agent is completed on the client for the first time. This file contains the full hardware inventory information forwarded to the SMS database.
- **Hardware Inventory Delta** The file (.hid extension) created during any subsequent hardware inventory process on the client. This file represents only the changes in hardware since the last time hardware inventory was run. If any changes are recorded, this file is forwarded to the SMS database.
- **Software Inventory Complete** The file (.sic extension) created when the software inventory agent is completed on the client for the first time. This file contains the full software inventory information forwarded to the SMS database.
- **Software Inventory Delta** The file (.sid extension) created during any subsequent software inventory process on the client. This file represents only the changes in software since the last time software inventory was run. If any changes are recorded, this file is forwarded to the SMS site and merged into the SMS database.
- **Status VarFile** The file (.svf extension) that contains status messages generated by both the server and the client. These status messages display in the SMS status system to notify SMS Administrators of system issues. In large sites, the status system can process thousands of status messages every day.
- **Site Control File** The ASCII text file (.ct2 extension) that holds the SMS site properties and hierarchy information.
- **Packages** Software distribution files recorded in the SMS site for distribution to the client.
- **Advertisements** Based on the recorded packages, advertisements are packages that are publicized to groups or SMS collections.

SMS Specific Performance Monitor Counters

To test the performance of the SMS system further, you can use the Windows NT/2000 Performance Monitor tool. When Performance Monitor is running on the SMS site server, the following SMS-specific PerfMon objects are available:

- **SMS Discovery Data Manager**
    - *DDRs Processed/minute*—The number of Discovery Data Record files that Discovery Data Manager processes in a minute.

- *Total Bad DDRs Processed*—The total number of corrupt or invalid Discovery Data Record files processed during the PerfMon session.
- *Total DDRs Enqueued*—The number of Discovery Data Record files waiting in the Discovery Data Manager queue, minus the total Discovery Data Record files processed.
- *Total DDRs Processed*—The total number of Discovery Data Records processed during the PerfMon session.

- **SMS Executive Thread States**
  - *Running Thread Count*—The number of running threads.
  - *Sleeping Thread Count*—The number of threads waiting for specific conditions in the SMS system to enact them.
  - *Yielding Thread Count*—The number of threads ready to run, but waiting to run because of a limit on concurrent threads.
- **SMS In-Memory Queues**
  - *Total Objects Dequeued*—Total number of objects queued since the PerfMon session started.
  - *Total Objects Enqueued*—Total number of objects completed since the PerfMon session started.
- **SMS Inventory Data Loader**
  - *MIFs Processed/minute*—The number of Management Information Files the Inventory Data Loader has processed since the PerfMon session started.
  - *Total Bad MIFs Processed*—Total number of corrupt or invalid Management Information Files the Inventory Data Loader has processed since the PerfMon session started.
  - *Total MIFs Enqueued*—Total number of Management Information Files waiting in the Inventory Data Loader queue, minus the total MIFs Processed.
  - *Total MIFs Processed*—The total number of Management Information Files processed by the Inventory Data Loader in the current PerfMon session.
- **SMS Software Inventory Processor**
  - *SINVs Processed/minute*—The number of Software Inventory Records processed in the most recent minute.

    - *Total Bad SINVs Processed*—The number of corrupt or invalid Software Inventory Records processed since the PerfMon session started.
    - *Total SINVs Enqueued*—The number of Software Inventory Files in the Software Inventory Processors input queue, minus the total number of Software Inventory Files processed.
    - *Total SINVs Processed*—The total number of Software Inventory Files processed since the PerfMon session started.
- **SMS Standard Sender**
    - *Average Bytes/sec*—The average throughput of the specified SMS sender.
    - *Current Bytes Being Sent*—The current number of bytes being written by all sending threads.
    - *Sending Thread Count*—The number of threads sending to a destination.
    - *Total Bytes Attempted*—The total number of bytes saturating network bandwidth, both successful and failed (retried).
    - *Total Bytes Failed*—The total number of bytes that failed to reach their destination.
    - *Total Bytes Sent*—The total number of bytes sent successfully to a destination.
- **SMS Status Messages**
    - *Corrupt*—The number of damaged status files received by the SMS_STATUS_MANAGER.
    - *Processed/sec*—The number of status messages processed in the last second.
    - *Received*—The number of status messages received.
    - *Replicated at High Priority*—The number of status messages received at the parent site sent with high priority.
    - *Replicated at Low Priority*—The number of status messages received at the parent site sent with low priority.
    - *Replicated at Normal Priority*—The number of status messages received at the parent site sent with normal priority.
    - *Reported To Application Event Log*—The number of status messages reported to the Windows NT Application event log.
    - *Written to SMS Database*—The number of status messages written to the SMS site database.

SQL Server Configuration for SMS

When you install SQL Server on a system other than the server that SMS resides on, you must create the database and transaction logs manually. In doing so, you must also configure the SQL Server for optimum performance to achieve the best interaction with the SMS site. Follow these steps when you create the SQL Server database manually:

1. Create a SQL account SMS can use to access the database.
2. If not completed already, give the *sa* (system administrator) account a password. When SQL Server is installed, the *sa* account's password is blank.
3. Create the Data devices and Transaction Log devices.
4. Tune SQL Server using the settings in Table 1-5.

When you allow SMS to set up the database and logs for you, it uses the following calculations. You should see these same calculations when setting up the SQL Server manually:

- SMS site data device size = Number of clients × 100K (minimum 50MB).
- SMS log device size = 20 percent of the data device size (minimum 10MB).
- Software metering data device size = Number of clients × 200K (minimum 10MB).
- Software metering log device size = 15 percent of the metering data device size (minimum 10MB).
- Tempdb data device = 20 percent as much space as all data devices on the SQL Server.
- Tempdb transaction log = 20 percent as much space as the Tempdb data device.

Secondary Site Server Installation

A *SMS Secondary site server* is a server that houses no SQL database and doesn't need a SQL database onsite. This device is best suited for smaller locations that don't have local SMS expertise available, but still need to inventory client computers and software distributions.

The Secondary site server is used as a point of contact for the client computers of that site. All inventory files are forwarded to the Secondary site server, and then forwarded to the Parent site up the SMS hierarchy, where the SMS database resides. The Secondary site

Parameter	Settings
User Connections	SMS requires at least 40 user connections for each primary site and 2 additional connections per SMS Administrator console that you plan to install at the site. This is the default setting based on the initial SMS installation. For each additional SMS Administrator console beyond five, add five SQL Server connections. If SQL Server supports other applications in addition to SMS, allocate sufficient user connections for the other applications. Each SQL Server connection requires 40K of memory. (NOTE: MMC consoles open no more than 30 SQL Server user connections at one time).
Open Objects	The Open Objects setting specifies the maximum number of database objects (tables, views, and stored procedures) that can be open at one time. Set the value of Open Objects to 1,000 or greater. Set Open Objects in the SQL Enterprise Manager Configuration settings. The default for the SMS installation is 500 open objects. For very large sites, the setting may need to be set above 5,000.
Memory	The optimum Memory option setting depends on how much RAM is installed on the computer running SQL Server and on which other services or applications run on the SQL Server computer. For SMS, set the maximum Memory value to at least 8,192. (The Memory setting is in increments of 2K, so this setting is equal to 16MB.) Set Memory in the SQL Enterprise Manager Configuration settings. Increasing the Memory value affects other processes on the computer running SQL Server. Before you change this option, see the SQL Server product documentation for performance and tuning information.
Locks	Locks should be set to a minimum of 10,000. When a SQL update procedure is performed, locks are used to prevent another user from accessing the same data, which could result in a database corruption.

Table 1-5. SQL Server Settings for SMS 2.0

server also houses software distributions and advertisements, so they are local to the site. This keeps the client computers from having to connect across the WAN to pull down large installations. The Secondary site server provides bandwidth management by giving the client computers a local point for login and retrieval. A Secondary site server should be considered for the following reasons:

- Small site (less than 100 users)
- The network connection (WAN) is slow

- SMS expertise isn't available
- Cost is an issue

NOTE: While the Secondary site server needs disk space to store packages and inventory files, it does have the RAM and processor requirements of a Primary or Parent site.

You can initiate the Secondary site installation in three ways: from the original SMS CD placed in the local CD drive at the Secondary site, over the WAN with the CD inserted into the CD drive at the Secondary site, or from the SMS Administrator console at the Primary site.

TIP: The local CD method is a better choice if the connection between sites is slow (using RAS or a slow network link) or if the installation must be performed during business hours.

You should plan the Secondary site installation for off-hours. You also need to be careful that other processes won't be in use during this time, such as inventory resynchs, schedule hardware and software inventory, large package distributions, and so forth. Making sure the Primary site isn't processing a large amount of data during the Secondary site deployment makes the installation quicker and smoother. Installing the Secondary site server after hours can at least take any stray processes out of the equation if you need to troubleshoot a failed or stalled installation.

CODE BLUE

Before the Secondary site installation is initiated, all extraneous processes should be stopped on the target server. Processes like Antivirus software, backup software, and Compaq Insight Agents should all be stopped before the installation.

Using the Secondary Site Installation Logs

During the Secondary site installation, SMS writes verbose information about the Secondary site installation. Every phase of the installation has an entry in an appropriate log file. SMS records everything, not only success or failure. Use the data in these logs in conjunction with the information in the following section, "Secondary Site Installation Checklist" to troubleshoot a failed Secondary site server deployment. Table 1-6 describes the logs produced on the Primary site server, and Table 1-7 describes the logs produced on the Secondary site server.

Server Component	Description	Log Files at Primary Site Server
SMS Provider	WMI provider that accesses the site database to provide data to the Administrator console.	SMS\Logs\SMSprov.log
Hierarchy Manager	SMS thread component that monitors the site database for site control file change requests, and then updates the site control file.	SMS\Logs\Hman.log
Scheduler	SMS thread component that manages the data transfer between sites on the specified sending schedule.	SMS\Logs\Sched.log
Sender	SMS thread component that manages the connection between sites, ensures the integrity of the transferred data, and recovers from errors.	SMS\Logs\Sender.log
Despooler	SMS thread component that decompresses and processes instruction files from the Sender.	SMS\Logs\Despool.log
Replication Manager	SMS thread component that works with the Sender and Scheduler to distribute (or replicate) objects between sites.	SMS\Logs\Replmgr.log

Table 1-6. Status Message Components and Their Related Log Files on the Primary Site Server During the Secondary Site Server Installation

Server Component	Description	Log Files on Secondary Site Server
SMS_Bootstrap Service	SMS service component used specifically to install other SMS components.	<Installation Drive>\SMS_bootstrap.log
Setup	SMS application used to install or remove the Secondary site.	<System Drive>\SMSsetup.log
Site Component Manager	SMS service component that installs and removes server components.	SMS\Logs\Sitecomp.log
Hierarchy Manager	SMS thread component that monitors the site database for site control file change requests, and then updates the site control file.	SMS\Logs\Hman.log
Replication Manager	SMS thread component that works with the Sender and Scheduler to distribute (or replicate) objects between sites.	SMS\Logs\Replmgr.log
Scheduler	SMS thread component that manages the data transfer between sites on the specified sending schedule.	SMS\Logs\Sched.log
Sender	SMS thread component that manages the connection between sites, ensures the integrity of the transferred data, and recovers from errors.	SMS\Logs\Sender.log

Table 1-7. Status Message Components and Associated Log Files on the Secondary Site Server During Secondary Site Installation

Secondary Site Installation Checklist

This section provides a checklist you can use for installing secondary site servers. The order of tasks is accompanied by checkpoints, which help you troubleshoot the process at each significant milestone. If your Secondary site installation is stalled at one of these checkpoints, use the data in the logs referenced in Tables 1-6 and 1-7 to determine the cause.

TIP: The logs contain a lot of information, so you should print the files to make finding and referencing any error messages easier.

The following functions occur during the installation. Significant checkpoints are noted at the appropriate places.

- Installation is initiated from the SMS Administrator console.
- The SMS Provider updates the site database with the new information in the sites table and site control table.
- Hierarchy Manager queries the sites table.
- Hierarchy Manager verifies network connections and requests the installation.
- Hierarchy Manager creates the minijob that sends the site Setup package to the Secondary site server.
- Hierarchy Manager creates the Bootstrp.ini file.
- Hierarchy Manager compresses the files into a Sitepkg.p* file in the \SMS\Inboxes\Hman.box directory on the Primary site server.

CHECKPOINT: Make sure the compressed Sitepkg.p* file is in the \SMS\Inboxes\Hman.box directory on the Primary site server.

- Hierarchy Manager creates a minijob.
- The *.job files are created in the SMS\Inboxes\Schedule.box\ directory on the site server.

CHECKPOINT: Make sure the *.job files are in the \SMS\Inboxes\Schedule.box\ directory on the Primary site server for the *.job files.

- Scheduler initiates a request to the sender to send the job.
- The *.srq (sender request) files are created in the \SMS\Inboxes\Schedule.box\ directory on the site server.

CHECKPOINT: Make sure the *.srq files are in the \SMS\Inboxes\Schedule.box\ directory on the Primary site server.

- Scheduler sends the *.pck (compressed package) and *.ins (instruction) files to the Secondary site server.

- Scheduler copies the Bootstrp.exe and Bootstrp.ini files to the root of the installation drive of the Secondary site server.
- Scheduler installs the SMS_Bootstrap service on the Secondary site server.

CHECKPOINT: Make sure the *.pck and *.ins files are on the Secondary site server. Look in the root of the installation drive for the Bootstrp.exe and Bootstrp.ini files, and review the Windows NT/2000 services list on the Secondary site server for the SMS_Bootstrap service to be sure the service is both installed and running.

- Bootstrap reads the information in the Bootstrp.ini file.
- Bootstrap locates the source files.
- Bootstrap creates the SMS directory and SMS*.tmp directories on the Secondary site server. This directory structure is used to decompress the *.pkg file.
- Bootstrap creates a Setup.ini file on the Secondary site server based on the contents of the Bootstrp.ini.

CHECKPOINT: Check for the existence of the SMS directory on the Secondary site server, as well as the Setup.ini file. You can also verify the contents of the Setup.ini file with the Bootstrp.ini file.

- Bootstrap starts the Setup on the Secondary Site server.
- Setup installs and starts the Site Component Manager service thread on the Secondary site server.
- The Sitectrl.ct0 file for the Secondary site server is written in the SMS\Inboxes\Sitectrl.box directory.

CHECKPOINT: Look in the \SMS\Inboxes\Sitectrl.box directory on the Secondary site server for the existence of the Site Control file.

- Bootstrap identifies when Setup has finished and deinstalls from the Secondary site.
- Site Component Manager reads the Install.map file for the list of components to be installed on the Secondary site server.
- Site Component Manager installs the SMS Executive service on the Secondary site server.

CHECKPOINT: Verify the SMS Executive service is installed by viewing the Windows NT/2000 services list on the Secondary site server.

- Site Component Manager installs the SMS_SERVER_BOOTSTRAP service on the Secondary site server. During this phase, Site Component Manager registers the *.DLL files on the Secondary site server. The SMS_SERVER_BOOTSTRAP service is installed, started, stopped, and removed several times to allow the *.DLL files to be registered.

CHECKPOINT: Verify the SMS_SERVER_BOOTSTRAP service is installed on the Secondary site server by viewing the Windows NT/2000 services list. You may need to refresh the list during this process, because the service is installed and deinstalled several times.

- Site Component Manager installs the components identified in the Install.map file.
- Site Component Manager creates a *.ct2 file and in the SMS\Inboxes\Hman.box directory on the Secondary site server.

CHECKPOINT: Make sure the *.ct2 file is located in the \SMS\Inboxes\Hman.box directory on the Secondary site server.

- Hierarchy Manager retrieves the *.ct2 file.
- Replication Manager retrieves the *.ct2 file in the form of a *.rpl file located in the SMS\Inboxes\Replmgr.box\Outbound\High directory on the Secondary site server and places it in the SMS\Inboxes\Replmgr.box\Process directory as a *.*<ParentSiteCode>* file.

CHECKPOINT: Check both the \SMS\Inboxes\Replmgr.box\Outbound\High and \SMS\Inboxes\Replmgr.box\Process directories on the Secondary site server for the existence of the *.rpl and *.*<ParentSiteCode>* files.

- Replication Manager moves the *.*<ParentSiteCode>* file from the SMS\Inboxes\Replmgr.box\Process directory and places it into the SMS\Inboxes\Replmgr.box\Ready directory. It then creates a minijob that will send the replicated objects to the Primary site server.

CHECKPOINT: Make sure the *.*<ParentSiteCode>* file exists in the \SMS\Inboxes\Replmgr.box\Ready directory on the Secondary site server.

- Scheduler receives the minijob and creates a compressed instruction file (*.i*).
- Scheduler creates a compressed package file (*.p*). The *.ct2 file is compressed into the package.
- Scheduler creates a *.srq (send request) file in the SMS\Inboxes\Schedule.box\Requests directory on the Secondary site server.

CHECKPOINT: Make sure the *.srq files are in the \SMS\Inboxes\Schedule.box\Requests directory on the Secondary site server.

- Scheduler moves the *.srq, *.i*, and package to the SMS\Inboxes\Outboxes\<*Sender*> directory on the Secondary site server.

CHECKPOINT: Make sure the *.srq, *.i*, and *.pck files are in the \SMS\Inboxes\Outboxes\<*Sender*> directory on the Secondary site server.

- Scheduler moves the instruction file and package to the SMS\Inboxes\Schedule.box\Tosend directory on the Secondary site server.

CHECKPOINT: Make sure the *.ins and *.pkg files are in the \SMS\Inboxes\Schedule.box\Tosend directory on the Secondary site server.

- Sender reads the send request and connects to the \\SMS_<*Servername*> share at the Primary site server.
- Sender retrieves the *.p* files and writes it as a *.pck file at the Primary site server in the SMS\Inboxes\Despoolr.box\Receive directory.

CHECKPOINT: Make sure the *.pck file is in the \SMS\Inboxes\Despoolr.box\Receive directory at the Primary site.

- Offer Manager creates a *.tmp file, and then renames it to a *.ins file.
- Despooler, at the Primary site, retrieves the minijob from the \SMS\Inboxes\Replmgr\Incoming directory.
- Despooler instructs Replication Manager to decompress the files.
- Replication Manager extracts the *.ct2 file from the *.rpl file.

- Replication Manager moves the *.ct2 file into the SMS\Inboxes\Hman.box directory, and then deletes the *.rpl file.

CHECKPOINT: Make sure the *.ct2 file is in the \SMS\Inboxes\Hman.box directory at the Primary site. Also verify the *.rpl file has been deleted.

- Hierarchy Manager processes the *.ct2 file by writing the information to the site database.
- Hierarchy Manager forwards the new site control information to all Parent sites in the SMS hierarchy.

When the Secondary site installation is complete, you should be able to view the information for the new site in the SMS Administrator console from all Primary, Parent, and Child sites in the hierarchy.

Installation Gotchas

Remember these other important considerations when you set up the SMS site. Following these best practices can help avoid pitfalls after SMS is deployed.

Use Multiple Client Connection Accounts

If Account Lockout is enabled in the domain in which SMS installed, you could have a problem with the client connection account being locked out. The client connection account contacts the SMS site for information on packages and advertisements, and to update client hardware and software inventory. The Client Access Account password is stored on all inventoried computers. Computers that haven't contacted the server in a while—either because they have been offline or are mobile computers—have an old, out-of-date Client Access Account password. When they connect to the SMS server the next time, they lock out the client account, which prevents all the organization's computers from contacting the SMS site.

While a quick fix is to avoid changing the Client Access Account password, this solution doesn't provide good security. For example, when an individual who knows the Client Access Account password leaves the company, you must change the password immediately.

A better, more secure solution to this dilemma is to maintain additional client connection accounts. Propagate the multiple connection accounts to all the client computers. When you're ready to change the password, another client account is still active, providing a connection with the SMS site. You can alternate between these accounts to provide uninterrupted connection.

Adequate OS License Plan

During the SMS installation, you could receive error messages indicating the CAP cannot be accessed. This is because of the Windows NT License Manager being configured *Per Server* licensing. You then either need to change the License Manager to *Per Seat* or purchase more licenses for Windows NT.

Naming Conventions

Installing SMS 2.0 into a folder that has a space in its name can cause serious problems. SMS indicates a successful installation, but when you try to open the Administrator console, the following error displays

Cannot find Mfc42u.dll in the existing path

When the SMS server is restarted, reboot fails with the following error

STOP: C000021a {Fatal System Error} The Windows Logon Process Failed to start normally

Computer Time Issues

If the time between the SMS server and the SQL server is out of synch, package distributions can fail, along with other SMS operations. (If SQL Server and SMS reside on the same computer, this issue doesn't arise). SMS itself doesn't provide a mechanism to determine if the time on both servers is in synch, so you need to use an additional tool to keep the time accurate. Note:

- For Windows NT/2000 computers: net time /domain:<*domain name*> /set
- For Windows 9*x* computers: net time /workgroup:<*domain name*> /set

This command should be run on a regular basis, so use it in a network logon script. When SMS is installed into a Windows 2000 Active Directory structure, the computer time issue becomes even more critical. If the Active Directory is out of synch by over five to ten minutes, the Active Directory will fail, causing all functions (including SMS), to stop.

Choose the Right Server Type

If at all possible, install SMS on a member server in the Windows NT/2000 domain. The amount of communication that takes place between *domain controllers* (*DCs*) makes them a poor choice for installing SMS, though this eases the administrative burden of account management and replication. If SMS must be installed on a DC, make sure to "beef-up" the server with plenty of RAM, hard disk space, and a fast and clean network connection.

Secondary Site Server Cautions

If the server you're installing as a Secondary site server has ever been inventoried as an SMS client, remove the client software before initiating the Secondary site installation. In addition, avoid FAT. SMS Secondary sites require a Windows NT/2000 NTFS partition. Never give a Secondary site server the role of CAP. Secondary site servers cannot coexist with the CAP for another SMS site server.

Check Trusts

When installing sites that span domains, be sure the proper Windows NT/2000 Trusts are in place. This includes any site below the Central site (Primary site, Child site, Secondary site).

NetWare Issues

OK, get over it. NetWare still exists in some organizations. If one of these organizations is your company, you need to pay special attention to the NetWare client running on all the SMS servers (as well as the client piece, covered in Chapter 2). With the introduction of SMS 2.0, Microsoft decided to halt development on its NetWare compatible client. If NetWare servers are going to be used in your organization as Client Access Points, Logon Points, and/or Distributions Points, Novell's own 32-bit client is required on any SMS server (Site Server, Parent Server, Secondary Server). The Novell client is available as a free download from Novell's download site: http://www.novell.com/download/.

You should monitor this Web site regularly. Novell releases upgraded clients and revisions at an alarming rate due, primarily, to bug fixes. If you experience any issues after installing the Novell client, check back at the site to see if a fix is available. Microsoft recommends version 4.5 or later.

A great way to keep up on updated patches and fixes is to visit FileWatch at http://www.filewatch.com. This site enables you to customize a profile that includes only the manufacturers and the manufacturer's products in which you are interested. When your tracked products are identified to have fixes and patches released, you can opt to have an e-mail automatically sent to you with the critical information.

Intersite Communication

During the installation of the Secondary site server, SMS creates the SMSServer_*sitecode* account. This account is used for communication between the Primary site server and the Secondary site server. To become the Secondary site server, if the server receiving the SMS components cannot contact the PDC in the master domain, the Secondary site installation will fail. Make sure the connection between the Secondary site and the Primary site is valid before starting the installation. This scenario is easy to back out of, but both frustrating and time-consuming.

Chapter 2

Client Configuration, Installation, and Discovery

The main focus of the SMS product is to provide end-to-end, kitchen-sink management for your organization's computers. By providing a rich feature set, SMS drives down the cost of owning and maintaining computers. Keeping this in mind, you can understand that the primary components of SMS are client driven. SMS attempts to make managing clients by automating the installation of the client agents as easy as possible.

Once the client agents are installed and the computer's information has been reported to the site's SMS database, the computer becomes a SMS client. An *SMS client* is defined as any computer (server/desktop/laptop) with the SMS agents installed, which has been assigned to an SMS site. Being assigned to an SMS site means the computer's data record has been written to the site database and it falls within the SMS Sites Subnet boundary.

While Microsoft has made great strides in automating the client agent installation, some potential problems exist. If you take special care with some key areas, however, you can ensure a successful SMS deployment.

Client Requirements

One consideration sometimes overlooked when preparing for SMS 2.0 is the client-side requirements. The initial load of the SMS agents on the computer can be intensive. If you prepare for this by ensuring that your company's computers meet the requirements and recommendations discussed in this section, you can avoid some of the common problems.

Clients require the following minimums:

- 32MB RAM
- Pentium 90 MHz processor

Each component of the SMS client has its own disk space stipulations, as follows:

- **Hardware Inventory**: 10 percent Free Disk Space
- **Software Inventory**: 3MB of virtual memory; 2MB of free disk space
- **Client Component Files**: 12MB-15MB (depending on the installed components)

The SMS client can be installed on any of the following operating systems:

- Windows 2000 (with SMS 2.0 SP2 applied to both the site and the client)
- Windows NT (Intel)
- Windows NT (Alpha)
- Windows 95/98
- Windows 3.1 and Windows for Workgroups

CODE BLUE

If you use Novell NetWare on your system, you could face serious problems if you don't take some preventative steps. If your system is using NetWare servers as CAPs, Logon Points, or Distribution Servers, you must install the Novell Netware 32-bit client on both the client computers and the SMS Primary server. This is an absolute requirement.

In addition, the Novell implementation of the IP stack is incompatible with the IP stack allowed by SMS. As a result, the only way to gain interoperability between NetWare and SMS is to maintain the IPX network protocol.

Client Installation Methods

SMS provides the following three methods for client installation:

- Logon Client Installation (for Windows Networking, NetWare Bindery Logon, and NetWare NDS Logon Client Installation)
- Windows NT Remote Client Installation
- Manual Installation

Client installation differs from Client Discovery (covered in the next section) in that the installation actually copies files, creates directories, and makes modifications to the computer's registry.

Logon Client Installation

Logon Client Installation uses network logon scripts to install and configure the client components on the computer. This automated method is probably the easiest way to perform a client installation.

SMSLS.BAT is run from the logon script. This batch file does a check for the operating system version and executes the component installation files:

- Slownet.exe, which determines the speed of the network connection.
- SMSBoot1.exe, which launches the client installation program.

When the batch file has completed its processes, SMSBoot1.exe runs the appropriate client installation program, after which the computer must reboot. Several versions of the client installation program exist, each of which is based on the operating system providing the logon mechanism:

- Boot32wn.exe is for 32-bit operating systems logging into a Windows 2000/NT domain.
- Boot32nd.exe is for 32-bit operating systems logging into a NetWare NDS tree.
- Boot32nw.exe is for 32-bit operating systems logging into a NetWare bindery environment.

For troubleshooting purposes, understanding exactly what the SMSLS.BAT does to initialize the client installation can help. If SMSLS.BAT stops or encounters problems, where the file stopped may help you determine why it didn't complete its mission. (Generally, if SMSLS.BAT stops during the batch process, check to see whether the client computer has lost the connection to the network). Reading the contents of the batch file before executing it helps you understand what the commands do (and what they're looking for).

Batch File For Windows Networks

The contents of SMSLS.BAT for Windows Networks (with comments added) are:

- @echo off
- REM Copyright (C) 1994–1999 Microsoft Corporation
- REMW
- REM echo Systems Management Server 2.0

The following lines check the OS type, computer name, and session name. If the OS is unknown or is Windows Terminal Server, SMSLS.BAT exits:

- if %SMS_UNSUPPORTED_OS%. == TRUE. goto END
- if not %WINSTATIONNAME%. == . goto END
- if not %SESSIONNAME%. == . goto END

The following lines check for the existence of Slownet.exe in the client directory and executes it if found:

- :OK_TO_PROCEED
- if %SMS_LOCAL_DIR%. == . goto SLOWNETUSER

- if not exist %SMS_LOCAL_DIR%\MS\SMS\CORE\BIN\SLOWNET.EXE goto SLOWNETUSER
- %SMS_LOCAL_DIR%\MS\SMS\CORE\BIN\SLOWNET.EXE %0
- if errorlevel 1 goto END

The following lines start the SMSBoot1.exe file. If the file isn't found in the standard location, it moves to the USER section: if not exist %SMS_LOCAL_DIR%\MS\SMS\CORE\BIN\SMSBOOT1.EXE goto USER

- %SMS_LOCAL_DIR%\MS\SMS\CORE\BIN\SMSBOOT1.EXE -S %0 -N -WINDIR=%WINDIR%
- goto END

If Slownet.exe was not found in the SMS client directory, SMSLS.BAT determines that Slownet.exe should be in the client's TEMP directory:

- :SLOWNETUSER
- if %SMS_LOCAL_DIR_USER%. == . goto SLOWNETTEMP
- if not exist %SMS_LOCAL_DIR_USER%\MS\SMS\CORE\BIN\SLOWNET.EXE goto SLOWNETTEMP
- %SMS_LOCAL_DIR_USER%\MS\SMS\CORE\BIN\SLOWNET.EXE %0
- if errorlevel 1 goto END

The following lines run SMSBoot1.exe if it wasn't found in the standard location:

- :USER
- if %SMS_LOCAL_DIR_USER%. == . goto SERVER
- if not exist %SMS_LOCAL_DIR_USER%\MS\SMS\CORE\BIN\SMSBOOT1.EXE goto SERVER
- %SMS_LOCAL_DIR_USER%\MS\SMS\CORE\BIN\SMSBOOT1.EXE -S %0 -N -WINDIR=%WINDIR%
- goto END

The following lines run Slownet.exe from the TEMP directory if it was not found in the SMS client directory. If Slownet.exe doesn't exist in the TEMP directory, the search moves to the Slownetserver section:

- :SLOWNETTEMP
- if not exist %TEMP%\SLOWNET.EXE goto SLOWNETSERVER
- %TEMP%\SLOWNET.EXE %0
- if errorlevel 1 goto END

The following lines run SMSBoot1.exe from the server location if it wasn't previously found in the SMS client directory location:

- :SERVER
- %0\..\SMSBOOT1.EXE -S %0 -N -WINDIR=%WINDIR%
- goto END

The following lines run SMSBoot1.exe from the Server:

- :SLOWNETSERVER
- %0\..\SNBOOT.EXE
- if errorlevel 1 goto END
- %0\..\SMSBOOT1.EXE -S %0 -N -WINDIR=%WINDIR%

The batch file ends:

- :END

NOTE: When troubleshooting installations by the SMSLS.BAT file, review the WN_LOGON.LOG file, which is located in the %WINDIR%\MS\SMS\Logs directory on the client computer.

Batch Files for NetWare Logins

The following two batch files are specific to NetWare logins. They use the same logical process as the SMSLS.BAT for Windows Networking, so this book won't include explanatory remarks. Each NetWare client also uses its respective SMSBootx.exe file. For NetWare in

Bindery mode, the file is Smsnw1.exe. For NetWare NDS, the file is Smsnds1.exe. The specific batch files can be found on the SMS server in the SMS\BIN\i386 directory. The SMS batch files can be placed into network login scripts manually or they can be automatically inserted into the current network login scripts by setting that option in the SMS site Properties.

SMSLS.BAT for NetWare Bindery

```
REM Copyright (C) 1994-1999 Microsoft Corporation
REM
REM This file is the Systems Management Server (SMS) logon script
REM include file for NetWare workstations.
REM It installs the SMS client components and collects hardware
REM and software inventory data.
REM Exit script if Windows Terminal Server remote session
IF "%<WINSTATIONNAME>." <> "." THEN GOTO SMS_END
IF "%<SESSIONNAME>." <> "." THEN GOTO SMS_END
NO_REM_TS:
IF "%<SMS_LOCAL_DIR>." = "." THEN GOTO TRY_USER_VAR
#%<SMS_LOCAL_DIR>\MS\SMS\CORE\BIN\SLOWNET.EXE %<SMS_LOGON> 0 /B
IF "%ERROR_LEVEL" = "1" THEN GOTO SMS_END
IF "%ERROR_LEVEL" <> "0" THEN GOTO TRY_USER_VAR
#%<SMS_LOCAL_DIR>\MS\SMS\CORE\BIN\SMSNW1.EXE -D -N -WINDIR=%<WINDIR>
IF "%ERROR_LEVEL" = "0" THEN GOTO SMS_END
TRY_USER_VAR:
IF "%<SMS_LOCAL_DIR_USER>." = "." THEN GOTO TRY_FROM_SERVER
#%<SMS_LOCAL_DIR_USER>\MS\SMS\CORE\BIN\SLOWNET.EXE %<SMS_LOGON> 0 /B
IF "%ERROR_LEVEL" = "1" THEN GOTO SMS_END
IF "%ERROR_LEVEL" <> "0" THEN GOTO TRY_FROM_SERVER
#%<SMS_LOCAL_DIR_USER>\MS\SMS\CORE\BIN\SMSNW1.EXE -D -N
-WINDIR=%<WINDIR>
IF "%ERROR_LEVEL" = "0" THEN GOTO SMS_END
TRY_FROM_SERVER:
#%<SMS_LOGON>\X86.bin\SNBOOT.EXE 0
IF "%ERROR_LEVEL" = "1" THEN GOTO SMS_END
#%<SMS_LOGON>\X86.BIN\SMSNW1.EXE -WINDIR=%<WINDIR>
SMS_END:
```

SMSlsnds.bat for NetWare NDS

```
REM IMPORTANT! DO NOT REMOVE THE LINES: Microsoft Systems Management
Server (start)
REM AND (end) OR ANY LINES BETWEEN THESE
REM ***PRODUCT*** Build ***BUILDNUM***
REM You need 3 backslashes to get the # command to run on W95 with
NetWare's IntraNetWare Client v2.2!
set SMS_LOGON="\***SMSLOGONDIR***"
REM Exit script if Windows Terminal Server remote session
IF "%<WINSTATIONNAME>." <> "." THEN GOTO SMS_END
IF "%<SESSIONNAME>." <> "." THEN GOTO SMS_END
NO_REM_TS:
IF "%OS." == "WINNT." THEN GOTO SMS_32BIT
IF "%<OS>." == "Windows_NT." THEN GOTO SMS_32BIT
IF "%OS." == "WIN95." THEN GOTO SMS_32BIT
IF "%OS." <> "MSDOS." THEN GOTO SMS_32BIT
IF "%OS_VERSION." == "V7.00." THEN GOTO SMS_32BIT
REM WRITE "WARNING: Unsupported client OS. Bootstrap will terminate."
REM WRITE "(SMS 2.0 NDS Logon Points only support WinNT, Win95, Win98
and MsDos v7.00 clients)"
GOTO SMS_END
SMS_32BIT:
IF "%<SMS_LOCAL_DIR>." = "." THEN GOTO TRY_USER_VAR
#%<SMS_LOCAL_DIR>\MS\SMS\CORE\BIN\SLOWNET.EXE %<SMS_LOGON> 0 /B
IF "%ERROR_LEVEL" = "1" THEN GOTO SMS_END
IF "%ERROR_LEVEL" <> "0" THEN GOTO TRY_USER_VAR
#%<SMS_LOCAL_DIR>\MS\SMS\CORE\BIN\SMSNDS1.EXE -D -N -WINDIR=%<WINDIR>
IF "%ERROR_LEVEL" = "0" THEN GOTO SMS_END
TRY_USER_VAR:
IF "%<SMS_LOCAL_DIR_USER>." = "." THEN GOTO TRY_FROM_SERVER
#%<SMS_LOCAL_DIR_USER>\MS\SMS\CORE\BIN\SLOWNET.EXE %<SMS_LOGON> 0 /B
IF "%ERROR_LEVEL" = "1" THEN GOTO SMS_END
IF "%ERROR_LEVEL" <> "0" THEN GOTO TRY_FROM_SERVER
#%<SMS_LOCAL_DIR_USER>\MS\SMS\CORE\BIN\SMSNDS1.EXE -D -N
-WINDIR=%<WINDIR>
```

```
IF "%ERROR_LEVEL" = "0" THEN GOTO SMS_END
TRY_FROM_SERVER:
#%<SMS_LOGON>\X86.bin\SNBOOT.EXE 0
IF "%ERROR_LEVEL" = "1" THEN GOTO SMS_END
IF "%ERROR_LEVEL" <> "0" THEN GOTO TRY_9XCSNW_FROM_SERVER
#%<SMS_LOGON>\X86.BIN\SMSNDS1.EXE -WINDIR=%<WINDIR>
IF "%ERROR_LEVEL" = "0" THEN GOTO SMS_END
REM Special case for Win9x running with the CSNW redirector.
TRY_9XCSNW_FROM_SERVER:
set SMS_LOGON="\***9XCSNWLOGONDIR***"
#%<SMS_LOGON>\X86.bin\SNBOOT.EXE 0
IF "%ERROR_LEVEL" = "1" THEN GOTO SMS_END
#%<SMS_LOGON>\X86.BIN\SMSNDS1.EXE -WINDIR=%<WINDIR>
IF "%ERROR_LEVEL" = "0" THEN GOTO SMS_END
SMS_END:
```

Windows 2000/NT Remote Client Installation

The Windows Remote Client Installation method is a "headless" installation. The SMS site identifies the Windows 2000/NT client computers, sends a bootstrap to the computer, and installs the client through a Windows 2000/NT service. Although this method of installation works well for all Windows 2000/NT clients, you'll find it particularly useful for Windows 2000/NT servers.

The target computer doesn't need to have a user logged on to install SMS client. As long as the computer's IP address falls within the subnet boundaries configured in the site's properties, the computer is discovered and the client is installed.

This is an excellent way to install Remote Control on servers so you can directly manage the server's screens from a window on your computer for troubleshooting and diagnosis.

Remember, the SMS Service account must have Administrator privileges on the target computer when you use the Remote Client Installation method.

(For more on the Windows NT Remote Client Installation method, see the Windows Remote Client Installation Checklist in this chapter).

Ccmbtlder.exe starts the client installation process for Windows NT Remote Client Installation. The computer doesn't need a reboot at completion. (Ccmbtlder.exe is for 32-bit computers only).

Excluding Computers from Remote Client Installation

While the Windows Remote Client Installation method is useful for distributing the SMS client to Windows 2000/NT computers, you should exclude some computers from this installation type (for example, a computer that doesn't meet the requirements outlined in Microsoft's Hardware Compatibility List or a computer that doesn't have an adequate amount of RAM or hard disk space).

You can prevent certain servers and workstations from participating by modifying the registry on the SMS site server:

1. Open a registry editor and navigate to HKEY_LOCAL_MACHINE\Software\Microsoft\SMS\Components.
2. Create a new subkey named sms_discovery_data_manager
3. Add a new data item to this subkey with the following characteristics:

   Data Type: REG_MULTI_SZ

   Value Name: ExcludeServers

   Value: <*computer names to exclude*> (enter each computer name on a separate line; use the Return key to place them on separate lines).

You needn't reboot the server to put these changes into effect.

CODE BLUE

After the system is discovered and is added into the Discovery database, if you remove the computer name from the ExcludeServer list, the SMS client software won't install. You must use one of the following methods to install the SMS client software:

1. Logon Discovery
2. SMSMan.exe

Note that: At this point, SMSMan.exe can be distributed using the software distribution mechanism.

Manual Client Installation

The Manual Client Installation method provides another option for installing the SMS client on target computers. The installation can be run interactively, distributed via a network logon script, or placed on an intranet page.

- **SMSMan.exe** starts the manual client installation process using the **Systems Management Wizard** from the logon point (can be run manually). The computer requires a reboot. SMSMan.exe is for 32-bit computers only.
- **SMSMan16.exe** starts the manual client installation process using the **Systems Management Wizard** from the logon point (can be run manually). The computer requires a reboot. SMSMan16.exe is for 16-bit computers only.

SMSMan.exe

SMSMan.exe is the utility for a manual SMS client component installation for computers with 32-bit operating systems. This utility is located in two places—on the server and on the client workstation (if the core components have been installed).

- **Server location:** \SMSLOGON\<OS platform>\00000409\SMSMAN.EXE
- **Client location:** %WINDIR%\MS\SMS\CORE\BIN\00000409\SMSMAN.EXE

The syntax for SMSMan.exe is: smsman.exe [*installation mode*]. Where *installation mode* is one of the following options:

- /S {*server name*}: Specifies a Windows 2000/NT server installation location.
- /D {*domain name*}: Specifies a Windows 2000/NT domain installation location.
- /B {*\\server\volume*}: Specifies a NetWare Bindery installation location.
- /C {*tree.org.orgunit*}: Specifies a NetWare NDS installation location.
- /A: Automatically selects an installation location.
- /U: Uninstalls all SMS client components.
- /Q: Specifies quiet mode.
- /H or /?: Displays the Help Screen for smsman.exe

If you don't enter a command line switch, the Installation Wizard opens, as shown in the following illustration.

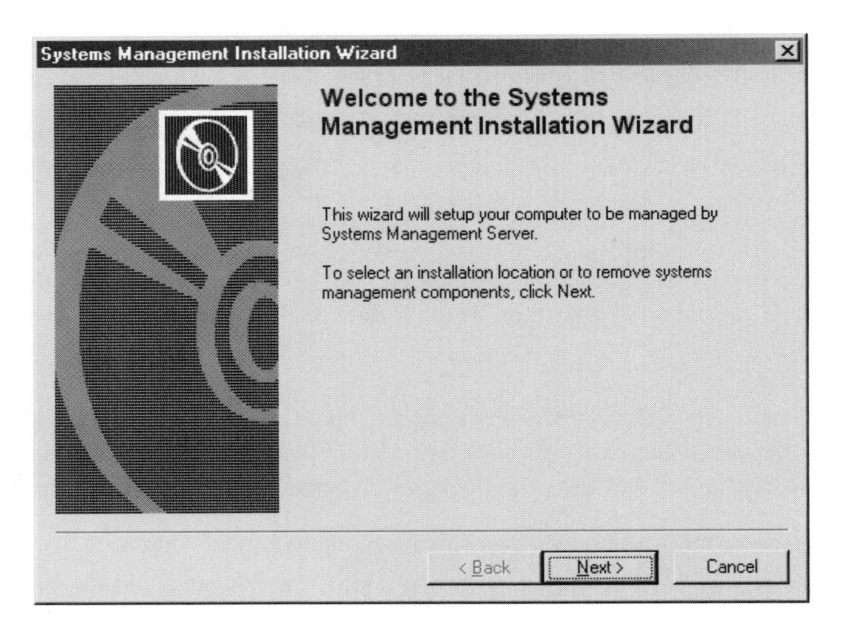

NOTE: SMSman16.exe is run the same way. The differences between SMSman16.exe and SMSman.exe are the operating system they are run on and that SMSman16.exe doesn't support the /A and /D command line switches.

Client Discovery

SMS 2.0 includes Resource Discovery of all objects on your network. Using the discovery method, you can have SMS find all the devices on your network and record the discovered device information into a reporting structure based on subnets.

These records known as *discovery data records* (*DDR*) are forwarded to the SMS site server database. Because SMS is fully customizable, you decide which discovery methods you do and which ones you don't to use with your site.

The decision of which Discovery Method to use at your site depends on how your site is configured. SMS 2.0 provides such a diverse collection of Discovery Methods, it can and will find all the devices on the network. The following Discovery Methods are available:

- Logon Discovery (Windows Networking, NetWare NDS, NetWare Bindery)
- Windows 2000/NT User Account Discovery
- Windows 2000/NT User Group Discovery
- Network Discovery
- Heartbeat Discovery
- SMS Server Discovery

NOTE: If you choose a custom installation of SMS 2.0, only the SMS Server Discovery method enables automatically, and you can choose any additional discovery methods you want to use. If you choose the express setup, all Discovery Methods are enabled except for Network Discovery.

Logon Discovery

As the name suggests, the Logon Discovery method finds clients as they log in to the network. The SMS 2.0 Logon Discovery method supports Windows Networking, NetWare NDS, and NetWare Bindery logon scripts.

NOTE: NetWare discovery is only available if you install NetWare support when you install the SMS 2.0 site.

Logon Discovery is a two-step process:

1. Define Logon Points (Windows 2000/NT Domain Controllers, NetWare Bindery Logon Servers, or a NetWare NDS container and volume.)
2. Logon Scripts modifications.

SMS 2.0 can be set to modify the logon scripts automatically. The script change can be put at the beginning or the end of the logon script. SMS 2.0 includes the files to be included in the logon scripts. SMSLS.BAT for Windows clients can be found in the SMS\Data\NT_logon directory and SMSls.scr for NetWare clients can be found in the SMS\Data\NW_logon directory.

Part of the Logon Discovery is the installation of the SMS client software on the target computer. When the client is discovered, a *discovery data record (DDR)* is forwarded to the site database. In addition, when you have the Logon Discovery method enabled, you can use the SMS Installation Wizard to discover the clients. This procedure allows the discovery of clients who are unaffected by logon scripts and clients for which login scripts are not enabled.

Three files are available with the SMS Installation Wizard to cover the types of clients SMS 2.0 supports:

1. SMSMan.exe (Windows 32-bit clients).
2. SMSMan16.exe (Windows 16-bit clients).
3. Manboot.exe (DOS clients).

These files can be executed on the client in a number of ways: directly on the client, from a network drive, from an intranet page, distributed via e-mail as an executable attachment, or from a floppy disk. The files can be found in the SMSLOGON share at the specified logon points.

The clients must be connected to the network for these files to run because they search for logon points to start the discovery and installation process. A useful feature with SMS 2.0 is that these installations include an uninstall procedure, which can be accessed via the standard Add/Remove Programs icon in the client's Control Panel.

User and Group Discovery

Windows NT User Account Discovery and Windows NT User Group Discovery are similar discovery methods. Incidentally, while NT is embedded in the name of the feature, these discovery methods work for both Windows 2000 and Windows NT.

User Account Discovery

When you enable the Windows NT User Account Discovery method, SMS 2.0 polls the Domain Controllers in the domains you specify, looking for Windows 2000/NT user accounts (domain accounts, not local user accounts). As SMS discovers each user account, a DDR is forwarded to the site server database.

SMS has the capability to discover items using the following methods:

1. Microsoft DHCP.
2. SNMP agents on the client computers.
3. The routers' ARP cache. Note that: The SMS service MUST have Read rights to the ARP cache.
4. User Manager polling.
5. Server Manager polling.
6. Discovery Agents.

NOTE: To become a "client," and before the *Client Configuration Request* (*CCR*) is generated, the discovered device must allow an Anonymous connection and return a supported OS name.

This method enables you to group users by domain to configure your collections. Because SMS 2.0 has the capability to discover the list of items, this method enables you to pare down the information into a manageable group for reporting, queries, and software distribution. You can schedule how often SMS should poll the Domain Controllers for updated information.

CAUTION: If you allow discovery across multiple domains, the SMS service account must have Administrator privileges in the domains you have specified for discovery.

User Group Discovery

As with the User Account Discovery method, the Windows NT User Group Discovery method polls the Domain Controllers you specify, looking for Windows 2000/NT Groups (domain groups, not local resource groups). A DDR for each discovered user group is forwarded to the site server database.

This method enables you to place NT Domain Groups into collections. You can schedule how often SMS should poll the Domain Controllers for updated information.

Network Discovery

The *Network Discovery* method is probably the most useful discovery feature of SMS 2.0 because it discovers system resources on your network such as, but not limited to, computers, routers, hubs, and printers. Not necessarily used for software distribution, this discovery method can help ascertain a large amount of data important to the operation and performance of your organization's network. SMS trace uses the data to provide information about the health of network links between the SMS sites.

CAUTION: The Network Discovery method increases the amount of traffic across the LAN/WAN, so it should be scheduled at a time when network resources aren't being used. It discovers all network devices across subnets, so you should work together with individuals at other sites to determine if this option is acceptable.

Network Discovery isn't enabled by default. Network Discovery is a manual method that must be enabled, and then scheduled to run.

You can specify three levels of Network Discovery. Each level builds on the previous discovery level:

- **Topology**, which uses SNMP to discover only routers and subnets.
- **Topology and the Client**, which uses SNMP, DHCP, and the NT Browser to discover routers, subnets, clients, and other devices, such as printers or gateways.
- **Topology, Client and the Client OS**, which uses SNMP, DHCP, NT Browser, and Windows Networking calls to discover routers, subnets, clients, and other devices listed above, plus the operating systems of the clients.

For the Network Discovery method to work, one of the following must be available:

- Microsoft DHCP (this must be *Microsoft* DHCP).
- SNMP agents installed and enabled on the client computers.
- Router's ARP cache (the SMS Service Account must have Read access to the router).

TAKE COMMAND

The ARP cache on the router can be configured to hold information for a specified period of time. If the SMS site is not receiving Discovery information from the router, you can determine the contents of the ARP cache by using the Windows NT/2000 ARP command: *ARP –a* <IP Address of the router>

Heartbeat Discovery

The *Heartbeat Discovery* method can be described as the "backup" or "CYA" system. Heartbeat Discovery can be set to a determined schedule, to update the SMS site database with refreshed records. The Heartbeat Discovery method is advantageous for detecting those clients not governed by another discovery method. A good example would be client computers (remote users) who seldom log on to their network server and the Logon Discovery method is not turned on.

CAUTION: The Heartbeat Discovery method is only active on computers that already have SMS client software installed.

SMS Server Discovery Method

Adding to the hoard of discovery methods, SMS must also determine and discover the other SMS site systems in a hierarchy. SMS provides two discovery methods to facilitate obtaining this information:

- Windows NT SMS Server Discovery
- NetWare Bindery SMS Server Discovery

The SMS Server Discovery method is the only discovery method you cannot configure or disable. This method is critical to the operation of SMS 2.0. The methods are fully automated by the SMS 2.0 system.

NOTE: Client software is installed on Windows 2000/NT SMS servers, but it isn't installed on NetWare Bindery SMS servers. This is because Windows 2000/NT servers can also serve as SMS clients, can be remote-controlled, and can receive and install software distributions. NetWare Bindery servers don't function this way.

Pre-Staging Client Installations

The SMS RESKIT (on the CD accompanying the SMS 2.0 Resource Guide) includes some helpful utilities for preloading client files on a computer.

The CliStage.ipf and NewUID.ipf (SMS Installer script files) are installed in the \BORK\SMS\CliStage directory. The CliStage.ipf compiles the client files for installation, while the NewUID.ipf verifies a unique SMS ID is not already installed on the target PC. The NewUID.ipf can be used in conjunction with the CliStage.ipf for assurance. Make sure you don't use the NewUID.ipf on a PC being upgraded from SMS 1.2 to 2.0. The old ID will be transferred during the upgrade.

The CliStage.ipf is extremely helpful if you distribute computers by deploying PC images. You can load the client files on the computer before creating the master image. When the PC logs into the network for the first time, the client files are already on the computer. This allows SMS to begin with the DDR, assigning the computer to a site and starting the hardware and software inventory. However, the primary reason for preloading the client files is to save network bandwidth. When a multitude of computers receive the client installation during the same period, the network becomes saturated. This method ensures all the company's computers get the initial installation of the SMS client, and it also saves the network from becoming slow and unresponsive.

For the 32-bit installation, prestaging the client saves roughly 5MB from transmitting across the network. For the 16-bit installation, the amount is a little over 2MB. The installed files are listed in Table 2-1 (32-bit) and Table 2-2 (non-32-bit).

Manual Pre-Staging

To understand any issues that arise with prestaging the client components, it helps to know what the CliStage.ipf does. CliStage.ipf copies only the core components to the client computer.

For 32-bit computers

1. A %WINDIR%\MS\SMS\BIN directory is created on the computer.
2. The following files are copied to the %WINDIR%\MS\SMS\BIN directory: Boot32wn.exe, Slwnt32.exe, Clicore.exe, and Snboot.exe.
3. Slwnt32.exe is renamed to Slownet.exe.

For 16-bit computers

1. A %WINDIR%\MS\SMS\BIN directory is created on the computer.
2. The files are copied to the %WINDIR%\MS\SMS\BIN directory: Boot16wn.exe, Clicor16.exe, and Snboot.exe.

Source	Destination
%smslogon%\%processor%.bin\clicore.exe	%windir%\ms\sms\core\bin\clicore.exe
%smslogon%\%processor%.bin\slwnt32.exe	%windir%\ms\sms\core\bin\slownet.exe
%smslogon%\%processor%.bin\boot32wn.exe	%windir%\ms\sms\core\bin\boot32wn.exe
%smslogon%\%processor%.bin\smsboot1.exe	%windir%\ms\sms\core\bin\smsboot1.exe
%smslogon%\%processor%.bin\00000409\smsman.exe	%windir%\ms\sms\core\bin\00000409\smsman.exe

Table 2-1. 32-Bit Files Source and Destination Locations

Source	Destination
%smslogon%\%processor%.bin\clicor16.exe	%windir%\ms\sms\core\bin\clicor16.exe
%smslogon%\%processor%.bin\slwnt16.exe	%windir%\ms\sms\core\bin\slownet.exe
%smslogon%\%processor%.bin\boot16wn.exe	%windir%\ms\sms\core\bin\boot16wn.exe
%smslogon%\%processor%.bin\smsboot1.exe	%windir%\ms\sms\core\bin\smsboot1.exe
%smslogon%\%processor%.bin\00000409\smsman16.exe	%windir%\ms\sms\core\bin\00000409\smsman16.exe

Table 2-2. Non-32-Bit Files Source and Destination Locations

At this point, all that remains to be done is to have the client run the SMS Installation Wizard. This can be deployed via a company intranet Web page or a link in an e-mail message. When the SMS Installation Wizard runs, it only assigns the client to the SMS site and starts the client components installation specified by the site properties. The Wizard recognizes the core components installed on the computer and it only finishes the installation from that point.

NewUID.ipf for Assurance

If a SMS ID already exists on the computer, NewUID.ipf does the following:

1. Removes the registry value from: HKEY_LOCAL_MACHINE\SOFTWARE\Microsoft\SMS\Client\Configuration\Client Properties\SMS Unique Identifier.
2. Finds and deletes all copies of the **SMSuid.dat** file from the hard drive of the computer.
3. Removes all registry keys from: HKEY_LOCAL_MACHINE\SOFTWARE\Microsoft\NAL\Client\AbExprtDB.

Discovery and Installation Logs

The logs described in this section contain information to help you troubleshoot failed installations. These logs should be used in conjunction with the appropriate checklists (covered in the following section). The following tables (Tables 2-3, 2-4, 2-5, and 2-6) cover the variety of logs you can use.

Thread	Log File
Installation through the SMSLS.BAT file	%WINDIR%\MS\SMS\Logs\WN_logon.log
Manual Installation using the SMSman.exe file	%WINDIR%\MS\SMS\Logs\WN_MANUAL.LOG
Launch32 process	%WINDIR%\MS\SMS\Logs\Launch32.log
SMS Client Service	%WINDIR%\MS\SMS\Logs\Clisvc.log
CCIM32 Client Maintenance	%WINDIR%\MS\SMS\Logs\Ccim32.log
Core Client Installation Process	%WINDIR%\MS\SMS\Logs\Clicore.log
Installing core component	%WINDIR%\MS\SMS\Logs\Ccim32.log
Installing optional components	%WINDIR%\MS\SMS\Logs\Ccim32.log %WINDIR%\MS\SMS\Logs\SMSapm32.log
Individual component installation	%WINDIR%\MS\SMS\Logs\individual logs

Table 2-3. 32-Bit Client Windows NT Logon Discovery and Installation

Thread	Log File
Installation through the SMSLS.BAT file	%WINDIR%\MS\SMS\Logs\WN_logon.log
Remote Installation	%WINDIR%\MS\SMS\Logs\WN_REMOTE.LOG
Launch16 process	%WINDIR%\MS\SMS\Logs\Launch16.log
Core Client Installation Process	%WINDIR%\MS\SMS\Logs\Clicore.log %WINDIR%\MS\SMS\Logs\Install.log
Installing optional components	%WINDIR%\MS\SMS\Logs\Cliex16.log

Table 2-4. 16-Bit Client Windows NT Logon Discovery and Installation

Server Component	Log File
Discovery Data Manager	%WINDIR%SMS\Logs\Ddm.log
Client Configuration Manager	%WINDIR%SMS\Logs\Ccm.log

Table 2-5. Windows NT Remote Client Installation Logs (Server-side)

Client Component	Log File
Core Client Installation Process	%WINDIR%MS\SMS\Logs\Clicore.log
Client Component Installation Manager	%WINDIR%\MS\SMS\Logs\Ccim32.log

Table 2-6. Windows NT Remote Client Installation Logs (Client-side)

Changing Maximum Log File Size on the Client

The default log file setting for the SMS client is 100K. In some cases, this log file size may not provide enough information to diagnose a problem. You can change the file size on the client by modifying the computer's registry: HKEY_LOCAL_MACHINE\Software\Microsoft\SMS\Client\Configuration\Client Properties

- **Value Name:** LogFileSizeforDebugging
- **Data Type:** DWORD
- **Value:** 400 (hexadecimal) for a 1MB maximum log file size

Client logging is an excellent tool for diagnosing client problems. Microsoft included a series of utilities on the SMS 2.0 CD in the \SUPPORT directory. One of these utilities enables you to turn verbose logging on at the client and to set the client logs threshold to 5MB. The client logging, by default, captures a lot of data. Enabling the increased logging can help pinpoint the problem when normal logging fails to capture it.

NOTE: Remember to turn off the additional client logging after you have diagnosed the problem. The amount of information input into the log files is vast, taking up valuable processor time on the client and causing a noticeable performance loss.

These are .reg files, located in the \RESKIT\BIN\<*platform*>\DIAGNOSE directory on the SMS 2.0 CD. The .reg files work well, but they must be run at the workstation. The .reg files included are:

- Turn_On_Nal_Logging.reg
- Turn_Off_Nal_Logging.reg.

These .reg files enable security logging to the client logs so the accounts security can be traced for failure.

You can take the same concept, using the information from the .reg files, and create a script to distribute the verbose logging.

The same idea was taken and incorporated into two SMS Installer files that can be set up as packages and advertised to the client, allowing remote installation and deinstallation. Then, you can remotely connect to the client with SMS Trace and search the log files to pinpoint the problems. The utilities (NALon and NALoff) are available for download from: http://www.admin911.com, or from http://swynk.com/trent/sections/ScriptUtils.asp.

Checklists

Here's your chance to track your plans and your activities as you work with SMS. In this section, a checklist is presented, along with the important checkpoints for the workflow. You can use the checkpoints to troubleshoot problems or to reassure yourself about successes.

32-Bit Client Windows Network Logon Discovery and Installation for New Installations Checklist

The following checklist walks through a brand new 32-bit client installation. It uses the same format as the other workflow checklists in the book. Take special note of the checkpoints in the event an issue arises in the previous area.

- The user logs onto the network.
- SMSLS.BAT is run through the network login script.

TAKE COMMAND

Slownet.exe is the SMS utility that determines the speed of the network from the SMS server to the client computer. By default, the network speed must be over 40 Kbps for the installation to continue, but you can configure Slownet.exe to accept a different speed requirement with the following syntax:
Slownet <*remote path*> [<*required speed*> | *0* for RAS Check only] </v>,
where /v causes Slownet.exe to display the retrieved information in verbose mode.

- SMSLS.BAT runs Snboot.exe from the server.
- Snboot.exe determines the operating system on the client computer.

NOTE: If the client has been prestaged (as described in the previous section), Boot32wn.exe, Slwnt32.exe, Clicore.exe, and Snboot.exe will be present on the computer already. When the SMSLS.BAT finds these files installed on the computer, it skips the portion of the batch file that copies the files from the Logon Point.

- Snboot.exe copies the operating specific Slownet.exe to the client computer.
- Snboot.exe runs Slownet.exe to determine the network speed. If the connection to the Logon Point is less than 40 Kbps or is a RAS connection, SMSLS.BAT is stopped.

NOTE: If the client computer is connecting using Terminal Server, SMSLS.BAT and SMSMan.exe will exit and halt the process.

CHECKPOINT: At this juncture, you can determine that the process has run successfully by finding Slownet.exe on the client computer. If the file exists, but the installation has stopped, SMS has determined the network speed is inadequate. Check that the computer has not lost its network connection. If the network connection is fine, verify the speed of the network link or check for a faulty network card. If this is a RAS connection, Slownet.exe checks for the existence of RASAPI32.DLL in memory and stops the progression of the SMSLS.BAT batch process.

- SMSLS.BAT runs SMSBoot1.exe from the SMS Logon Point.

NOTE: During the running of the specific SMS programs, you can verify they are running on a 32-bit client. For Windows 2000/NT, open Task Manager, click the Processes tab, and find the program's name in the Image Name list. You can verify it isn't hung by looking in the CPU and CPU Time columns for the Image Name and making sure it is getting CPU time. For a Windows 9x computer, use CTRL-ALT-DEL to bring up the Windows 9x version of the Task Manager. The program name is listed in the dialog box. If the program is hung, it displays (not responding) next to the program name.

- SMSBoot1.exe verifies the MS\SMS directory exists on the client computer and, if it is not found SMSBoot1.exe creates it.
- SMSBoot1.exe double-checks the operating system type.

- If Boot32wn.exe has already been copied to the client, SMSBoot1.exe verifies Boot32wn.exe is the correct date, time, and size between the client version and the server version.
- SMSBoot1.exe creates a SMSboot.ini file that contains information for Boot32wn.exe to continue the installation. The information includes the path to the Logon Point and the location of the client installation files on the computer.
- SMSBoot1.exe executes Boot32wn.exe.
- SMSBoot1.exe terminates.

CHECKPOINT: At this part of the installation process, you can verify Boot32wn.exe is running on the computer by using the OS specific Task Manager. SMSBoot1.exe should now be absent from the list. You can also check the computer's hard drive for the existence of the SMSBoot.ini file.

- Boot32wn.exe reads the information from the SMSBoot.ini file.
- Boot32wn.exe deletes the SMSBoot.ini file.

CHECKPOINT: Verify the SMSBoot.ini file has been deleted.

- Boot32wn.exe runs a second copy of Boot32wn.exe, and then terminates, leaving the second copy to continue the installation.
- Boot32wn.exe checks the Copylog.tcf file located in the \\<Servername>\SMSLOGON\Config directory. This file contains information as to the location of the files needed for installation, as well as the specific site from which the files will be installed.

NOTE: The Copylog.tcf file is critical to the clients being installed as part of the SMSLS.BAT or SMSMan.EXE process. The data contained within the Copylog.tcf file points to the appropriate \\<Servername>\SMSLOGON\Sites\<Sitecode> folder to determine the following key pieces of configuration information. See the following numbered list.

1. CLI_INST.CFG—The CLI_INST.CFG file contains all the SMS registry information that must be applied to the client computer.
2. CAPLIST.INI—The CAPLIST.INI file contains the list of CAPs and their respective paths.

3. NETCONF.NCF—The NETCONF.NCF file contains the list of subnets configured for the site.
4. COMPVER.INI—**New in Service Pack 2.** The COMPVER.INI file contains SMS component versioning information that stops SMS from downloading an older version of CliCore.exe to the client computer.

Boot32wn.exe (second copy from here on out) reads the Winnt.tcf or Win95.tcf or file from the \\<Servername>\SMSlogon\Config directory at the Logon Point. The Win*.tcf file contains some site-specific information such as: logon server paths, installation sites, information to be registered to the computer's registry, site options, and so forth.

NOTE: If Boot32wn.exe senses the server is running Terminal Services or the connection is over a Terminal Services link, Boot32wn.exe exits and the installation process halts.

- Boot32wn.exe copies SMSBoot1.exe and Clicore.exe from the \\<Servername>\SMSlogon\x86.bin directory to the MS\SMS\Core\Bin directory on the client computer.

NOTE: If using the Service Pack 2 upgrade in your SMS Site, the following Code Blue outlines the changes to the Boot32wn.exe process.

CODE BLUE

New in SP2 The following portion of the checklist has been inserted to reflect the changes as of the release of SMS 2.0 Service Pack 2. Microsoft has enabled Boot32wn.exe with more processing features to protect the client computer from receiving and installing the wrong version of the components.

- Boot32wn.exe launches and retrieves the Sitecode from the Copylog.tcf file. The Sitecode is listed in the FILE SOURCE section of the Copylog.tcf file and referenced by the X86.BIN\CLICORE.EXE=<Sitecode> line, shown in the following example:

```
[FILE SOURCE]

  x86.bin\smsboot1.exe=ROD
```

```
x86.bin\boot32wn.exe=ROD

X86.BIN\CLICORE.EXE=ROD

x86.bin\00000409\SMSMan.exe=ROD

x86.bin\boot16wn.exe=ROD

x86.bin\00000409\SMSMan16.exe=ROD

x86.bin\CLICOR16.EXE=ROD
```

NOTE: Copylog.tcf can be opened using Notepad to review the information contained therein and is located in the SMSLOGON\CONFIG directory.

- Boot32wn.exe retrieves the client component version information from the Compver.ini file (shown in the next example), located in the SMSLOGON\Sites\Sitecode directory.

```
[COMPONENT VERSION INFORMATION]

Component version=2.00.1493.2009
```

NOTE: The Compver.ini file contains information on the most current client version available for the site. The information contained within the file can be viewed using Notepad.

- Boot32wn.exe compares the Clicore.exe version located in the Logon Point to the version listed in the Compver.ini file.

NOTE: If the Compver.ini file cannot be found, Boot32wn.exe calls either the Cliver.DLL (SP2 specific) or Cliex32.DLL file to verify the version installed on the client against the one located at the Logon Point. Cliver.DLL is new to SP2 and is used exclusively for checking the client versions. It performs a complete file and date check of the CliCore.exe on the client computer.

- If the version of Clicore.exe installed on the client computer is the same version or older, Boot32wn.exe copies SMSBoot1.exe and Clicore.exe from the \\<Servername>\SMSlogon\x86.bin directory to the MS\SMS\Core\Bin directory on the client computer.

NOTE: If the client computer has an earlier version of CliCore.exe installed, but isn't assigned to the site containing the newer components (the site name retrieved from the Copylog.tcf file), then Boot32wn.exe exits.

CHECKPOINT: At this part of the process, you can verify the Temp.tcf file exists in the MS\SMS\Core\Data directory on the client computer.

- If the Temp.tcf file doesn't already exist, Boot32wn.exe creates the SMS Unique Identifier (SMSUID) in the computer's registry: *HKEY_LOCAL_MACHINE\SOFTWARE\Microsoft\SMS\Client\Configuration\Client Properties\SMS Unique Identifier*

CHECKPOINT: Verify the existence of the SMSUID in the computer's registry. If you have locked down the registry as part of the organization's security policies, Boot32wn.exe could have trouble creating the registry key.

- Cliex32.dll reads the Temp.tcf file and retrieves the discovery data properties for the site. Any program that can read ASCII text files can read the Temp.tcf file. Structured like a standard INI file, the Discovery Properties section will look like this example:

```
[DISCOVERY PROPERTIES]
 SMS Unique Identifier=SMSDISCV.DLL,GetSMSDiscoveryProperty
 NetBIOS Name=SMSDISCV.DLL,GetSMSDiscoveryProperty
 IP Addresses=SMSDISCV.DLL,GetSMSDiscoveryProperty
 IP Subnets=SMSDISCV.DLL,GetSMSDiscoveryProperty
 IPX Addresses=SMSDISCV.DLL,GetSMSDiscoveryProperty
 IPX Network Numbers=SMSDISCV.DLL,GetSMSDiscoveryProperty
 MAC Addresses=SMSDISCV.DLL,GetSMSDiscoveryProperty
 Resource Domain OR Workgroup=SMSDISCV.DLL,GetSMSDiscoveryProperty
 Operating System Name and Version=SMSDISCV.DLL,GetSMSDiscoveryProperty
 Last Logon User Name=SMSDISCV.DLL,GetSMSDiscoveryProperty
 Last Logon User Domain=SMSDISCV.DLL,GetSMSDiscoveryProperty
 Client=SMSDISCV.DLL,GetSMSDiscoveryProperty
 SMS Installed Sites=SMSDISCV.DLL,GetSMSDiscoveryProperty
 Client Version=SMSDISCV.DLL,GetSMSDiscoveryProperty
```

- Cliex32.dll collects the discovery data by calling (SMSDISCV.DLL) each line in the Discovery Properties section of the Temp.tcf file.
- Cliex32.dll creates a SMSdisc.ddr file in the MS\SMS\Core\Data directory. The SMSdisc.ddr file contains all the information Cliex32.dll received from calling the SMDISCV.DLL properties in the Temp.tcf file.

CHECKPOINT: Check for the existence of the SMSdisc.ddr file in the MS\SMS\Core\Data directory. If the file doesn't exist, the Temp.tcf file is missing or corrupt, or Cliex32.dll had errors calling SMSDISCV.DLL. In either event, you may need to start the installation process over again.

- Cliex32.dll copies the new DDR to the \\<Servername>\SMSlogon\Ddr.box\ directory. It renames the DDR file <UniqueID>.DDR.

NOTE: If Logon Discovery isn't enabled, the DDR isn't copied to the Logon Point. Also, if the client isn't assigned to a site at this point, the installation process stops. The following steps in the checklist are specific to the client Discovery after the client is installed.

- Boot32wn.exe calls Clicore.exe. Clicore.exe is the installation package that installs the client's core components. Clicore.exe is run with the following command line:

  Clicore.exe /s inst (where /s is for silent mode installation)

CHECKPOINT: To see if the process is still moving, you can look in the %WINDIR%\MS\SMS\CORE directory structure on the client computer. After Clicore.exe has completed installing the files, the following directory structure is created %WINDIR%\MS\SMS\CORE\BIN\00000409.

- Boot32wn.exe reads the information in the CAPlist.ini and Cli_inst.cfg files from the SMSlogon share in the \Sites\<Sitecode> (Sitecode = three-letter site code) directory, and then updates the computer's registry with the list of assigned *client access points* (*CAP*).
- Boot32wn.exe installs the SMS client service.
- Boot32wn.exe starts the SMS client service.
- Boot32wn.exe registers Ccim32.dll with the computer and starts the process.
- Boot32wn.exe terminates.

CHECKPOINT: To verify the SMS client service is installed and started on a Windows NT/2000 computer, open the Services Control Panel applet. On Windows 9*x* computers, bring up the running services dialog box (CTRL-ALT-DEL) and check for the clisvcl.exe file. Boot32wn.exe should be absent from the running tasks list.

- If the locally logged-on user doesn't have Administrator rights on the computer, then Ccim32.dll calls the Cliex32.dll file.
- Cliex32.dll creates a Client Configuration Record (*.ccr) on the CAP.
- On the CAP, Inbox Manager or Inbox Manager Assistant copies the *.ccr file from the CAP to the SMS Site server into the SMS\Inboxes\Ccr.box directory.

CHECKPOINT: Verify the *.ccr file does, indeed, exist in the Ccr.box directory.

- CCM.dll attempts to connect to the \\<ClientName>\Admin$ share. If the connection fails, CCM.dll exits and the installation fails.
- CCM.dll copies and updates the CCMCore.exe and CCMbtlder.exe files on the client computer.
- CCM.dll executes the CCMbtlder.exe file.
- CCMbtlder.exe calls the CCMCore.exe file. CCMCore.exe extracts the Network Abstraction Layer (NAL) files and registers the NAL with the CAP.
- CCMbtldr.exe copies and updates the CliCore.exe and CCMBoot.exe files from the CAP.
- CCMbtldr.exe executes the CCMBoot.exe file.
- CCMBoot.exe installs and starts the SMS Client Service.

CHECKPOINT: On Windows 2000 and Windows NT computers, the SMS Client Service should now appear in the list of services and be running. On Windows 95 and Windows 98, verify the service is running by reviewing the list of running tasks (CTRL-ALT-DEL). The installation and starting of the SMS Client Service is recorded in the CCIM32.log file.

- Ccim32.dll creates the client's SMS Unique ID (if it isn't already present).
- CliCore.exe finishes the process by installing the remaining SMS Core Components.
- Mlaunch.dll installs the following client base application components*: Available Programs Manager (APM)* and Windows Management Instrumentation.

- Ccim32.dll calls Cliex32.dll. Cliex32.dll returns the list of Discovery Data that should be discovered on the client computer.
- Cliex32.dll reads the Temp.tcf file and, again, the discovery data is retrieved.
- Cliex32.dll creates a SMStemp.ddr file in the MS\SMS\Core\Data directory on the client computer.

CHECKPOINT: Check for the SMStemp.ddr file in the MS\SMS\Core\Data directory on the client computer.

- Cliex32.dll verifies each site to which the client is assigned.

NOTE: If the client is assigned to the site, the process continues to the next step in the progression. If the client is NOT assigned to the site, Ccim32.dll removes the specific site from the client computer's site list, and reruns the verify for each site code available to the SMS hierarchy. When Ccim32.dll finds the site the client is assigned to, the next step in the progression is followed.

- Cliex32.dll retrieves the information from the CAPlist.ini file in the SMSlogon\Sites\<Sitecode> directory on the SMS server share.
- Cliex32.dll updates the client's registry with the CAP list information.
- Ccim32.dll checks the heartbeat interval specified in the site server settings.
- Cliex32.dll creates the DDR and sets the heartbeat interval on the client computer. It copies it to the Ddr.box on the CAP with a <unique name>.ddr format.
- If the heartbeat interval has been reached and a DDR needs to be created, Cliex32.dll creates one and copies it to the CAP.

CHECKPOINT: Verify the *.ddr file exists in the Ddr.box on the Windows NT CAP share on the SMS server.

- Ccim32.dll checks for any component advertisements retrieved from Cliex32.dll. The optional component advertisements are specified in the SMS site settings and include Hardware Inventory, Software Inventory, Remote Control, Software Metering, WBEM, NT Event to SNMP Trap Translator, and Software Distribution.

NOTE: Ccim32.dll also verifies the version of the installed components. If the client components are installed and an old version is found, Ccim32.dll submits an upgrade command to APM. If the client components are installed but the versions are current, Ccim32.dll submits a verify command to the APM. If any components are no longer active for the site, Ccim32.dll deinstalls the components. All processing is recorded in the Ccim32.log file on the client computer.

- Ccim32.dll goes to sleep for the default value of 23 hours. If errors have occurred during the installation of the optional components, it sleeps for one hour and starts the process again.

CHECKPOINT: The client installation and discovery process is complete. You should see the core and optional components installed. You can check their status in the Systems Management Properties Control Panel applet.

16-bit Client Windows Network Logon Discovery and Installation for New Installations Checklist

The 16-bit Client Windows Network Logon installation is similar to the 32-bit client installation with a few exceptions. The 16-bit installation uses different files to run the client installation and it also modifies the 16-bit Windows files, such as the WIN.INI file. 16-bit Windows, computers don't have a registry, so the .INI files are used to store information.

NOTE: 16-bit clients boot first to DOS, and then run Windows. The client installation starts after the user logs into the network from a DOS prompt, and continues after 16-bit Windows is initiated. Typing WIN at the DOS prompt or including the command in the computer's Autoexec.bat file normally runs this.

- User logs on to the network.
- SMSLS.BAT is run.
- SMSLS.BAT executes SMSBoot1.exe.
- SMSBoot1.exe verifies the existence of the MS\SMS directory on the client. If it doesn't exist, it is created.
- SMSBoot1.exe verifies the client's operating system.

- SMSBoot1.exe retrieves Boot16wn.exe and copies it to the client computer.
- SMSBoot1.exe writes to the Run section of the computer's WIN.INI file. It inserts the entry: Run=Boot16wn.exe
- SMSBoot1.exe writes the server and client paths to the WIN.INI:
- SMSServerPath = \\<Logonpoint>\SMSlogon
- SMSClientPath = C:\WINDOWS\
- SMSBoot1.exe writes the bootstrap information to the WIN.INI:
- Bootstrap2Parameters = -S <driveletter>:\SMSls –N –WINDIR=
- SMSBoot1.exe terminates

CHECKPOINT: Troubleshooting a 16-bit client installation is limited to verifying the existence of files installed and copied to the computer and modifications to the INI files. At this juncture, look in the WIN.INI file for Run=Boot16wn.exe, SMSServerPath = \\<Logonpoint>\SMSlogon, SMSClientPath = C:\WINDOWS\, and Bootstrap2Parameters = -S <driveletter>:\SMSls –N –WINDIR=. You can also verify the Boot16wn.exe file exists on the computer.

- Boot16wn.exe reads the path to server information in the WIN.INI file.
- Boot16wn.exe retrieves the information from the Win16.tcf file at the Logon Point. The Win16.tcf file is located in the SMSlogon\Config directory.
- Boot16wn.exe copies the SMSBoot1.exe and Clicor16.exe files from the Logon Point to the MS\SMS\Core\Bin directory on the client computer.
- Boot16wn.exe copies the Win16.tcf file from the Logon Point to the MS\SMS\Core\Data directory on the client computer. The file is renamed Temp.tcf.

CHECKPOINT: Verify the Temp.tcf exists in the MS\SMS\Core\Data directory on the client computer. Also, check for the existence of SMSBoot1.exe and Clicor16.exe in the MS\SMS\Core\Bin directory.

- Boot16wn.exe executes Clicor16.exe with the following command-line: *Clicor16.exe /s disc*. The */s* switch makes the installation silent, while the *disc* switch causes the files compressed in the package to extract.
- Boot16wn.exe calls Cliex16.dll.

- Boot16wn.exe reads the SMScfg.ini file for the SMS path information.
- If the SMS UID (Unique IDentifier) isn't found for the client computer, Boot16wn.exe creates it and writes the information to the SMScfg.ini file.

CHECKPOINT: Look in the SMScfg.ini file for the computer's SMS Unique ID assignment.

- Boot16wn.exe gets the list of discovery data properties from the Temp.tcf file in the MS\SMS\Core\Data directory.
- Boot16wn.exe uses Cliex16.dll to discover each property retrieved from the Temp.tcf file.
- Cliex16.dll creates the DDR on the client in the MS\SMS\Core\Data\SMSdisc.ddr file. The SMSdisc.ddr file contains the list of property names and values.
- If Windows Logon Discovery is enabled for the site, Boot16wn.exe copies the client's DDR to the SMSLogon\Ddr.box directory on the SMS Logon Server.

CHECKPOINT: At this juncture, you can look in the client's MS\SMS\Core\Data directory for the client DDR and the SMSLogon\Ddr.box directory on the SMS Logon Server.

- If Logon Installation is enabled for the site, Boot16wn.exe reads the Netconf.ncf file from the SMSlogon\Sites\<Sitecode> directory on the Logon Server to determine if the client is assigned to a site. It retrieves the list of configured IP subnets and IPX Network numbers. If Logon Installation isn't enabled, Boot16wn.exe ends the installation process.
- Boot16wn.exe executes Clicor16.exe and installs the client core files for setup with the *Clicor16.exe /s inst* command line.
- Boot16wn.exe retrieves the Client Access Points from the CAPlist.ini file on the Logon Server. The CAPlist.ini file resides in the SMSlogon\Sites\<Sitecode> directory.
- Boot16wn.exe writes the CAP information to the SMScfg.ini file on the client computer.
- Boot16wn.exe creates the NAL abstract export from the caplist.ini file on the SMS Logon Point.

NOTE: The NAL abstract export contains a listing of the CAPs in NAL format.

- Boot16wn.exe registers Ccim16.exe and Clearque.exe with the Launch16.exe file.
- Boot16wn.exe executes Launch16.exe.
- Launch16.exe executes Ccim16.exe and Clearque.exe. Note that: Launch16.exe is placed in the RUN line of the client computer's Win.ini file.
- Boot16wn.exe terminates.
- Ccim16.exe verifies the assignments for each SMS site.
- Ccim16.exe retrieves the list of discovery data properties from the Temp.tcf file. This file is located in the %WINDIR%\MS\SMS\Core\Data directory on the client computer.
- Ccim16.exe calls Cliex16.dll. Cliex16.dll discovers the exact properties.
- Ccim16.exe creates a SMSTemp.ddr file in the %WINDIR%\MS\SMS\Core\Data directory on the client computer. The SMSTemp.ddr file contains the properties that were discovered.
- If Heartbeat Discovery is enabled, Ccim16.exe gives a unique name to the SMSTemp.ddr file and copies it to the CAP into the DDR.box directory. If Heartbeat Discovery isn't enabled for the site, Ccim16.exe retrieves the client component advertisement data for each assigned site, gets a list of components that should be installed on the client, and retrieves the advertisement information from the site.
- If any pending SMS component installation advertisements exist, Ccim16.exe calls the APM, writes the offer information to the SMScfg.ini file, and the APM installs the advertised applications; then progression continues. If no SMS component installation advertisements are pending, Ccim16.exe progression continues.
- Ccim16.exe configures Launch16.exe to execute the Ccim16.exe cycle in 23 hours.

CHECKPOINT: This ends the client installation for 16-bit Windows computers. The client computer should have the 16-bit components installed, have a SMS Unique ID, and display in the SMS Administrator Console. If any errors occur during the final Ccim16.exe process, Ccim16.exe configures Launch16.exe to restart the Ccim16.exe cycle in one hour.

Windows NT Remote Client Installation for New Installations Checklist

The following checklist walks through the Windows NT Remote Client Installation.

- Discovery Data Manager retrieves all the Windows NT and Windows 2000 information from the current site.
- Discovery Data Manager creates a DDR for each computer found.

NOTE: For each computer found in the site, Discovery Data Manager checks that the computer's Architecture is set to System and verifies the OS is Windows NT or Windows 2000. It can also retrieve IP Network, User, and User Group information. Before continuing, Discovery Data Manager also checks the HKEY_LOCAL_MACHINE\SMS\Components\SMS_Discovery_Data_Manager\Exclude Servers key in the registry for the list of excluded servers. To verify, Discovery Data Manager confirms the NetBIOS name listed in the .DDR file against the retrieve value.

- Discovery Data Manager creates a Client Configuration Request file and places it in the \\SMS\Inboxes\Ccr.box directory.
- Client Configuration Manager retrieves the CCR from the Ccr.box directory.
- Client Configuration Manager connects to the Admin$ share on the remote computer.

CHECKPOINT: If the Client Configuration Manager cannot connect to the remote computer, it places the CCR into the Ccrretry.box directory on the SMS site server. Client Configuration Manager then retries the Client Configuration Request for every hour up to seven days. If the CCR file exists in the Ccrretry.box, you should first verify you are able to connect to the remote computer from the SMS server. One method for doing this is to PING the IP address and host name of the server. If the IP Address returns a valid connection, but the host name doesn't resolve, look at the DNS structure in your organization. If no valid connection is returned, you should look at the remote computer itself for possible problems. If you receive a valid connection from both the IP address and host name, the SMS server might not have the appropriate rights on the remote computer. The SMS Service account must be able to connect to the Admin$ share on the remote computer. If it's unable to connect to this share, verify the SMS Service has Administrator rights on the remote computer. The Ccm.log file will contain information as to why the connection cannot be made.

- Ccm.dll copies Ccmcore.exe (SMS core file) and Ccmbtldr.exe (SMS loader file) to the %WINDIR%\MS\SMS\Core\Bin directory on the remote computer.
- Ccm.dll initiates Ccmbtldr.exe on the remote computer.

CHECKPOINT: To verify the process is working, check the %WINDIR%\MS\SMS\Core\Bin directory on the remote computer for the Ccmcore.exe and Ccmbtlder.exe files. Also, verify Ccmbtlder.exe is running by viewing the running Processes in the Task List on the remote computer.

- Ccmbtldr.exe on the remote computer executes Ccmcore.exe to extract the Network Abstraction Layer (NAL) files.
- Ccmbtlder.exe on the remote computer registers the NAL path to the CAP.
- Ccmbtlder.exe on the remote computer retrieves and copies Clicore.exe and Ccmboot.exe from the CAP to the local hard drive.
- Ccmboot.exe installs and starts the SMS Client Service.

CHECKPOINT: You can look on the remote computer to verify Clicore.exe and Ccmboot.exe exist on the hard drive in the MS\SMS\Core\Bin directory. You can also check the Windows NT/2000 services on the remote computer to make certain the SMS Client Service is installed and started.

- Ccmboot.exe registers Ccim32.dll with the remote computer.
- Ccmboot.exe terminates.

CHECKPOINT: This ends the Windows NT Remote Client Installation's involvement with installing the SMS client. Ccmboot.exe should be absent from the Process list in the remote computer's Task List. At this point, the Windows Networking Logon Discovery method process is used to finish the client installation (see the 32-bit Client Windows Network Logon Discovery and Installation for New Installations Checklist for the insertion point).

Uninstalling the SMS Client

When you attempt to diagnose issues with SMS client components, you may find the process is complicated by loaded application. For example, a driver or program loaded in memory could cause the SMS Client installation to fail, or it could cause some components to run improperly. For troubleshooting purposes, you may need to remove the SMS client, which you can accomplish in any of several ways. Those methods are covered in this section.

Manual Uninstall

You can start the deinstallation of the SMS 2.0 client by adding the following string value and data to the registry on the client computer:
HKEY_LOCAL_MACHINE\Software\Microsoft\SMS\Client\Configuration\Client Properties

Value Item to add: SMS Client Deinstall

Data: TRUE

Then, to complete the deinstallation process, take the appropriate step, as follows:

- **For Windows 95:** Run Clisvc95.exe.
- **For Windows 2000/NT:** Stop and restart the SMS Client Service.

Uninstall Using the Systems Management Installation Wizard

SMSMan.exe, the program that starts the SMS client installation, can also be used to remove the client. Running it from the command line enables you to select the Remove Systems Management Components option. On the client computer, SMSMan.exe is located in the %WINDIR%\MS\SMS\CORE\BIN\00000409 directory.

You can also use the /U command-line switch to skip the wizard interface and just remove the client. Using the /Q switch with the uninstall command makes the removal completely silent.

Uninstall with 20Clicln.bat

The SMS 2.0 Resource Guide includes a batch file, 20clicln.bat, that removes the SMS 2.0 client. The batch file determines the OS type, reads the components installed, removes items from memory, stops services, and deletes the client files. The batch file calls three dependency files:

- Hammer.exe (SMS Installer compiled executable that does the actual removal)
- Kill.exe (for removing running processes)
- Setevnt.exe (for logging the success or failure in the Windows NT event log)

Uninstall by Removing the Client's Subnet or Network Number from the Site Boundary

Another method for removing the SMS client software is to remove the client's subnet or network number from the SMS site's boundary. This method removes all the clients assigned to that particular SMS site. To remove the subnet or network number from the site boundary, perform the following steps in the Systems Management Server Administrator console:

1. Expand the Site Database property.
2. Expand the Site Hierarchy property.
3. Right-click the site and click Properties on the shortcut menu.
4. Click the Boundaries tab.
5. Right-click the subnet/network number to remove and click Delete on the shortcut menu.

During the next maintenance interval, the client software will be deinstalled. Or, you can force the immediate deinstallation of the SMS client by restarting the computer.

Supporting Mobile Users

SMS 2.0 adds a lot of functionality for remote and mobile users. One of the best components exists in, and must be maintained at, the client.

When mobile users travel from office to office, or even to a client site that has SMS 2.0 implemented, they may log in to the remote network. Logging in to a SMS 2.0 network would automatically move the client PC to the new SMS site. Use Traveling mode (found in the Systems Management Control Panel applet on the client) to keep this from happening.

Mobile computer

☑ This computer connects to the network from different locations

When Traveling mode is turned on and the user logs into another SMS 2.0 boundary, the user is prompted to uninstall the original SMS site and install the new site. If the user chooses not to install the new site, she won't be prompted again for 30 days, even if she logs in to that boundary every day for the next 30 days.

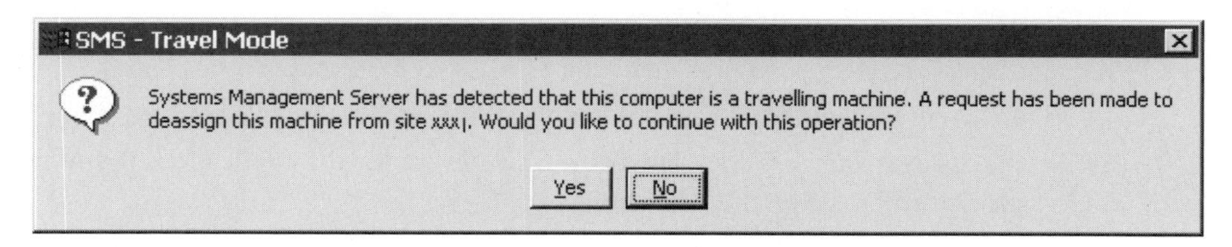

CAUTION: On Win9x clients, the user is allowed to set Traveling mode options. On Windows 2000/NT clients (Workstation and Server), the user must have Administrator rights on the client PC to set the Traveling mode options.

Client Utilities

A number of client utilities on the market are designed to help troubleshoot client problems. One excellent source, referred to many times in this book, is the *Microsoft Systems Management Server 2.0 Resource Guide* (*SMS 2.0 Resource Guide*). This guide includes a CD-ROM that contains a horde of great client utilities. If you want to be technically fluent with SMS, this resource guide is a critical first step.

This section covers some of the client utilities offered by the *SMS 2.0 Resource Guide* to make troubleshooting and diagnosing client problems easier.

Cliutils.exe

The Client Utilities tool (Cliutils.exe) performs various client-side functions for clients running 32-bit operating systems. It's extremely useful for stopping and starting failed components, and can perform a complete cycle of the client components. Performing the cycle enables you to propagate changes to the client computer immediately, instead of waiting until the next scheduled site cycle.

The Client Utilities tool relies on the existence of SMSCLReg.dll, which is located in the %WINDIR%\MS\SMS\CORE\BIN directory. If this file doesn't exist, you receive an application error.

Cliutils.exe can be sent as a SMS package to the client computer or can be run manually from the client computer. The syntax is, **CliUtils** [*<command> <parameter>*]

The following commands and parameters are available:

- **/KICK *<Registered Name>*** KICK signals the STARTCYCLE event for the client component. Components used with KICK are client processes that run on a schedule.
- **/STOP *<Registered Name>*** STOP signals the STOP event for the application. Running SMS services are affected by this command.
- **/START *<Registered Name>*** START starts the application. Stopped SMS Services are affected by this command.
- **/SCHED *<Schedule String>*** SCHED is used to decode the Schedule List string.
- **/APPREG** APPREG registers an application to be started by the client launchers.

Registered Names:

- Advertised Programs Monitor
- Available Programs Manager
- Client Configuration Installation Manager
- Clisvcl (Client Service NT)
- Clisvc95 (Client Service 95/98)
- Hardware Inventory Agent
- Software Inventory Agent
- System Offer Data Provider
- WNet User Groups Offer Data Provider

AddSystem.exe

AddSystem.exe is the command-line equivalent of the SMS Manual Discovery tool, described after this section. It can be obtained from the BackOffice Resource Kit 4.5 or the *SMS 2.0 Resource Guide*. The tool is installed into the \BORK\SMS\Diagnose directory by default. AddSystem.exe must be run from the site server console.

Based on the command line switches, it creates a DDR for the specified Windows 2000/NT client, which is processed on the site server and uses the NT Remote client installation to install the client components. The tool only provides discovery and installation for Windows 2000/NT computers. The syntax is: **AddSystem** <System> <Domain> <IpAddr> <SubnetAddr> [file.ddr]

If you don't want to wait for the scheduled refresh of the collection membership, open the SMS Administrator and Update the Collection Membership, then Refresh the Collection. The new computer record shows up in the All Systems collection almost immediately. The file SMSRsGen.dll is required to be in the same working directory as Addsystem.exe.

AddSysGui.exe

The SMS Manual Discovery tool addsysgui.exe is a graphical version of the AddSystem.exe tool, which is also part of the BackOffice Resource Kit 4.5 or the *SMS 2.0 Resource Guide*.

Executing the command **addSysGui** starts the tool, which installs itself into the \BORK\SMS\Diagnose directory by default. Then you can run the tool from the site server console. This utility only provides discovery and installation for Windows 2000/NT computers.

The following information is required to complete the manual discovery:

- System Name (NetBIOS name)
- Windows NT Domain (Domain in which the WinNT computer is installed)
- IP Address (IP Address of the WinNT computer)
- IP Network Number (Subnet)

After you enter the information, if the computer is found, you see a message to that effect. Then you see another message, indicating the DDR was successfully created. Depending on the load of the site server, the DDR record is added to the database in less than five minutes.

If the target computer is on the local *LAN* (*local area network*), the client software installation may take up to ten minutes. A *WAN* (*wide area network*) computer (depending on the bandwidth and WAN traffic) could take up to 30 minutes. If it goes beyond 30 minutes, check for WAN connectivity problems.

If you don't want to wait for the scheduled refresh of the collection membership, open the SMS Administrator and Update the Collection Membership, and then refresh the Collection. The new computer record appears in the All Systems collection almost immediately.

Pview95.exe

Another useful tool included with the *SMS 2.0 Resource Guide* is the Process Viewer, Pview95.exe. This is a graphical Windows 9*x*-only utility that performs many of the same functions as the Windows 2000/NT Task Manager (see the following illustration for a view of the interface). Process Viewer aids your troubleshooting efforts by identifying running processes and enabling you to determine which tasks are hung. Process Viewer also works remotely.

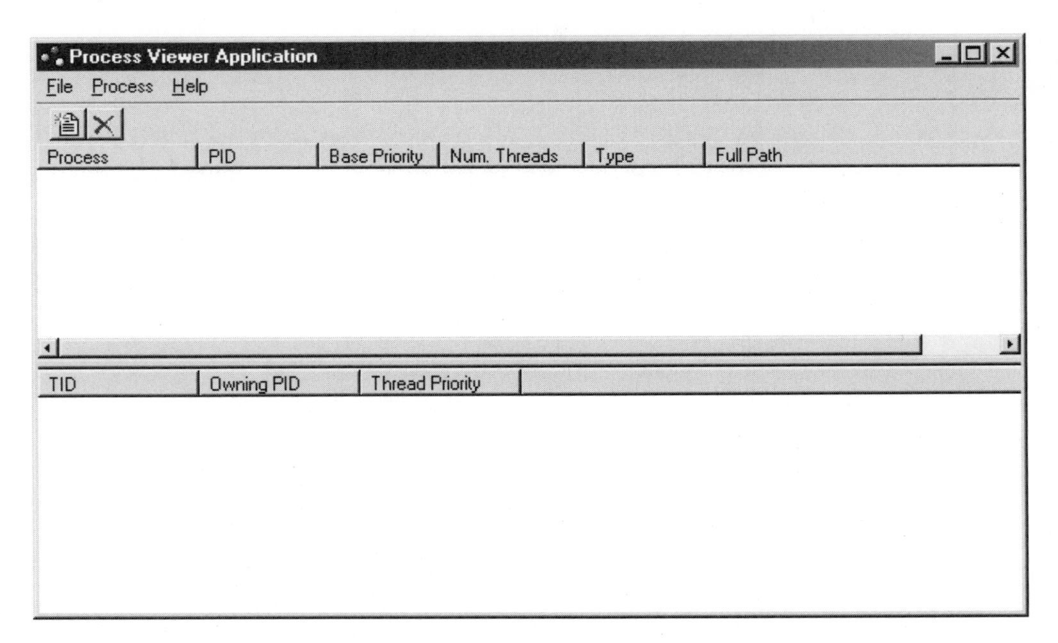

Discdump.exe

The *SMS 2.0 Resource Guide* includes the Dump Discovery Data tool, discdump.exe. This tool retrieves the network discovery data information from the local computer's DDR record and displays it in a readable format. This information goes a long way in helping you to identify computer discovery errors.

The following is an example of the information this tool enables you to see:

--Begin discdump.exe output

SMS Unique Id: GUID:9EC78B60-2075-11D4-A725-00104B343E6C

NetBIOS Address: EINSTEIN

IP Addresses - COMPLETE

[0]: 10.15.10.3

IP Subnets - COMPLETE

[0]: 10.15.10.0

IPX Addresses - COMPLETE

[0]: 00000000:00104B343E6C

```
IPX Network Numbers - COMPLETE
   [0]: 00000000
### NO Token Ring ID
MAC Addresses - COMPLETE
   [0]: 00:10:4B:34:3E:6C
Resource Domain / Workgroup: UNIVERSE
OS Name & Version: Microsoft Windows NT Advanced Server 4.0
Last Logged On User Name: Administrator
Last Logged On User Domain: UNIVERSE
Is Client Installed: 1
Installed Sites - COMPLETE
   [0]: ROD
Client Version: 2.00.1239.0000
### NO Preferred Server Name
### NO Preferred Tree Name
### NO NDS Name Context
--End discdump.exe output
```

Client Installation Gotchas

This section covers some of the traps and problems you can encounter during client installation processes.

Windows 9x Scandisk

Some organizations schedule Scandisk to check the computer's hard disk for errors. If Scandisk starts before or during the SMS client installation, it displays an error.

When you're deploying the SMS client, turn off the scheduled event before you begin.

Inaccessible CAP

During the SMS 2.0 client installation, if an error message is recorded in the Ccim32.log that the CAP is not accessible (WaitForCAPAccess), the Windows 2000/NT server that houses the SMS site services and database could be out of licenses. This can occur when the server is set to "Per Server" licensing.

When an SMS client computer connects to the CAP, it can use several licenses because it's trying to connect under multiple user contexts. Changing the server licensing from "Per Server" to "Per Seat" enables the client to install.

NOTE: Other reasons exist why a client cannot connect to the CAP, such as rights issues or the network being unavailable, but the licensing occurrence is the most common.

Valid Temp Directory Required

The computer on which the SMS client will be installed must have a valid temp directory defined in the system environment variables. This issue is particularly critical when performing a SMS 1.2 client upgrade to the SMS 2.0 client agents. SMS 2.0 attempts to write a temporary system.ini file to the computer's Temp directory before making modifications. If the Temp directory variable doesn't exist on the computer, the Windows directory is used, overwriting the current system.ini file.

Cliex32.dll Error 126 Error in Wnmanual.log

If you try to install the SMS client from a directory other than the \x86.bin\00000409 directory on the SMSLOGON share, an error message is generated and the client installation fails. The Wnmanual.log file records the following information:

```
Begin CliEx processing.~
ERROR: Load of DLL CliEx32.dll failed:
(C:\WINNT\MS\SMS\CORE\BIN\cliex32.dll),126
ERROR: Initializing CliEx failed error code 126~
Unable to continue; exiting~
```

Installation Must Finish Properly

Installation of the SMS client is a long process. If the process doesn't complete properly, the client may not be fully installed. Part of the client installation process is performing the first hardware and software inventory of the computer. On Windows 9*x* clients, this is performed after the first restart of the computer.

Depending on the speed of the computer, you should plan on the first inventory process taking between ten and thirty minutes. During this period of time, a Windows 9*x* computer can noticeably lose performance. The unsuspecting user may think something is wrong with the computer and try to reboot it. This can cause unexpected results for the completion of the client installation. For instance, the Windows 9*x* client may never be assigned to the SMS site. When deploying the SMS installation, inform the user base of the potential slowdown of the computer and direct them not to reboot.

For Windows 2000/NT clients who log in to a domain, a potential issue exists with Network Discovery and Remote Client Installation. If the computer is restarted within 15 minutes of logging in to the network, the Wuser32 service hangs and gives the infamous "End Task" message. The Permitted Viewers of the SMS site is based on the Windows accounts assigned to the group. The Wuser32 agent must authenticate with this Access Control List (ACL). If the authentication is interrupted, Wuser32 hangs.

Unsupported Network Redirectors

Organizations plan their infrastructures around a variety of network redirectors. For example, some companies use a third-party TCP/IP stack or an older version of a networking client.

Older versions of the Novell IntraNetWare client aren't supported, and you can acquire information about supported redirectors on Microsoft's SMS site at http://www.microsoft.com/smsmgmt/deployment/SMSwithNovell.asp.

When you initiate the installation with SMSLS.BAT or SMSMan.exe, an unsupported network redirector could cause the installation to hang. To determine if this issue is plaguing your installations, enable NAL logging on the client computer. On the SMS 2.0 CD-ROM, in the Support\Reskit\I386\Diagnose directory, is a registry file called Turn_on_nal_logging.reg. Running this file against the computer's registry turns on the NAL logging. Then check the Wn_manual.log file for the following error message: NAL [2]—Warning: this version of the redirector is not supported.

Client Components

You must verify the client has the correct client versions installed. When applying a HotFix or a service pack to the SMS site, the client computers receive the new components on the next login. If the client hasn't received the upgraded components, client-side functions won't operate.

You can find the client versions (base components) by looking in the *\SMS\Inboxes\Clicomp.src\Base\Compver.INI* file on the site server.

Compver.INI File:

[COMPONENT VERSION INFORMATION]

Component version=2.00.1380.1000

You can fix the client components by sending a client resynch or by running SMSman.exe on the computer.

SMS Client Page Faults, Illegal Operations, and GPFs

Generally, if you experience any problems with the SMS client files on Windows 95 and Windows 98, this is because the Microsoft Foundation Class Library files are older or incompatible versions. Installing applications on Windows 95 that use the *Microsoft Foundation Class Library* (*MFC*) can overwrite versions needed for the SMS Client. The MFC is a set of files that provide the base API functions of Microsoft operating systems. The wrong versions of the MFC files can cause the SMS client to fail and, in turn, cause Windows 95 to perform general protection faults and illegal operations. Always keep the latest MFC files installed on the Windows 95 computer. See the following link to download the latest MFC files: http://www.microsoft.com/windows95/downloads/contents/WURecommended/ S_WUServicePacks/MFCLibrary/Default.asp

Workstations Showing as Devices Only

Microsoft released a white paper on workstation security a few years ago. Based on this white paper, you can lock down a system by modifying the following registry key and changing the data value to '1': HKEY_LOCAL_MACHINE\System\Currentcontrolset\control\lsa\restrictanonymous

When this value is changed, however, Network Discovery finds the workstations, but doesn't identify them as anything except devices. This limits the client discovery process methods to only Logon Discovery. Changing the data value back to '0' can fix the problem.

WBEM and DCOM

The latest version of the *Distributed Component Object Model files* (*DCOM*) is required on Windows 95 computers. If the latest version isn't installed, hardware inventory may not run and the computer record won't show up in the SMS collections. If you experience this issue:

1. Obtain the latest DCOM installation from http://www.microsoft.com/com/tech/dcom.asp.
2. Open the Systems Management Properties control panel applet.
3. Click the Components tab.
4. Highlight the Windows Management component and click the Repair Installation button.

Dual Boot Clients

The SMS UID can only exist once on any given computer, even if you dual-boot between operating systems. When this situation is present, program advertisements and package distributions are distributed to both operating systems. If applications targeted at specific operating systems are distributed, an installation on the wrong OS can potentially cause serious computer problems. If you or someone must use a dual-boot system (for example, some software developers use dual-boot systems to test applications on multiple OSs), try to configure the advertisements and packages so they are specific to an operating system.

When creating the packages, specify the operating system type in the Program Properties shown in the following illustration. As an added measure of security, set up collections based on specific operating systems, and distribute the packages and advertisements to the collections.

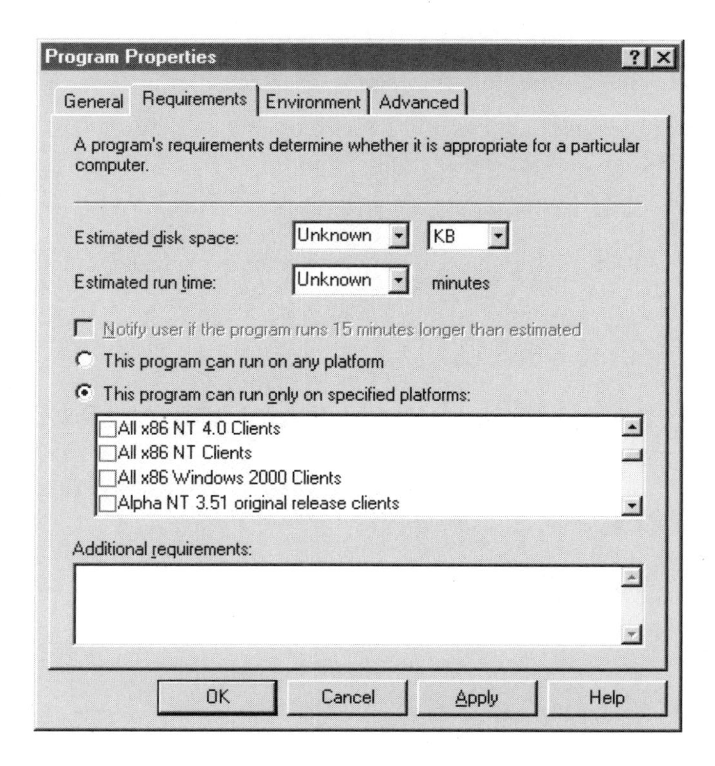

Remote Subnets Not Showing Domain Participation

When Network Discovery runs, it discovers the client by querying the DHCP server, retrieving SNMP information from the client, and pulling information from the ARP cache on the router. You may notice the client information is showing up in the SMS site database, but the client is not shown as being assigned to a domain. To discover domain information, you must enable Topology, Client, and Client Operating System Discovery in the SMS site properties.

Client Reinstalls Itself

To ensure that SMS 2.0 is not reinstalling your clients every four weeks, look in the following logs: CLICORE.LOG; INSINV.LOG; INHINV.LOG. View the information in these logs to see when your clients were last installed. If your clients are reinstalling themselves every four weeks, the workaround is to edit your Site Control File.

1. Stop SMS_EXEC & SMS_SITE_COMPONENT_MANAGER.
2. Back up your Site Control File (\SMS\inboxes\sitectrl.box\sitectrl.ct0)
3. Remove the following line: PROPERTY <Component Verify Interval><REG_SZ><00011700001000F0><0>.
4. Restart the SMS Services.

The BASE.CFG file will be updated in the \SMS\inboxes\clicfg.src directory along with \CAP_XXX\clicomp.box directory on each CAP.

✦ SMS 2.0 and McAfee Virus Scan

Fatal Exception When Logging on to NetWare with Windows 95

For Windows 95 clients, when you install the SMS client via a login script to a NetWare 3.*x* server, a fatal exception error occurs if you have McAfee VirusScan set to load VShield at startup. The issue is the order of loading.

To work around this issue, disable *Load VShield at Startup* in VShield Configuration Manager. Then, create a shortcut to Vshwin32.exe in the Windows 95 startup group. This allows the SMS script to run *before* VShield loads.

Zero Administration Kit

Windows NT 4.0 clients with the *Zero Administration Kit* (*ZAK*) installed can cause Clicore.exe to fail during the installation of the client components. No error message is associated with the failed installation in the Clicore.log file. If you walk through the checklists (in this chapter), you will notice Cliex32.dll never starts its process.

ZAK adds a couple of registry values to the client computer that causes the SMS client installation to fail. The problem is the format of the data values. ZAK adds these values as REG_SZ and they should be REG_EXPAND_SZ. To fix this problem, you must first delete the two registry values, and then add them back using the correct format.

Change the following registry values:

In HKEY_LOCAL_MACHINE\SYSTEM\CurrentControlSet\Control\Session Manager\Environment, the value is temp=%SystemDrive%\temp.

In HKEY_LOCAL_MACHINE\SYSTEM\CurrentControlSet\Control\Session Manager\Environment the value is tmp=%SystemDrive%\temp.

For more information on this issue, see the Microsoft Knowledge Base article: Q222967. For more information on the Zero Administration Kit, see http://www.microsoft.com /NTWorkstation/downloads/Recommended/Featured/NTZAK.asp

Line Continually Added to Autoexec.bat

Windows 95 and Windows 98 client computers could receive an error message indicating the computer is "Out of Environment Space" when installing the client software. This is because of the following line being truncated in Autoexec.bat:

if not "%OS%"=="Windows_NT" if "%COMSPEC%"=="C:\WINDOWS\COMMAND.COM" set SMS_LOCAL_DIR=C:\WINDOWS

When the SMS client is installed, this line is added to Autoexec.bat. Each time the SMS Client service is started, it verifies this line exists in the Autoexec.bat. If the line doesn't exist, it adds it. If the line is truncated, SMS considers the line not installed and continually reads the line until the computer runs out of environment space and locks up.

Chapter 3

Hardware Inventory Installation, Collection, and Processing

Inventory is the key to unlocking information for SMS clients. Once the SMS Core Components have been installed on the computer, install the Hardware Inventory Agent. The *Hardware Inventory Agent* performs a comprehensive scan of the computer's hardware and reports the information to the SMS site for inclusion in the SQL database. Once the data is accessible in the SMS database, it is available for retrieving, viewing, and manipulating.

The specific hardware components inventoried are determined by the site's SMS_DEF.MOF file (described later in this chapter). This file contains the standard hardware inventory set across the organization. Based on your requirements, this file can be modified to collect a small or large amount of hardware inventory. This capability allows complete customization to meet your organization's information requirements.

Hardware Inventory Agent Directory Structure

When the Hardware Inventory Agent is installed on the client computer, it creates a specific directory structure as shown in Table 3-1. This directory structure provides for both the storage of the Hardware Inventory Agent program files and also a working directory structure for hardware inventory processing.

Directory	Description
%WINDIR%\MS\SMS\CLICOMP\HINV	The HINV directory is the core directory for the Hardware Inventory Agent. It includes the Hardware Inventory Agent executable (hinv32.exe for 32-bit clients; hinv16.exe for 16-bit clients), the deinstallation file (dehinv32.exe for 32-bit clients; dehinv16.exe for 16-bit clients), and the SMS site's default hardware inventory file (SMS_DEF.MOF).
%WINDIR%\MS\SMS\CLICOMP\HINV\OUTBOX	The OUTBOX directory temporarily stores the hardware inventory data before it is forwarded to the CAP for processing.
%WINDIR%\MS\SMS\CLICOMP\HINV\TEMP	The TEMP directory is a working directory for the Hardware Inventory Agent. This directory stores temporary files before they are converted to inventory files readable by the SMS processes.

Table 3-1. Hardware Inventory Directory Structure

Hardware Inventory Agent Client Registry Key

When the Hardware Inventory Agent is installed on the client computer, information and properties are stored in the computer's registry. This information is key to inventory running properly. The registry information is polled for values to start and complete the process. The Hardware Inventory Agent information is stored under the HKEY_LOCAL_MACHINE hive.

HKEY_LOCAL_MACHINE

The following example data has been stored on a SMS client assigned to a site with the three-letter site code ROD.

- **SOFTWARE\Microsoft\SMS\Client\Client Components\Hardware Inventory Agent**

Executable Path
Type: REG_SZ
Data: C:\WINNT\MS\SMS\clicomp\hinv\hinv32.exe
Last Inventory Cycle
Type: REG_DWORD
Data: 0x395de2b0
Last Inventory Cycle OpCode
Type: REG_DWORD
Data: 0x30
Last Inventory Schedule
Type: REG_SZ
Data: 0994678000100038
MOF Checksum
Type: REG_DWORD
Data: 0xc4539749

- **SOFTWARE\Microsoft\SMS\Client\Client Components\Hardware Inventory Agent\Installation Properties**

 # Consecutive Verifies
Type: REG_DWORD
Data: 0
Base Component
Type: REG_SZ
Data:

Deinstall Command Line
Type: REG_SZ
Data: C:\WINNT\MS\SMS\clicomp\hinv\dehinv32.exe /s
Installed Languages
Type: REG_MULTI_SZ
Data: 0x00000409
Installed OS Version
Type: REG_MULTI_SZ
Data: WIN NT
I386
04.00.1381.6
Installed Version
Type: REG_SZ
Data: 2.00.1493.2000
Language Support Type
Type: REG_DWORD
Data: 0
Last Operation Time
Type: REG_SZ
Data: 3942735C
Manual Run App
Type: REG_SZ
Data: Hardware Inventory Agent
Pending Command
Type: REG_DWORD
Data: 0x1
Pending Language Support Type
Type: REG_DWORD
Data: 0
Pending Operation Languages
Type: REG_MULTI_SZ
Data: 0x00000409
Pending Operation OS Version
Type: REG_MULTI_SZ
Data: WIN NT
I386
04.00.1381.6

Pending Operation Program Name
Type: REG_SZ
Data: WIN NT (I386) Verify program name
Pending Operation Sites Requesting This Component
Type: REG_MULTI_SZ
Data: ROD
Pending Operation Time
Type: REG_SZ
Data: 2000:07:01:08:12:47
Pending Operation Version
Type: REG_SZ
Data: 2.00.1493.2000
Sites Requesting This Component
Type: REG_MULTI_SZ
Data: ROD
SMS Client Installation State
Type: REG_SZ
Data: Installed
Verify Interval Offset (# hours)
Type: REG_DWORD
Data: 0xc4

- **SOFTWARE\Microsoft\SMS\Client\Client Components\Hardware Inventory Agent\Sites**

Site List
Type: REG_MULTI_SZ
Data: ROD

- **SOFTWARE\Microsoft\SMS\Client\Client Components\Hardware Inventory Agent\Sites\ROD**

Last Inventory Resync
Type: REG_SZ
Data: 0x01BFD95C48FF4690

The technologies incorporated in the SMS hardware inventory process are complicated, but they are standard across the industry. These standards enable vendors to write applications that can "talk" to SMS and the SMS hardware processes. One particular vendor, Computing Edge (http://www.computingedge.com) has a product called Inventory + Solutions, which is described in the section "Hardware Inventory Utilities" later in this chapter.

Overview of SMS Hardware Management Technologies

Understanding the underlying technologies SMS uses to produce its hardware inventory information can help you better understand the hardware inventory processes and the information available.

WBEM

Web-Based Enterprise Management (*WBEM*) is a set of technologies created by the standards committee, *Distributed Management Task Force* (*DMTF*). These standards were created to provide unification of Enterprise Management technologies. Any vendor working within these standards can create enterprise-level applications that work across different platforms. WBEM provides to the industry the capability to deliver a well-integrated set of standard-based management tools, leveraging emerging technologies such as:

- Common Information Model (CIM), described in more detail later in this chapter
- XML (Extensible Markup Language)
- Desktop Management Interface (DMI)
- Managed Object Format (MOF)

The WBEM model is a framework that includes *Application Programming Interfaces* (*API*), syntax, and an object model. WBEM is the mediator between the application layer and the provider, as shown in Figure 3-1. These applications can be developed around any language that allows interaction with the WBEM interface. Some of these languages are VBScript, JScript, COM, and Windows Scripting Host.

WBEM provides a point of integration through which data from management sources can be accessed, and it complements and extends existing management protocols and instrumentation such as *Simple Network Management Protocol* (*SNMP*), *Desktop Management Interface* (*DMI*), and *Common Management Information Protocol* (*CMIP*).

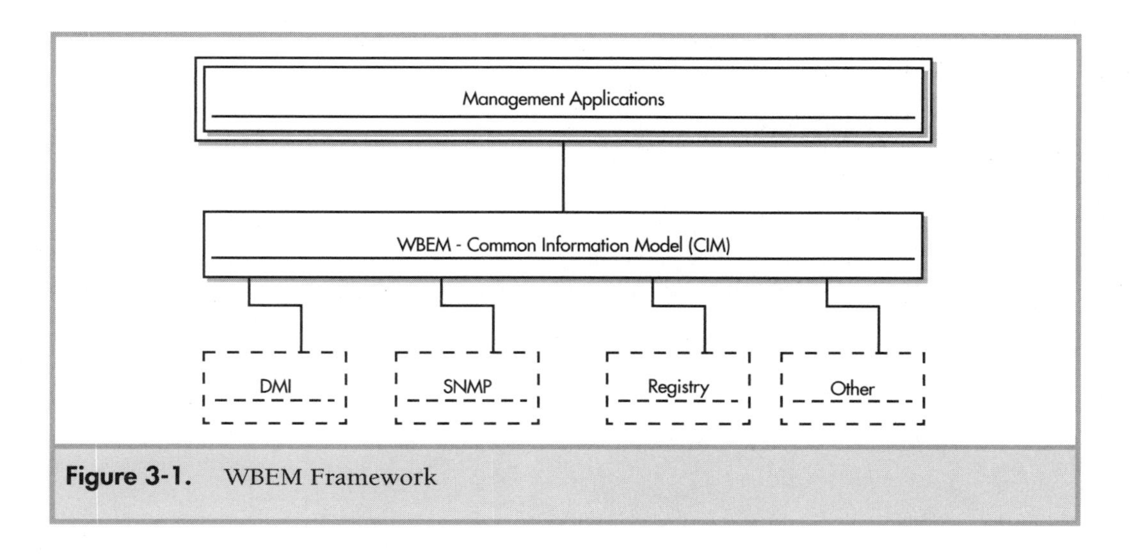

Figure 3-1. WBEM Framework

For detailed, technical data on WBEM, visit the DMTF Web site at http://www.dmtf.org/wbem/.

SMS WBEM Classes and Attributes

SMS uses the Microsoft implementation of the WBEM standards to provide hardware inventory information through queries to the SMS site database. This implementation is organized into a tree in the following order:

- Super classes
- Child classes
- Attributes

At the lowest tree level (attributes), each attribute can contain more attributes. Providing this type of hierarchal structure allows a wealth of information to be retrieved and used.

The following shows the elements in the SMS WBEM tree.

- **WBEM SuperClass**
  - SMS_Resource
- **Child Classes of SMS_Resource**
  - SMS_R_UserGroup

- SMS_R_User
- SMS_R_System
- SMS_R_IPNetwork

NOTE: The SMS_R_UserGroup and SMS_R_User child classes represent information derived from Windows 2000/NT security group information. These child classes have no properties or attributes of their own and cannot be queried using WBEM or WMI methods.

- **Attributes of SMS_R_System**
  - AgentName
  - AgentSite
  - AgentTime
  - Client
  - IPAddresses
  - IPSubnets
  - IPXAddresses
  - LastLogonUserDomain
  - LastLogonUserName
  - MACAddress
  - Name
  - NetBIOSName
  - OperatingSystemNameandVersion
  - ResourceDomainOrWorkgroup
  - ResourceID
  - ResourceNames
  - ResourceType
  - SMSAssignedSites

  - SMSUniqueIdentifier
  - SNMPCommunityName
  - SystemRoles
  - UserDomain
- **Attributes of SMS_R_IPNetwork**
  - AgentName
  - AgentSite
  - AgentTime
  - Name
  - ResourceID
  - ResourceType
  - SMSAssignedSites
  - SubnetAddress
  - SubnetMask

Viewing the SMS WBEM Discovery Data

You can view the SMS Discovery Data for the SMS site by running the Wbemtest.exe utility installed as part of the *Windows Management Instrumentation* (*WMI*) services. Windows 2000 computers have these services installed by default, whereas, Windows 95, Windows 98, and Windows NT computers receive the services as part of SMS installation.

On Windows NT computers, Wbemtest.exe is the Web-based Enterprise Management Common Information Model Object Manager Tester. On Windows 2000 computers, the Wbemtest.exe program name has been changed (thank God!) to Windows Management Instrumentation Tester. As you see later in the WMI description section, the name was modified to identify the technology better as a Microsoft specific implementation of WBEM.

To view the Discovery Data, follow these steps:

1. Choose Start | Run and enter **wbemtest** in the space provided.
2. Click OK to execute the wbemtest program.

3. Once wbemtest is running, click the Connect button.

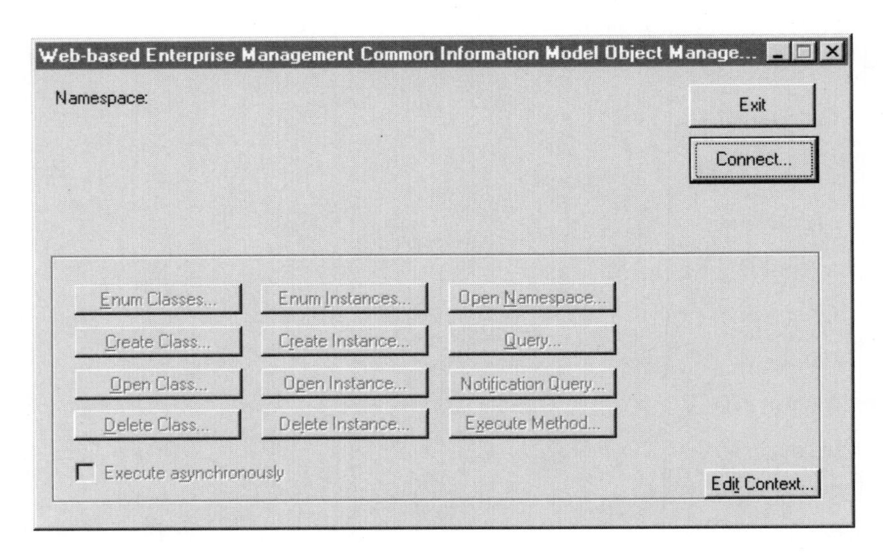

4. In the Server\Namespace box, type **root\SMS\site_<*sitecode*>**.

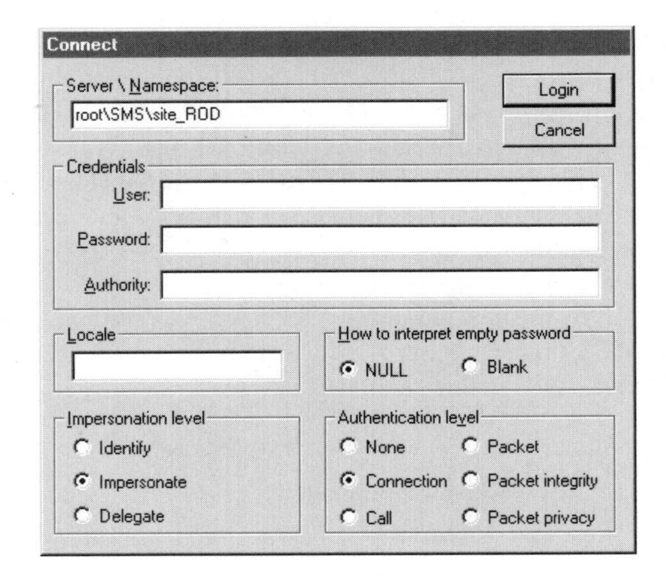

5. Click Login.
6. At the main screen, click Query.

7. On the Query screen, type the following: **select * from sms_r_system**.

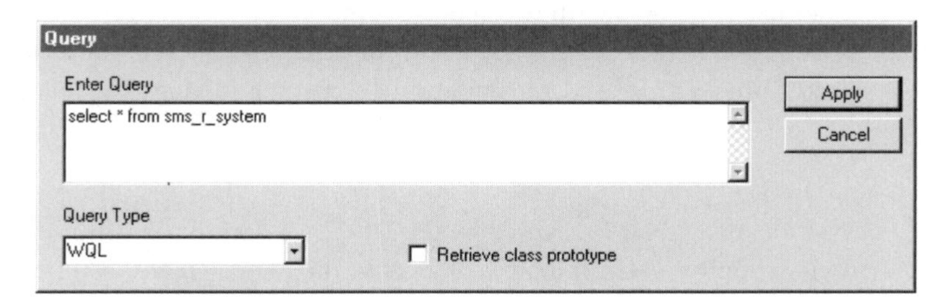

8. Click Apply.

NOTE: The select statement in step 7 is a WBEM Query Language (WQL) query. WQL is similar to the SQL query language.

After a short time (the query could take a while depending on the load of the SMS site server), a list of the system resource objects displays. These objects represent the items that have been inventoried through the hardware inventory process.

Double-clicking a listed object displays the complete DDR information pertaining to the resource.

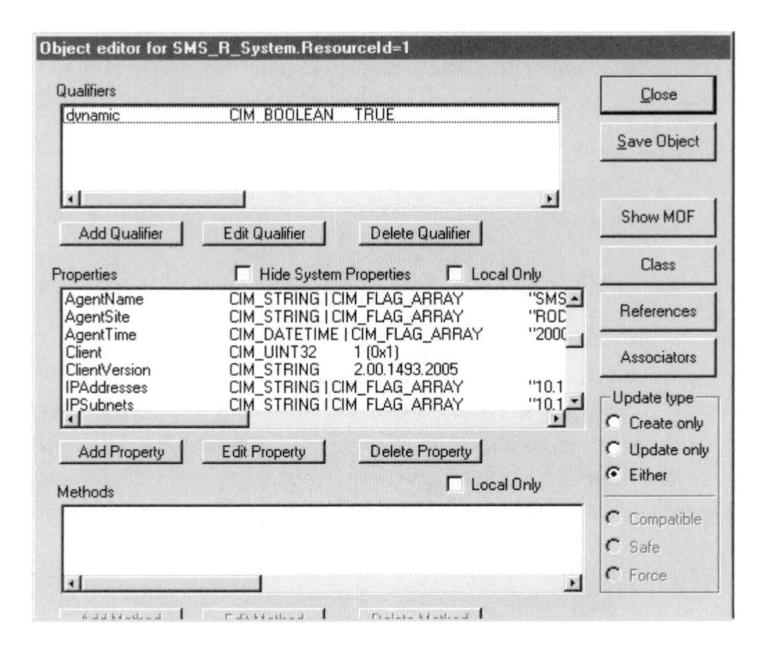

Reinstalling WBEM Components

If the client computer has problems with the WBEM components, the WBEM components can be reinstalled using the WBEMCORE.exe file on the SMS 2.0 CD. If a newer version exists on the computer, the WBEMCORE installation detects it and stops the installation.

CIM

The *Common Information Model* (*CIM*), created by the DMTF as part of the WBEM initiative, provides a unified view of physical and logical objects in the managed environment. To represent managed objects, developers use the object-oriented structures supported by CIM. These include classes that describe managed objects, class properties that define common characteristics and features of particular classes, class and property qualifiers that provide additional information, and methods that can be invoked on managed objects. Properties describe data, and methods describe behavior. The core of CIM is platform-independent with support for platform-specific extensions. The Windows Management Instrumentation technology includes an extension of the CIM schema—the Win32 extension schema—for the Microsoft Windows platforms. CIM defines the following:

- A core model that establishes a basic classification of the elements and associations of the managed environment, and describes objects that apply to all management domains.
- Several common models—extensions of the core model. The common models address systems, devices, networks, applications, users, and service-level agreements. They include a base set of classes that represent the managed objects specific to the individual management areas, but which are implementation- and technology-independent.
- Extensions to the common models—includes classes representing managed objects that are technology-specific additions to the common models. These classes typically apply to specific platforms such as UNIX or the Microsoft Win32 environment.

WMI

Windows Management Instrumentation (*WMI*) is Microsoft's version of WBEM. WMI provides a layer of services to make 32-bit operating systems easier to manage. WMI is installed on the SMS client as a set of providers. These providers allow SMS to interact with the hardware on the computer. They work as mediators between the computer hardware, the processes, and the SMS site components. WMI extends the CIM to represent management objects in Windows-based managed environments. The WMI technology provides the following:

- Access to monitor, command, and control any managed object through a common, unifying set of interfaces, regardless of the underlying instrumentation mechanism. WMI is an access mechanism.
- A consistent model of Windows 2000 operating system operation, configuration, and status.
- A COM *Application Programming Interface* (*API*) that supplies a single point of access for all management information.
- Interoperability with other Windows 2000 management services. This approach can simplify the process of creating integrated, well-architected management solutions.
- A flexible, extensible architecture. Developers can extend the information model to cover new devices, applications, and so on by writing code modules called WMI providers, described later in this document.
- Extensions to the *Windows Driver Model* (*WDM*) to capture instrumentation data and events from device drivers and kernel-side components.
- A powerful event architecture. This allows management information changes to be identified, aggregated, compared, and associated with other management information. These changes can also be forwarded to local or remote management applications.
- A rich query language that enables detailed queries of the information model.
- A scriptable API that developers can use to create management applications.

NOTE: The scripting API supports several languages, including Microsoft Visual Basic, Visual Basic for Applications, Visual Basic Scripting Edition (VBScript), Microsoft JScript, and Perl. Additionally, you can use the Windows Scripting Host or Internet Explorer to write scripts that use this interface. Windows Scripting Host, like Internet Explorer, serves as a controller engine of ActiveX scripting engines. Windows Scripting Host supports scripts written in VBScript, JScript, and Perl.

WMI Version 1.5

Version 1.5 is the current revision of WMI and is installed as part of the Windows 2000 operating system. A key feature of version 1.5 is the capability to gather information from the computer's *BIOS* (*Basic Input/Output System*). The BIOS stores information about the manufacturer, the product, the version, the serial number, and the default hardware settings. Hardware vendors whose products support SMBios version 2.1 (Systems Management BIOS, formerly known as DMI BIOS) can take full advantage of the WMI version 1.5.

Table 3-2 shows some of the information available through SMBios support and WMI version 1.5, and you can see how valuable it is to implement WMI version 1.5 in your organization.

MIF Attribute	Group	Description	Type
DMTF|ComponentID|001	Component ID Group MIF Description	Manufacturer	String
DMTF|ComponentID|001	Component ID Group MIF Description	Product	String
DMTF|ComponentID|001	Component ID Group MIF Description	Version	String
DMTF|ComponentID|001	Component ID Group MIF Description	Serial Number	String
DMTF|System BIOS|001	System BIOS Group MIF Definition	Version	String
DMTF|System BIOS|001	System BIOS Group MIF Definition	BIOS ROM Size	Integer
DMTF|System BIOS|001	System BIOS Group MIF Definition	BIOS Starting Address	INT64
DMTF|System BIOS|001	System BIOS Group MIF Definition	BIOS Ending Address	INT64
DMTF|System BIOS|001	System BIOS Group MIF Definition	BIOS Release Date	DATE
DMTF|BIOS Characteristic|003	BIOS Characteristic Group Definition	BIOS Characteristic Index	Integer
DMTF|BIOS Characteristic|003	BIOS Characteristic Group Definition	BIOS Number	Integer
DMTF|BIOS Characteristic|003	BIOS Characteristic Group Definition	BIOS Characteristics	ENUM
DMTF|BIOS Characteristic|003	BIOS Characteristic Group Definition	BIOS Characteristics Description Type	String
DMTF|BIOS Characteristic|003	BIOS Characteristic Group Definition	Processor Family	ENUM
DMTF|BIOS Characteristic|003	BIOS Characteristic Group Definition	Processor Upgrade	ENUM
DMTF|BIOS Characteristic|003	BIOS Characteristic Group Definition	Number of Expansion Slots	Integer
DMTF|BIOS Characteristic|003	System Cache	System Cache Index	Integer
DMTF|BIOS Characteristic|003	System Cache	System Cache Speed	Integer

Table 3-2. List of SMBios Attributes

MIF Attribute	Group	Description	Type
DMTF|BIOS Characteristic|003	System Cache	System Cache Size	Integer
DMTF|BIOS Characteristic|003	System Cache	System Cache Write Policy	ENUM
DMTF|BIOS Characteristic|003	Parallel Ports	Connector Type	ENUM
DMTF|BIOS Characteristic|003	Parallel Ports	Connector Pinout	ENUM
DMTF|BIOS Characteristic|003	Parallel Ports	Parallel Port Capabilities	Integer
DMTF|BIOS Characteristic|003	System Slots	Slot Index	Index
DMTF|BIOS Characteristic|003	System Slots	Slot Type	INT64
DMTF|BIOS Characteristic|003	System Slots	Slot Width	ENUM
DMTF|BIOS Characteristic|003	System Slots	Current Use	Integer
DMTF|BIOS Characteristic|003	System Slots	Slot Description	String
DMTF|BIOS Characteristic|003	System Slots	Slot Category	ENUM
DMTF|BIOS Characteristic|003	System Slots	Virtual Slot	ENUM
DMTF|BIOS Characteristic|003	System Slots	Resource User ID	Integer

Table 3-2. List of SMBios Attributes *(continued)*

As mentioned, WMI version 1.5 comes with Windows 2000. To take advantage of the SMBios features with SMS and Windows 95, Windows 98, or Windows NT 4.0, you need to deploy the latest WMI version on the client computers and install SMS 2.0 Service Pack 2 or better in your SMS site hierarchy.

WMI version 1.5 for Windows 9*x* and Windows NT can be downloaded from Microsoft's Web site at http://msdn.microsoft.com/downloads/sdks/wmi/default.asp.

NOTE: Windows 95 MUST have Distributed Component Object Model (DCOM) installed before installing WMI version 1.5. DCOM is available from Microsoft's Web site at http://www.microsoft.com/com/dcom/dcom95/download.asp.

MIF Files

Management Information Format files (MIF) are the crux of all SMS information. SMS inventory information is inserted into these files, and then replicated from the client computer to the SMS site. MIF files have a specific format, which allows SQL Server to read and retrieve the information contained within.

You can also create your own MIF files for inventorying specific items that may not be included with the normal SMS inventory scan. The capability to create custom MIF files further extends the data SMS can provide.

Custom MIFs and SMS 2.0

If you used custom MIFs with your SMS 1.2 implementation, you should remember the following three things as you are implementing to SMS 2.0. Changes exist to the way SMS 2.0 reads MIF files. The structure of the MIF has changed slightly. Also, the local path in which SMS 2.0 looks for the IDMIFs and NOIDMIFs has been relocated on the SMS 2.0 client.

First, understanding the difference between IDMIF and NOIDMIF helps. You may no longer need the IDMIF files, but still want to use the NOIDMIF. SMS 2.0 is able to collect a richer amount of hardware information, so extending the hardware Architecture with the IDMIF may be unnecessary.

By default, a lot of the hardware inventory detail is turned off in SMS 2.0 (SMS_DEF.MOF file, described in this chapter) because the amount of information that can be collected would overwhelm the server and the client computer. Use MOF Manager (described later) to view the hardware inventory details available to determine if you still need to use MIF files. The information you used MIF files to obtain in SMS 1.2 may already be available in SMS 2.0.

The IDMIF file enables you to add entirely new Architectures to the SMS database. The NOIDMIF enables you to add new classes to the new Architecture or an already existing Architecture. Think of it as a stack of blocks in the SMS database. The Architecture (object) is the top block in the column and its Classes (or properties) are the blocks that sit below. Each specific Architecture in the database has its own column and its own Class blocks below it. Depending on the number of specified properties collected about an object, the Architecture (column of blocks) could be very small or very large.

For example, a computer is a database system Architecture. Each property of the computer, such as RAM, BIOS version, number of hard disks, and so forth is a Class of the computer Architecture.

If you use the IDMIF file to create a new Architecture in the database, remember, this Architecture does not show up in SMS 2.0 Resource Explorer. You need to create a Query to pull this information from the SMS database. Using a NOIDMIF file to add classes to a current, default SMS 2.0 Architecture puts the data under the present Architecture, and it is available via the Resource Explorer.

The Inventory Data Loader on the SMS 2.0 primary site server processes IDMIF files. NOIDMIFs are used in conjunction with third-party utilities to process information on the client PC. This information is usually information collected through manual input by the user via custom input forms.

Changes During the SMS 1.2 to SMS 2.0 upgrade, the IDMIF and NOIDMIF files are erased from the server location in which they were stored. If you want to keep these files, you need to store them in a different path, outside the SMS directory tree. MIF files on the SMS 1.2 server are stored in the <*driveletter*:>\SMS\Logon.srv\Isvmif.box directory. Copy the contents of this directory to another location.

The data that already exists in the database from the inclusion of these files is retained and upgraded to the SMS 2.0 database structure.

CODE BLUE

The files that exist on the client are kept, but SMS 2.0 cannot read them because SMS 2.0 IDMIF files have a slight change incorporated. The SMS 1.2 files can be modified to work with the SMS 2.0 MIF syntax.

SMS 2.0 incorporates a new Delta Header into the IDMIF file. SMS 2.0 reads the Delta Header and uses the data to understand what the SMS processes should do with the information. The following are the Delta Headers introduced by SMS 2.0:

- //AgentID <agent name>
- //FullResync <0 or 1>
- //ResyncAgent <0 or 1>
- //ResyncClass <*class name*> <0 or 1>
- //Architecture <*architecture name*>
- //UniqueID <*unique value*>

The only required headers are the Architecture and the UniqueID. The Architecture header reference is a new Architecture as mentioned before. The UniqueID is an ID assigned to the Architecture. Every Architecture in the database must have a unique ID associated with it.

To include IDMIF and NOIDMIF files with your SMS 2.0 installation, the files need to be directed to the new MIF file locations on the client. Two registry keys on the client point to the new MIF file locations:

- The data item NOIDMIF in HKEY_LOCAL_MACHINE\Software\Microsoft\SMS\Client\Configuration\Client Properties\NOIDMIF Directory has the value %WINDIR%\MS\SMS\Noidmifs.

- The data item IDMIF in HKEY_LOCAL_MACHINE\Software\Microsoft\SMS\Client\Configuration\Client Properties\IDMIF Directory has the value IDMIF: %WINDIR%\MS\SMS\IDMIFS.

When third-party vendors create their custom MIF files, they query these registry keys to determine the correct MIF directory path. When migrating your existing NOIDMIF and IDMIF files, these are the directories in which the files should be placed.

Again, remember, IDMIF and NOIDMIF files are hardware inventory components. No matter what information you collect (for example, specific registry key information, logon user name, or MS Outlook settings), the information is stored in a hardware data Architecture and only NOIDMIF information displays in the Resource Explorer. Information such as an Office location or a User's Social Security number is stored under hardware Architecture. The Hardware Inventory Client Agent (HINV32) processes these files on the client. HINV32 processes the information and forwards it on to the site server where the Inventory Data Loader enters the information into the site database.

Custom MIF Example

The following example MIF file is installed as part of the Q252718 HotFix. This HotFix, installed on the SMS site servers, is one of the required prerequisites before upgrading the SMS site to Service Pack 2.

NOTE: When HotFixes are installed on the SMS site, a NOIDMIF file is placed in the %WINDIR%\MS\SMS\NOIDMIFS directory. The MIF filename that the HotFix installation creates is named after the Microsoft Knowledge Base article created for the HotFix. In this case, the following example MIF's filename is Q252718.mif. Not only does this enable you to retrieve HotFix information from the SMS Administrator console (because of the MIF entry into the site's SQL database), but you can also take a quick look in the NOIDMIFS directory on the server to determine this. If you are sitting in front of the server, this is a convenient way to determine whether client components are up to date without opening the SMS Administrator console. Similarly, if you are logged into the server using an account that doesn't have certain view rights in the SMS Administrator console, you can still identify the HotFixes that have been applied.

```
--Start Custom MIF

Start Component

  Name = "Machine"

    Start Group

        Name = "QFE Update"

        ID = 1

        Class = "MICROSOFT|UPDATE|1.0"

        Pragma = "Hardware"

        Start Attribute

            Name = "UpdateID"

            ID = 1

            Access = READ-ONLY

            Storage = SPECIFIC

            Type = String(8)

            Value = "Q252718"

        End Attribute

        Start Attribute

            Name = "ProductName"
```

```
    ID = 2
    Access = READ-ONLY
    Storage = SPECIFIC
    Type = String(8)
    Value = "SMS 2.0"
End Attribute
Start Attribute
    Name = "Description"
    ID = 3
    Access = READ-ONLY
    Storage = SPECIFIC
    Type = String(80)
    Value = "TBD"
End Attribute
Start Attribute
    Name = "Type"
    ID = 4
    Access = READ-ONLY
    Storage = SPECIFIC
```

```
    Type = String(40)

    Value = "Update"

End Attribute

Start Attribute

    Name = "IsInstalled"

    ID = 5

    Access = READ-ONLY

    Storage = SPECIFIC

    Type = Int

    Value = 2

End Attribute

Start Attribute

    Name = "InstallDate"

    ID = 6

    Access = READ-ONLY

    Storage = SPECIFIC

    Type = Date

    Value = "20000608222759.000000+000"

End Attribute
```

```
        Start Attribute
            Name = "InstalledBy"
            ID = 7
            Access = READ-ONLY
            Storage = SPECIFIC
            Type = String(20)
            Value = "Administrator"
        End Attribute
    End Group
End Component
--End Custom MIF
```

SMS_DEF.MOF

The SMS_DEF.MOF file is a database that SMS uses to relay standard site hardware requirements. This standard is replicated to all child sites and all client computers. The *MOF* extension stands for *Managed Object Format*. The primary SMS_DEF.MOF file copied to the client computer is stored in the \SMS\Inboxes\Clifiles.src\Hinv directory on the site server. This file is installed on to the client during the hardware inventory component installation and is installed in the %WINDIR%\MS\SMS\CLICOMP\HINV directory on the client computer.

NOTE: 16-bit hardware is not customizable. Modifying the SMS_DEF.MOF file has no affect on 16-bit hardware inventory. Full inventory is performed on the 16-bit client every time hardware inventory is run.

When the SMS site is installed, the installation process creates a default SMS_DEF.MOF file. By default, many of the available hardware options are not enabled. As you see in the following sections, the SMS_DEF.MOF file is fully customizable.

CODE BLUE

Be careful when editing the SMS_DEF.MOF file. The file is not designed to run with all the options enabled. The size of a normal hardware inventory MIF file is around 100K. As you add more hardware items to the inventory, the file size increases substantially.

This adversely affects both the performance on the client during hardware inventory and network transmission. If hundreds of clients are inventorying at the same time, the network can become saturated with MIF transmissions.

Manually Editing the SMS_DEF.MOF File

SMS 2.0 incorporates features that enable you to customize your environment, and specify the amount and detail of hardware inventory. This capability provides total customization to meet the inventory needs of your organization.

Editing SMSDEF.MOF with the MOF Manager Utility

The **SMS_DEF.MOF** file is the site template for the hardware inventory preferences. SMS 2.0 uses this file to propagate the hardware inventory rules to other child sites and client PCs. By default, not all Classes and Properties are enabled. This is primarily because the amount of data would overwhelm both the client and the site server during the first inventory process.

CODE BLUE

Editing the SMS site SMS_DEF.MOF file directly could cause serious problems. A direct edit risks damaging the hardware inventory parameters of the site and could cause hardware inventory to stop processing completely.

Instead, copy the site SMS_DEF.MOF file to a workstation to modify it. Once you are satisfied with the changes, test the modified file on a single client. When you are positive the new file works, copy it to the SMS site for replication to the other sites and client computers.

Don't do any of this until you back up the site's SMS_DEF.MOF file.

The following is an example of the PC BIOS section in the SMS_DEF.MOF file:

```
[SMS_Report(TRUE),
    SMS_Group_Name("BIOS"),
    ResID(300),ResDLL("SMS_RXPL.dll"),
    SMS_Class_ID("MICROSOFT|PC_BIOS|1.0")]
class Win32_BIOS : SMS_Class_Template
{       [SMS_Report(TRUE)]
    string          BuildNumber;
    [SMS_Report(FALSE)]
    string          Caption;
    [SMS_Report(FALSE)]
    string          CodeSet;
    [SMS_Report(TRUE)]
    string          Description;
    [SMS_Report(FALSE)]
    string          IdentificationCode;
    [SMS_Report(FALSE)]
    datetime        InstallDate;
    [SMS_Report(FALSE)]
    string          LanguageEdition;
```

```
[SMS_Report(TRUE)]

string          Manufacturer;

[SMS_Report(TRUE),key]

string          Name;

[SMS_Report(FALSE)]

string          OtherTargetOS;

[SMS_Report(FALSE)]

boolean         PrimaryBIOS;

[SMS_Report(TRUE)]

datetime        ReleaseDate;

[SMS_Report(TRUE)]

string          SerialNumber;

[SMS_Report(FALSE)]

string          SoftwareElementID;

[SMS_Report(FALSE)]

uint16          SoftwareElementState;

[SMS_Report(FALSE)]

string          Status;

[SMS_Report(FALSE)]

uint16          TargetOperatingSystem;
```

```
    [SMS_Report(TRUE)]

    string          Version;

};
```

Microsoft included the MofMan utility on the SMS 2.0 CD in the \Support\ResKit\Bin\<platform>\MofMan directory. MOF Manager is a graphical interface for modifying the SMS_DEF.MOF file. The utility is specific to the SMS_DEF.MOF file and won't work with any other MOF file.

The interface is simple, as shown in Figure 3-2.

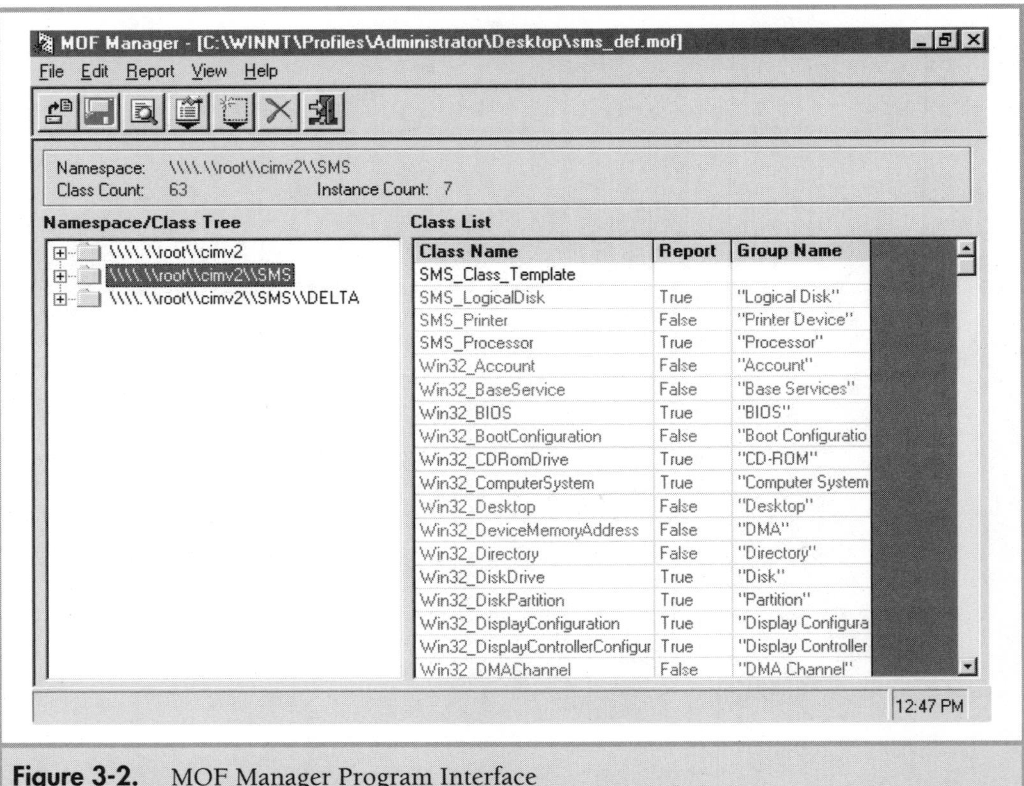

Figure 3-2. MOF Manager Program Interface

For this example, the same information from the PC BIOS section of the SMS_DEF.MOF file is shown in the following illustration, but in the MOF Manager format (default values).

Property List

Property Name	Type	Report	Key	Unit
BuildNumber	string	True		
Caption	string	False		
CodeSet	string	False		
Description	string	True		
IdentificationCode	string	False		
InstallDate	datetime	False		
LanguageEdition	string	False		
Manufacturer	string	True		
Name	string	True	True	
OtherTargetOS	string	False		
PrimaryBIOS	boolean	False		
ReleaseDate	datetime	True		
SerialNumber	string	True		
SoftwareElementID	string	False		
SoftwareElementStat	uint16	False		
Status	string	False		
TargetOperatingSyst	uint16	False		
Version	string	True		

Certain properties in the SMS_DEF.MOF file are set as False by default. The more Properties that are marked True, the larger the information packet sent back to the site server.

To enable a Property, double-click its listing to change the Property to True. This informs the Hardware Inventory Agent that this item should be included during the inventory process.

For true customization of your organization, you should determine what Properties of Classes are needed in your organization, enable those Properties, and distribute the standard throughout the enterprise.

Editing SMSDEF.MOF with Any Text Editor

Situations may occur where you don't have access to MOF Manager and have to edit the SMS_DEF.MOF file manually. In this case, understanding the MOF structure is imperative. You can open the SMS_DEF.MOF file in any text editor.

NOTE: Again, the SMS_DEF.MOF file is stored on the SMS 2.0 site server in the \\<site_server>\<share>\SMS\Inboxes\clifiles.src\hinv.

CAUTION: Always back up the file, and then copy it to another machine or another location before you make any changes. Never edit the file directly on the site server location.

To enable reporting on an item in the class, replace FALSE with TRUE on the SMS_Report line that coincides with the item you want to turn on. The opposite is true if you want to disable inventory on a hardware item.

After editing and saving the SMS_DEF.MOF file, copy the new version over the one on the site server. The new version is available to the client PCs after the next SMS site maintenance schedule.

CAUTION: Don't change the file structure in any way. Use the SMS MOF Manager if at all possible. If you accidentally modify the structure, the SMS_DEF.MOF file could contain a syntax error. When this happens, the Hardware Inventory Agent cannot update the hardware inventory schema. The SMS Status Message system will display a 10507 error message. You can use the MofComp.exe utility, located in the %SYS32%\WBEM directory to verify the viability of the SMS_DEF.MOF file, but you probably will need to replace the file with a backup file.

The following example is an excerpt from the SMS Group Name "User Accounts." Notice the SMS class is Win32_UserAccount indicated on the fifth line of the group header. A great deal of good information is in this group and, by default, it is all turned off.

```
[SMS_Report(FALSE),

     SMS_Group_Name("User Accounts"),

     ResID(5900),ResDLL("SMS_RXPL.dll"),

     SMS_Class_ID("MICROSOFT|USER|1.0")]

class Win32_UserAccount : SMS_Class_Template

{

     [SMS_Report(FALSE)]

     uint32           AccountType;

     [SMS_Report(FALSE)]

     string           Caption;

     [SMS_Report(FALSE)]
```

```
string          Description;
[SMS_Report(FALSE)]
boolean         Disabled;
[SMS_Report(FALSE),key]
string          Domain;
[SMS_Report(FALSE)]
string          FullName;
[SMS_Report(FALSE)]
datetime        InstallDate;
[SMS_Report(FALSE)]
boolean         Lockout;
[SMS_Report(FALSE),key]
string          Name;
[SMS_Report(FALSE)]
boolean         PasswordChangeable;
[SMS_Report(FALSE)]
boolean         PasswordExpires;
[SMS_Report(FALSE)]
boolean         PasswordRequired;
```

```
    [SMS_Report(FALSE)]

    string          SID;

    [SMS_Report(FALSE)]

    uint8           SIDType;

    [SMS_Report(FALSE)]

    string          Status;

};
```

TIP: If you look at the hardware inventory parameters for your site in the SMS_DEF.MOF file, many of the inventory options are turned off. This is to protect your site from being overwhelmed by the amount of data SMS 2.0 can collect. You can manually customize the SMS_DEF.MOF file to your site's needs or use the MOF Manager program that comes with the SMS 2.0 Support tools on the SMS 2.0 CD. Using Notepad to make modifications to the SMS_DEF.MOF file is better. Also, note Mofman.exe in Sp1 is broken, use Notepad, SP2 version, or Resource Kit version.

CODE BLUE

Mofman.exe, which comes as part of Service Pack 1, doesn't work correctly. If you want to edit the SMS_DEF.MOF, you must either use Notepad or the version that comes with Service Pack 2.

For example, suppose you have been asked to find out the Icon Spacing (of all things) on each computer in a specific department. You won't need the data after the initial inventory and the specific collection doesn't need to be run on the entire site. You already have a Collection defined based on the department through a workgroup parameter or an environment variable.

Because all the processes, such as hardware and software inventory, reside on the client, the same SMS_DEF.MOF file that resides on the CAP is propagated to the client. This makes inventory for your site a uniform process.

The SMS_DEF.MOF file is propagated from the \Clifiles.Box\Hinv directory on the CAP to the %Windir%\Ms\Sms\Sitefile\<*Sitename*>\Hinv and %Windir%\Ms\Sms\Clicomp\Hinv directories on the client. The location under \Sitefile is a backup copy for repairing the hardware inventory component.

To inventory additional components, perform the following steps:

1. Copy the SMS_DEF.MOF file from the CAP to your local machine.
2. Use MOF Manager to customize the SMS_DEF.MOF file for the custom inventory.
3. Create a SMS Installer package that installs the new SMS_DEF.MOF file to the %Windir%\Ms\Sms\Clicomp\Hinv directory on the client.
4. Create a distribution package of the compiled script.
5. Distribute the package to the targeted collection (this can also be distributed to one client if that's the focus).
6. Wait for the new inventory.

NOTE: At the next CCIM cycle, the SMS_DEF.MOF file on the client computer is overwritten with the site's default .MOF file. Also, if you modify an individual SMS_DEF.MOF file on a client, SMS overwrites it with the .MOF on the site server.

CODE BLUE

The best troubleshooting is preventive maintenance. Once you develop a hardware inventory schedule for your site, plan to deploy the distribution right before a hardware inventory is scheduled. Or, include an external command in the deployment package to run the hardware inventory immediately after the new SMS_DEF.MOF file is installed. The command file is Hinv32.exe in the %Windir%\Ms\Sms\Clicomp\Hinv directory.

Also, take note of the following to insure a trouble-free deployment:

- If you're afraid the distribution might not run before the hardware inventory, make the distribution mandatory.
- For mobile clients, send the package via e-mail or have them pull it from a Web page.
- When a resynch is performed on the client computer, the site SMS_DEF.MOF file will be repropagated to the client, so the new inventory schema must be run before this happens.

SMS_DEF.MOF Inventory Classes

The SMS_DEF.MOF file contains the information SMS uses to collect hardware inventory. Table 3-3 lists the hardware inventory classes contained in the SMS_DEF.MOF file, the WMI object name, the SMS Class Name for using in queries, and whether the specific class is collected by a default installation. For more information on how to query using the SMS Class Name, see "Queries" in Chapter 10. You can also use this table for planning for your organization. Sit down with a group of people and decide what hardware information is important to have available.

Name	WMI (WBEM) Name (Listing in MOF Manager)	SMS Class Name	Collected by Default?
Account	Win32_Account	SMS_G_System_ACCOUNT	No
Base Services	Win32_BaseService	SMS_BaseService	No
BIOS	Win32_BIOS	SMS_G_System_PC_BIOS	Yes
Boot Configuration	Win32_BootConfiguration	SMS_G_System_BOOT_CONFIGURATION	No
CD-ROM	Win32_CDRomDrive	SMS_G_System_CDROM	Yes
Computer System	Win32_ComputerSystem	SMS_G_System_COMPUTER_SYSTEM	Yes
Desktop	Win32_Desktop	SMS_G_System_DESKTOP	No
Directory	Win32_Directory	SMS_G_System_DIRECTORY	No
Disk	Win32_DiskDrive	SMS_G_System_DISK	Yes
Display Configuration	Win32_DisplayConfiguration	SMS_G_System_DISPLAY_CONFIGURATION	Yes
Display Controller Configuration	Win32_DisplayControllerConfiguration	SMS_G_System_DISPLAY_CONTROLLER_CONFIGURATION	Yes
DMA	Win32_DeviceMemoryAddress	SMS_G_System_DEVICE_MEMORY_ADDRESS	No
DMA Channel	Win32_DMAChannel	SMS_G_System_DEVICE_MEMORY_ADDRESS	No
Driver – VXD	Win32_DriverVXD	SMS_G_System_DRIVER_VXD	Yes
Environment	Win32_Environment	SMS_G_System_ENVIRONMENT	No
Groups	Win32_Group	SMS_G_System_GROUP	No
IRQ Table	Win32_IRQResource	SMS_G_System_IRQ	No

Table 3-3. SMS_DEF.MOF Hardware Inventory Classes

Name	WMI (WBEM) Name (Listing in MOF Manager)	SMS Class Name	Collected by Default?
Keyboard	Win32_Keyboard	SMS_G_System_KEYBOARD_DEVICE	Yes
Load Order Group	Win32_LoadOrderGroup	SMS_G_System_LOAD_ORDER_GROUP	No
Logical Disk	Win32_LogicalDisk	SMS_G_System_LOGICAL_DISK	Yes
Memory	Win32_LogicalMemoryConfiguration	SMS_G_System_X86_PC_MEMORY	Yes
Modem	Win32_POTSModem	SMS_G_System_MODEM_DEVICE	Yes
Motherboard	Win32_MotherboardDevice	SMS_G_System_MOTHERBOARD_DEVICE	Yes
Network Adapter	Win32_NetworkAdapter	SMS_G_System_NETWORK_ADAPTER	Yes
Network Adapter Configuration	Win32_NetworkAdapterConfiguration	SMS_G_System_NETWORK_ADAPTER_ CONFIGURATION	Yes
Network Client	Win32_NetworkClient	SMS_G_System_NETWORK_CLIENT	Yes
Network Connection	Win32_NetworkConnection	SMS_G_System_NETWORK_CONNECTION	No
Network Login Profile	Win32_NetworkLoginProfile	SMS_G_System_NETWORK_LOGIN_PROFILE	No
NT Event Log File	Win32_NTEventlogFile	SMS_G_System_NT_EVENTLOG_FILE	No
NT Log Event	Win32_NTLogEvent	SMS_G_System_NT_LOG_EVENT	No
Operating System	Win32_OperatingSystem	SMS_G_System_OPERATING_SYSTEM	Yes
Operating System Recovery Configuration	Win32_OSRecoveryConfiguration	SMS_G_System_OS_RECOVERY_CONFIGURATION	No
Pagefile	Win32_PageFile	SMS_G_System_PAGE_FILE	No
Parallel Port	Win32_ParallelPort	SMS_G_System_PARALLEL_PORT	Yes
Partition	Win32_DiskPartition	SMS_G_System_PARTITION	Yes
Pointing Device	Win32_PointingDevice	SMS_G_System_POINTING_DEVICE	Yes
Ports	Win32_PortResouce	SMS_G_System_PORT	No

Table 3-3. SMS_DEF.MOF Hardware Inventory Classes *(continued)*

Name	WMI (WBEM) Name (Listing in MOF Manager)	SMS Class Name	Collected by Default?
Printer Configuration	Win32_PrinterConfiguration	SMS_G_System_PRINTER_ CONFIGURATION	No
Printer Device	Win32_Printer	SMS_G_System_PRINTER_ DEVICE	No
Print Jobs	Win32_PrintJob	SMS_G_System_PRINT_JOB	No
Process	Win32_Process	SMS_G_System_PROCESS	No
Processor	Win32_Processor	SMS_G_System_PROCESSOR	Yes
Protocol	Win32_NetworkProtocol	SMS_G_System_PROTOCOL	No
Program Group	Win32_ProgramGroup	SMS_G_System_PROGRAM_ GROUP	No
Registry	Win32_Registry	SMS_G_System_REGISTRY	No
SCSI Controller	Win32_SCSIController	SMS_G_System_SCSI_ CONTROLLER	Yes
Serial Ports	Win32_SerialPort	SMS_G_System_SERIAL_PORT	No
Serial Port Configuration	Win32_SerialPortConfiguration	SMS_G_System_SERIAL_PORT _ CONFIGURATION	No
Services	Win32_Service	SMS_G_System_SERVICE	Yes
Shares	Win32_Share	SMS_G_System_SHARE	No
Sound Devices	Win32_SoundDevice	SMS_G_System_SOUND_ DEVICE	Yes
System Account	Win32_SystemAccount	SMS_G_System_SYSTEM_ ACCOUNT	No
System Drivers	Win32_SystemDriver	SMS_G_System_SYSTEM_ DRIVER	No
System Memory Resource	Win32_SystemMemory Resource	SMS_G_System_SYSTEM_ MEMORY_ RESOURCE	No
Tape Drive	Win32_TapeDrive	SMS_G_System_TAPE_DRIVE	Yes
Time Zone	Win32_TimeZone	SMS_G_System_TIME_ZONE	No
Universal Power Supply	Win32_PowerSupply	SMS_G_System_POWER_ SUPPLY	No
User Accounts	Win32_UserAccount	SMS_G_System_USER	No
Video	Win32_VideoConfiguration	SMS_G_System_VIDEO	Yes

Table 3-3. SMS_DEF.MOF Hardware Inventory Classes *(continued)*

When you look at the Collected by Default column, you may find default items that are unnecessary in your organization. You can use the MOF Manager Utility to turn off the default hardware inventory classes. Or, you can turn on the hardware items that make sense for your company. Remember, the more items that are enabled, the larger the collection file will be, the longer hardware inventory will take to process, and the more network bandwidth will be used when transferring the files to the CAP, and then on to the SMS site server.

Hardware Inventory Logs

The logs listed in Table 3-4 and Table 3-5 should be used when you are troubleshooting the hardware inventory process. The tables are sorted by the name of the SMS thread, and include the log location (Server, CAP, Client) and the path to the log file. When you use the Hardware Inventory Checklist in the following section, refer to the specific log file based on the thread in use.

Thread	Location	Log file
Hardware Inventory Agent	Client	<%windir%>\MS\SMS\Logs\Hinv32.log
Client Component Installation Manager	Client	<%windir%>\MS\SMS\Logs\Ccim32.log
Client Service (CliSvcl)	Client	<%windir%>\MS\SMS\Logs\Clisvc.log
Copy Queue	Client	<%windir%>\MS\SMS\Logs\Cqmgr32.log
Inbox Manager	Site Server	SMS\Logs\Inboxmgr.log
Inbox Manager Assistant	CAP	SMS\Logs\Inboxast.log
Inventory Processor	Site Server	SMS\Logs\Invproc.log
Inventory Data Loader	Site Server	SMS\Logs\Dataldr.log
Replication Manager	Site Server	SMS\Logs\Replmgr.log

Table 3-4. Hardware Inventory Logs (32-bit Client)

Thread	Location	Log file
Hardware Inventory Agent	Client	<%windir%>\MS\SMS\Logs\Hinv.log
Client Component Installation Manager	Client	<%windir%>\MS\SMS\Logs\Ccim16.log
Copy Queue	Client	<%windir%>\MS\SMS\Logs\Clearque.log
Inbox Manager	Site Server	SMS\Logs\Inboxmgr.log
Inbox Manager Assistant	CAP	SMS\Logs\Inboxast.log
Inventory Processor	Site Server	SMS\Logs\Invproc.log
Inventory Data Loader	Site Server	SMS\Logs\Dataldr.log
Replication Manager	Site Server	SMS\Logs\Replmgr.log

Table 3-5. Hardware Inventory Logs (16-bit Client)

Hardware Inventory Process Checklists

For the hardware inventory process to begin, hardware inventory must be enabled for the SMS site. If it isn't, the hardware inventory component "wakes up," checks the site configuration, and then stops. This checklist is divided into two phases: Client Phase and SMS Site Server Phase. The division of the processes refers to where the processing is occurring.

32-bit Client Checklist

The client services and threads start the process by performing the inventory and creating the inventory files. The inventory files are then passed to the CAP where they are retrieved by the threads on the SMS site server. The CAP provides no processing; it is only a holding box for the inventory files.

Client Phase The SMS hardware inventory process determines if hardware inventory is installed on the client. If it isn't, the Client Component Installation Manager (Ccim32.dll) starts the process.

- Ccim32.dll creates the Hinv directory in the %WINDIR%\MS\SMS\Clicomp directory on the client computer.
- Ccim32.dll installs the files for the Hardware Inventory Client component in the newly created Hinv directory.

- Ccim32.dll executes Mofcomp.exe.
- Mofcomp.exe compiles the SMS_DEF.MOF for the client. The SMS_DEF.MOF file stores the hardware inventory defaults designated for the SMS site. When hardware inventory is run, SMS_DEF.MOF is used to determine what pieces of hardware to inventory.
- Ccim32.dll schedules hardware inventory to "kick-off" after ten minutes of the component installation.

CHECKPOINT: Verify the hardware inventory component has been correctly installed. Confirm the Hinv directory has been created, and the component files have been inserted into the directory. The directory structure looks like the following: %WINDIR%\SMS\MS\Clicomp.

```
└→Hinv
   └→Outbox
   └→Temp
```

The Outbox and Temp directories should be empty because the Hardware Inventory process has not kicked off yet. In the Hinv directory, the following files should be present:

- DeHinv32.exe (the hardware inventory component deinstallation program)
- Hinv32.exe (the hardware inventory component that runs the process)
- The computer's SMS_DEF.MOF file (the hardware inventory specifications as defined in the site properties).

To verify a successful installation, also check the Hinv32.log. Hardware inventory isn't run on the computer until 15 to 30 minutes have elapsed after the installation. If an hour or more has passed and hardware inventory hasn't run, look in the Clisvc.log for errors.

NOTE: Clisvcl.exe (Windows 2000/NT clients) and Clisvc95.exe (Windows 9x clients) determine the hardware inventory frequency. The inventory frequency is stored in the computer's registry at HKEY_LOCAL_MACHINE\SOFTWARE\MS\SMS\Client\Sites\System\<SiteCode>\Client Components\Hardware Inventory Agent in a data item named Inventory Schedule.

- If hardware inventory is already installed on the client computer, Hinv32.exe queries the WMI CIM for the stored hardware inventory values defined by the computer's SMS_DEF.MOF file.

- Hinv32.exe checks for any NOIDMIF files (*.MIF) in the %WINDIR%\MS\SMS\NOIDMIFS directory.
    - If any NOIDMIF files exist, Hinv32.exe reads the contents of the files.
    - Hinv32.exe writes the information from the NOIDMIF files into the CIM Object Manager.

CODE BLUE

SMS requires the custom MIF files follow a specific criteria. If the files don't meet the criteria, Hinv32.exe pulls the files from the %WINDIR%\MS\SMS\NOIDMIFS directory and puts them into the %WINDIR%\MS\SMS\NOIDMIFS\BADIDMIFS directory. Here are the criteria for custom MIF files:

- MIF files must be less than the size indicated in the site settings of the SMS Administrator console. You can modify the accepted size of a custom MIF file by opening the properties of the Hardware Inventory Client Agent. To accomplish this:

1. Open Site Database—Site Hierarchy—Site (three-letter site code) —Site Settings—Client Agents—properties of the Hardware Inventory Client Agent.
2. Set the size in K. The minimum is 1K; the maximum SMS can handle is 5,000K (5MB). The default for the SMS installation is 250K.

If the MIF file is over the specified amount, it is moved to the process's relative \BADMIFS directory.

The maximum MIF size can be increased by modifying the registry data item **Max MIF size**, which is located in the following registry key at the Site Server: HKEY_LOCAL_MACHINE\SOFTWARE\Microsoft\SMS\Components\SMS_Inventory_Dataloader.

- MIF files cannot change the system information as outlined by the standard inventory.
- MIF files cannot add, delete, or update any System Architecture properties defined by the Hardware Inventory Agent in the SMS site database.
- The MIF file must be able to be parsed.

CHECKPOINT: Check for the existence of any files in the %WINDIR%\MS\SMS\NOIDMIFS\BADIDMIFS directory.

- Hinv32.exe enumerates the hardware inventory information in the CIM Object Manager (the *CIM Object Manager* is the conduit between the client applications, the CIM Repository, and the providers).
- Hinv32.exe writes the information to a temporary file in the %WINDIR%\MS\SMS\Clicomp\Hinv\Temp directory on the client computer.
- Hinv32.exe renames the temporary file to Hinvdat.hic or Hinvdat.hid (see the following NOTE for differences between the two types of Hinvdat files) and copies it to the %WINDIR%\MS\SMS\Clicomp\Hinv directory.

CHECKPOINT: This process moves along quickly, so you may be unable to catch the files in the TEMP directory. If a .hic or .hid file is present in the %WINDIR%\MS\SMS\Clicomp\Hinv directory, you can be sure the process is functioning properly.

NOTE: If the hardware inventory process has run on the client before, Hinv32.exe renames the file to Hinvdat.hid (.hid = Hardware Inventory Delta) instead of Hinvdat.hic (.hic = Hardware Inventory Complete). The first time hardware inventory is run, the hardware inventory process does a complete inventory of the computer's hardware and renames the file to Hinvdat.hic. For subsequent hardware inventory processes, SMS compares the complete inventory to anything that may have changed on the computer. The .hid file represents only the changes since the last hardware inventory was run. This creates a smaller file, which is transferred to the CAP, and then to the site database. Transferring a smaller file preserves network bandwidth, especially if your site is configured to perform hardware inventory frequently.

- Hinv32.exe copies either the Hinvdat.hic or Hinvdat.hid to the %WINDIR%\MS\SMS\Clicomp\Hinv\outbox directory.
- Hinv32.exe renames the .hic or .hid extension to an .inv file extension and prompts the Copy Queue to start the transfer of the .inv file to the CAP.
- Hinv32.exe deletes the .hic or .hid file.

CHECKPOINT: Verify an .inv file exists in the %WINDIR%\MS\SMS\Clicomp\Hinv\outbox directory.

- Hinv32.exe detects any IDMIF files in the %WINDIR%\MS\SMS\IDMIFS directory.

NOTE: IDMIFS follow the same criteria for all MIF files shown in the previous section of the checklist describing the processing of bad NOIDMIF files. If Hinv32.exe cannot process an IDMIF file, it is moved to the %WINDIR%\MS\SMS\IDMIFS\BADMIFS directory.

- Hinv32.exe renames the .inv file to .nhm (No History MIF) and moves it, as well as any .mif files (NOIDMIF and IDMIF), to the Inventry.box directory in the CAP_<sitecode> share on the site server.
- Hinv32.exe deletes all .inv files on the client computer.

CHECKPOINT: At this point, you should see, at least, an .nhm file in the Inventry.box on the CAP. Any .mif files that were processed are also in this directory. Check the \BADMIFS directory for any .mif files that couldn't be processed. If any exist, determine the reason based on the MIF file criteria. Verify all .inv files have been deleted on the computer. If the files (.nhm and .mif) don't exist on the CAP, double-check the connection between the client computer and the CAP. Remember, the Inbox Manager Assistant may have hit its wake-up interval and have already removed the files from the CAP (see the next section on the SMS Site Server Phase). The Cpmgr32.log file informs you of any connectivity issues between the computer and the CAP. On the CAP, view the Inboxast.log to determine if the CAP received the .nhm file.

SMS Site Server Phase

- Inbox Manager Assistant retrieves the .nhm and/or .mif files from the CAP and moves them to the SMS\Inboxes\Inventry.box on the site server.
- Inventory Processor renames any .nhm files to .mif and moves all the .mif files to the SMS\Inboxes\Dataldr.box (Data Loader Inbox).
- When the Inventory Data Loader detects .mif files in its inbox, it retrieves the files to the SMS\Inboxes\Dataldr.box\Process directory and begins processing the .mif files (it loads the data, hence, the name *Data Loader*).

CHECKPOINT: Identify that the .nhm and/or .mif files are present either in the Inventry.box or the Dataldr.box (depending on where the MIF files are in the process). You can view the Invproc.log to determine if the Inventory Processor successfully processed the .nhm file and renamed it to a .mif format.

NOTE: The Inventory Data Loader checks its processing directory every 15 minutes. When it finds .mif files in the processing directory, the Inventory Data Loader processes them until the inbox is empty.

- Inventory Data Loader tries to parse the .mif file. If it is successful, it writes the .mif information to the SMS site database.

NOTE: The Inventory Data Loader performs the same checks and balances Hinv32.exe does on .mif files. This is second-level protection in case an inventory file has become corrupt because of network disturbances, such as faulty NICs, failed connections, client or server problems with defective storage controllers, or garbage along the communication lines. If a corrupt .mif file were to be processed and entered into the site database, the site database could become corrupt. If the .mif file doesn't parse correctly, it is moved to the SMS\Inboxes\Dataldr.box\BADMIFS directory and the process stops.

CHECKPOINT: The Dataldr.log helps identify any issues if the Data Loader has problems processing the MIF files or writing the information to the SMS site database. Check the BADMIFS directory for any MIF files that either didn't meet the criteria or may be corrupt.

- If a parent site is defined, Replication Manager forwards the .mif file to the parent site's SMS\Inboxes\Dataldr.box where the parent site goes through the same process.

CHECKPOINT: Check the SMS\Inboxes\Dataldr.box at the parent site for the .mif files. If they aren't present, verify the connection.

- Inventory Data Loader updates the site's database statistics.

CHECKPOINT: At this point, the Hardware Inventory process is complete. If the inventory information doesn't show up in the computer's record in the SMS Administrator console, check the SQL Server error logs for more information. Also, double-check that the SQL Services are running.

16-bit Client Checklist

The 16-bit Client hardware inventory process isn't as involved as the 32-bit client. The 16-bit process performs no client-side verifications of possible corrupted files. The entire verification process is left to the Inventory Data Loader on the site server.

Client Phase

- Hinv16.exe inventories the hardware of the client computer and writes the information to a .tmp file in the %WINDIR%\MS\SMS\Clicomp\Hinv\Temp directory.
- Hinv16.exe renames the .tmp file to a .raw file and places it in the %WINDIR%\MS\SMS\Clicomp\Hinv\Outbox directory.

NOTE: The .raw file created by Hinv16.exe is preceded by an eight-digit filename. For the first hardware inventory completed, the filename will be: 00000000.raw. Every time hardware inventory is run, the filename is incremented by one digit, hence, for a computer that has been inventoried 17 times, the filename will be: 00000017.raw.

CHECKPOINT: Check for the existence of the .raw file in the %WINDIR%\MS\SMS\Clicomp\Hinv\Outbox directory.

- Hinv16.exe presents the .raw files to ClearQue.exe (the 16-bit Copy Queue thread).
- ClearQue.exe copies the .raw files from the %WINDIR%\MS\SMS\Clicomp\Hinv\Outbox directory to the CAP_<sitecode>\Hinv.box directory on the CAP.

NOTE: ClearQue.exe runs on a one-hour schedule. Every hour, ClearQue.exe checks the hardware inventory outbox for any new or remaining .raw files and transfers them to the CAP.

- ClearQue.exe deletes the .raw files from the %WINDIR%\MS\SMS\Clicomp\Hinv\Outbox directory that have been successfully transferred to the CAP.

CHECKPOINT: Verify the xxxxxxxx.raw file has been successfully transferred to the CAP and placed in the CAP_<sitecode>\Hinv.box directory. If the file was successfully transferred, the same filename shouldn't be present on the client computer. If the file is not found on the CAP, verify the client computer hasn't lost network connectivity.

SMS Site Server Phase

- Inbox Manager Assistant retrieves the .raw files from the CAP and moves them to the SMS_<sitecode>\Inboxes\Inventry.box directory on the SMS site server.

CHECKPOINT: The specific .raw file should no longer be in the CAP_<sitecode>\Hinv.box directory on the CAP and should be found in the SMS_<sitecode>\Inboxes\Inventry.box directory on the SMS site server. If the .raw file isn't present in the SMS site server directory, verify the SMS_EXECUTIVE service is running.

- Inventory Processor retrieves the .raw files from the Inventry.box and reformats them into MIF format.
- Inventory Processor renames the .raw files to a .MIF extension.
- Inventory Processor moves the new .mif files to the SMS\Inboxes\Dataldr.box directory.

CHECKPOINT: Verify the .MIF files are now located in the SMS\Inboxes\Dataldr.box directory.

- Inventory Data Loader retrieves the .MIF files from the Dataldr.box directory and moves them to the SMS\Inboxes\Dataldr.box\Process directory.

CHECKPOINT: Check the SMS\Inboxes\Dataldr.box\Process directory for the new .MIF files.

NOTE: The Inventory Data Loader checks its processing directory every 15 minutes. When it finds .MIF files in the processing directory, it processes them until the inbox is empty.

- Inventory Data Loader processes the .mif files in the Process directory.
- Inventory Data Loader tries to parse the .mif file. If it's successful, it writes the .MIF information to the SMS site database.

CHECKPOINT: The Dataldr.log helps identify issues if the Data Loader has problems processing the MIF files or writing the information to the SMS site database. Check the \BADMIFS directory for any MIF files that either didn't meet the criteria or may be corrupt.

- If a parent site is defined, Replication Manager forwards the .MIF file to the parent site's SMS\Inboxes\Dataldr.box where the parent site goes through the same process.

CHECKPOINT: Check the SMS\Inboxes\Dataldr.box at the parent site for the .MIF files. If they aren't present, verify the connection.

- Inventory Data Loader updates the site's database statistics.

CHECKPOINT: At this point, the Hardware Inventory process is complete. If the inventory information doesn't show up in the computer's record in the SMS Administrator console, check the SQL Server error logs for more information. Also, double-check that SQL Services are running.

Hardware Inventory Resynch Checklist

A Hardware Inventory Resynch can be initiated at the SMS site server. When this happens, the Inventory Data Loader has already begun its process of checking the site for bad .MIF files and has either found a corrupt .MIF file or discovered a .MIF file that is trying to update a nonexistent row in the SMS SQL database.

The Resynch is a protective measure to verify MIF files and keep the SMS database from becoming corrupt. The following Checklist assumes the Data Loader has identified one of the criteria for starting the resynch. The Hardware Inventory Resynch takes place in two phases: SMS Site Server Phase and the Client Computer Phase. These phases identify where the Resynch processing is taking place and what location can be researched to identify any problems.

Site Server Phase

- Inventory Data Loader verifies the Client.lkp (client lookup) file in the SMS\INBOXES\CLIDATA.SRC directory on the site server has an associated entry for the computer that submitted the MIF file.
- Inventory Data Loader creates an index based on the client's SMS Unique ID.
- Inventory Data Loader initiates a Resynch request and writes a .CFG file to the SMS\Inboxes\Clidata.src directory on the SMS site server.

NOTE: If the Inventory Data Loader doesn't find an entry for the identified client in the Client Lookup file (LKP), it creates a .CFG file for the client and adds the client information to the Client Lookup file for next time.

- Inbox Manager retrieves the new .CFG file and the Client.LKP file.
- Inbox Manager copies the .CFG and Client.LKP files to the CAP\Clidata.box directory on the CAP.

CHECKPOINT: Verify the Client.LKP file and the new .CFG file are present in the CAP\Clidata.box directory on the CAP. The Client.LKP file can be viewed to determine the actual name of the .CFG file for which you should be looking. The client's SMS Unique ID precedes this .CFG name. The Client.LKP file is in ASCII text format. Here's an example of the contents of the Client.LKP file: GUID:9EC78B60-2075-11D4-A725-00104B343E6C IUSH4YZ5.cfg

Client Computer Phase

- CCIM (Client Component Installation Manager) sleeps until its scheduled wake-up interval and connects to the CAP. The scheduled wake-up period is 23 hours, by default.

CHECKPOINT: You can verify CCIM has started its wake-up polling by viewing the running services on the client computer:

- CCIM reads the specific client information as indicated in the Client.LKP file. The Client.LKP file points to the new .CFG file on the CAP.
- CCIM reads the .CFG file and modifies the client computer's registry with the updated information. The registry key modified is *HKEY_LOCAL_MACHINE\SOFTWARE\Microsoft\SMS\Client\Sites\Share\<Sitecode>\Configuration\Dataloader Properties\Last Resync Request*.
- CCIM sends a message to the SMS Client Service to indicate the registry key has been updated.
- The SMS Client Service executes the Hardware Inventory Agent.

CHECKPOINT: Verify the Hardware Inventory Agent is running.

- The Hardware Inventory Agent checks the **Last Resync Request** data item in HKEY_LOCAL_MACHINE\SOFTWARE\Microsoft\SMS\Client\Sites\Share\<Sitecode>\ Configuration\Dataloader Properties against the **Last Resync Request** data item in HKEY_LOCAL_MACHINE\SOFTWARE\Microsoft\SMS\Client\Client Components\ Hardware Inventory Agent\Sites\<Sitecode>. If the values match, the Resynch is halted.

CHECKPOINT: If the Resynch has trouble completing at this point in the process, check that the process has access to the client's registry. If you look at the contents of the .CFG file shown in the previous Checkpoint, as referenced by the Client.LKP file, you can see the Last Resync Request information written to the client computer's registry (see following list).

.CFG Contents

```
[Dataloader Properties]
(REG_SZ)Last Resync Request=0x01BFD95C48FF4690
TargetPlatforms=ALL
[Client Components]
LastUpdate=29350236, 1224689296
```

- If the registry key values don't match, the Hardware Inventory Agent starts the hardware inventory cycle on the client.

CHECKPOINT: If the Hardware Inventory Resynch has reached this far, you can use the Hardware Inventory Process Checklist to follow the hardware inventory process.

Hardware Inventory Scheduling

When SMS is installed, Hardware Inventory is set to run every seven days by default. This option cannot be modified during the initial installation; it can only be modified after the site software is installed and running. Hardware in a computer rarely changes, so the seven-day default is a sensible standard.

In some unique situations, however, the seven-day period may not make sense. A specific example is a lab environment where hardware changes frequently. Or, another possibility is a software developer dependent on swapping hardware for testing purposes. Then again, individuals in these situations may not want the hardware inventoried by SMS at all.

The Hardware Inventory schedule can be modified to the particular needs of the organization. Some companies prefer to inventory hardware every day, some once a month, and others feel the seven-day default is adequate.

The Hardware Inventory schedule is modified through the SMS Administrator console in the Hardware Inventory Agent properties. You can access this property screen by opening Site Database | Site Hierarchy | Site Name | Site Settings | Client Agents.

The more frequently Hardware Inventory is set to run, the more network traffic is required to transfer the inventory files. If you must set Hardware Inventory to run on a frequent basis, plan to schedule it during a period when network activity is at its lowest. The time of day that produces the heaviest load on the network is usually the morning, as people start logging into the network. The second heaviest is between 11:45A.M. and 1:00P.M. (as employees start coming back from lunch).

As shown in the following illustration, the Hardware Inventory Client Agent Properties can be modified for a simple inventory schedule and a full schedule.

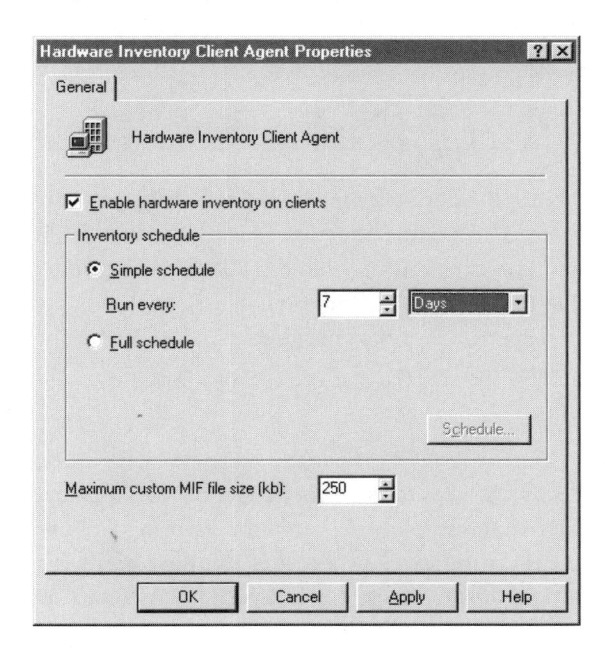

The Simple Schedule section enables you to quickly modify the schedule that is best for your organization. The Full Schedule can be used to provide a more comprehensive method for assigning scheduling to the SMS site.

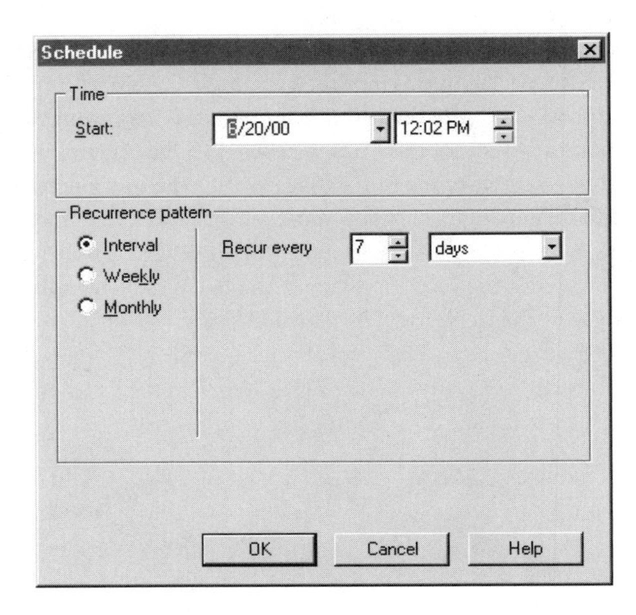

In addition to modifying the hardware inventory schedule, you can set the maximum size of the custom MIF file. This relates directly to how large the MIF file can be before SMS considers the file is "bad" and dropped into the BADMIFS directories.

Also note, the Enable Hardware Inventory on Clients check box is on the Hardware Inventory Client Agent Properties screen. This check box MUST be checked for hardware inventory to run in the SMS hierarchy.

Best Practices

As mentioned, an aggressive hardware inventory schedule can create a horde of MIF files flying across the network; this results in a saturated network. Hardware inventory on the client computer is a processor-intensive procedure. Running hardware inventory every day could upset the user population. It should already be a practice in your organization to sit down and hammer-out standards for technology and its processes. SMS hardware inventory should be added to this list.

The big concerns for deploying the SMS hardware inventory schedule should keep to the following points:

- **Network Connections**—Are the network connections fast or slow? If the communication lines connecting child sites to the SMS site are slow, consider scheduling processing off-hours.
- **Client Configuration**—What type of hardware is installed at your site? What processor types? How much RAM? If the client computers are inadequate, you might not want to run hardware inventory every day. You might even consider running hardware inventory once a month and notifying the user-base of the schedule.
- **Client Computer Type**—Is the user-base mostly LAN-locked, using desktop computers? Is your organization highly mobile using laptop computers? If the bulk of computers in the organization are desktop computers, it would make sense to keep the hardware inventory schedule once a week or once a month. Having individual users open the case on the desktop computer and swap parts isn't a common practice. Laptop computers, on the other hand, can frequently change hardware. With the plug-and-play capability of the operating system, and the types of ports available on the laptop computer (PCMCIA, USB, and so forth), the computer's hardware makeup can change quickly.
- **SMS Hierarchy Configuration**—Is your SMS site spread out across WAN links with multiple child sites or secondary sites? If the SMS site is large and hardware inventory takes a while to process completely, it would make sense to make the hardware inventory more frequent.
- **Tolerance**—Although the SMS Hardware Inventory process runs as a background process, it can still slow the performance of the computer. How tolerant will the user-base be to running hardware inventory once a day versus running it once a week or once a month? And, more important, how tolerant will management be if processing power is slowed and a critical report needs to be sent?

NOTE: Remember, duplicate SMS Unique IDs can cause hardware inventory and software inventory to perform poorly. When duplicate IDs exist, inventory data can flood the servers, causing stress on both the servers and the network connection. Also, duplicate IDs cause constant hardware and software resynchs.

Forcing Client Inventory

With SMS 1.2 you could force a client inventory by running the Hardware Inventory Agent with the /f switch (invwin32 /e /f). With the out-of-the-box implementation of SMS 2.0, the only clearly evident way to force inventory is by going through the Control Panel applet on the client computer—going to components—selecting the hardware or software component—and starting the component. This requires end-user participation and interaction.

You can force hardware inventory from the client computer by following these steps:

1. In Control Panel, double-click Systems Management.
2. Click the Components tab.

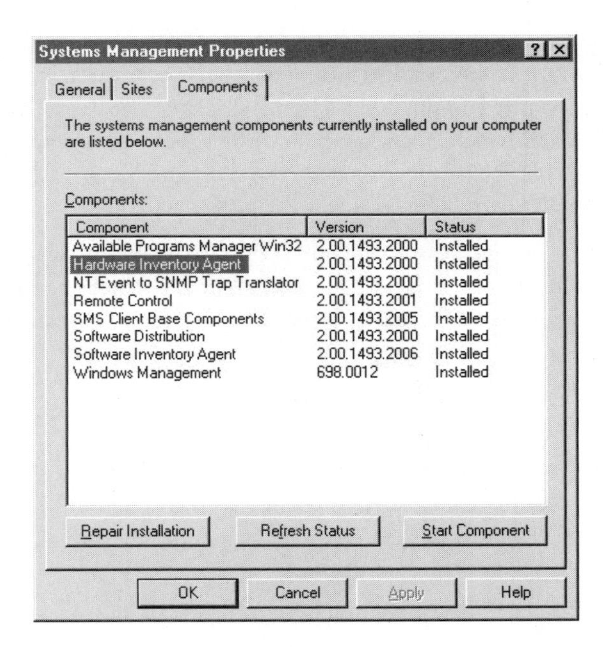

3. Select Hardware Inventory Agent.
4. Click Start Component.

The Hardware Inventory Agent starts and takes inventory on this client.

NOTE: Performing hardware and software inventory is processor-intensive, so the client computer will seem to operate more slowly while the inventory process is running.

InvSync.exe

The InvSync.exe tool is included on the SMS 2.0 CD in the \Support\Reskit\Bin\Platform\Diagnose directory. This tool sends a hardware or software inventory resynchronization request to the client based on parameters. InvSync.exe must be copied to the SMS\Bin\i386 directory on the site server.

The syntax for invsync is: **InvSync [hw | sw]** ***client_NetBiosName***

For example: InvSync sw MyComputerName

InvSync.exe is also dependent on the following files (verify their existence in the SMS\Bin\i386 directory):

- Encrypt.dll
- BaseObj.dll
- BaseSQL.dll
- Basesvr.dll
- BaseUtil.dll
- SMSPerf.dll

NOTE: InvSync.exe can only be run from the site server. It won't run on a client that belongs to a child site.

NTForceInv.exe

SMS Scriptmania (http://sms.scriptmania.com) is a relatively new Internet site. This site is just getting started, but has a good quantity of SMS specific scripts and utilities. One utility of particular interest is the NTForceInv.exe utility. NTForceInv.exe can be sent via a SMS package or advertisement. The utility forces the hardware (and software) inventory to run on a computer running Windows NT or Windows 2000. CCIM does not have to trigger the event for the utility to start gathering computer inventory.

The syntax is: **NTForceInv.exe /pc:*ComputerName* /hw:[y or n] /sw:[y or n]**

Typing in **NTForceInv.exe /?** brings up the command-line options screen shown in the following illustration.

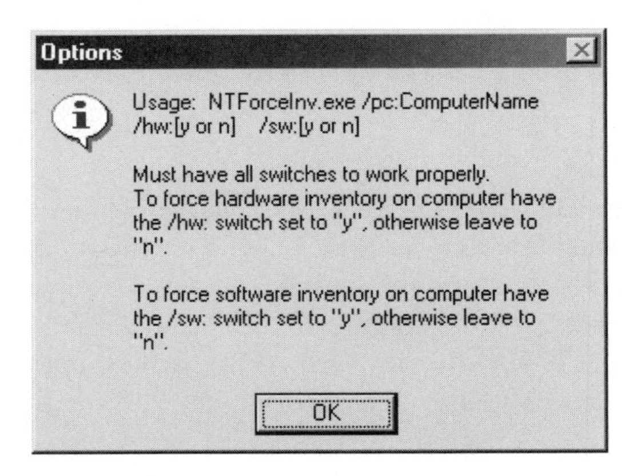

Forcing Windows 9x Inventory

Not to leave Windows 95 and 98 computers out, you can force the Windows 9*x* computers to run hardware inventory, as well. The following script is a SMS Installer script that retrieves the computer path to the SMS directory from the Windows registry. It then starts Hinv32.exe from the %SMSLOC%\Clicomp\Hinv\Hinv32.exe directory.

This script starts hardware inventory on Windows 95, Windows 98, Windows NT, and Windows 2000 computers. SMS Installer is an add-on tool that is part of the SMS 2.0 installation. It is available as an installable option during the setup. SMS Installer is primarily a repackaging tool, allowing you to create uniform SMS distributions, but it is also a high-level scripting tool that is easy to master. For more on SMS Installer, you can refer to: *Microsoft SMS Installer*, ISBN 0-07-212447-4.

---Begin Script

```
item: Get Registry Key Value

  Variable=SMSLOC

  Key=SOFTWARE\Microsoft\SMS\Client\Configuration\Client Properties

  Default=NOTFOUND
```

```
  Value Name=Local SMS Path

  Flags=00000100

end

item: Execute Program

  Pathname=%SMSLOC%\clicomp\hinv\hinv32.exe

  Default Directory=%SMSLOC%\Core\Bin

  Flags=00000100

End

---End Script
```

This script is also available for download in SMS Installer (.IPF) format from: http://www.swynk.com/trent/Articles/forcehardware.asp and http://www.admin911.com. Using this script, it is important to know that even though Hinv32.exe is located in the %SMSLOC%\clicomp\hinv directory, the compiled executable must be run from the %SMSLOC%\Core\Bin directory (notice the "Default Directory" line in the SMS Installer script). When the SMS client installs, it registers its DLL files with the operating system as being located in the BIN directory. The client components are dependent on these files to run. Therefore, Hinv32.exe is called to execute, but it is actually starting execution from the Core Components directory. Trying to run a client component from its "home" directory will produce an error message.

Hardware Inventory Utilities

The utilities discussed in this section are extremely useful for extending SMS hardware inventory, as well as aiding in troubleshooting hardware inventory problems.

MIFCHECK.exe

The MIF Checker Tool, included as part of the Microsoft Systems Management Server 2.0 Resource Guide, is a perfect tool to verify that a MIF file is valid. This command line tool checks for syntax and semantic errors in the MIF file. MIF Checker is primarily for software vendors using MIF files to extend SMS inventory, but should your organization need to extend the inventory, it can be used internally.

NOTE: When using the MIF Checker Tool, the MIF file that is being verified must be in the same directory as MIFCHECK.EXE. Also, MIFCHECK.EXE will only find one error at a time. If an error is found, the tool must be run against the MIF file again after the error is fixed to finish the verification.

The MIF Checker Tool also allows you to "dump" MIF files into a readable format, which can be opened in any text editor.

- Syntax for checking the MIF file: **mifcheck.exe** ***filename*****.MIF**
- Syntax for dumping the MIF file: **mifcheck.exe /dump** ***filename*****.MIF**

MIFGen.exe and MIFWin.exe

The MIF Form Generator Tool and the MIF Entry Tool come with the Microsoft Systems Management Server 2.0 Resource Kit. These tools allow you to extend inventory by generating and distributing user-entry forms. These forms prompt the user for information such as user name, social security number, phone number, location, etc. You create the form and customize it as needed, creating the specific fields required by your organization. The MIF Form Generator Tool allows you to distribute and retrieve specific user information.

The output of the MIF Form Generator Tool is an .XNF file, which can be utilized on the client computer by running the MIF Entry Tool. The .XNF file must be installed to the %WINDIR%\MS\SMS\BIN directory on the client computer. You can create a SMS Installer script that installs the specific forms to the client directory.

NOTE: The MIF Form Generator Tool only runs on Windows 2000 and Windows NT.

The MIF Entry Tool must also be installed on the client computer. If you create multiple forms, you can run the MIFWin.exe with the name of the form on the command line to run the specific form.

PowerMIF

PowerMIF, by CompTrends Corporation (http://www.comptrends.com), is similar in functionality to the MIF Form Generator included in the Microsoft Systems Management Server 2.0 Resource Guide. PowerMIF is probably the best custom MIF form available for SMS. PowerMIF takes the work out of collecting user specific data by utilizing a customized wizard-style interface, environment specific questions, logo usage, summary-only options and detailed descriptions.

Now fully supporting SMS 2.0 clients with backwards compatibility, PowerMIF is your total solution for retrieving custom user information. You can view a PowerMIF slide show online at: http://www.comptrends.com/images/powermif.gif. This demo-ware version is fully functional and will demonstrate PowerMIF's functionality from beginning to end. For pricing information, call (888) 833-3084.

Inventory + Solution

Inventory + Solution from Computing Edge (http://www.computingedge.com), is a full-featured solution to extend the SMS hardware inventory.

Computing Edge's Inventory + Solution is an easy to install and easy-to-configure component. Inventory + Solution is installed on the same server on which SMS 2.0 is installed. The product works seamlessly as either an add-on component to SMS, or a stand-alone product using Computing Edge's free Notification Server component. Notification Server can be configured to forward the information received from the Inventory + Solution client runtime to the SMS server database, or the information can be viewed in Notification Server.

Interface

Notification Server uses the standard Microsoft Management Console (MMC) interface to display and configure the Computing Edge Server component. It uses the same interface to display reports for the information gathered by the Inventory + Solution client run-time, but it also goes one better than SMS. Every view for Notification Server is displayed in HTML. This makes it easy to click quickly between views, reports, configurations, components, and so forth. And, because Notification Server is built entirely on HTML, it provides a perfect platform for offering reports on a company intranet or Internet with Computing Edge's Web Reports. Because Notification Server uses the MMC, it makes for an easy snap-in into the current SMS Administrator console. Create a company standard SMS MMC in administrative mode, complete with the SMS Administrator console and Computing Edge's Notification Server, and you can easily monitor, configure, and administer both products from one interface. The Notification Server interface, because of the HTML format, is quite a bit faster than the SMS Administrator console.

Installation

Computing Edge does a good job of providing all the tools needed to get Inventory + Solution installed right the first time. Placing the CD into the CD drive automatically brings up the Notification Server Prerequisite installation component. The Prerequisite component inventories the server and identifies missing Notification Server requirements. Based on the information, the Prerequisite component displays the list and enables you to install the missing requirements, most of which are included on the Computing Edge CD-ROM (see Table 3-6).

Configuration

After all the required components are installed, Notification Server must be configured. Notification Server is configured through its Web-type interface in the MMC. Each new

Requirement	Included on CD
Windows NT 4.0 w/SP 4 or better	No
Microsoft Internet Information Server (IIS) 4.0 or better	No
Microsoft Data Access Control (MDAC) 2.1	Yes
Windows Management Service 698.0001	Yes
Microsoft Management Console (MMC) 1.1	Yes
Microsoft Windows Installer Service 1.10+	Yes
Microsoft Foundation Classes (MFC Library) 6.0.8447.0	Yes
Microsoft Internet Explorer 5 or better	Yes
Microsoft Database Engine (SQL Server) 7.0	Yes
Computing Edge Notification Server	Yes

Table 3-6. Inventory + Solutions Requirements

MMC folder you click displays an HTML page with easy-to-follow instructions for configuring the Notification Server. The bulk of the time setting up Notification Server is spent installing the requirements. If you already have the requirements installed on your Windows NT server, the time from installation of Notification Server to complete configuration is less than 20 minutes.

Customization

Because Inventory + Solutions runs on a Microsoft SQL Server, it is completely customizable through SQL query statements. Just as with SMS, you configure the inventory and collections, and then create your custom reports and queries.

Client

The client piece for Inventory + Solutions is a small, quick executable that can be run in network logon scripts, distributed via an SMS package, e-mailed, distributed in a floppy disk set, or scheduled through the stand-alone Notification Server. This makes the client easy-to-distribute, even to remote users. This small executable means nothing has to be installed on the computer. With Notification Server running in your organization, you won't even need a SMS client installed on the computer. The information will be collected and made accessible by the Notification Server installed in your organization.

Running With SMS

Computing Edge has long provided excellent integrating components for SMS. With the release of SMS 2.0 came hope that this release would finally fix the woes of SMS 1.2. While this statement is somewhat true, shortcomings still exist that can only be addressed through internal development or third-party add-ons and utilities. Computing Edge makes great products that extend SMS to give it the rich amount information you would expect. Inventory + Solutions is easy to install and configure, fully customizable, and adds value to your SMS investment.

Running Without SMS

For those organizations without SMS, Inventory + Solution is great as a stand-alone product and can easily be deployed throughout your company. The Inventory + Solution client runs on any Windows 95/98, Windows NT, and Windows 2000 computer. Notification Server can be set up in a hierarchal fashion based on your organization, administrative requirements, and standards, similar to SMS. Computing Edge provides additional products similar to SMS in functionality. So, if you need more than what Inventory + Solution alone offers, but have not yet invested in the SMS, you can get the same type of functionality through the other Computing Edge products. New products are being developed all the time to provide solutions for the voids in industry systems management.

Performance Monitor

You can use the Windows 2000/NT Performance Monitor on the SMS site server to help troubleshoot possible hardware inventory problems.

Inventory Data Loader

The following PerfMon counters are used to determine inventory processing problems for the Inventory Data Loader thread.

MIFs Processed/minute The MIFs Processed/minute counter records the number of MIF files processed in the past minute.

Total Bad MIFs Processed The Total Bad MIFs Processed counter records the number of bad MIF files processed during the current PerfMon session.

Total MIFs Enqueued The Total MIFs Enqueued counter records the total number of MIF files in the Inventory Data Loader queue subtracted by the number of MIF files processed.

Total MIFs Processed The Total MIFs Processed counter records the total number of MIF files processed during the current PerfMon session.

Hardware Inventory Gotchas

The following topics highlight some areas you should be aware of for the hardware inventory process.

"Insert Disk in Drive A:" During Hardware Inventory

You may be experiencing this message on some of your Windows 95, Windows 98, Windows NT, and Windows 2000 clients. Here is the workaround:

1. Using MOF Manager, open the SMS_DEF.MOF file in the SMS\Inboxes\Clifiles.src\Hinv directory on the site server.
2. Navigate to the Win32_LogicalDisk class.
3. Highlight the Win32_LogicalDisk class and select No on the Report selection.
4. Propagate the new SMS_DEF.MOF file to all site servers.

Updating SMS BIOS Information

When the BIOS is updated on the computer, the new information is not inventoried by SMS. You can force a hardware inventory resynchronization using the INVSYNC.EXE tool (detailed earlier in this chapter) from the *Microsoft Systems Management Server 2.0 Resource Guide* that will capture this new BIOS information.

MIF Files Are Not Being Processed on the Site Server

MIF files contain the hardware information gathered during the hardware inventory process. The Inventory Data Loader processes the files and enters the information into the SMS database. This section provides some things to look for if MIF files aren't processing.

If this is a child site, the MIF files could be processing slowly because of communication problems with the parent site. Not only does the Inventory Data Loader process have the responsibility of processing and writing for the local site, it also has the responsibility of transferring the MIF files on to the parent site. Processing could be slow, but could pick up dramatically once communication has been completed. Be patient.

Check the SQL Server services. If MIF files seem to backlog in the Process directory, the SQL Server services could be hung or stopped because of another process. Inventory Data Loader tries to process MIF files every ten minutes. If the MIF files are backlogged the queue can fill up quickly.

Check the Dataldr.log file regularly to identify problems before they become critical issues.

NOTE: SMS Duplicate IDs and 0 byte *.sic and *.sid files are the most common causes of server backlogs. SMS Duplicate IDs, and 0 byte *.sic and *.sid files are the most common causes of backlogs occurring on SMS Servers.

10501, 10502, and 10511 Errors

The SMS Status Message system records everything. If you receive a 10501, 10502, or 10511 error in the status system, check that the WMI is installed and running properly on the computer. Reinstall the latest version if it isn't installed or is failing.

Insufficient Disk Space

Keep a close eye on the disk space of the client computers. Run a query or report at least once a month to monitor disk space use. A low-disk situation on a client computer can cause the Hardware Inventory Agent to stop functioning. An indication this has occurred would be a 10504 error in the SMS Status Message system. The Hardware Inventory Agent requires at least 3MB of virtual memory and 500K of hard disk space to initiate the inventory cycle.

BADMIFs Directory

Constantly monitor the SMS\Inboxes\Dataldr.box\BADMIFs directory on the SMS site server. Files in this directory indicate hardware inventory resynchs. Numerous files in this directory could indicate an inventory problem. If a hardware inventory problem occurs, this directory could fill up quickly. By default, SMS deletes the MIF files in the BADMIFs directory every 14 days. This number can be modified at the following location in the site server's registry:

HKEY_LOCAL_MACHINE\SOFTWARE\Microsoft\SMS\Components\SMS_INVENTORY_DATA_LOADER\Delete Bad MIFs Older Than.

Windows 9x Clients Hang After Service Pack 2 Is Applied

After upgrading the SMS 2.0 site hierarchy to Service Pack 2, Windows 95 and Windows 98 clients can hang for ten minutes or more during hardware inventory. The client computer's Hinv32.log file contains the following error information:

```
WARNING 1 - Failed to update new cycle info !!! Hardware Inventory Agent

7/01/2000 11:47:37 AM 4294127983 (0xFFF3316F)

ERROR 1 - Cannot get schedule for previous cycle !! Hardware Inventory Agent

7/01/2000 11:47:37 AM 4294127983 (0xFFF3316F)
```

To fix this problem, you must install both WMI 1.5 and the latest version of DCOM. WMI 1.5 requires DCOM version 1.3 be installed on the Windows 9*x* computer.

NOTE: DCOM **MUST** be installed before WMI.

DCOM version 1.3 can be obtained from Microsoft's Web site at the following location:

http://www.microsoft.com/com/resources/downloads.asp.

WMI 1.5 can also be obtained from Microsoft's Web site, but from the following location:

http://msdn.microsoft.com/downloads/sdks/wmi/download.asp.

Once DCOM 1.3 and WMI 1.5 are installed, the client will update properly and the problem will resolve.

If you can, you should plan to install DCOM 1.3 and WMI 1.5 before the Service Pack 2 deployment. Perform an inventory of the version of DCOM and WMI on your Windows 95 and Windows 98 computers (you can inventory DCOM by obtaining the version of the DCOMExt.DLL file on each computer; you can inventory WMI by obtaining the version of the WMI.DLL file on each computer). Distribute DCOM 1.3 to the computers that need the upgraded component, and then apply SMS 2.0 Service Pack 2 to your site.

Chapter 4

Software Inventory Installation, Collection, and Processing

Microsoft Systems Management Server's Software Inventory provides a comprehensive scan of the computer's installed software. In previous versions of SMS, software inventory identified installed software through manual entry. If you wanted a specific software package inventoried, you would need to know the file details of that package. For example, if you wanted to inventory Microsoft Office, you would need to tell SMS that Microsoft Office must be inventoried based on the existence of the mso.exe file. And, even further, if you needed to know which computers have Microsoft Office 97 versus Microsoft Office 2000, you had to tell SMS the exact time and date of the MSO.EXE file for the inventory process to identify the proper version. This made it harder to perform queries and to produce reports when upgrading software across the enterprise. You had to do a lot of research beforehand to produce useable software inventory data.

SMS 2.0 eliminates this time-consuming process. When SMS 2.0 inventories software, it reads the binary header information from the application's file. Most software application vendors place a small 2k header in the executable (.exe) and dynamic link library (.dll) files. This header contains information about the file. For example, the file properties shown in the next illustration are included in the file header for WinWord.exe (Microsoft Word for Windows 2000). SMS 2.0 retrieves this information and forwards it to the SMS site server for inclusion in the SQL database, where it can be viewed through Resource Explorer and managed through queries and reports.

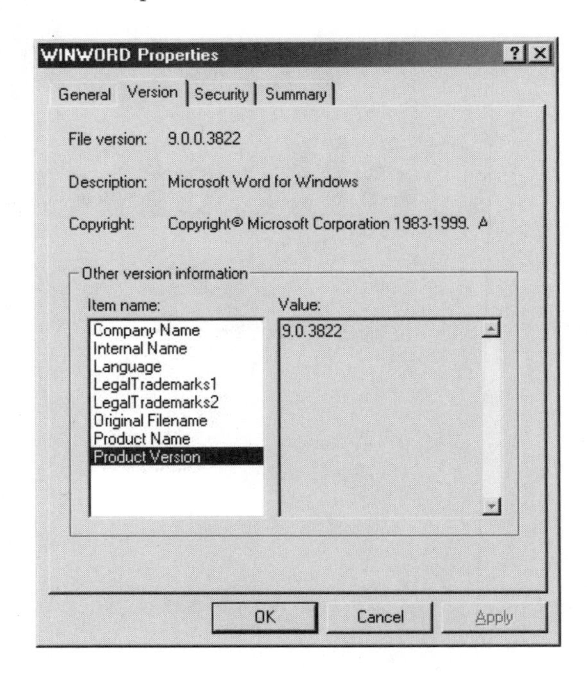

When SMS inventories the software on the client computer, it tries to retrieve all the following information:

- Filename
- File Version
- File Size
- Date and Time of File Creation
- File Description
- Company Name
- Product Name
- Product Version
- Product Language

Most application vendors include this information in the header of their application files. If the header information cannot be retrieved from the file, the specific file details are listed in the Unknown Software category in the Resource Explorer for the particular computer.

If you configure the software inventory on the SMS site to inventory other file types, such as .BMP, .INI, .BAT, and so forth, those files don't contain the resource information found in .EXE and .COM files.

Files you should consider collecting are those with the extensions .EXE, .COM, .DLL, .OCX (these are the default file types selected by the SMS installation). The resource information contained in these files can be critical when planning for software upgrade distributions. Knowing the resource information of a file can help when you need to diagnose a flaky application. For example, if an older version DLL file has been installed on the computer, Microsoft Word may lock up. The software inventory record can help you quickly resolve the problem.

When SMS displays the data in the Resource Explorer, the following fields are shown by default:

- Filename
- File Description
- File Version
- File Size (in bytes)
- File Count (how many copies of the file were found on the reference computer)
- Creation Date (the date and time the file was created)

When you configure the software inventory component of the site, you can also modify the Company and Product associations using the Inventory Names property. This feature (shown in the following illustration) gives you the capability to associate the inventoried Company and Product names with a specific value. When SMS reads the binary header and finds the company and product names, it inventories this information verbatim. As shown in the illustration, the Inventoried Names field displays the different ways Microsoft Corporation has been coded into the file header. Modifying this information to associate with a single version of the display name aids in making your queries and reports uniform.

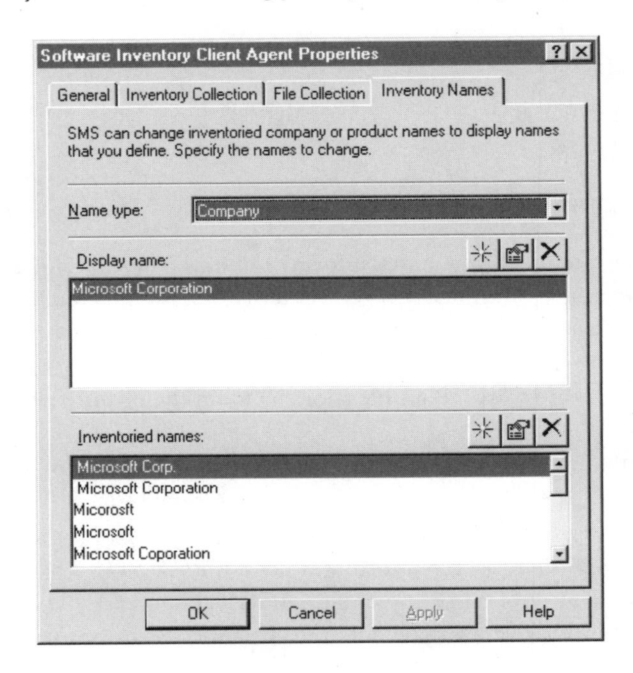

Inventorying Internet Explorer

To see why a comprehensive file-detailed software inventory is so critical, imagine trying to inventory Microsoft Internet Explorer. You probably have multiple versions deployed, and perhaps even multiple revisions of the same version. For example, Microsoft has distributed several patches for Internet Explorer 5.0. These patches were developed to fix bugs and fill security holes. Each time IE is patched, the revision level is updated. An example of the revision level for Internet Explorer 5.5 is shown in the next illustration. The Internet Explorer version is 5.5, but the revision number is 5.50.4030.2400.

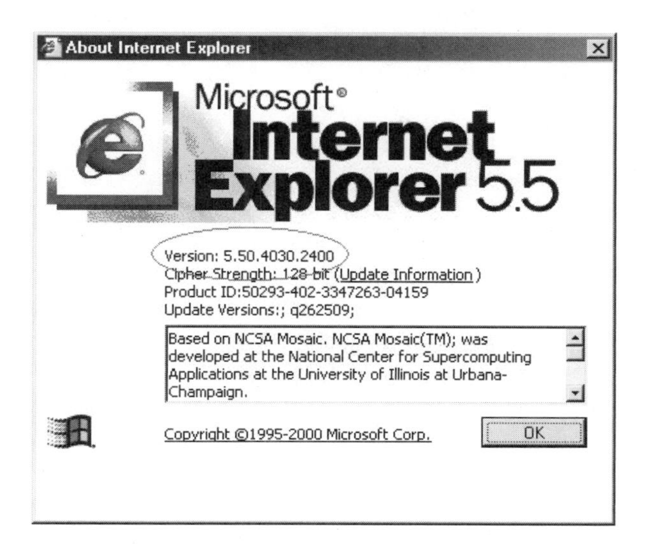

CODE BLUE

When Microsoft releases beta software, that software is usually available to anyone who can access Microsoft's Web site. If users install beta code, serious computer problems could result: applications might stop working or the computer could even fail to boot. If a user calls the HelpDesk with a peculiar problem, you can use the Inventory feature to see whether the user has installed a beta update.

The best way to inventory Internet Explorer is to account for the SHDOCVW.DLL file. This DLL is installed with all Internet Explorer versions 3.0 or later. On Windows 9*x* systems, it is in the C:\WINDOWS\SYSTEM directory. On Windows 2000 and Windows NT systems, the DLL is in the C:\WINNT\SYSTEM32 directory. If this file doesn't exist, Internet Explorer is not installed correctly or it isn't installed at all. As shown in Table 4-1, the inventory information from SHDOCVW.DLL gives you the Internet Explorer revision.

The SMS Software Inventory process retrieves the versioning information from the SHDOCVW.DLL file. This information can be viewed by using the Resource Explorer for the specific computer resource. Or, it can be quickly retrieved for multiple computers by using a Collection, Query, or generated Report (described in detail in Chapter 10).

Version	Product
4.70.1155	Internet Explorer 3.0
4.70.1158	Internet Explorer 3.0 (OSR-2)
4.70.1215	Internet Explorer 3.01
4.70.1300	Internet Explorer 3.02 and 3.02a
4.71.1008.3	Internet Explorer 4.0 PP2
4.71.1712.5	Internet Explorer 4.0
4.72.2106.7	Internet Explorer 4.01
4.72.3110.3	Internet Explorer 4.01 Service Pack 1
4.72.3612.1707	Internet Explorer 4.01 SP2
4.72.3711.2900	Internet Explorer 4.*x* with Update for "Server-side Page Reference Redirect" Issue installed
5.00.0518.5	Internet Explorer 5 Developer Preview (beta 1)
5.00.0910.1308	Internet Explorer 5 beta (beta 2)
5.00.2014.213	Internet Explorer 5
5.00.2314.1000	Internet Explorer 5 (Office 2000)
5.00.2516.1900	Internet Explorer 5.01 (Windows 2000 beta 3, build 5.00.2031)
5.00.2614.3500	Internet Explorer 5 (Windows 98 Second Edition)
5.00.2717.2000	Internet Explorer 5 with Update for "Malformed Favorites Icon" Security Issue installed
5.00.2721.1400	Internet Explorer 5 with Update for "ImportExport Favorites()" Security Issue installed
5.00.2723.2900	Internet Explorer 5.0 with Update for "Server-side Page Reference Redirect" Issue installed
5.00.2919.800	Internet Explorer 5.01 (Windows 2000 RC1, build 5.00.2072)
5.00.2919.3800	Internet Explorer 5.01 (Windows 2000 RC2, build 5.00.2128)
5.00.2919.6307	Internet Explorer 5.01
5.00.2919.6400	Internet Explorer 5.01 with Update for "Server-side Page Reference Redirect" Issue installed
5.00.2920.0000	Internet Explorer 5.01 (Windows 2000, build 5.00.2195)
5.50.3825.1300	Internet Explorer 5.5 Developer Preview (beta)
5.50.4134.600	Internet Explorer 5.5 Released Version

Table 4-1. Internet Explorer Versions Based on the SHDOCVW.DLL File

Software Inventory Installation

When you install the Software Inventory Agent, you create the directory structure and file locations shown in Table 4-2.

Directory	Description
%WINDIR%\MS\SMS\CLICOMP\SINV	The SINV directory is the core directory for the Software Inventory Agent. It includes the Software Inventory Agent executable (sinv32.exe for 32-bit clients; sinv16.exe for 16-bit clients), and the deinstallation file (desinv32.exe for 32-bit clients; desinv16.exe for 16-bit clients).
%WINDIR%\MS\SMS\CLICOMP\SINV\OUTBOX	The OUTBOX directory receives the software inventory data before it is forwarded to the CAP for processing.
%WINDIR%\MS\SMS\CLICOMP\SINV\TEMP	The TEMP directory is a working directory for the Software Inventory Agent. This directory receives temporary files before they are converted to inventory files readable by the SMS processes.
%WINDIR%\MS\SMS\CLICOMP\SINV\FILECOL	The FILECOL directory stores actual files that are collected from the client computer and forwarded to the SMS site server.

Table 4-2. Software Inventory Client Directories and Files

Maintenance Tasks

Part of maintaining the SMS site is performing regular checks on the software inventory and the Software Inventory process. Being proactive about maintenance can save headaches later. A smart practice is to keep written historical data on the SMS site. During the scheduled software inventory period, keep track of server utilization to be aware of any server issues that may arise in the future. Verify enough storage space is on the server and the network is not bogged down with a lot of other tasks.

Monitoring Software Inventory

The Software Inventory process consists of more than just an application that runs on the client. The SMS Software Inventory process actually consists of components, threads, processes, applications, services, network bandwidth, and client and server capabilities. Each of these elements should be monitored before, during, and after the scheduled Software Inventory period.

Monitoring *before* the inventory process enables you to gather baseline data for off-time. Monitoring during the process enables you to gather baseline data for peak time. Monitoring after the process is important to determine if the system has survived. Monitoring during all three phases helps you to plan appropriately for future capacity, identify possible problems, and learn how your site performs.

Monitoring the Server

Monitoring the SMS server can help you determine the efficiency of the SMS site. The best way to accomplish this is with the Windows 2000/NT Performance Monitor program. You can use the Windows 2000/NT Performance Monitor on the SMS site server to help troubleshoot possible inventory problems. The data can also be used to determine if more capacity should be added for RAM, disk space, and network bandwidth. The following PerfMon counters record information specific to the Software Inventory Processor thread on the SMS site server.

- SINVs Processed/minute records the number of software inventory files processed in the past minute.
- Total Bad SINVs Processed records the number of bad software inventory files processed during the current PerfMon session.
- Total SINVs Enqueued records the number of software inventory files queued subtracted by the number of software inventory files processed.
- Total SINVs Processed records the total number of software inventory files, both good and bad, processed during the current PerfMon session.

NOTE: Keep a critical eye on the DATALDR.BOX directory on the site server. A large number of files could indicate a backlog. A frequent backlog of MIF files in this directory indicates it's time to upgrade the server's RAM, hard disk, and processor or number of processors. A backlog of MIF files could also indicate you have computer records with duplicate SMS Unique IDs. You can determine if this is the case by running the following query:

```
select * from sms_g_system_SYSTEM as g INNER JOIN
sms_gh_system_SYSTEM as h on g.ResourceId = h.ResourceId where
g.Name <> h.Name
```

Monitoring the Client

Over time, some client problems may arise that slow the performance of the Software Inventory process on the client.

Low Disk Space Always monitor the client computers through the SMS Administrator Console. Conduct queries to determine the available space on the client's hard disks. A weekly or monthly report on the amount of available hard disk space should be adequate. Any hard disks with less than 50MB of free space usually experience problems when running applications, storing data, and printing.

Any low-disk space error on the client is reported to the Status Message system of the SMS Server. The Software Inventory process requires at least 3MB of virtual memory and 500K of disk space on the client to begin the inventory process. When either of these requirements is missing, a 10601 error displays in the status system and the client's inventory cycle could be delayed by as much as eight hours.

Similarly, if you see a 10602 error in the SMS Message Status system, you should check the disk space on the specified client computer. When the Software Inventory Agent collects files, it collects a copy of each file specified in the site properties. In effect, the client computer must have space twice the size of the file. If you are gathering large files and the computer is low on disk space, the Software Inventory Agent will be unable to complete the collection.

Fragmented Hard Disk Over time, as the hard drive reads and writes information, the data and application files become fragmented. This causes the hard drive to take longer when retrieving files because they are farther apart on the hard disk. This fragmentation can slow hard drive access considerably. Running a good defragmentation program regularly can help ensure the Software Inventory process is optimum on the client computer.

Corrupted Software Inventory Agent Any of several problems can cause the Software Inventory Agent to become corrupt:

- **Computer Lockups.** A computer can lock up for a number of different reasons, including virus infection, corrupt or incompatible hardware drivers, corrupt system files, or mismatched system files.
- **Mismatched SMS Component Files.** When the SMS site is upgraded with a new service pack, the new client files are propagated to the computers assigned to the SMS site. If the upgrade is being performed as a user shuts down, the sum of the SMS files could be different versions. All the SMS client agents are reliant on the DLL files in the %WINDIR%\MS\SMS\Core\Bin directory. If the Core Components are only partially updated, the SMS agents could cease to function.
- **Deleted files.** God forbid, the user has access to the SMS client directory but, in some cases, he does. In Windows 95, for instance, not much in the way of directory security exists to protect the Windows directory. A user could potentially delete any files within the Windows directory structure. If a SMS file gets deleted, the particular agent will fail to run. In Windows 2000 and Windows NT, this access can, and should, be restricted.

Repairing the Software Inventory Agent

After the cause of a corrupted Software Inventory Agent has been identified and resolved, you can repair the Software Inventory Agent through the Systems Management applet in the

Control Panel. As shown in the following illustration, the Software Inventory Agent is on the Components tab. Select the Software Inventory Agent and click the Repair Installation button. Make sure the computer is connected to the network and has access to the SMS site. The repair should take about 15 minutes.

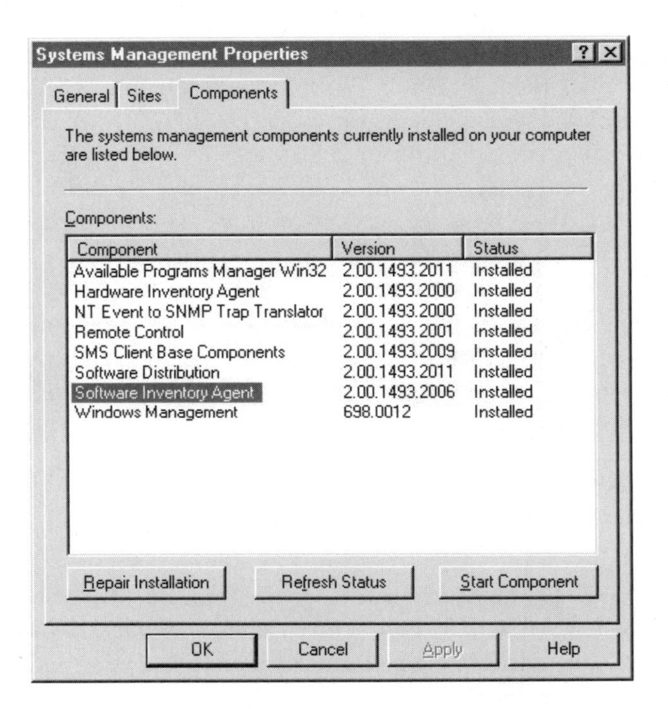

NOTE: When you click the Repair Installation button, an Advertised Program Manager (APM) is made to the CAP. When the request is received, the Software Inventory Agent installation is distributed to the client.

Scheduling Software Inventory

You can modify the Software Inventory schedule through the SMS Administrator Console to meet your company's specific needs. The initial screen of the Software Inventory Client

Agent, shown in the next illustration, enables you to change the Software Inventory schedule for your SMS site. By default, the Simple Schedule is selected for the site. The Simple Schedule enables you to choose a schedule quickly by number of hours, days, and weeks. This scheduling technique may be adequate for your organization.

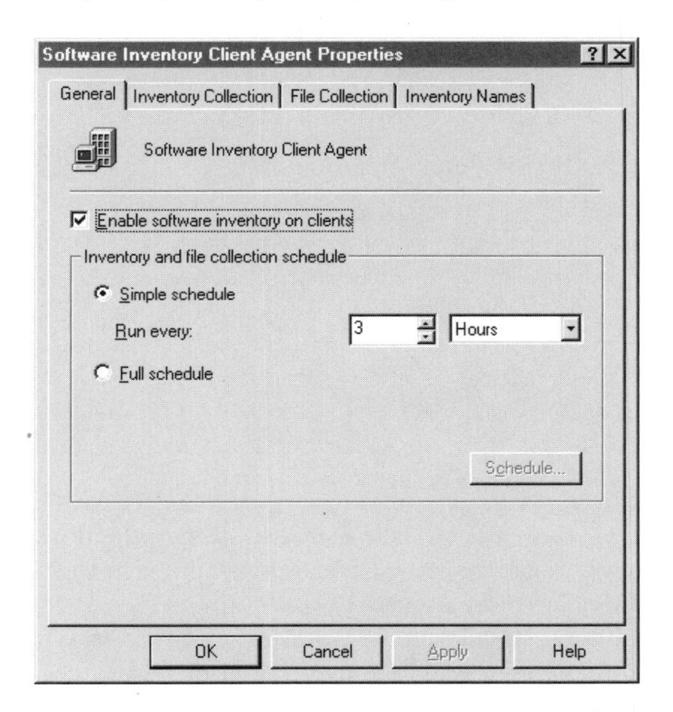

If the Simple Schedule method doesn't produce the desired results, you can use the Full Schedule option (shown in the following illustration) to create as comprehensive an inventory schedule as you need. The Full Schedule uses days, weeks, and months to schedule the inventory, but it also allows for full customization. For example, you can choose the date and time the Full Schedule should start. In the Weekly mode, you could schedule software inventory to recur every seven weeks and only on Tuesdays. In Monthly mode, you can modify the schedule so software inventory only runs every six months on the first Wednesday of that month.

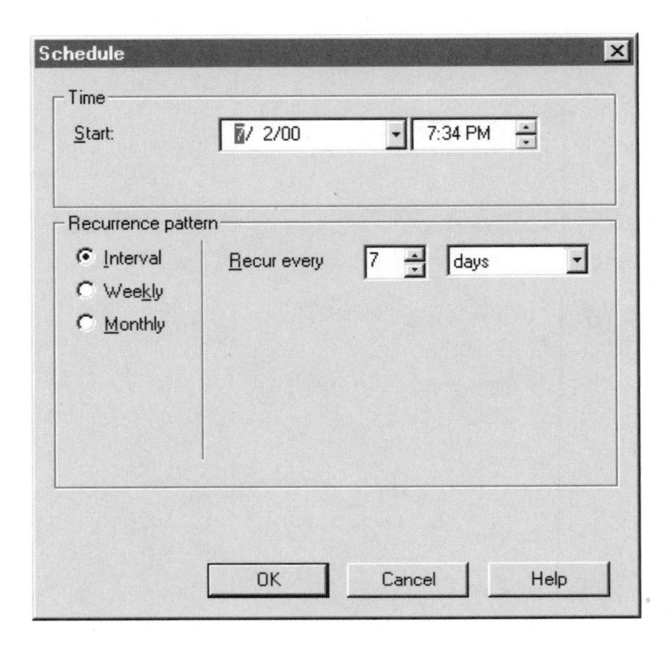

Most companies prefer to run software inventory every seven days. This certifies that the data in the SMS database is current. If you have individuals in your organization who love to install the latest chat software and corporate policy prohibits it, you might want to set a more aggressive Software Inventory schedule.

The Software Inventory schedule may need periodic modification. When you distribute a new software application, you need to record the installation. Obtaining this information is critical for creating queries and building reports. You can adjust the schedule and the new information is then propagated to the client computer. You can also forego this method and still get the needed information by forcing a software inventory cycle. Methods for forcing inventory are described later in this chapter.

Modifying File Inventory

In addition to modifying the Software Inventory schedule, you can also choose the types of files inventoried. Why would you want to change the inventory type after the initial setup? Viruses are the main reason. New viruses are written every day, and then unleashed on the public. Most new viruses are written to take advantage of various Microsoft software features. Windows Scripting Host, introduced later in this chapter, is a common target of virus developers. If you know a virus is on the loose that runs with a WSH extension, you can quickly modify the Inventory Collection (shown in the following illustration) to scan for that file extension and locate the virus easily.

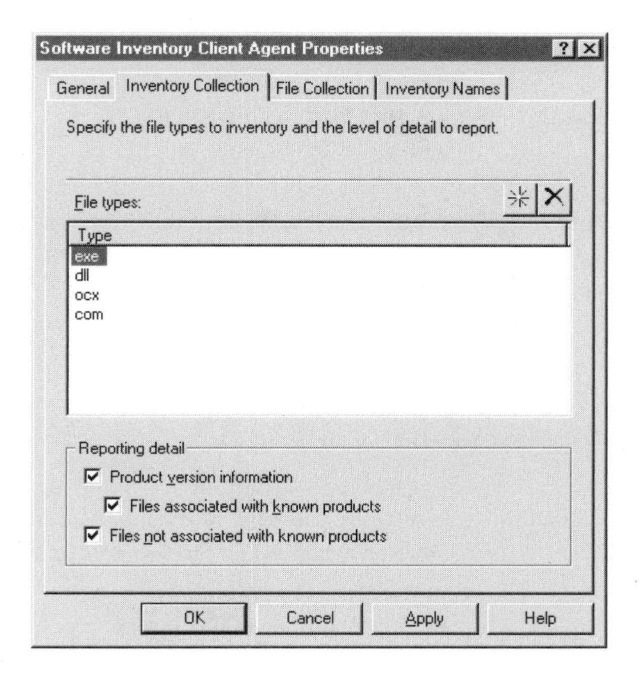

Software Inventory Logs

Tables 4-3 and 4-4 list the log filenames, their associated threads, and the location for 32-bit and 16-bit clients. These log files should be used in conjunction with the Software Inventory

Thread	Log file	Location
Software Inventory Agent	<%windir%>\MS\SMS\Logs\Sinv32.log	Client
Client Component Installation Manager	<%windir%>\MS\SMS\Logs\Ccim32.log	Client
Client Service (CliSvcl)	<%windir%>\MS\SMS\Logs\Clisvc.log	Client
Copy Queue	<%windir%>\MS\SMS\Logs\Cqmgr32.log	Client
Inbox Manager Assistant	SMS\Logs\Inboxast.log	Server
Software Inventory Processor	SMS\Logs\Sinvproc.log	Server
Replication Manager	SMS\Logs\Replmgr.log	Server

Table 4-3. Software Inventory Logs (32-bit Client)

Thread	Log File	Location
Software Inventory Agent	%WINDIR%\MS\SMS\Logs\Sinv.log	Client
Client Component Installation Manager	%WINDIR%\MS\SMS\Logs\Ccim16.log	Client
Copy Queue	%WINDIR%\MS\SMS\Logs\Clearque.log	Client
Inbox Manager Assistant	SMS\Logs\Inboxast.log	Server
Software Inventory Processor	SMS\Logs\Sinvproc.log	Server
Replication Manager	SMS\Logs\Replmgr.log	Server

Table 4-4. Software Inventory Logs (16-bit Client)

Checklists discussed in the following section. These log files contain all the information you need to diagnose and resolve the problem if a step in the process fails or stalls.

Software Inventory Process Checklists

The following checklists walk through the Software Inventory process. When you are troubleshooting inventory problems, these checklists help you discover where the process is stalled. When used in combination with the Software Inventory log files, any issues can be quickly resolved.

Software Inventory Checklist 32-bit Client

The Software Inventory for the 32-bit client is processed in two phases: Client Phase and Site Server Phase. Before the Software Inventory process is initiated, the SMS client verifies the Software Inventory Agent is:

1. Enabled for the site.
2. Installed on the client.
3. Installed, but not missing components (or a corruption of the components).

If Software Inventory isn't enabled for the site, the process stops. If the Software Inventory Agent is not installed on the client computer, the Client Component Installation Manager (CCIM32.DLL) starts the installation process. Similarly, if the current installation is corrupted or has missing files, CCIM32.DLL then repairs the Software Inventory application before continuing with the inventory.

If the Software Inventory Agent doesn't install, it could be due to the client not being within the Site's IP or IPX boundary. As shown in the next illustration, you can confirm the site's boundary by opening the Site Properties and navigating to the Boundaries tab. On the client computer, you can then verify the client falls within the configured boundary.

- On Windows 9*x* computers, run WinIPCFG from the START | RUN command.
- On Windows 2000 and Windows NT computers, run IPCONFIG from the command prompt.

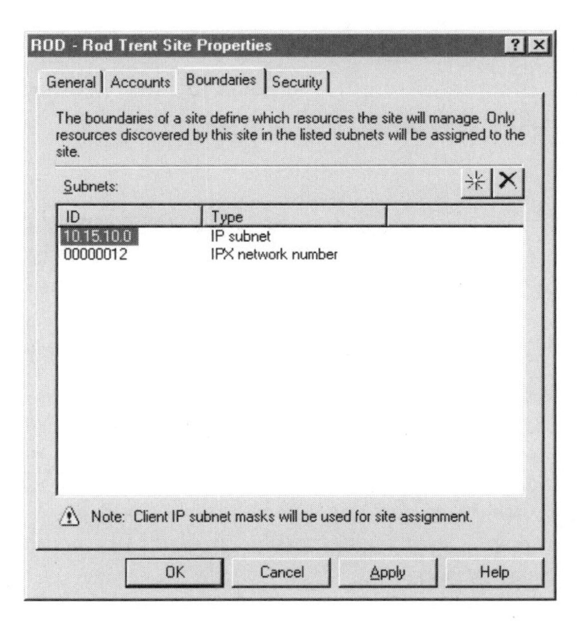

CODE BLUE

If Software Inventory is not being performed on the client, first verify that Software Inventory is enabled for the site. Next, check the directory structure of the Software Inventory application on the computer to confirm the application is installed. If the application is installed, but still not running, you can try to repair the installation manually by going into the Systems Management Control Panel applet, clicking the Components tab, highlighting the Software Inventory Agent component, and clicking the Repair Installation button. If Software Inventory still doesn't start, verify the client has a valid connection to the CAP. Check for both a live network connection and a valid user account.

When the Software Inventory Agent is installed for the first time, or is repaired either manually or by the Client Component Installation Manager, the Software Inventory process starts automatically within approximately 20 minutes. The SMS Client Service (Clisvcl.exe) starts the inventory process. If the Software Inventory process has been initiated, the Sinv32.exe file should be resident in the computer's memory. You can also verify the inventory cycle has started by looking in the Sinv32.log file.

The following checklist assumes the Software Inventory Agent is installed correctly on the client computer and this is the first Software Inventory process performed on the computer. If Software Inventory is enabled for the site, Ccim32.dll installs the Software Inventory components on the client computer into the %WINDIR%\MS\SMS\Clicomp\Sinv32 directory. Then, 20 minutes after the Software Inventory components have been installed, Clisvcl32.exe initiates the first software scan.

Client Phase

The SMS Client Service (Clisvcl32.exe) starts the Software Inventory process by executing Sinv32.exe which then retrieves the information that describes the types of files that should be inventoried. This information is stored at the SMS site in the Software Inventory properties. Sinv32.exe creates a Software History (Sinv.his) file from any Software Complete (Sinvdat.sic) file that exists. Sinv32.exe always creates this history file, even if inventory has previously been gathered.

CHECKPOINT: Check the Sinv.his file located in the %WINDIR%\MS\SMS\Clicomp\Sinv directory for a current date and time stamp. If the date and time of the file is not current, view the Software Inventory Agent log for possible problems. The Software Inventory Agent may have had problems starting.

CODE BLUE

If File Collection has been enabled for the site, the specified files are gathered during the same time as the software inventory is being run. The Software Inventory Agent (Sinv32.exe) provides the file gathering mechanism. Any files designated for collection are retrieved and placed into the %WINDIR%\MS\SMS\Clicomp\Sinv\Filecol directory on the client computer. For subsequent file collections, Sinv32.exe checks against the Sinv.his file to identify any collected files that have changed since inventory. The old versions of the files found in the \Filecol directory are replaced with the updated files. File collection impacts the overall Software Inventory process in the following ways:

- More disk space is required on the client computer to store the collected files during the Software Inventory process.
- More disk space is required on the Primary Site server to store the collected files. If collection has been enabled, the site server extracts and stores the specified files from every resource assigned to the site. Do not collect large files! Instead, you can limit the size of data collected in the Software Inventory Client Agent properties on the site server. The default collection value is 1MB. Watch this. If you are collecting a file larger than 1MB, this value will need to be altered. If you see a 10603 error in the SMS Status Message system, this indicates the maximum size of the collected files has exceeded the setting. By default, the Software Inventory process stores retain up to five copies of the collected files on the site server. You can change this number by modifying a registry key on the site server: HKEY_LOCAL_MACHINE\Software\Microsoft\SMS\Components\SMS_Software_Inventory_Processor\Maximum Collected Files.
- The time for the Software Inventory process to complete is doubled. The Software Inventory agent spends extra time identifying the file to be collected, gathering the file, and then compressing it into the software inventory file.
- A larger data stream is sent to the CAP and on to the site server. The more files and the larger the files collected, the larger the amount of data that must be replicated to the server for storage. Network bandwidth can be severely affected. Files collected are appended (compressed) to the Software Complete or the Software Delta file. When they are compressed into the inventory file, Sinv32.exe deletes them from the \Filecol directory.

Based on the client status, Sinv32.exe performs either a full or partial software scan and writes the information to the Software Complete (Sinvdat.sic) or the Software Delta (Sinvdat.sid) file in the %WINDIR%\MS\SMS\Clicomp\Sinv directory on the client computer.

NOTE: If Software Inventory has been gathered before, Sinv32.exe compares the newly created history file with the old one. Based on the changes, Sinv32.exe creates a Software Inventory Delta (%WINDIR%\MS\SMS\Clicomp\Sinv\Sinvdat.sid) file. The delta file contains only the changes, as opposed to the complete inventory file. The capability to propagate only the changes in inventory saves network bandwidth when the inventory is reported to the site. Then, Sinv32.exe replaces the old history file (%WINDIR%\MS\SMS\Clicomp\Sinv\Sinv.his) with the new one from the working directory (%WINDIR%\MS\SMS\Clicomp\Sinv\Temp).

CHECKPOINT: Verify the Sinvdat.sic or Sinvdat.sid file exists in the %WINDIR%\MS\SMS\Clicomp\Sinv\ directory on the client computer. For this type of write access, the SMS Service account needs the proper security authorization to the MS directory structure.

- Sinv32.exe copies the Sinvdat.sic or the Sinvdat.sid file to the %WINDIR%\MS\SMS\Clicomp\Sinv\Outbox directory.
- Sinv32.exe renames the Sinvdat.sic or the Sinvdat.sid file with a *.inv extension. The actual filename of the *.inv file is an eight-character name that is randomly generated. The renamed file resides in the %WINDIR%\MS\SMS\Clicomp\Sinv\Outbox directory.
- After the *.inv file is created, Sinv32.exe deletes the original Sinvdat.sic or Sinvdat.sid file from the %WINDIR%\MS\SMS\Clicomp\Sinv directory.

CHECKPOINT: Check both the %WINDIR%\MS\SMS\Clicomp\Sinv and %WINDIR%\MS\SMS\Clicomp\Sinv\Outbox directories. The *.sic or *.sid files should be deleted and the *.inv file should be waiting in the Software Inventory Outbox.

- Sinv32.exe calls the Copy Queue Manager (Cqmgr32.dll) process to begin the process of copying the *.inv file to the CAP.
- Cqmgr32.dll renames the *.inv file to a new *.sic or *.sid file with a unique eight-character filename.
- Cqmgr32.dll moves the new *.sic or *.sid file to the CAP into the \Sinv.box directory.

CHECKPOINT: If the client doesn't have network connectivity to the CAP, the inventory files won't be copied. If the inventory files aren't present on the CAP, verify the network connection, as well as the security rights of the logged-in user.

Site Server Phase:

- As the *.sic or *.sid file is moved from box to box, the random eight-character filename is changed by the process acting upon it.
- Inbox Manager Assistant moves the *.sic or *.sid file from the CAP to the SMS\Inboxes\Sinv.box on the SMS site server.

NOTE: If the discovery data for the client doesn't exist in the SQL database, Software Inventory Processor moves the *.sic or *.sid file to the SMS\Inboxes\Sinv.box\Orphans directory. The Data Discovery Record (DDR) must be processed and recorded in the SMS site database before the software inventory information can be written. Without a corresponding DDR in the site database, the software inventory cannot be tied to the record. The Software Inventory Processor checks for the client's DDR every ten minutes. When the DDR is available, it is placed in the SMS\Inboxes\DDM.box directory for processing. When the DDR is processed and the information is written to the SQL database, then the *.sic or *.sid file is acted upon.

- Software Inventory Processor checks the date stamp of the *.sic or *.sid file and compares it to the date stamp of the software inventory already stored in the SQL database for the client. If the date stamp is older, the *.sic or *.sid file is deleted and the Software Inventory process is halted.
- If the date stamp of the *.sic or *.sid file is newer than the information stored in the SQL database, Software Inventory Processor checks the syntax of the file.
- If the syntax of the *.sic or *.sid file is correct, Software Inventory Processor processes the files. If the syntax is incorrect, resulting in a corrupt or invalid inventory file, Software Inventory Processor moves the *.sic or *.sid file to the SMS\Inboxes\Sinv.box\Badsinv directory. Software Inventory Processor then forces a Software Inventory Resync (shown later in this chapter), which requests a new complete inventory of the identified client.

CHECKPOINT: Check the SMS\Inboxes\Sinv.box\Badsinv directory for any *.sic or *.sid files. You can also verify no *.sic or *.sid files exist in the SMS\Inboxes\Sinv.box\Orphans directory.

NOTE: If file collection has been enabled, Software Inventory Processor separates the actual information from the compressed, collected files. The compressed information is written back into the original files, with the original extension, to the SMS\Inboxes\Sinv.box\Filecol\<ClientResourceID> directory. A directory is created under \Filecol for every DDR recorded in the site database. Each client DDR contains a unique Client Resource ID. This ID is used to create the individual directory. Each client assigned to the site receives its own directory and Software Inventory Processor stores five versions of the collected file. Each file has a unique character name with the file's original extension. If you are collecting multiple files, the random filename makes it hard to identify exactly what is being stored in the client's ID directory.

- Software Inventory Processor writes the inventory information to the SQL database. This data includes the software inventory information, as well as the collected file's header information.

CHECKPOINT: Once the data has been written to the SMS SQL database, the new information is viewable through the Resource Explorer of the specific client. If the information isn't available, check the SQL logs for problems that may have arisen due to SMS writing to the SQL database. The Software Inventory process is complete.

Software Inventory Checklist 16-bit Client

The Software Inventory process for the 16-bit client is different from the 32-bit client process only in the client phase. Once the 16-bit client phase has been completed, the Site Server Phase listed in the 32-bit Client Checklist is the same across both platforms.

As with the 32-bit client, the Software Inventory Agent for the 16-bit client verifies Software Inventory is enabled for the site. Also, the 16-bit client does a check to determine if the Software Inventory program is installed. If it isn't installed, the Client Component Installation Manager (Ccim16.exe) initiates the Software Inventory installation.

Because the 16-bit Software Inventory installation differs slightly than the 32-bit version, the following minichecklist walks through the 16-bit installation. For a 16-bit Software Inventory Installation Checklist, see the following bulletpoints.

- Ccim16.exe reads the inventory frequency from the Sinv.cfg file located on the CAP in the \Clicomp.box directory.
- Ccim16.exe sends an installation package (Insinv16.exe) request to the Advertised Programs Manager (APM) and adds the component configuration data to the SMScfg.ini file.

- APM executes the Insinv16.exe package.
- Insinv16.exe creates the %WINDIR%\MS\SMS\Clicomp\Sinv directory on the client computer, and then installs the 16-bit version of the Software Inventory into the directory structure.
- Launch16.exe launches the Sinv16.exe (both files installed by the Insinv16.exe package). Sinv16.exe waits for approximately 30 minutes, and then begins the initial software inventory (listed in the following section: 16-bit Client Software Inventory Process Checklist).

For a 16-bit Client Software Inventory Process Checklist see the following bulletpoints.

- Sinv16.exe gathers file information from the Sinv.cfg file. This file information includes the file extensions designated for software inventory through the SMS site properties.
- Sinv16.exe creates an SMSsoft.old file. (The history file (*.his) created by the 32-bit process, is relative to the 16-bit version with the *.old extension.)

TIP: 16-bit Software Inventory also supports file collection. If this is the first time files have been collected, Sinv16.exe identifies all specified files and compresses them into a SMS File Collection History (SMSfcoll.his) file. For all subsequent file collections, Sinv16.exe compares the files' versions and dates with those stored in the SMSfcoll.his file, and only updates those that have changed. The SMSfcoll.his file is stored in the %WINDIR%\MS\SMS\Clicomp\Sinv directory on the client computer.

- If this is the first time inventory has been run on the computer, Sinv16.exe creates a Software Inventory Complete (*.sic) file in the %WINDIR%\MS\SMS\Clicomp\Sinv directory on the client computer. If this is a subsequent inventory, Sinv16.exe compares the new inventory to the old inventory contained in the SMSsoft.old file and creates a Software Inventory Delta (*.sid) file in the %WINDIR%\MS\SMS\Clicomp\Sinv directory. When the *.sid file is created, Sinv16.exe updates the SMSsoft.old file with the new inventory information.

CHECKPOINT: At this point, you can verify the *.sic or *.sid file has been created. Also, check to make certain the time and date stamp of the SMSsoft.old file is current.

NOTE: When Sinv16.exe creates a *.sic or *.sid file, it assigns the file a name based on a consecutive eight-digit, numerical value. The numerical value starts with 00000000 and progresses one count each time inventory is run. For example, the filename, 00000012.sid, would indicate that Software Inventory has been collected 12 times on the computer.

- Sinv16.exe makes a call to the Copy Queue (Clearque.exe) to initiate the *.sic or *.sid file to be transferred to the CAP.
- Clearque.exe copies the *.sic or *.sid file to the \Sinv.box directory on the CAP, and then deletes the old *.sic or *.sid file.

CHECKPOINT: The client portion of the 16-bit Software Inventory process is complete. From this point, the rest of the processing is left up to the SMS site server as shown in the Site Server Phase in the 32-bit Client Checklist. If the client doesn't have network connectivity to the CAP, the inventory files won't be copied. If the inventory files aren't present on the CAP, verify the network connection and also the security rights of the logged-in user. If the *.sic or *.sid file isn't deleted from the client computer, this is an indication the client cannot contact the CAP.

Software Inventory Resynch Checklist

A Software Inventory Resynch is a request to reinventory the client computers assigned to the SMS site. An inventory resynch usually means some problem has been identified with the inventory files passed to the site for processing. When a resynch is requested, a full, complete inventory is processed on the client computer. The Software Inventory Processor on the site server requests a Software Inventory Resynch if either of the following two conditions exist:

1. A bad Sinvdat.sic or Sinvdat.sid file has been passed to the site for processing. As indicated earlier in the chapter, the syntax of the inventory file is checked before it is processed and the information is written to the site database. If the syntax is incorrect, it is moved to the SMS\Inboxes\Sinv.box\Badsinv directory. If any files exist in this directory, the Software Inventory Processor requests an inventory resynch for the specific client. Identifying bad inventory files keeps the SQL database from becoming corrupt.
2. A Sinvdat.sic or Sinvdat.sid has been identified as containing information that will update a nonexistent row in the database. If you think of the database structure as a tree, the row is the lowest limb. The rest of the tree must be in place before the limbs are able to grow. As an example, when the inventory file is checked, SMS sees file

versioning information in the file, but it doesn't see a reference to the application in the database. An earlier inventory file for the client may have been missed, so the Software Inventory Processor requests the resynch to retrieve the software information before writing the version information.

Site Server Phase:

- Software Inventory Processor checks the Client Lookup file (Client.lkp) for a valid entry for the client that has invalid hardware information. If an entry for the client doesn't exist, one is added.
- Software Inventory Processor uses the client's SMS Unique ID as an index to create a *.cfg file.
- Software Inventory Processor adds a resync request to the *.cfg file, and then writes the *.cfg file to the SMS\Inboxes\Clidata.src directory on the site server.
- Inbox Manager retrieves the *.cfg and Client.lkp files from the site server and places them in the Clidata.box on the CAP.

Client Phase:

- *Client Component Installation Manager* (*CCIM*) wakes up from its 23-hour cycle, connects to the CAP, and reads the *.cfg file. It uses the Client.lkp file to identify which *.cfg file should be read.
- CCIM enters the information contained in the *.cfg file to the computer's registry at HKEY_LOCAL_MACHINE\SOFTWARE\Microsoft\SMS\Client\Sites\Shared\<Sitecode>\Configuration\Software Inventory Processor\Last Resync Request and notifies clisvc.exe that it has updated the registry. This initiates the Clisvc.exe.
- SMS Client Service (Clisvc.exe) launches the Software Inventory Agent.
- Software Inventory Agent compares the two registry keys: HKEY_LOCAL_MACHINE\SOFTWARE\Microsoft\SMS\Client\Sites\Shared\<Sitecode>\Configuration\Software Inventory Processor\Last Resync Request and HKEY_LOCAL_MACHINE\SOFTWARE\Microsoft\SMS\Client\Client Components\Software Inventory Agent\Sites\<Sitecode>\Last Resync Request. If the values of these keys aren't identical, the keys are updated to match and a Software Inventory cycle is started (see the Software Inventory Checklists earlier in the chapter).

NOTE: When the Software Inventory cycle is initiated because of the registry key update, a Hardware Inventory process is also started.

Forcing Software Inventory

The Software Inventory process contains checks and balances to keep the inventory data current. At times, however, you might need to force the Software Inventory process to execute before the scheduled time. For example, you may need to look for the presence of a virus.

Control Panel Applet

With the out-of-the-box implementation of SMS 2.0, the only clearly evident way to force inventory is by using the Control Panel applet on the client computer: going to components, selecting the Software Component, and starting the component. This requires end-user participation and interaction.

You can force software inventory from the client computer by following these steps:

1. In Control Panel, double-click Systems Management.
2. Click the Components tab (see the next illustration).
3. Select Software Inventory Agent.
4. Click Start Component.

The Software Inventory Agent executes and takes inventory on this client.

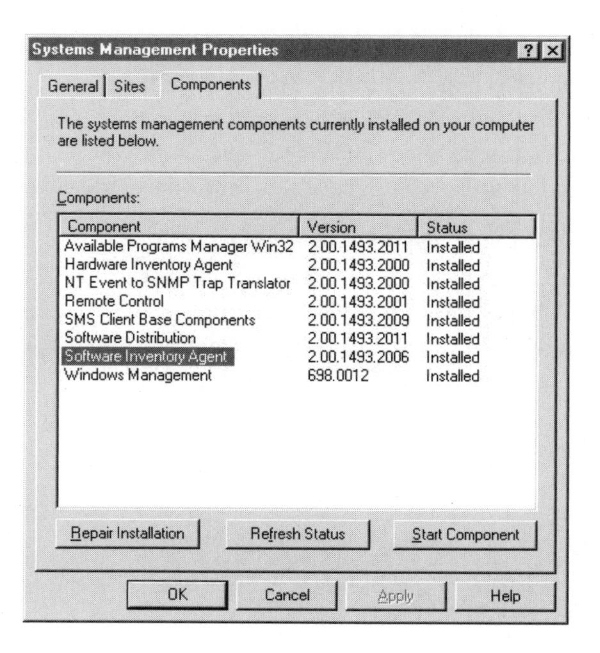

NOTE: Performing hardware and software inventory is processor-intensive, so the client computer seems to operate more slowly while the inventory process is running.

SMS Installer

Microsoft SMS Installer provides a great way of distributing a software inventory package to the client computer. SMS Installer enables you to script a batch of external commands quickly and easily, such as the executable that starts the Software Inventory process. When the script is complete, it is compiled into a one-file executable that can be distributed through the SMS Software Distribution mechanism. The following SMS Installer script first retrieves the client's path to the SMS directory from the registry, and then it runs Sinv32.exe. This script works with Windows 2000, Windows NT, Windows 95, and Windows 98.

This script is available for download from: http://www.swynk.com/trent/Articles/forcesoftware.asp *and* http://www.admin911.com.

```
--Begin Script
item: Get Registry Key Value
  Variable=SMSLOC
  Key=SOFTWARE\Microsoft\SMS\Client\Configuration\Client Properties
  Default=NOTFOUND
  Value Name=Local SMS Path
  Flags=00000100
end

item: Execute Program
  Pathname=%SMSLOC%\clicomp\sinv\sinv32.exe
  Default Directory=%SMSLOC%\Core\Bin
  Flags=00000100
end

--End Script
```

InvSync.exe

The InvSync.exe tool is included on the SMS 2.0 CD in the \Support\Reskit\Bin\Platform\Diagnose directory. This tool sends a hardware or software inventory resynchronization request to the client based on parameters. InvSync.exe must be copied to the SMS\Bin\i386 directory on the site server.

The syntax for Invsync is InvSync [hw | sw] *client_NetBiosName*

For example: InvSync sw *MyComputerName*

InvSync.exe is also dependent on the following files (verify their existence in the SMS\Bin\i386 directory):

- Encrypt.dll
- BaseObj.dll
- BaseSQL.dll
- Basesvr.dll
- BaseUtil.dll
- SMSPerf.dll

NOTE: InvSync.exe can only be run from the site server. It does not operate on a client that belongs to a child site.

NTForceInv.EXE

As noted in Chapter 3, NTForceInv.exe is a utility to force hardware and software inventory on the local or remote computer.

The utility can be downloaded from http://sms.scriptmania.com.

Turning Off Software Inventory for a Single Computer

For most organizations, software inventory is run on an aggressive schedule because the software on the computer could change frequently. For servers, this aggressive Software Inventory schedule can cause undue stress on the processing power, the disk I/O, and even exhibit itself in a slowdown of network adapter performance. You can turn off software inventory for a single computer by following these steps:

1. Create a dummy file called: **SKPSWI.DAT**
2. Copy this file to the root directory of each hard disk drive letter on the computer.
3. Change the **SKPSWI.DAT's** file attribute to Hidden (H).

When the Software Inventory Agent starts, it sees this file and skips the inventory on each drive letter where the file is found.

Inventorying a Single DLL File

SMS, by default, does not enable DLL files to be inventoried as part of the standard Software Inventory process. This is actually a good thing, considering the number of DLL files that can exist on the computer. Adding the DLL extension to the list of file types SMS should scan for increases the length of the Software Inventory process, which, in turn, eats client computer processing power.

When the Software Inventory Agent inventories software, it reads the header information contained in the file's binary code. This is the information you see in the Resource Explorer and the information displayed in query output.

Based on this comprehensive interrogation of the installed files, if you need to inventory a DLL file (for example, determining the version of DCOM installed on the computer), create a SMS Installer script that copies the specific DLL file to the same directory or another directory you choose, and then renames it with an .EXE extension. Because the Software Inventory process already inventories .EXE files, the .DLL file information is included in the next software scan.

Inventory for Non-Networked Computers

One of the drawbacks to the SMS system is the inability to install and inventory computers that aren't connected to the network. If your organization is highly mobile, you may have individuals that report directly to the customer's site. In some cases, you never see these people because they rarely stop into the office, except for quick meetings or to gather mail. They may never even log in to your network. They may refuse to log in to your network because the customer's network configuration is completely different. Or, you may have set up a small network at the customer's site specifically for those employees to function outside the company's environment. So, how do you get software and hardware inventory from these computers?

If you are using some kind of computer imaging process in your organization you should be pre-installing the SMS Core files (see "Pre-Staging Client Installations," Chapter 2). If you aren't, the SMS Core files need to be installed. This is outlined in the following section. If the Core files are, indeed, preinstalled on the computer, you can skip to the section on "Running Inventory on the Non-Networked Computer."

To start the process, you need to manufacture some way of getting the installation and SMS site files to the nonnetworked computers. Because there are a lot of files, a CD image of the directories is the best method.

Place the following Windows 2000/NT specific SMS shares on the CD (make sure to keep the same share names when copying the files to the CD):

1. CAP_<sitecode>
2. SMSLogon

Installing the SMS Applications on a Non-Networked Computer

The CD should include some automated way for individuals to run the installation and inventory. You can use batch files, SMS Installer scripts, or Windows Scripting Host files to provide the automation. To create these automated scripts for installing the Core components, do the following:

1. Use the Windows 2000/NT NET command to share the SMSLogon directory on the CD.
2. Use the Windows 2000/NT NET command to share the SMS_<sitecode> directory on the CD.
3. Change to the \x86.bin directory on the CD and run: SMSBOOT1.EXE -S %0 -N -WINDIR=%WINDIR%.
4. Wait for Clisvcl.exe and CliCore.exe to finish the installation.
5. On the CD, change to the \Clicomp.box\WBEM\i386 directory and run the WBEM installation with the silent switch: WBEMSDK.EXE –s.
6. Reboot the computer.

Once the computer has been restarted and the user has logged back in, follow the steps in the next section to run the initial software and hardware inventory.

Running Inventory on the Non-Networked Computer

The CD you prepare should provide a way to start the software and hardware inventory automatically, using the following steps.

1. Use the Windows 2000/NT NET command to share the SMSLogon directory on the CD.
2. Use the Windows 2000/NT NET command to share the SMS_<sitecode> directory on the CD.
3. Change to \Clicomp.box\Sinv\i386 directory on the CD and run the software inventory installation with the silent switch: Insinv32.exe –s.

4. Change to the \Clicomp.box\Sinve\i386 directory on the CD and run the hardware inventory installation with the silent switch: Inhinv32.exe –s.
5. IMPORTANT: After the hardware and software applications are installed, the computer's registry must be modified in the following areas to reflect the assignment to the correct SMS site:
    - [HKEY_LOCAL_MACHINE\SOFTWARE\Microsoft\SMS\Client\Sites\System**<site code>**)]
    - [HKEY_LOCAL_MACHINE\SOFTWARE\Microsoft\SMS\Client\Sites\System**<site code>**\Client Components]
    - [HKEY_LOCAL_MACHINE\SOFTWARE\Microsoft\SMS\Client\Sites\System**<site code>** \Client Components\Remote Control]
    - [HKEY_LOCAL_MACHINE\SOFTWARE\Microsoft\SMS\Client\Sites\System**<site code>**\Client Components\Software Inventory Agent]
    - [HKEY_LOCAL_MACHINE\SOFTWARE\Microsoft\SMS\Client\Sites\System**<site code>**\Client Components\Hardware Inventory Agent]
    - [HKEY_LOCAL_MACHINE\SOFTWARE\Microsoft\SMS\Client\Sites\System**<site code>**\Client Components\SMS Client Base Components]
    - [HKEY_LOCAL_MACHINE\SOFTWARE\Microsoft\SMS\Client\Sites\System**<site code>**\Client Components\SMS Client Base Components\Copy Queue]
6. Force the hardware inventory by running the command line: %WINDIR%\MS\SMS\Clicomp\Hinv\Hinv32.exe.
7. Force the software inventory by running the command line: %WINDIR%\MS\SMS\Clicomp\Sinv\Sinv32.exe.
8. After the hardware and software inventory is forced, it takes approximately ten to twenty minutes for the hardware and software inventory to complete.
9. Once the hardware and software inventory is complete, the inventory files must be retrieved for inclusion in the company's SMS site. The following files can be copied to a floppy disk, posted to a corporate intranet page/FTP site, or sent via e-mail:
    a. %WINDIR%\MS\SMS\CORE\DATA*.DDR
    b. %WINDIR%\MS\SMS\SINV\OUTBOX*.INV
    c. %WINDIR%\MS\SMS\HINV\OUTBOX*.INV

10. Once you receive the inventory files through your chosen procedure, they need to be inserted into the SMS site for processing.
    a. The *.DDR file is inserted into the <Siteserver>\CAP_<sitecode>\DDR.box directory.
    b. The Hardware *.INV files are inserted into the <Siteserver>\CAP_<sitecode>\Inventry.box directory.
    c. The Software *.INV files are inserted into the <Siteserver>\CAP_<sitecode>\Sinv.box directory.
11. The SMS site will now process the computer inventory properly.
12. Stop the SMS Client Service on the computer and set the Startup Option to manual. With the SMS Client Service set to manual, the inventory process won't run automatically. You can create a procedure to start the process manually when you need current inventory for the non-networked computer.

NOTE: The procedure in step 9 should be automated using your favorite scripting method. You should also consider compressing the files into one and using a unique identifier for the specific computer's compressed file.

Other Software Inventory Tools

The tools outlined in this section can help troubleshoot software inventory problems on the client as well as the server.

Software Inventory Viewer (SinvView.exe)

The Software Inventory Viewer (contained in the SMS Resource Guide) enables you to view the data inside the *.sic, *.sid, and *.his files. Using this tool can help in two ways:

1. You can pipe the output of the program to a text file, for manual review of software inventory. The information inside the text file can also be used for inclusion in a SMS Installer script variable. Once the text file information has been retrieved into the SMS Installer variable, the data can be used with the entire script.
2. You can review the data file on the client and compare it to the related data file on the server. This enables you to verify software inventory is being reported correctly. Syntax of SinvView.exe: **Sinvview** *filename*

The following code listing is example data from the Software Inventory Viewer Output.

```
SINVVIEW Software Inventory File Viewer for SMS v2.0
Copyright 1994 - 1998 by Microsoft Corp.  All rights reserved.
Win32 Software Inventory File
#############################
Version #     : 2.0
Client ID     : GUID:9EC78B60-2075-11D4-A725-00104B343E6C
Netbios Name : EINSTEIN
IP Address    : 10.15.10.3
IPX Address   : 00000000:00104B343E6C
MAC Address   : 00:10:4B:34:3E:6C
OPCode        : 7
Dated On      : 07/01/2000 08:14:39

*** Product ***
(0) Microsoft Corporation     Microsoft Systems Management Server Installer
2.0.92.00      English (United States)
File: (2) wbemsdk.exe    Microsoft Systems Management Server Installer 2.0.92.00
6855316  05/02/2000 18:06:11 x4
File: (2) wbemsdk.exe    Microsoft Systems Management Server Installer 2.0.92.00
3794092  05/02/2000 18:06:14 x5

*** Product ***
(0) DSP GROUP, INC.           DSP GROUP Windows NT(TM) TrueSpeech DLL
1.03           English (United States)
File: (0) tsd32.dll      DSP Group TrueSpeech(TM) Audio Encoder & Decoder 1.03
19216    10/13/1996 21:38:00 x1

*** Product ***
(0) Microsoft Corporation     Tabular Data Control
1, 2, 0, 0031  English (United States)
File: (0) TDC.OCX        TDC ActiveX Control                         1, 2, 0, 0031
73120    05/02/2000 18:58:55 x1

*** Product ***
(0) Microsoft Corporation     RichText
6.00.8418      English (United States)
File: (0) RICHTX32.OCX   RichTx32.OCX                                6.00.8418
204296   06/08/2000 20:26:52 x1
```

Windows Scripting Host

Windows Scripting Host (*WSH*) is a tool developed by Microsoft to allow easier administration of systems. WSH 2.0 comes loaded with Windows 2000. Version 1.0 is available as an installation option on Windows 98 computers, and is an add-on for Windows 95 and Windows NT. The most current version of WSH can be downloaded from Microsoft's MSDN Web site: http://msdn.microsoft.com/scripting.

WSH provides direct interaction with the computer and its resources. It is a complete Win32 application that allows scripts to be run in the Windows environment. WSH scripts can be as simple or as complicated as you want, and still provide a high-level of power. The scripting language is simple, enabling nonprogrammers to create batch processes for managing systems. But, WSH also provides enough functionality for experienced programmers to enjoy the benefits of the scripting language quickly. The language is fully COM-compliant and based on the VBScript and JScript programming languages. WSH integrates fully with WMI (described in Chapter 3), so you can use the scripting tool to retrieve all the data available to the Windows system.

Several Web sites are dedicated to WSH. These sites are an excellent resource for tips, source code, and learning the tool. The following Web sites provide good information to get you started with WSH, as well as giving you a great resource to keep going back.

Windows Scripting Host FAQ: http://wsh.glazier.co.nz/

The Windows Scripting Host FAQ has it all, but one of the best features of the site is the *Frequently Asked Questions* (*FAQ*) section. This Web site provides a great search tool to find topics on nearly any scripting subject.

WinScripting: http://cwashington.netreach.net/main_site/default.asp?topic=news

WinScripting offers a scripting community where you can upload scripts you've created and download scripts posted by other individuals. WinScripting does a great job keeping up on the latest scripting news and providing links to obtain the latest scripting tools. The site also has an innovative layout built entirely by using scripting resources.

WinScripter.com: http://www.winscripter.com/

WinScripter.com contains a library of scripting code for download that helps you understand the scripting languages. Probably the best features of the site are the How-To section and the Message Board. The Message Board is comprised of posts by individuals, which leads you to a comprehensive location for retrieving solutions to specific problems. Don't be concerned about the incorrect dates on the Message Board. "100" means 2000. Obviously, Y2K didn't smile kindly on the site.

WSH is effective at pulling any kind of information from the computer, and can be used to retrieve hardware and software information. WSH uses the same Win32 classes to retrieve hardware as defined in the SMS_DEF.MOF file (described in Chapter 3). In this section, you learn how it can be used to troubleshoot software inventory on the local computer. If you suspect software inventory is not processing correctly on the client, you can use the functionality of WSH and WMI to resolve those concerns. The idea is to run some WSH scripts on the local computer, and then verify the information with what is in the SMS database.

TIP: When running WSH files, two methods are available: compiled with Wscript.exe or compiled with Cscript.exe. By default, WSH scripts are run using the Wscript.exe compiler. Wscript.exe runs with a Graphic User Interface just like any other Windows application. It displays dialog boxes and offers command buttons. The following script code examples are better when run through the DOS prompt because of the amount of information presented. When the "NEXT" item is used in the scripts, each line displayed is shown in its own Windows dialog box. When gathering an extensive amount of information, this can be tedious to get completely through the script. If you run the script code examples using the Cscript.exe compiler, they run in a command interpreter window. Not only does this let all the information be displayed at one time, it also enables you to pipe the information to a text file for viewing and printing later. The command line syntax for the Cscript.exe compiler will look like this: **cscript filename.vbs**

The scripts included in this section are available for download from http://www.admin911.com.

APP_SCHEMA.VBS

The following script example retrieves the qualifiers, properties, and methods from the Win32_Products WMI Class. After the information is retrieved, you can use the properties to retrieve specific product names, as shown in the following WinApps.VBS section. The Win32_Products Class represents the information WMI has gathered for applications that have been installed using the Windows Installer service. When any application is installed using the Windows Installer service, it is registered in its own database. WMI has access to this information.

Command Line: Cscript.exe APP_SCHEMA.VBS

```
'***************************************************************************
'
' WMI Sample Script - Schema browsing (VBScript)
'
' This script demonstrates browsing of qualifiers, properties and methods for
the ' Win32_Product Class
'
'***************************************************************************
```

```
On Error Resume Next
Set Process = GetObject("winmgmts:Win32_Product")
WScript.Echo ""
WScript.Echo "Class name is", Process.Path_.Class

'Get the properties
WScript.Echo ""
WScript.Echo "Properties:"
WScript.Echo ""
for each Property in Process.Properties_
       WScript.Echo " " & Property.Name
next

'Get the qualifiers
WScript.Echo ""
WScript.Echo "Qualifiers:"
WScript.Echo ""
for each Qualifier in Process.Qualifiers_
       WScript.Echo " " & Qualifier.Name
next

'Get the methods
WScript.Echo ""
WScript.Echo "Methods:"
WScript.Echo ""
for each Method in Process.Methods_
       WScript.Echo " " & Method.Name
next


if Err <> 0 Then
       WScript.Echo Err.Description
       Err.Clear
end if
```

APP_SCHEMA.VBS script The following listing is the output of the APP_SCHEMA.VBS script. The Properties section contains the information you should know. The specific properties are used to gather the information in a readable format.

```
Class name is Win32_Product

Properties:

 Caption
 Description
 IdentifyingNumber
 InstallDate
 InstallLocation
 InstallState
 Name
```

```
 PackageCache
 SKUNumber
 Vendor
 Version

Qualifiers:

 dynamic
 Locale
 MappingStrings
 provider
 UUID

Methods:

 Install
 Admin
 Advertise
 Reinstall
 Upgrade
 Configure
 Uninstall
```

WinApps.VBS

WinApps.VBS is written to take advantage of the Name property retrieved from the Win32_Product class. The other properties are also useful but, in this instance, the names of the applications installed by the Windows Installer service is the data you want to retrieve.

Command Line: Cscript.exe WinApps.VBS

```
'***************************************************************************
'
' WMI Sample Script - Information Installed Windows Installer Products
'
' This script demonstrates how to retrieve the info about the installed Windows
Installer ' applications.
' Win32_Product Class.
'
'***************************************************************************
Set SystemSet = GetObject("winmgmts:").InstancesOf ("Win32_Product")


for each System in SystemSet
       WScript.Echo System.Name
Next
```

Partial Output of WinApps.VBS

```
Directory Services
Maps Samples
Network Diagrams Samples
Office Layout Samples
Organization Charts Samples
Release Notes Professional
Microsoft Visual Studio Service Pack 3
McAfee VirusScan
Windows 2000 Administration Tools
Visio 2000
Visio
Active Directory Migration Tool
Program Files
ActivePerl Build 613
ReaderWorks Standard
Microsoft Project 2000
Microsoft Office 2000 SR-1 Premium
Microsoft Office 2000 SR-1 Disc 2
WebFldrs
Windows 2000 Support Tools
Technical Information June 2000
```

GroupApps.VBS

The following WSH script retrieves the applications installed on the local computer by querying the WMI. Instead of querying the Windows Installer database for the information, this script checks the local user profiles and reports back with a list of the applications and their associated shortcuts, as identified in the Windows Program Groups. This information is particularly useful when you are verifying the software inventory data in the SMS database.

Command Line: Cscript.exe GroupApps.VBS

```
'**************************************************************************
'
' WMI Sample Script - Information about the Installed Apps by Group (VBScript)
'
' This script demonstrates how to retrieve the info about the Installed Apps by
Group on the ' local machine from instances of
' Win32_OperatingSystem.
'
'**************************************************************************
Set SystemSet = GetObject("winmgmts:").InstancesOf ("Win32_ProgramGroupOrItem")

for each System in SystemSet
       WScript.Echo System.Name
Next
```

Partial Output of GroupApps.VBS The following is a partial list of information produced by the GroupApps.VBS script.

```
All Users:Start Menu\Programs\SMS 2.0 Support Tools\Tools Help.lnk
All Users:Start Menu\Programs\SMS 2.0 Support Tools\Tools.lnk
All Users:Start Menu\Programs\SMS 2.0 Support Tools\Uninstall.lnk
All Users:Start Menu\Programs\Startup\Microsoft Office.lnk
All Users:Start Menu\Programs\Systems Management Server\Active Directory Collection
Sync Manager.lnk
All Users:Start Menu\Programs\Systems Management Server\Active Directory Discovery
Agent.lnk
All Users:Start Menu\Programs\Systems Management Server\Network Monitor Control Tool.
lnk
All Users:Start Menu\Programs\Systems Management Server\Network Monitor.lnk
All Users:Start Menu\Programs\Systems Management Server\SMS Administrator Console.lnk

All Users:Start Menu\Programs\Systems Management Server\SMS Administrator's Guide.lnk

All Users:Start Menu\Programs\Systems Management Server\SMS Courier Sender.lnk
All Users:Start Menu\Programs\Systems Management Server\SMS Release Notes.lnk
All Users:Start Menu\Programs\Systems Management Server\SMS Setup.lnk
All Users:Start Menu\Programs\Windows 2000 Support Tools\Deployment Planning
Guide.lnk
All Users:Start Menu\Programs\Windows 2000 Support Tools\Error and Event Messages.lnk

All Users:Start Menu\Programs\Windows 2000 Support Tools\Release Notes.lnk
All Users:Start Menu\Programs\Windows 2000 Support Tools\Tools Help.lnk
All Users:Start Menu\Programs\Windows 2000 Support Tools\Tools\Active Directory Admin
```

Using Windows Scripting Host with SMS Queries

If you need to query the SMS site for software inventory, but you don't have access to the SMS Administrator Console, you can use WSH to pull the information. When you create queries on the SMS site, in the SMS Administrator Console, the query language can be reused in WSH.

As you look through the following WSH code, you can see the query run with a "strQuery" command. Any query created through the SMS Administrator Console can be copied and pasted into a WSH script. The new scripts can be saved and reused throughout the organization.

Checking for Software In the following WSH script, the original SMS query looks like this:

```
select distinct SMS_G_System_COMPUTER_SYSTEM.Name,
SMS_G_System_COMPUTER_SYSTEM.UserName, SMS_G_System_SoftwareProduct.ProductName
from  SMS_R_System inner join SMS_G_System_COMPUTER_SYSTEM on
SMS_G_System_COMPUTER_SYSTEM.ResourceID = SMS_R_System.ResourceId inner join
SMS_G_System_SoftwareProduct on SMS_G_System_SoftwareProduct.ResourceID =
SMS_R_System.ResourceId order by SMS_G_System_COMPUTER_SYSTEM.Name,
SMS_G_System_SoftwareProduct.ProductName
```

Command Line: Cscript.exe <filename>.VBS

```
'The following line connects to the SMS Server through the WMI layer.
'For SERVER put in your SMS Server name.
'For XXX put in the site code for that server
winmgmt1 =
"winmgmts:{impersonationLevel=impersonate}!//SERVER\root\sms\site_XXX"

'The following section echoes the connection then gets the object.
WScript.ECho winmgmt1
Set SystemSet = GetObject( winmgmt1 )

'Here is the query to list Machine Name, User Name, and Product Name.
strQuery = "select distinct SMS_G_System_COMPUTER_SYSTEM.Name,
SMS_G_System_COMPUTER_SYSTEM.UserName, SMS_G_System_SoftwareProduct.ProductName
from  SMS_R_System inner join SMS_G_System_COMPUTER_SYSTEM on
SMS_G_System_COMPUTER_SYSTEM.ResourceID = SMS_R_System.ResourceId inner join
SMS_G_System_SoftwareProduct on SMS_G_System_SoftwareProduct.ResourceID =
SMS_R_System.ResourceId order by SMS_G_System_COMPUTER_SYSTEM.Name,
SMS_G_System_SoftwareProduct.ProductName"
'The following section echoes all the instances found by the query.
Set objEnumerator = SystemSet.ExecQuery(strQuery)
for each instance in objEnumerator
WScript.Echo "-> " & instance.SMS_G_SYSTEM_COMPUTER_SYSTEM.Name & " " &
instance.SMS_G_System_COMPUTER_SYSTEM.UserName & " " &
instance.SMS_G_System_SoftwareProduct.ProductName
Next
```

Partial Output from the Software Check The following is displayed in the command prompt window as the script continues retrieving each installed application.

```
> EINSTEIN Administrator VDOnet corp.Ltd VDOLiv32 Player
> EINSTEIN Administrator Visual Basic
> EINSTEIN Administrator Visual Basic 4.0
> EINSTEIN Administrator VSFlexGrid 7.0 Pro
> EINSTEIN Administrator WBEM SDK
> EINSTEIN Administrator Web Administrator
> EINSTEIN Administrator Windows Installer - Unicode
> EINSTEIN Administrator Windows Management Instrumentation
> EINSTEIN Administrator Windows NT Server, Enterprise Edition Installer
> EINSTEIN Administrator Word for Windows Export Format DLL for Crystal Reports

> EINSTEIN Administrator WRSaver Module
> EINSTEIN Administrator Year 2000 Microsoft Product Analyzer
```

Checking the Software Installed on the SMS Server The following WSH script enables you to check the software inventory on the SMS site server, itself. This is useful to determine quickly if the SMS server is running the proper software and software versions. The original SMS query looks like this:

```
select
SMS_R_System.Name,SMS_G_System_SoftwareProduct.ProductName,SMS_G_System_SoftwarePro
```

```
duct.ProductVersion from SMS_R_System inner join SMS_G_System_SoftwareProduct on
SMS_G_System_SoftwareProduct.ResourceID = SMS_R_System.ResourceId
```

Command Line: Cscript.exe <filename>.VBS

```
'The following line connects to the SMS Server through the WMI layer.

'For SERVER put in your SMS Server name.

'For XXX put in the site code for that server


winmgmt1 = "winmgmts:{impersonationLevel=impersonate}!//SERVER\root\sms\site_XXX"

'The following section echoes the connection then gets the object.

WScript.ECho winmgmt1
Set SystemSet = GetObject( winmgmt1 )

'In the following section, the SMS query is run against the SMS database.

strQuery = "select
SMS_R_System.Name,SMS_G_System_SoftwareProduct.ProductName,SMS_G_System_SoftwarePro
duct.ProductVersion from SMS_R_System inner join SMS_G_System_SoftwareProduct on
SMS_G_System_SoftwareProduct.ResourceID = SMS_R_System.ResourceId"

'The following section displays all the instances of the gathered information.

Set objEnumerator = SystemSet.ExecQuery(strQuery)
for each instance in objEnumerator
WScript.Echo "-> " & instance.SMS_R_System.Name & " " &
instance.SMS_G_System_SoftwareProduct.ProductName & " " &
instance.SMS_G_System_SoftwareProduct.ProductVersion
next
```

Partial Output of SMS Server Applications The following output is displayed in the command prompt window during script's retrieval of the installed SMS Server applications.

```
> EINSTEIN Systems Management Server 2.00.1493.2009
> EINSTEIN Systems Management Server 2.00.1493.2008
> EINSTEIN Systems Management Server 2.00.1493.2007
> EINSTEIN Systems Management Server 2.00.1380.1105
> EINSTEIN Systems Management Server 2.00.1380.1125
> EINSTEIN Microsoft Systems Management Server Installer 2.0.90.00
> EINSTEIN Microsoft Visual FoxPro for Windows 5.0a (Build 402)
> EINSTEIN Microsoft Systems Management Server 2.00.1493.2009
> EINSTEIN Systems Management Server 2.00.1493.2013
> EINSTEIN Systems Management Server 2.00.1380.1101
> EINSTEIN Systems Management Server 2.00.1239.0047
> EINSTEIN Systems Management Server 2.00.1239.0055
> EINSTEIN Systems Management Server 2.00.1493.2011
> EINSTEIN Microsoft(R) Network Monitor SMS
> EINSTEIN Microsoft (R) Visual C++ 6.0.100
```

```
> EINSTEIN Microsoft Systems Management Server Installer 2.0.91.07
> EINSTEIN Systems Management Server 2.00.1239.0064
> EINSTEIN Systems Management Server 2.00.1239.0062
```

Software Inventory Gotchas

Most software inventory issues have been resolved with SMS 2.0 Service Pack 2, but common issues always occur that cannot be fixed by a SMS revision patch. For example, a 10604 error in the SMS Status system indicates a corrupt file has been identified on the client computer. If the Software Inventory Agent has trouble compressing a corrupt file, it then reports the error back to the status system. Reinstalling or removing the file from the client computer is the only way to resolve this issue. As mentioned in this chapter, if you follow wise guidelines for maintaining the client computer's RAM, hard disk, and file structure, software inventory should run flawlessly.

If you take the time to monitor the software inventory process, most server problems can be resolved ahead of any potential issues.

The SMS Status Message system contains information formatted in a way to be very comprehensive. For detailed information on the SMS Status Message system, read through Chapter 9. This message system should be the first place to go for software inventory issues. After the status messages have been reviewed, the log files indicated in this chapter should be the next place to check for detailed information. To help identify the log files, the SMS Server Log Viewer tool should be downloaded and installed from http://sms.scriptmania.com. The tool must be run from the SMS site server, but it installs quickly and makes all the log files easily accessible as shown in the following illustration.

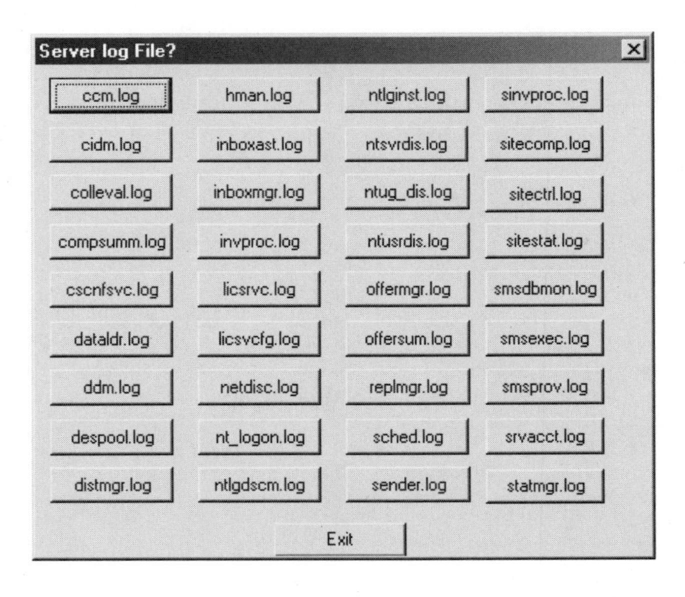

Chapter 5

Software Distribution and Advertisements

Without an automated system in place, software distribution is a costly project. SMS offers automated software package creation and deployment, as well as status information on both the delivery to the computer and the installation's success or failure.

SMS also provides a feature for packages to be "advertised" to Windows 2000/NT computers, enabling the end user to install applications on an as-needed basis. This even provides a way to deploy software to a user instead of a computer. Because software is distributed to Windows 2000 and Windows NT global groups, a user can log on to any computer and the software is immediately available for installation based on the user's group membership.

NOTE: Software distribution through advertisement doesn't work for local groups; it works only for global groups.

Software Installation

Software distribution and the Advertisement Programs Agent are installed as part of the client applications, after the core components are installed. For software distribution to work, the client computer must have both the core components and the client applications installed. It must also be entered into the SMS site database as a computer resource. You cannot distribute software to a computer that doesn't exist in the database and doesn't appear in the SMS Administrator console.

Directory Structure

Tables 5-1 and 5-2 list the notable directories and files that are part of the client's software distribution process and software advertisement process, respectively.

Directory	Description
%WINDIR%\MS\SMS\Clicomp\SWDist32	The general directory for software distribution.
%WINDIR%\MS\SMS\Clicomp\SWDist32\00000409	The 00000409 directory houses the DLL files needed for the software distribution process: CPLRes.DLL (for the Control Panel applet), MonRes.DLL (for the Software Monitor), and the WizRes.DLL (for the Software Wizard).

Table 5-1. Software Distribution Directory Structure

Directory	Description
%WINDIR%\MS\SMS\Clicomp\SWDist32\bin	The BIN directory contains the files needed for software distribution. It contains the Advertised Programs Monitor (SMSMon32.exe), the Advertised Programs Wizard (SMSWiz32.exe), the Offer Data Provider System (ODPSYS32.exe), the Offer Data Provider User (ODPUSR32.exe), and the uninstall program (SWDUnIns.exe).
%WINDIR%\MS\SMS\Clicomp\SWDist32\Cap	Houses the System, User, and User Group Lookup files.
%WINDIR%\MS\SMS\Clicomp\SWDist32\help\00000409	The Help directory contains the help file (SMSMon32.hlp) for Advertised Programs.

Table 5-1. Software Distribution Directory Structure *(continued)*

Directory	Description
%WINDIR%\MS\SMS\Clicomp\Apa	The general client directory for the Advertised Programs Agent.
%WINDIR%\MS\SMS\Clicomp\Apa\Bin	The BIN directory contains the program files for the Advertised Program Agent. These files include the Program Execution Agent (PEA32.exe), the Advertised Programs Manager (SMSAPM32.exe), and the uninstall file (APAUnIns.exe).
%WINDIR%\MS\SMS\Clicomp\Apa\Data	The general working directory for the files created by the advertisement process. These files include information on status, history, and available programs. Also, an environ.tmp file exists in this directory. The Advertised Programs Agent reads this file for the client's operative Temporary directory for processing.
%WINDIR%\MS\SMS\Clicomp\Apa\Data\Complete	Houses the files created when the advertisements have been completed. SMS uses these files to determine whether the program has been run.
%WINDIR%\MS\SMS\Clicomp\Apa\Data\Jobs	Contains the files that indicate any current advertisement jobs.
%WINDIR%\MS\SMS\Clicomp\Apa\Data\New	Houses the files for any new jobs. Also offers files that have been noted by the end user, but are still available for execution.
%WINDIR%\MS\SMS\Clicomp\Apa\Temp	The working directory for advertisement processing.

Table 5-2. Advertised Programs Agent Directory Structure

Targeting Distributions

In SMS 1.2, you distributed software by dragging-and-dropping on to a single computer or a computer group. The job was created and the software was deployed to the computer(s) for installation. In SMS 2.0, the method for targeting computers for package distribution is completely different. Software must be distributed by targeting collections.

Collections are based on criteria and SMS queries. For example, if you want to distribute Microsoft Office 2000 as an upgrade, you create a collection based on all the computers running an earlier version.

The inability to target a single computer for software distribution has frustrated the SMS community. Some workarounds for this dilemma are discussed in the next few sections.

Unique Collection

One method to target specific computers is to create a collection based on something specific to the computer. You can set up the collection based on explicit criteria, such as the inventoried user name or computer name. The following SMS query creates a collection based on the user name. (This method could create a problem if several people log on to that particular computer.) This collection is configured to add all computers that have been logged in to using the account "Administrator."

```
select SMS_G_System_COMPUTER_SYSTEM.UserName,
SMS_G_System_COMPUTER_SYSTEM.Name from  SMS_R_System inner join
SMS_G_System_COMPUTER_SYSTEM on SMS_G_System_COMPUTER_SYSTEM.ResourceID
= SMS_R_System.ResourceId where SMS_G_System_COMPUTER_SYSTEM.UserName =
"Administrator" order by SMS_G_System_COMPUTER_SYSTEM.UserName,
SMS_G_System_COMPUTER_SYSTEM.Name
```

The next query configures a new collection based on the specific name of the computer. The computer name is the computer's NetBIOS name that is assigned through the System Properties Control Panel applet on Windows 2000 computers and through the Network Properties applet for Windows NT and Windows 9*x* systems.

```
select SMS_G_System_COMPUTER_SYSTEM.UserName,
SMS_G_System_COMPUTER_SYSTEM.Name from  SMS_R_System inner join
SMS_G_System_COMPUTER_SYSTEM on SMS_G_System_COMPUTER_SYSTEM.ResourceID
= SMS_R_System.ResourceId where SMS_G_System_COMPUTER_SYSTEM.Name =
"EINSTEIN" order by SMS_G_System_COMPUTER_SYSTEM.UserName,
SMS_G_System_COMPUTER_SYSTEM.Name
```

A better method of creating a collection with a single resource is to identify the resource by the network interface card's (NIC) *Media Access Control* (*MAC*) address. The MAC address is a unique number assigned by the manufacturer to every network card.

The following query creates a collection based on the MAC address being 00:10:4B:34:3E:6C.

```
select SMS_G_System_COMPUTER_SYSTEM.UserName,
SMS_G_System_NETWORK_ADAPTER.MACAddress from  SMS_R_System inner join
SMS_G_System_NETWORK_ADAPTER on SMS_G_System_NETWORK_ADAPTER.ResourceID
= SMS_R_System.ResourceId inner join SMS_G_System_COMPUTER_SYSTEM on
SMS_G_System_COMPUTER_SYSTEM.ResourceID = SMS_R_System.ResourceId where
SMS_G_System_NETWORK_ADAPTER.MACAddress = "00:10:4B:34:3E:6C" order by
SMS_G_System_COMPUTER_SYSTEM.UserName,
SMS_G_System_NETWORK_ADAPTER.MACAddress
```

Add2Collection Utility

Add2Collection, from KND B.V., is an excellent tool for rapidly adding a computer to a collection. It integrates the SMS Administrator console by adding a menu option for every computer resource. This enables you to add the selected computer resource to a collection, and then distribute software to that single computer.

When Add2Collection is installed, a SMS Tools option is added to the list of options you see when you right-click a computer resource. Click SMS Tools to see the Add2Collection program, shown in the next illustration.

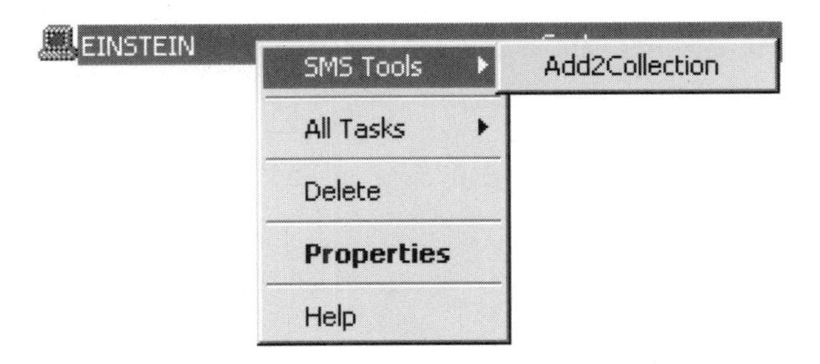

When you click the Add2Collection tool, the program enumerates, and then displays the collections currently installed at your SMS site, as shown in Figure 5-1.

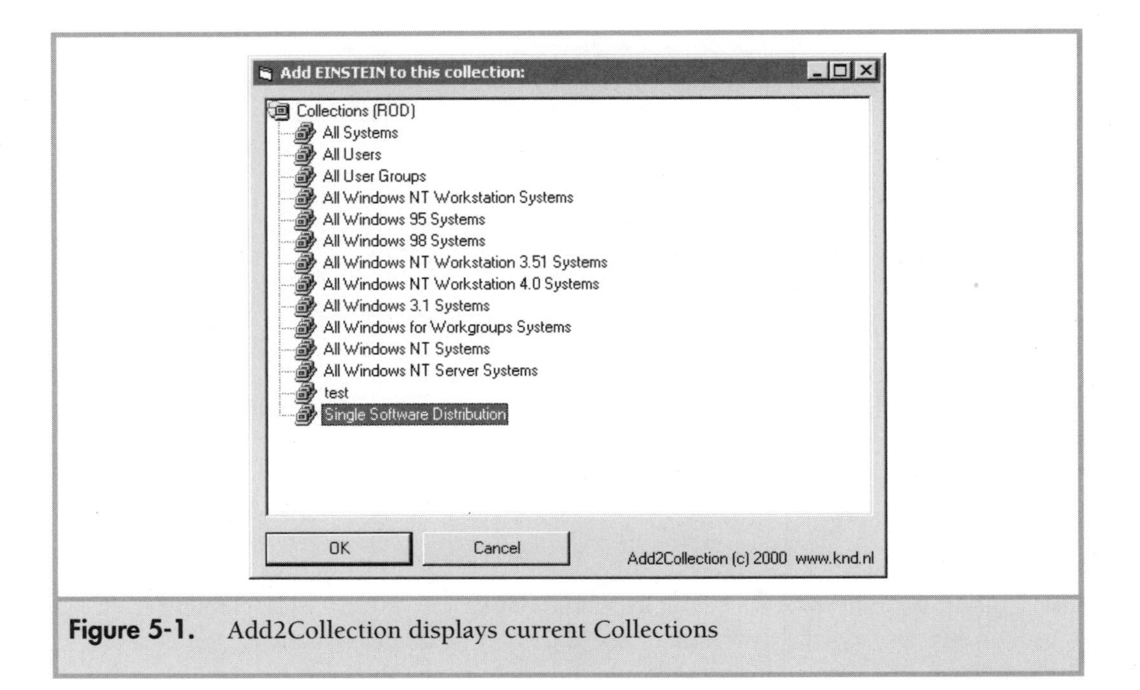

Figure 5-1. Add2Collection displays current Collections

TIP: Create a dummy collection used specifically for this feature. Call it something like "Single software distribution." To create a dummy collection, just add and save a new collection, giving it only a name. Don't add any criteria to the collection.

When the collections window is displayed, select the collection you want to add the computer resource to and click OK. The computer resource is added to the collection in a matter of seconds. Once the collection is populated with the computer resource, you can distribute software to the single computer. Note that: Add2Collection is a free program, available for download from: http://www.knd.nl/.

Creation

Software distribution and software advertisements are basically the same concept and you perform similar steps to create them. For a software advertisement to be available for distribution, you must first create a package and carry out an additional step of making the package an advertisement. Both processes are for distributing software, the difference is in how they are offered to the end user.

Packages

A *package* is a loose term that represents some type of program to be sent to a SMS collection, either through a Distribution or as an Advertisement. A package can be almost anything that needs to be installed on the client computer, provided the SMS package properties contain a valid command line. This command line can contain .REG files, .BAT files, .EXE files, .CMD files, and so forth. The package can be used to distribute software installations, software upgrades, patches, service packs, changes to the computer, and even to execute programs that already exist on the computer.

Package Types

When SMS packages are created, the "program" or command line that is identified can take many forms. It can be represented as a one-file executable, a batch file, a Wrapper program, a collection of application files, or any type of automation file created by a scripting program such as Windows Scripting Host or SMS Installer.

One-File Executable A *one-file executable* is a compressed version of the entire software application installation. This type of distribution is usually scripted with a "snapshot" program, such as SMS Installer.

SMS Installer (and similar applications) provides the capability to "watch" the installation of an application, and then to record all the changes made to the computer. These changes include registry modifications, file installations, and file changes. After the changes have been recorded into the SMS Installer script, the script is compiled into a compressed executable file. This executable contains all the computer modification information that SMS Installer recorded, as well as all the files installed by the application.

NOTE: Microsoft doesn't support the repackaging of MSI (Windows Installer) applications. You can use the Wrapper Program method (described in the next sections) to run the MSI executable to distribute the Windows Installer format application. See the section on "Distributing MSI Applications" in this chapter for more details.

Distributing a one-file executable through SMS provides many benefits over the other methods.

- **Compression saves bandwidth.** The compressed format of the application saves bandwidth as the package is distributed across the network to the SMS distribution points.
- **Compression saves disk space.** The compressed file also preserves disk space on the destination hard drives of the distribution points.

- **Zip-compatible file format.** SMS Installer has a unique feature of adding Zip compliancy to the compressed executable. When applications fail because of a corrupt file, the SMS Installer executable can be opened with a Zip-compatible program and the single file can be retrieved to fix the issue.
- **Network bandwidth.** Distributing one file instead of many files keeps down the amount of network bandwidth needed to replicate the file to the distribution points.
- **Status MIF.** SMS Installer has the option to create its own Status MIF file that is read by the SMS inventory. This Status MIF notifies the SMS system if a software application has been installed correctly or it has failed. It can also notify the system if the application is uninstalled.
- **Uninstall capability.** Scripting programs, such as SMS Installer, also provide a complete uninstall path for the application. Because the program has recorded the complete information about the application's installation, it also knows the complete method for putting the computer back to the original configuration (before the application was installed). This also enables you to distribute programs through the SMS software distribution mechanism that initiates the Uninstall process if the application is no longer needed.

The powerful scripting facility of SMS Installer can also be used to create scripts that make modifications to the destination computer, as well as executing programs that already exist on the PC.

As an example of a computer modification, the following SMS Installer script removes the My Network Places icon on the Windows 2000 desktop by changing some settings in the computer's registry. Making a change like this is useful to keep the end user from changing Windows 2000 network configuration settings.

```
--Begin Script
item: Edit Registry
  Total Keys=2
  item: Key
    Key=Software\Microsoft\Windows\CurrentVersion\Policies\Explorer
    New Value=01000000
    Value Name=NoNetHood
    Root=1
    Data Type=4
  end
  item: Key
    Key=S-1-5-21-1409082233-2146866087-1801674531-
1108\Software\Microsoft\Windows\CurrentVersion\Policies\Explorer
```

```
    New Value=01000000
    Value Name=NoNetHood
    Root=3
    Data Type=4
  end
end
--End Script
```

As an example of running a program that already exists on the computer, the following SMS Installer script uses the Windows 2000 RunDLL32.exe command to make an API call against the PrintUI.DLL system file. The PrintUIEntry /il option of PrintUI.DLL causes the Windows 2000 Add Printer Wizard to start. For more information on using the PrintUI.DLL file and the hoard of options available, see: http://www.swynk.com/trent/Articles/PrintUI.asp.

```
--Begin Script
item: Set Variable
  Variable=OPTIONS
  Value=/il
end
item: Execute Program
  Pathname=%SYS%\rundll32.exe
  Command Line=printui.dll,PrintUIEntry %OPTIONS%
end
--End Script
```

Batch Files You can use batch files to initiate application installations. The batch file contains the commands needed to start the program's Installation process by connecting to a network share and executing the setup program from there. For the batch file method to work, the end user needs the proper access rights to the share.

When the package is set up in the SMS Administrator Console, the batch filename (with the file extension, usually .BAT or .CMD) is used as the program's executable. As an example, the following batch file commands start the installation of Microsoft Office by running the setup executable from a Windows 2000 server share.

```
@echo off
\\<servername>\<sharename>\MSOffice\Setup.exe
```

Remember, the user needs the proper access to the server and the Windows 2000/NT share for the Batch file process to work. The default software installation account SMSCLITOKN only allows installations from the distribution point. You can create a separate software installation account specifically for accessing installations that aren't located on a distribution point. As shown in the next illustration, you can set up a specific Windows 2000/NT account that runs when the package installation begins. This account can be given the appropriate access rights to the source directory.

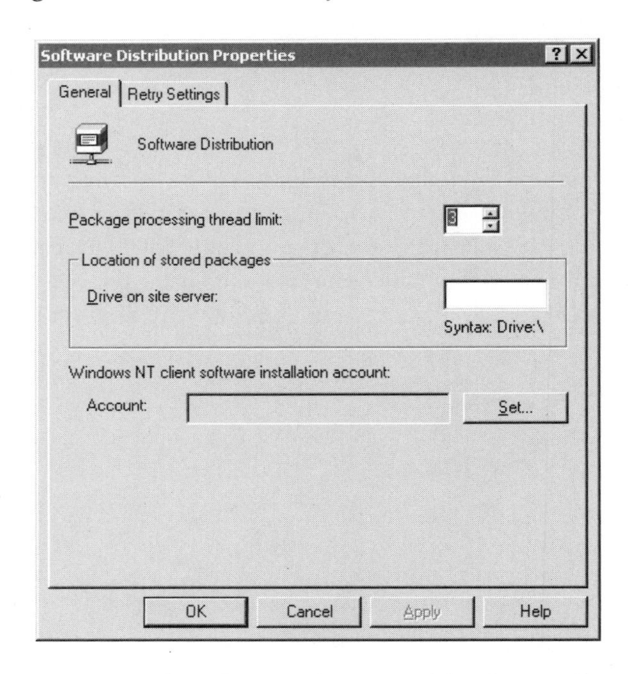

Some installations require a drive letter to be mapped for the installation to run. The following batch program maps the drive letter, and then runs the setup file.

```
@echo off
3net use I: \\<servername>\<sharename>
I:\MSOffice\Setup.exe
```

Wrapper Program Using a Wrapper program is similar to using the Batch File method of software distribution, except the batch commands are scripted. A *Wrapper* program is basically a combination of the one-file executable and the batch file methods. A script is created with commands that point to a network drive or share where the application's setup file is located. In addition to running the application installation, the tool used to script the Wrapper program can include other modifications. One common modification is to change the registry so the computer logs in automatically when the computer is restarted. This AutoAdminLogon technique is great for forcing the computer to restart under an Administrative context and running an installation that requires the special context. The AutoAdminLogon technique is described at the end of this chapter.

CODE BLUE

Another critical modification that should be employed is to shut down AntiVirus services during an installation. AntiVirus programs can be configured to be aggressive when scanning the system for viruses. Any virus-like activity will be identified and stopped. Some installations may confuse the AntiVirus program into thinking its operation warrants an alert. When this happens, the installation will fail. By using a Wrapper program, you can shut down the virus-scanning services before the installation and restart them after the installation is complete. On Windows 2000 and Windows NT, the AntiVirus services run as a standard system service and can be shut down easily. On Windows 95 and Windows 98, the services run as background processes, making it harder to disable them without the use of an extra utility. See your AntiVirus vendor's Web site for detailed information on how to disable and reenable the program.

The following script was created with SMS Installer and performs the same function as the batch file. It puts the location of the Windows 2000 share into the %SHARELOC% variable, and then executes the setup.exe from the share. As with the batch file method, the user must have the required rights to the share.

```
item: Set Variable
  Variable=SHARELOC
  Value=\\<ServerName>\<ShareName>\MSOffice\
end
item: Execute Program
  Pathname=%SHARELOC%
  Command Line=Setup.exe
end
```

NOTE: The Wrapper Program is the best method for distributing Microsoft Service Packs. Microsoft Service Packs come with their own installation routines and great care is taken to verify the update installs correctly.

CODE BLUE

Never repackage a service pack for distribution. Distributing a repackaged version of a service pack can fail if all files are not updated correctly. When the operating system is running, files and hardware drivers are held open by the OS's services, thread, and processes. If a repackage installation doesn't update all files correctly, the computer could stop functioning or even fail to boot.

Windows Scripting Host Windows Scripting Host provides the same functionality as the batch file package type, but it provides additional capabilities. WSH may be a little overkill for software distribution, but if you're skillful with the scripting tool, it could well be used to distribute applications.

For Windows Scripting Host to run external programs, you use the `Run()` method, as the following shows. The first script runs the setup program from a server share; the second script starts the installation from a drive letter and path.

```
Set shell = CreateObject("WScript.Shell")
shell.Run \\<ServerName>\ShareName\MSOffice\Setup.exe

Set shell = CreateObject("WScript.Shell")
shell.Run "I:\MSOffice\Setup.exe"
```

NOTE: Windows Scripting Host must be installed on the target machine for the script to work.

Application Files You can also deliver the entire file structure to the distribution point and point to the setup executable when you create the package. When SMS creates a package from the specified source directory, it includes all files in that directory, as well as the subdirectory structure. The only real advantage to using this method is the user already has the required access to the distribution point to run the installation. The big disadvantage of distributing software this way, assuming you have enough disk space to house the file structure, is the amount of bandwidth used when SMS moves the entire file set and directory structure to the distribution point. Most applications are large. If you look at the MS Office Professional 2000 CD set, you notice the entire installation comes on four CDs. One CD holds approximately 650MB. Copying a full 650MB across the network can consume the network bandwidth. In addition, the distribution point and the package source must store the file content. Secondary site servers are used to install applications to locations where a smaller number of users are present. For this reason, Secondary site servers are generally not purchased and configured with a lot of horsepower, RAM, and disk space. Several software distributions using the complete file distribution method could cause the Secondary site server to run out of disk space.

Testing the Packages

One of the most important aspects of dispensing applications through Distribution and Advertisement is to test, test, test, and test some more. Software distributions can fail for a number of reasons:

- User rights. If the user doesn't have the appropriate Windows 2000/NT user or group rights to install software or access the distribution point, the program will fail.
- Software Distribution Accounts. When Software Distribution Accounts are created for package distribution, SMS uses these to contact the distribution point or another specified directory location across the network. These accounts must have the proper rights assigned for access to the program's source.
- Account Lockouts. If you have aggressive security policies enabled in the Windows 2000 or Windows NT domain, the SMSCLITOKN account could become locked out.
- Failed or slow network connections. Of course, a failed network connection definitely means a distribution won't take place. Even slow network connections can cause distributions to take longer than expected, though, and cause replicated files to become corrupt.
- Incomplete collections. If a targeted collection is empty, the distribution status will always indicate it is pending.
- Corrupt .PKG and .OFR files. When sent over slow networks or over networks with intermittently failing hardware, .PKG and .OFR files can become corrupt.
- End user issues. If the end user decides he wants to restart his computer during a package installation, the distribution could fail. Similarly, if someone cancels an installation, the distribution reports a failure.
- Inaccessible distribution points. And, of course, if a server hardware failure occurs at a distribution point, the distribution won't complete for some of the computers.

The optimum way to avoid these issues is to test the packages as completely as possible. During testing, you may discover a better way to distribute the package. For example, to keep the end user from canceling a package, you may want to dispense the program using a method that makes the installation completely silent. Or, to keep the end user from restarting the computer, you may decide that disabling the mouse and keyboard before the installation is the best bet.

A lab environment is the ideal atmosphere in which to test packages. Build the lab to simulate your organization's environment as closely as possible.

If you don't have the luxury of a lab, test the distribution on a small group of users. Make sure to include users with varying levels of computer experience. When you distribute applications, you want the installation to be as easy-to-navigate and complete as possible. You can judge the success of a software distribution based on the number of HelpDesk calls it generates, not by the SMS System returning a success status.

Security

SMS 2.0 provides granular security. In addition to adhering to Windows 2000 and Windows NT domain security for the SMS service and installation accounts, SMS enables you to give individual users the rights to Classes and Instances in the Administrator console MMC. If you think of the SMS Administrator console as a tree structure, the *class* is the tree limb and the *instances* are its branches. An example of a class is the group collections. An instance of the collections is a specific collection, for example, all Windows 2000 Pro Workstation Systems. This security method is useful for limiting individuals' access to specific computer groups. For example, you may have a group of support people specifically assigned to work with financial applications and they should have access only to those computers in the collection (for example, All Financial Computers).

In many organizations, software distribution is considered a function of the local support HelpDesk. A SMS Administrator who has full access rights to the software packages for the SMS site generally creates the actual packages available for distribution. But, the management of the actual package distribution can be given to specific personnel. Because of the granular security of SMS, user rights can be limited to the SMS Site. Table 5-3 defines the SMS Object and the minimum-security permissions needed to be able to distribute applications.

Software Distribution Checklists

The following process checklists are separated into the Server-side and Client-side sections. The Server side part of software distribution is comprised of the creation, distribution, and replication of the Packages and Advertisements. The Client-side processes start when the client computer identifies that an assigned package is waiting.

Server-Side

Three distinct processes relate to software distribution on the SMS site server: Package Creation, Advertisement Creation, and Package and Advertisement Distribution. When following the Server-side software distribution checklists, use the associated log files listed in Table 5-4 to find detailed information about any errors.

SMS Object	Security Permissions
Advertisements	Read, Create, Modify, Delete (or Administer)
Collections	Read, Advertise, Read Resource
Packages	Read, Create, Distribute, Modify, Delete (or Administer)

Table 5-3. Objects and Permissions for Software Distribution

Package Creation Checklist

The package is created through the SMS Administrator console. The SMS Provider writes the information about the new package to the SMS database. A SQL Trigger is initiated that creates a Package Notification, and then SQL Monitor writes the Package Notification to a file in the SMS_<SiteCode>\Inboxes\Distmgr.box directory. The filename is the Package ID assigned by the SMS server, plus the .PKN extension.

Component	Logs	Process
SMS Provider	SMS\Logs\SMSProv.log	Advertisements, Packages, Creation, and Distribution
Offer Manager	SMS\Logs\Offermgr.log	Advertisements
SMS SQL Monitor	SMS\Logs\SMSdbmon.log	Advertisements, Packages, Creation, and Distribution
Distribution Manager	SMS\Logs\Distmgr.log	Advertisements, Packages, Creation, Distribution, and Courier Sender
Inbox Manager	SMS\Logs\Inboxmgr.log	Advertisements, Packages, Creation, and Distribution
Replication Manager	SMS\Logs\Replmgr.log	Packages, Creation, and Distribution
Scheduler	SMS\Logs\Sched.log	Packages, Creation, and Distribution
Sender	SMS\Logs\Sender.log	Packages, Creation, and Distribution
Despooler	SMS\Logs\Despool.log	Distribution
Courier Sender	SMS\Logs\Coursend.log	Courier Sender

Table 5-4. Server Logs for Troubleshooting Software Distribution and Advertisements

CHECKPOINT: To verify the SQL Trigger has been initiated, check the Distmgr.box directory for the specific .PKN file. The .PKN file is only in the directory for a few seconds, so you should open a window to the directory before the creation of the package is completed. The SMSdbmon.log file also identifies if any issues concerning SQL Server exist.

NOTE: On Secondary sites, this .PKN file is named <SiteCode>PackageID.pkg and resides in the \\Servername\SMS\Inboxes\Pkginfo.box and CAP_<SiteCode>\Pkginfo.box directories. The <SiteCode>PackageID.pkg file is a reference to the actual package. Every time the package gets updated, this file is changed across all Secondary sites. When the .PKN file is processed at the Primary site, the information is inserted into a table in the SQL database. This assures all Parent sites receive the information by accessing the SQL table directly. Secondary sites don't access the SQL table, they rely on the <SiteCode>PackageID.pkg file for the information.

- Distribution Manager compresses the source directory where the package command has been specified. It compresses the package into a working directory with the name of _s_m<RandomID>.tmp.
- Distribution Manager stores the compressed package into the \SMSpkg share directory with a <PackageID>.PCK filename.
- Distribution Manager decompresses the package to a _s_m<RandomID>.tmp temporary working file.

NOTE: During the package creation and distribution process, the package actually needs three times the size of the original package file. Make note of this as you are distributing packages. If a distribution point doesn't have the appropriate disk space to accommodate the additional package size, the distribution will fail.

- Distribution Manager copies the decompressed version of the package to the distribution points into the \SMSpkg<DriveLetter>$ share directory.

NOTE: An inseparable part of the package creation process involves the distribution of the created packages to the distribution points and the CAPs. This is part of the distribution process. The specific components of the distribution process are covered later in this section.

- Distribution Manager creates the package file, the Distribution Point List, and the package icon files. The files are created in the \SMS\Inboxes\Pkginfo.box directories, with the following names:
  - Package = <PackageID>.PKG

- Distribution Point List = <PackageID>.NAL
- Icon files = \<PackageID>.ICO\<SequentialNumber>.ICO
- \SMS\Inboxes\Pkginfo.box\<PackageID>.PKG
- \SMS\Inboxes\Pkginfo.box\<PackageID>.NAL
- \SMS\Inboxes\Pkginfo.box\<PackageID>.ICO\<SequentialNumber>.ICO

CHECKPOINT: At this point, Distribution Manager has completed processing of the created package. Use the Distmgr.log to identify any creation issues and verify if the process was successful. You can verify the file processing is successful by checking the following directories for the appropriate files. You need to verify these files exist on all the distribution points configured in the package properties.

NOTE: During package creation, you can assign different icons to the package. This is the icon displayed to the user when the package becomes available. SMS includes these icon files with the distributed package at the distribution points.

- Inbox Manager copies the package files to the CAPs in the \Pkginfo.box directory, using the same names as created on the SMS Site Server.

CHECKPOINT: The package creation process is complete. You can verify the Inbox Manager process is successful by viewing the Inboxmgr.log file and also verifying the .PKG, .NAL, and .ICO files exist at the CAPs in the \Pkginfo.box directory. The full distribution process begins at this point.

Advertisement Creation Checklist

The advertisement is created through the SMS Administrator console. SMS Provider writes the advertisement to the SMS database. The Offer Notification is triggered. Offer Manager creates the offer file in the SMS\Inboxes\Offerinf.box directory. The offer file is named with the offer ID and an .OFR extension.

CHECKPOINT: Verify the <OfferID>.OFR file exists in the \Offerinf.box directory. The Offermgr.log file indicates any issues. If problems occur with the Offer Notification, check the SMSdbmon.log file for information that could signify a problem exists with SQL Server.

- Offer Manager identifies the types of collections the advertisement is meant for and creates the appropriate Look-up files.

- System = \SMS\Inboxes\Offerinf.box\System.LKP
- User = \SMS\Inboxes\Offerinf.box\User.LKP
- User Group = \SMS\Inboxes\Offerinf.box\Usrgrp.LKP

- Inbox Manager replicates all the advertisement files (.OFR, .LKP, and .INS) to the CAPs in the \Offerinf.box directory.

CHECKPOINT: The advertisement Creation process is complete. The Inboxmgr.log file can be reviewed for information and the \Offerinf.box directory on the CAPs can be searched for the advertisement files. The full distribution process begins at this point.

Package and Advertisement Distribution Checklist

Package distribution primarily consists of the Distribution Manager starting the replication of the package information to the distribution points at the child sites. The distribution process relies on several different components. You should verify the success of the distribution process after each component has completed its task.

- Distribution Manager creates a replication file in the SMS\Inboxes\Replmgr.box\Outbound\<Frequency> directory on the SMS site server. The file will receive an object ID and be named: <ObjectID>.RPT.

CHECKPOINT: Check the \<Frequency> directory for the specific .RPT file. If issues exist with the creation of the replication file, the Distmgr.log file should be reviewed.

NOTE: The <Frequency> directory is actually three different directories under \Outbound: \Low, \Normal, and \High. The replication file is placed in the appropriate frequency directory based on the distribution's priority. As shown earlier in this chapter, this is established by using the Sending Priority option in the package properties.

- Replication Manager creates a <SequentialNumber>.JOB file in the SMS\Inboxes\Schedule.box directory.

CHECKPOINT: Confirm the .JOB file has been created in the \Schedule.box directory. The Replmgr.log file should be reviewed for any issues.

- Schedule compresses the items identified for transfer into the SMS\Inboxes\Schedule.box\ToSend directory on the SMS site server. It then creates a request-to-send (.SRQ file) in the SMS\Inboxes\Schedule.box\Outboxes\<SenderType> directory. The filename of the .SRQ is randomly generated.

CHECKPOINT: Examine the \ToSend directory for the compressed package. You can check the creation date and time on the .SRQ files in the \<SenderType> directory to identify the process's specific .SRQ file. The Sched.log file can be reviewed for any issues.

NOTE: The Sender Types are identified in the site settings of the SMS Hierarchy in the SMS Administrator Console: Standard Sender, Asynchronous RAS Sender, ISDN RAS Sender, X25 RAS Sender, and SNA RAS Sender. These describe the different methods that SMS sends data to other sites. As shown earlier in this chapter, the Preferred Sender can be set for each package through the package Properties.

- Sender renames the .SRQ files to a .SRS extension and sends the items identified for transfer from the SMS\Inboxes\Schedule.box\ToSend directory on the SMS site server to the SMS_<SiteCode>\Inboxes\Despooler.box\Receive directory at the child site.

CHECKPOINT: Verify the .SRS file has been transferred into the \Receive directory at the child site. The Sender.log file indicates any errors with the Sender process.

- Despooler on the child site decompresses the transferred objects. They are decompressed back into their original filenames (*.RPL, *.RPT, and *.PCK) into the following directories:
  - RPL and RPT = SMS\Inboxes\Replmgr.box\Incoming
  - Package Source Files (PCK) = \SMSpkg

CHECKPOINT: Make sure the transferred objects have been decompressed and they exist in the appropriate directories. The Despool.log file can be reviewed to identify any issues from the file decompression.

- Replication Manager moves the transferred objects into the child site's distribution and offer boxes at:
  - Distribution = SMS\Inboxes\Distmgr.box\<PackageID>.PKG
  - Offer = SMS\Inboxes\Offerinf.box\<OfferID>.OFR

CHECKPOINT: View the Replmgr.log file for any issues that may arise during the transfer of the .PKG and .OFR files to the distribution and offer boxes. Make certain the files exist in the \Offerinf.box and Distmgr.box directories.

- Distribution Manager updates the child site's database with the new package information.
- Inbox Manager distributes all the decompressed package property files to the CAPs.

CHECKPOINT: Certify the package property files have been distributed to the CAPs. Review the Inboxmgr.log file for any errors.

The server processing of the package is complete. You can now refer to the specific Client-side process to follow the package distribution and execution on the computer.

Client-Side

When following the Client-side software distribution checklists, use the associated log files in Table 5-5 to find detailed information about any errors.

As shown in Table 5-5, three different offering types exist: System, User, and User Group.

NOTE: The three offering types are only available for Windows 2000 and Windows NT client computers. On Windows 95, Windows 98, and 16-bit clients, all distributions are run under the User context.

- **System Distribution** When the System Offer Data Provider (Odpsys32.exe) runs, it finds the .INS file for the unique SMS identifier in the \\CAP_<Sitecode>\Offerinf.box\<Sitecode>systm.lkp (System Lookup) file on the CAP. Based on the recorded information in the .INS file, it loads the proper offerings listed in the .OFR file, and then sends the offer to the Advertised Programs Manager. When the offer is executed as a System type, the package is run using the Administrative context.
- **User Distribution** The User Offer Data Provider (Odpusr32.exe) finds the .INS file for the Windows 2000/NT user account in the \\CAP_<Sitecode>\Offerinf.box\<Sitecode>user.lkp (User Lookup) file on the CAP. Based on the recorded information in the .INS file, it loads the proper offerings listed in the .OFR file, and then sends the offer to the Advertised Programs Manager. When the offer is executed as a User type, the package is run using the User context.
- **User Group Distribution** The User Offer Data Provider (Odpusr32.exe) finds all the .INS files for all Windows 2000/NT user group memberships in the \\CAP_<Sitecode>\Offerinf.box\<Sitecode>usrgp.lkp (User Group Lookup) file on the CAP. Based on the recorded information in the .INS file, it loads the proper offerings listed in the .OFR file, and then sends the offer to the Advertised Programs Manager. When the offer is executed as a User Group type, the package is run using the User context.

Client Agent	Log	Client Type
Windows System Offer Data Provider	%WINDIR%\MS\SMS\Logs\Odpsys32.log	Windows 2000/NT Windows 95/98
Windows System Offer Data Provider	%WINDIR%\MS\SMS\Logs\Odpsys16.log	16-bit Client
Windows User Offer Data Provider	%WINDIR%\MS\SMS\Logs\Odpusr32.log	Windows 2000/NT
Windows User Offer Data Provider	%WINDIR%\MS\SMS\Logs\Odpusr9x.log	Windows 95/98
Windows User Offer Data Provider	%WINDIR%\MS\SMS\Logs\Odpusr16.log	16-bit Client
Windows User Group Offer Data Provider	%WINDIR%\MS\SMS\Logs\Odpwnt32.log	Windows 2000/NT
Windows User Group Offer Data Provider	%WINDIR%\MS\SMS\Logs\Odpwnt9x.log	Windows 95/98
Windows User Group Offer Data Provider	%WINDIR%\MS\SMS\Logs\Odpwnt16.log	16-bit Client
Advertised Programs Manager	%WINDIR%\MS\SMS\Logs\SMSapm32.log	Windows 2000/NT Windows 95/98
Advertised Programs Manager	%WINDIR%\MS\SMS\Logs\SMSapm16.log	16-bit Client
Offer Data Provider for System Collection Target	%WINDIR%\MS\SMS\Logs\Odpsys32.log	Windows 2000/NT Windows 95/98
Offer Data Provider for System Collection Target	%WINDIR%\MS\SMS\Logs\Odpsys16.log	16-bit Client
Offer Data Provider for User Collection Target	%WINDIR%\MS\SMS\Logs\Odpusr32.log	Windows 2000/NT
Offer Data Provider for User Collection Target	%WINDIR%\MS\SMS\Logs\Odpusr9x.log	Windows 95/98
Offer Data Provider for User Collection Target	%WINDIR%\MS\SMS\Logs\Odpusr16.log	16-bit Client
Offer Data Provider for User Group Collection Target	%WINDIR%\MS\SMS\Logs\Odpwnt32.log	Windows 2000/NT
Offer Data Provider for User Group Collection Target	%WINDIR%\MS\SMS\Logs\Odpwnt9x.log	Windows 95/98
Offer Data Provider for User Group Collection Target	%WINDIR%\MS\SMS\Logs\Odpwnt16.log	16-bit Client

Table 5-5. Client Logs for Troubleshooting Software Distribution and Advertisements

Windows 2000/NT Client

The following checklist for the Windows 2000/NT software distribution starts after the offer type has been identified.

Receiving the Offer The Advertised Programs Manager (SMSapm32.exe) reads the .PKG file(s) for the package information. It reads the .ICO file(s) to retrieve the package icon information, and the Advertised Programs Manager records the offer IDs in the following directories:

- %WINDIR%\MS\SMS\Clicomp\Apa\Data\New\<Sitecode><SequentialNumber>\Show.OFR
- %WINDIR%\MS\SMS\Clicomp\Apa\Data\New\<Sitecode>skip.OFR
- %WINDIR%\MS\SMS\Clicomp\Apa\Data\New\<Sitecode>seen.OFR

CHECKPOINT: Verify the .OFR files have been created in the proper directories. You can review the SMSapm32.log file for any information if the files don't exist.

Running the Package The package is run under the following conditions:

- The program is distributed as mandatory. A countdown timer is displayed. When the limit is reached, the program executes.
- The program's schedule data has been reached. A countdown timer is displayed. When the limit is reached, the program executes.
- The end user selects the advertisement from the Advertised Programs Monitor and executes it manually.
  - Advertised Programs Manager calls the Program Information Provider (%WINDIR%\MS\SMS\Clicomp\APA\Bin\PipCAP32.dll).
  - Program Information Provider reads the following information:
- **Package Information** = from the CAP, \CAP_<Sitecode>\Pkginfo.box\<PackageID>.PKG
- **Distribution Point Information** = from the CAP, \CAP_<Sitecode>\Pkginfo.box\<PackageID>.NAL
- **Icon Information** = from the CAP, \CAP_<Sitecode>\Pkginfo.box\<PackageID>.ICO\<SequentialNumber>.ICO
  - Advertised Programs Manager records the program execution status and history information in the following locations:

- **Status Directory** = %WINDIR%\MS\SMS\Clicomp\APA\Data\Jobs
- **History Directory** = %WINDIR%\MS\SMS\Clicomp\APA\Data\Complete

CHECKPOINT: Review the \Jobs and \Complete directories on the client computer to verify the existence of the program execution records. The SMSapm32.log file should be perused for any error messages.

- Two different Program Execution files exist: Program Execution Agent (%WINDIR%\MS\SMS\Clicomp\Bin\Pea32.exe) and Program Execution Manager (%WINDIR%\MS\SMS\Clicomp\Bin\Pem32.dll). Depending on the offer type (System, User, or User Group) the appropriate one executes the program. Pea32.exe is for User and User Group contexts. Pem32.dll is for the System/Administrative context.

Windows 95 and Windows 98 Clients

When different offer types are distributed (System, User, and User Group) to Windows 95 and Windows 98 computers, Windows Offer Data Provider (Odpwin9x.exe) must still verify the offer type because the server processes operate the same despite the client operating system. The relative lookup files identify the offer type as listed in this chapter. And, even though Windows 95 and Windows 98 computers run the program under the User context only, the offer type is recorded with different filenames in the client's SMS directory structure:

- System Type = %WINDIR%\MS\SMS\Clicomp\APA\Data\New\<Sitecode>seen.OFR
- User and User Group Types = %WINDIR%\MS\SMS\Clicomp\APA\Data\New\<Username><Sitecode>seen.OFR

Receiving the Offer The Advertised Programs Manager (SMSapm32.exe) retrieves the program information from the .PKG file(s), and it records the received offer IDs in the following locations:

- %WINDIR%\MS\SMS\Clicomp\APA\Data\New\<Sitecode><SequentialNumber>show.OFR
- %WINDIR%\MS\SMS\Clicomp\APA\Data\New\<Username>\<Sitecode><SequentialNumber>show.OFR
- %WINDIR%\MS\SMS\Clicomp\APA\Data\New\<Sitecode>ship.OFR

CHECKPOINT: Ensure the .OFR files exist in the correct locations on the client computer. Also, inspect the SMSapm32.log file for any error messages.

Running the Package The package is run under the following conditions:

- The program is distributed as mandatory. A countdown timer is displayed. When the limit is reached, the program executes.
- The program's schedule data has been reached. A countdown timer is displayed. When the limit is reached, the program executes.
- The end user selects the advertisement from the Advertised Programs Monitor and executes it manually.
- Advertised Programs Manager (SMSapm32.exe) calls the Program Information Provider file (PipCAP32.dll).
- Program Information Provider reads the following information:
  - **Package Information** = from the CAP, \CAP_<Sitecode>\Pkginfo.box\<PackageID>.PKG
  - **Distribution Point Information** = from the CAP, \CAP_<Sitecode>\Pkginfo.box\<PackageID>.NAL
  - **Icon Information** = from the CAP, \CAP_<Sitecode>\Pkginfo.box\<PackageID>.ICO\<SequentialNumber>.ICO
- Advertised Programs Manager records the program execution and history in the following locations:
  - **Status Directory** = %WINDIR%\MS\SMS\Clicomp\APA\Data\Jobs
  - **History Directory** = %WINDIR%\MS\SMS\Clicomp\APA\Data\Complete

CHECKPOINT: Look at the \Jobs and \Complete directories on the client computer to confirm the existence of the program execution records. The SMSapm32.log file should be reviewed for any error messages.

- The Program Execution Manager (Pem32.dll) executes the program (PackageID) from the distribution point. The distribution point directory location is \\<Servername>\SMSpkg<Driveletter>$\. The distribution point can also be a custom Windows 2000/NT share defined in the Program Properties.

16-bit Client

The following 16-bit client checklists are separated into two phases: receiving the offer and running the package.

Receiving the Offer The Advertised Programs Client Agent (APM16agt.exe) checks the CAP periodically and when a program becomes available:

- Advertised Programs Client Agent reads the System Lookup file at the CAP (\CAP_<Sitecode>\Offerinf.box\<Sitecode>systm.lkp) and finds the .INS file for the system's SMS Unique ID.
- Advertised Programs Client Agent loads the advertisement(s) information from the .OFR file(s) listed in the .INS file.

Running the Package The package is run under the following conditions:

- The program is distributed as mandatory. A countdown timer is displayed. When the limit is reached, the program executes.
- The program's schedule data has been reached. A countdown timer is displayed. When the limit is reached, the program executes.
- The end user selects the advertisement from the Advertised Programs Monitor and executes it manually.
- The Advertised Programs Manager (Apm16svc.dll) retrieves the following information:
- **Package Information** = from the CAP, \CAP_<Sitecode>\Pkginfo.box\<ObjectID>.PKG
- **Distribution Point Information** = from the CAP, \CAP_<Sitecode>\Pkginfo.box\<ObjectID>.NAL
- **Icon Information** = from the CAP, \CAP_<Sitecode>\Pkginfo.box\<ObjectID>.ICO\
- The Advertised Programs Manager executes the program from the distribution point (\\<SiteServerName\SMSpkg<Driveletter>$\<Object ID>) or from a Windows 2000/NT share.

Package Status

SMS provides a comprehensive reporting system for monitoring the SMS processes throughout the hierarchy. SMS uses message numbers to identify errors, warnings, and information. The System Status section in the SMS Administrator Console provides this detailed information and enables you to proactively monitor package and advertisement status. When you navigate the System Status in the MMC, you see advertisement status and package status, as shown in the following illustration. These sections give you a quick status summary of the package or advertisement condition.

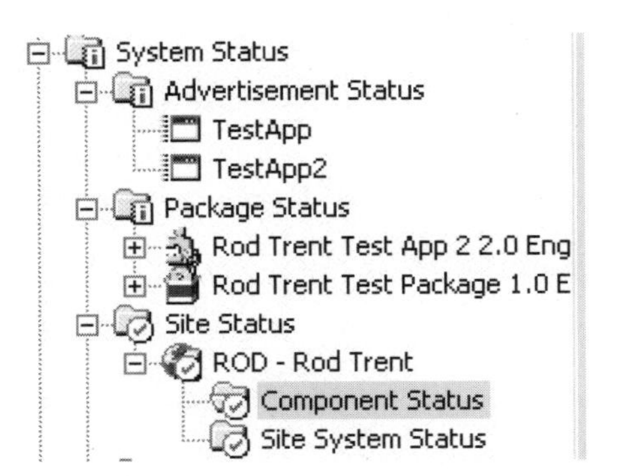

Advertisement Summary Status

The advertisement status gives you the following information:

- Site name
- Received
- Failures
- Programs Started
- Program Errors
- Program Success
- Summary Date

Package Summary Status

The package status gives you the following information:

- Site Name
- Source Version
- Targeted
- Installed
- Retrying
- Failed
- Summary Date

Comprehensive Status

For more detailed information on package and advertisement status, use the SMS status message queries. The stock queries provide instant access to the SMS site status information. The status messaging system is covered in more detail in Chapter 9, but you should be aware of some specific status message queries for software distribution. These can help when you're troubleshooting software distribution and advertisements.

- Advertisements created, modified, or deleted
- All status messages for a specific advertisement at a specific site
- All status messages for a specific package at a specific site
- Clients that deinstalled the advertised programs Client Agent
- Clients that failed to unstall the advertised programs Client Agent
- Clients that failed to run a specific advertisement program successfully
- Clients that failed to start a specific advertised program
- Clients that ran a specific advertised program successfully
- Clients that received a specific advertised program
- Clients that rejected a specific advertised program
- Clients that started a specific advertised program
- Packages created, modified, or deleted
- Programs created, modified, or deleted

When any of these status message queries are selected and run (as shown in the following illustration), the SMS status message viewer displays the results of the specific query. The SMS status message viewer is shown in Figure 5-2.

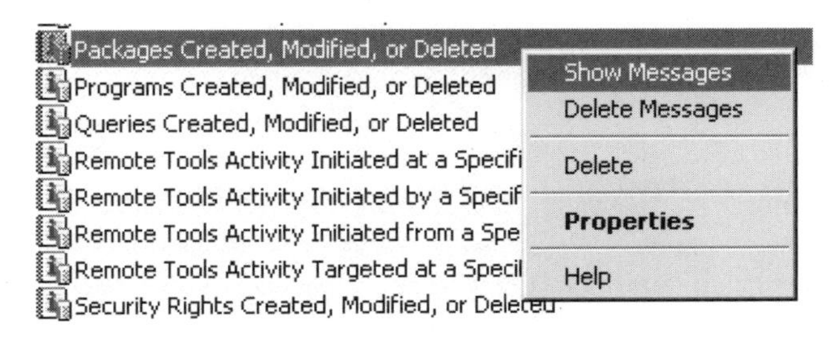

A valuable new tool, released with SMS 2.0 Service Pack 2, is the Comprehensive Advertisement Status Viewer. This tool provides quick status on the software distribution process outside of the SMS Administrator Console. For more information on the

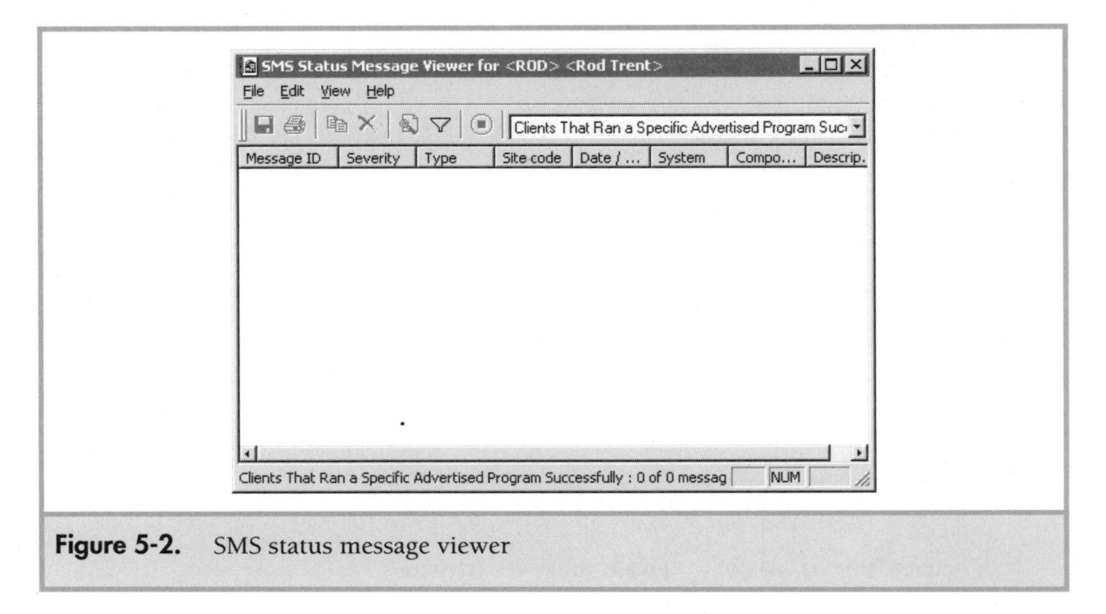

Figure 5-2. SMS status message viewer

Comprehensive Advertisement Status Viewer, see the Distribution Tools section later in this chapter.

In addition to using the status message queries installed with SMS, you can create your own queries using the message ID numbers listed in the next section.

Status Message IDs for Software Distribution

The SMS Advertised Programs Client Agent uses status message numbers 10000 to 10021, as shown in Table 5-6. You employ these status message numbers to monitor the software distribution process and also to build your own status message queries. The status message queries that come installed with SMS are based on these message ID numbers. The message ID numbers with an asterisk (*) by them indicate the common IDs for identifying general success and failure. Use these IDs when creating the status message queries for regular status information.

Exit Codes for Software Distribution Status

As mentioned in the status message IDs list in Table 5-6, the Advertised Programs Manager (APM) looks first for a generated status MIF file to determine software distribution status. If a status MIF file isn't found, the program's Exit Code is retrieved to relay the status information back to the SMS site.

Exit codes aren't always consistent because the return value that indicates success in one program might not be the same as in another program. After executing a program, the APM looks at MIF files found in the Temp or Windows directories and compares the filename, manufacturer, product, and version for matches with the properties of the installation that just completed. If a match is found, the status MIF success state and description string are put into a SMS 2.0 status message, which is copied to the CAP. The status MIF file is then deleted. If no match is found, the exit code indicates the status. When the installation returns a code of zero, the APM signals the installation was a success. If the resulting code is a nonzero value, APM returns a failure status, except for the following codes:

- 3010
- 3011
- 1641
- 1604

Message ID Number	Message Type	Process	Information
10000	Error	Distribution	The .OFR file for this advertisement is corrupt.
10001	Error	Distribution	The .PKG file for this package is corrupt.
10002	Information	Distribution	Indicates the advertisement was received from the originating site.
10003	Error	Installation	The executable assigned to the package cannot be found. This can be because a drive letter wasn't assigned to the package or the specified Windows NT Client software installation account doesn't have the appropriate permissions.
10004	Error	Installation	Indicates the executable file assigned to the package is corrupt or invalid.
10005	Information	Installation	Indicates the advertisement's assigned program started successfully.
10006	Error	Installation	A Status MIF couldn't be found for the program after execution. When this scenario happens, the Advertised Program Manager uses the installation's exit code as status. The exit code denoted an error.

Table 5-6. Software Distribution Status Messages

Message ID Number	Message Type	Process	Information
*10007	Error	Installation	The installed program created a Status MIF that indicated the installation failed. This is the general error message for a failed installation. When viewing System Status on packages and advertisements, you need to create a filter for this message ID number in the SMS Status Message Viewer to determine the failed installations. You can also use this message ID for creating a specific status message query for monitoring package failure.
10008	Information	Installation	A Status MIF couldn't be found for the program after execution. When this scenario happens, the Advertised Program Manager uses the installation's exit code as status. The exit code signified a success.
*10009	Information	Installation	This informational message ID is a full success for the program. The installation completed successfully and a MIF status file was generated and found. When viewing system status on packages and advertisements, you need to create a filter for this message ID number in the SMS status message viewer to determine the successful installations. You can also use this message ID for creating a specific status message query for monitoring package success.
10010	Error	Uninstallation	This message ID number reveals the uninstall of a program was unsuccessful because the program's uninstall command line wasn't found in the computer's registry.
10011	Error	Uninstallation	This message ID number indicates the uninstall of a program was unsuccessful because the command line found is invalid or the executable is corrupt.
10012	Information	Uninstallation	This informational message ID number designates the uninstall for the specified program started successfully.

Table 5-6. Software Distribution Status Messages *(continued)*

Message ID Number	Message Type	Process	Information
10013	Error	Uninstallation	A Status MIF couldn't be found for the uninstall program after execution. When this scenario happens, the Advertised Program Manager uses the uninstall's exit code as status. The exit code denoted an error.
*10014	Error	Uninstallation	The MIF file was generated successfully and it indicated the uninstall failed. When viewing system status on packages and advertisements, you need to filter using this message ID number in the SMS status message viewer to determine the failed uninstalls. You can also use this message ID for creating a specific status message query for monitoring uninstall failure.
10015	Information	Uninstallation	A Status MIF couldn't be found for the uninstall after completion. When this scenario happens, the Advertised Program Manager uses the installation's exit code as status. The exit code confirmed a successful uninstall of the program.
*10016	Information	Uninstallation	This informational Message ID is a full success of the program's uninstall. The uninstall completed successfully and a MIF status file was generated and found. When viewing system status on packages and advertisements, you need to filter using this message ID number in the SMS status message viewer to determine the successful uninstalls. You can also use this message ID for creating a specific status message query for monitoring successful uninstallations.
10017	Error	Uninstallation	The uninstall failed because the uninstall information specified in the Program's Properties of the SMS Administrator Console didn't match the uninstall information in the computer's registry.

Table 5-6. Software Distribution Status Messages *(continued)*

Message ID Number	Message Type	Process	Information
10018	Warning	Installation	The advertisement reached the client, but the client's operating platform wasn't specified in the Program's Properties, so the advertisement failed.
10019	Warning	Installation	The advertisement failed because it had expired by the time the client received it. This can happen if you set aggressive expiration dates on advertisements for individuals that don't frequent the office often.
10020	Information	Installation	This message ID number shows the client computer's network speed isn't adequate for the package to install. This would be a sign the network connection is slow or the computer is connected through a RAS line. The advertisement will be available to the client computer the next time the proper connection is made.
10021	Error	Installation	The computer was restarted before the installation was complete.

Table 5-6. Software Distribution Status Messages *(continued)*

The codes previously listed signify a successful installation, but the computer must be rebooted before the Installation process is complete.

If the exit codes aren't being read correctly by APM, a good chance exists the program's code could be incompatible. You can fix the exit code problem by repackaging the application with SMS Installer. SMS Installer has the capability to create Status MIF files that emit the proper exit codes.

Readvertising Advertisements

When an advertisement runs on the client computer, it is marked as completed, whether the installation was a success or failure. If you send additional advertisements that include the *same* program, those advertisements won't run. This makes resending offered software to the client computer difficult and you may need this functionality.

To readvertise an advertisement to the collection, you need to create an additional Assignment. As shown in the following illustration, you access the Advertisement Schedule Window for the specific package, and then you add another Assignment by clicking the new button and creating the additional entry. The new Assignment is shown in the second illustration. When the new Assignment is created, the advertisement is distributed to the same collection.

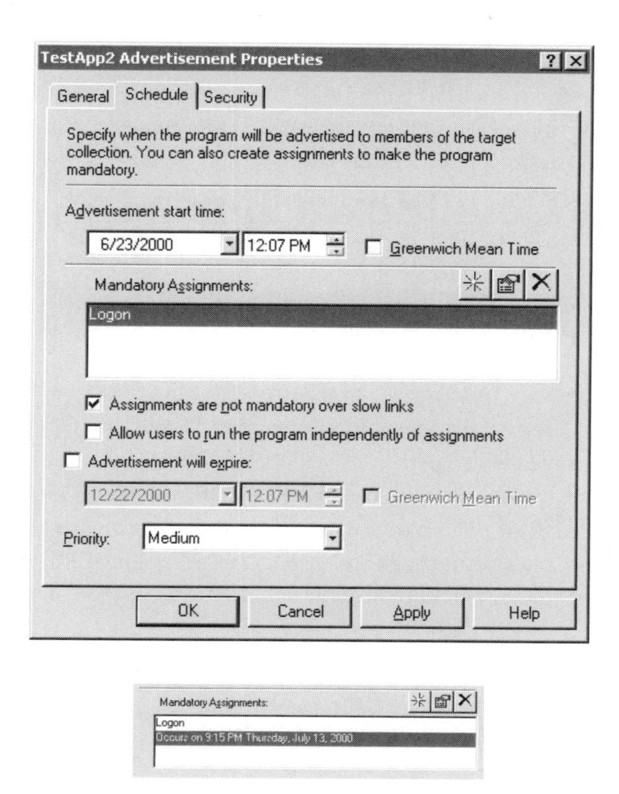

Rerunning an Advertisement on a Single Client

When an advertisement is run on a client, it never runs again. This is an important feature for keeping advertisements from running in a loop. Unfortunately, if an advertised program runs and returns a success exit code (described in the previous section on package status in this chapter), even though the package may not have completed, the advertisement will never run again. For example, if an advertisement contains multiple programs (defined on the Advanced Tab of the specific package's program properties), and the first program runs successfully, but the following program does not, the advertisement may still be marked as successful by the exit code.

You can trick SMS into rerunning an advertisement. To perform this process, find the advertisement you want to rerun, along with its advertisement ID in the SMS Administrator Console. Stop the SMS Client Service on the client, and find the file that refers to the advertisement ID in the %WINDIR%\MS\SMS\Clicomp\APA\Data\Complete directory.

The files in the \Complete subdirectory are created and given a filename based on a sequential number, which doesn't relate to the advertisement's ID. You must open each file in the \Complete directory in an ASCII text program such as Notepad and look for the AdvertID line in the file.

Delete the advertisement file that contains the correct advertisement ID and restart the SMS Client Service. The advertisement automatically runs again in a short time.

Modifying the Countdown Timer

When a Mandatory (or Assigned) advertisement is scheduled to run, a countdown timer is displayed. By default, the client installation of the software distribution Agents installs the countdown timer to be enabled, and the countdown time period is set to five minutes. If you have allowed the end user to modify the advertisement settings, he can stop the countdown time and modify the number of minutes the timer will count. If you have disabled the ability for the end user to make these modifications, you can still change these through editing the computer's registry.

To disable the countdown timer, go to: HKEY_CURRENT_USER\SOFTWARE\Microsoft\SMSClient\Monitor and change the **Countdown Signal** value to 0.

To change the countdown minutes go to: HKEY_CURRENT_USER\SOFTWARE\Microsoft\SMSClient\Monitor and change the **Refresh Minutes** to the minute value you prefer.

Distribution Tools

The tools discussed in this section help you troubleshoot software distribution and advertisements and can also help you deploy software packages.

AdvInfo

The Advertisement Information Tool (AdvInfo.exe), part of the SMS 2.0 Resource Guide, can help rapidly identify the package information contained within the .OFR and .PKG files. When you don't have immediate access to the SMS Administrator Console, you can use this command line utility to understand what the advertisement or package is meant to accomplish: **Syntax:** AdvInfo.exe *PackageID.PKG* or *OfferID.OFR*

NOTE: On the SMS site server, the PKG files are located in the SMS\Inboxes\Offerinf.box directory and the OFR files are located in the SMS\Inboxes\Pkginfo.box directory.

AdvertView

Relatively new to SMS, the Comprehensive Advertisement Status Viewer is part of the SMS 2.0 Support Tools installed from the SMS 2.0 Service Pack 2 image. You can locate the installation for these tools in the \SUPPORT directory on the SMS 2.0 SP 2 image.

The AdvertView graphical interface, shown in Figure 5-3, provides a quick view of advertisement status on individual SMS clients or collections. It provides the following features:

- Displays the status of a given advertisement on all of the targeted clients.
- Shows you which clients haven't received the advertisement, for example, mobile users.
- Displays % complete statistics such as the percentage of clients that have successfully run the advertisement, the percentage that haven't yet received it, and so forth.
- Handles the situation where an advertisement is targeted to a collection and all its subcollections by issuing recursive queries to determine the total client set in the collection and subcollections.

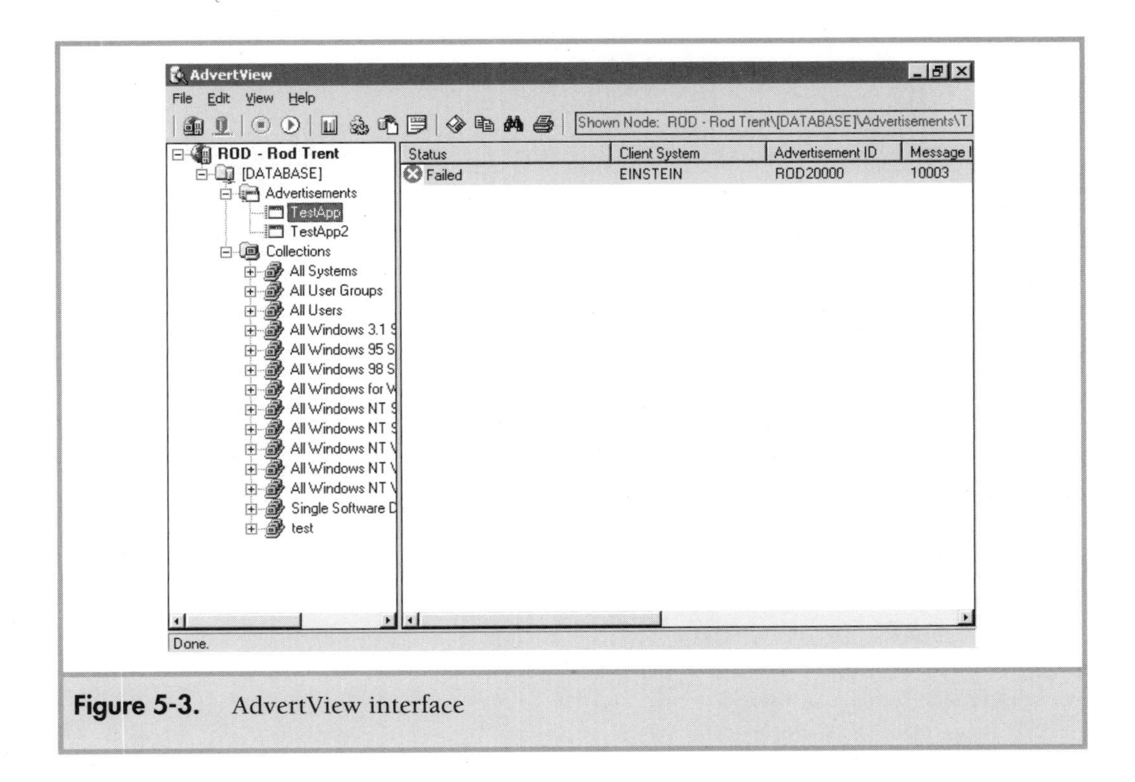

Figure 5-3. AdvertView interface

- Displays the status of all the advertisements for a given collection that each machine in the collection should receive. The status is not limited to only the advertisements targeted to that collection, but also includes those targeted to any collections to which each of those clients belong.
- Displays the raw text of the status messages, along with text of all WMI classes associated with a given status message.
- Status can be printed, saved, and copied into other applications.

Delete PDF

The SMS Resource Kit includes a utility called Delete PDF (DeletePDF.exe). Once *Package Definition Files* (*PDFs*) have been imported into the SMS 2.0 site, they cannot be deleted from the *SMS Administrator console*. The Delete PDF utility gives you this functionally outside of the Admin console.

If you install the CD from the Resource Kit using the defaults, the DeletePDF.exe is located in the Program Files\Resource Kit\SMS\DELETPDF directory.

The Delete PDF utility works from both Windows 9*x* and Windows NT/2000 computers, but the person using the utility needs Delete permissions on packages in the SMS Hierarchy, and the client PC must have the SMS Client software installed.

When the Delete PDF utility is run, you type in the SMS server name, SiteCode, login credentials (Domain\Username format if connecting across domains), and password.

After clicking OK, the utility connects to the SMS Site database and retrieves the list of registered packages that reference a PDF file. You can delete one item in the list or multiselect by checking the check boxes, and then clicking the Delete Selected button.

Gravity Square Inc. Advanced Scheduler

GSI Advanced Scheduler enables you to configure the time availability schedules for SMS advertised programs. Administrators often want to configure their SMS advertised programs to run only during specific hours, for example, nonbusiness hours. This functionality is currently integrated into SMS 2.0 (via advertisement's present time, mandatory assignment time, and expiration time) but is limited by the necessity for manual reconfiguration if the advertised program hasn't been successfully executed on all targeted clients before the expiration time.

Considering the fact that in many organizations, most software distribution cannot be completed within short time periods, an automated method of changing advertisement availability schedules is desirable.

GSI Advanced Scheduler enables you to configure automatic rescheduling of SMS 2.0 advertisements from the SMS Administrator Console object right-click menu. You never have to change the present, mandatory, or expiration times manually again. The GSI Advanced Scheduler service, running on the SMS Provider site system, does it all for you. The service has a configurable pulling interval and consumes virtually no system resources. All the advertisement rescheduling data is stored in the Windows Management repository, making GSI Advanced Scheduler compliant with SMS 2.0 programming access methods.

If your SMS hierarchy includes Microsoft Windows 2000/NT clients and your distributed software can run in the unattended mode, download and install the evaluation version of GSI Advanced Scheduler from http://www.gravitysquare.com/download.

NOTE: Instruct your users to leave their computers on all the time.

Gravity Square Inc. Distribution Load Balancer

The GSI Software Distribution Load Balancer enables you to split large software distribution jobs (for example, an SMS advertisement targeting a large SMS collection) into a set of smaller ones. Such load distribution decreases network use and loads inserted on distribution point SMS site systems and, in effect, increases the level of success of the software distribution.

GSI Software Distribution Load Balancer is especially useful in organizations that distribute software (with mandatory assignments) to a large number of SMS client machines. In these scenarios, all SMS clients access the distribution points at the same time, which causes high use of the infrastructure supporting SMS functionality. This, in effect, prevents successful change and configuration management, so the recommendation is that you don't advertise large distribution programs/packages to many SMS clients at once if you want to keep infrastructure use at a moderate level. This can be accomplished by decreasing the size of the SMS collections targeted by the software advertisements or, in other words, splitting the original collection into a number of smaller ones, each including a small number of SMS client machines.

The SMS software distribution job can be split manually. This involves the following tasks:

- Creation of *n* collections, each containing a subset of the original collection
- Creation of *n* advertisements, each targeting the newly created collection
- Configuration of each new SMS advertisement with the mandatory assignment(s)

The GSI Software Distribution Load Balancer, based on the following two parameters, does all the above automatically:

- The desired number of SMS clients accessing a single DP at once (for example, 20).

- The time between each miniadvertisement (for example, ten minutes) or the total time available for software distribution (for example, five hours—the equivalent of the time between miniadvertisements multiplied by the number of miniadvertisements).

The GSI Software Distribution Load Balancer is a Microsoft Management console (MMC) SMS Administrator console extension. It is easily installed on any SMS Administrator Console machine and is available from the right-click menu of the SMS advertisement object. This utility accesses SMS data via Windows Management Instrumentation APIs and is fully compatible with SMS 2.0 SP1 and SP2, on both Windows NT 4.0 and Windows 2000 machines. The GSI Software Distribution Load Balancer is licensed based on the number of SMS clients contained in the targeted SMS collection. A 30-day evaluation can be downloaded from http://www.gravitysquare.com/download.

Microsoft SMS Installer

On the SMS 2.0 CD, Microsoft includes a unique scripting utility called *SMS Installer*, which is a repackaging utility. *Repackaging* means taking an application installation and recording the Installation process verbatim into a reusable script. The script can be customized or left as-is and compiled into a distributable executable.

The compressed files include everything needed to install a software package, including the files, the program shortcuts (and icons), and information for modifications to the client PC (such as modifying system files and the registry). SMS Installer takes a "snapshot" of the computer before the software installation, runs the installation, and then takes another snapshot after the software installation completes. Whatever options are selected during the installation, SMS Installer records these verbatim in a stand-alone script. Just like a movie script, SMS Installer records the steps to complete the custom installation from beginning to end. Using SMS Installer enables you to issue applications using the one-file distribution method.

SMS Installer provides even further customization of the software package after the snapshot has been taken and recorded. It does this through both an easy-to-use Wizard and a powerful scripting facility.

The latest version of SMS Installer can be installed from the \SMSSETUP\SMS_INST\ <platform> directory on the SMS 2.0 CD.

For an in-depth guide on SMS Installer, check out *Microsoft SMS Installer* from McGraw-Hill, ISBN: 0072124474. Several Web sites are also dedicated to creating great SMS Installer scripts, such as http://www.swynk.com/trent, http://www.comptrends.com, http://sms.Scriptmania.com, and http://www.appdeploy.com/.

As mentioned, SMS Installer also includes a powerful scripting utility. Not only can you distribute applications with SMS Installer, you can create your own tools to help diagnose software distribution problems. For example, you can create a simple script to push through the software distribution system to identify any issues. Using the checklists in this chapter, monitor the file through the entire distribution process to determine where a problem may lie.

The following SMS Installer script runs a simple procedure to display a message to the recipient of the package. The screen is shown in the next illustration.

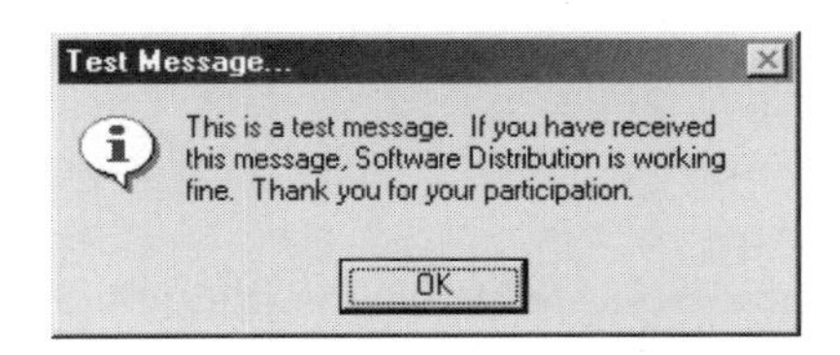


```
item: Display Message
  Title English=Test Message...
  Text English=This is a test message.  If you have received this message,
Software Distribution is working fine.  Thank you for your participation.
  Flags=00100100
end
```

RunAs

Windows 2000 introduced the RunAs service. *RunAs* is both an executable and a service that runs on Windows 2000 computers. Using the RunAs service, you can deploy SMS packages that require being run under a different security context than the logged-on user. For instance, if a package needs administrator rights to the computer, you can use the RunAs command and initiate the package using the administrator account: **Syntax: runas** [/profile] [/env] [/netonly] /user:<*UserName*> program

- **Command Line Options:**
  - **/profile** if the user's profile needs to be loaded
  - **/env** use current environment instead of user's
  - **/netonly** use if the credentials specified are for remote access only
  - **/user** <*UserName*> should be in the form user@domain or domain\user
  - **program** command line for .exe

- **Examples:**
  - runas /profile /user:mymachine\administrator cmd
  - runas /profile /env /user:mydomain\admin "mmc %windir%\system32\dsa.msc"
  - runas /env /user:user@domain.microsoft.com "notepad \"my file.txt\""

SMS WakeUp from 1E

SMSWakeUp integrates with SMS 2.0 to provide administrators with an easy method of booting PC's that have been powered down into low power or sleep mode. When a PC is operating in this mode, the network adapter can listen for a specific type of packet, which when received, instructs the network adapter to restore the power supply to full power.

The main use for this within SMS is to enable distribution of software to large numbers of machines that have been powered off overnight by intercepting software advertisements. Using SMSWakeUp you can instruct the machines to boot, install the software, and then using SMS 2.0, power down again.

SMSWakeUp uses Magic Packet technology, which was developed by AMD and is now implemented by most major network card vendors. A limited evaluation version of SMSWakeUp can be downloaded from http://www.1e.com/Software/SMS2/SMSWakeUp/default.htm.

Deploying Windows 2000 Professional with SMS

You can use SMS to deploy Windows 2000 to upgrade the computers in your organization. To identify which computers meet the requirements to run Windows 2000, deploy the Microsoft Windows 2000 Readiness Analyzer Tool via SMS. The Windows 2000 Readiness Analyzer Tool is available for download from http://www.microsoft.com/smsmgmt/zipdocs/windows2000readiness.exe. The download is comprised of several tools:

- **A Wrapper program.** The Wrapper program for the Windows 2000 Analyzer allows easy deployment and execution of the utility. When the SMS package runs, no user interaction is needed.

- **W2KMIFG.exe.** W2KMIFG.exe is a utility that generates a NOIDMIF file collected by the SMS Inventory process. The information from the NOIDMIF file is available for access to the Windows 2000 Analyzer's recorded results.
- **A Package Definition File (PDF).** The PDF file imports into the SMS system for quick setup of the SMS package.
- **SMS queries.** The queries extracted from the download import into the SMS system and provide the criteria for reporting noncompliant computers.
- **Crystal Info report.** A Crystal Info report is included in the download—Windows 2000 Noncompliant Systems by Site.

For more information on the Windows 2000 Readiness Analyzer and the steps to deploy the tool, see http://www.microsoft.com/smsmgmt/deployment/readiness.asp.

Preparing the Windows 2000 Upgrade Package

The following section assumes a Windows 2000 Professional upgrade of a Windows NT Workstation computer.

Start by creating a directory on the network and copying the entire I386 directory structure into it (the volume needs at least 650MB of free space). Share the directory and provide the appropriate rights.

Use a specific Software Distribution Access Account for the deployment. Create a new Windows 2000/NT account in the domain and give it domain administrator rights and a secure password. This account will be used later when configuring the properties of the SMS package.

Creating the SMS Package

The next step is to create the SMS package. The stock PDF files on the SMS site server are located in the \SMS\Scripts\00000409\PDFStore\Load directory, and new PDF files are installed there so SMS can retrieve them.

NOTE: PDF files for SMS 2.0 have a .sms extension. In earlier versions of SMS, the PDF files had a .pdf file extension.

Right-click Packages, click New, and choose Package From Definition (as shown in the next illustration) to start the Create Package from Definition Wizard.

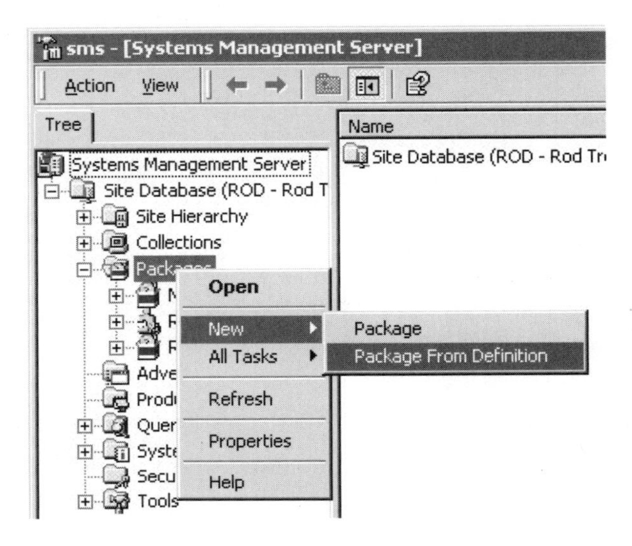

1. Move through the wizard, and choose Windows 2000 Professional from the list presented.
2. On the Source Files Wizard screen, select Create a Compressed Version of the Source.
3. On the Source Directory screen, enter the path to the Windows 2000 Professional files directory you set up earlier.
4. Click Finish to allow SMS to create the new package.
5. After the package for Windows 2000 Professional is created, click Programs, and then double-click the Automated Upgrade from Win9x, NTW3.51/4.0 (x86) option.
6. Confirm the PDF import settings are correct.

Once the Program has been configured and verified, open the Access Accounts of the package and delete the Guests and Users Access Accounts. Then add the Windows NT Software Distribution Access Account mentioned at the beginning of this section.

To add the account to the package properties, right-click the Access Accounts, choose New, and then choose the Windows NT Access Account. Click Set and add the account in the format Domain\User.

TIP: Deleting the Guests and Users Access Accounts ensures the Windows 2000 setup files are not accessed and executed by an end user. When the Windows 2000 package is distributed to the computers, instead, it uses the Windows NT Access Account you created.

Distributing Windows 2000

After you create the package, you can distribute the upgrade. This step must be carefully planned using the following considerations:

- **Test the distribution** Test the Windows 2000 package thoroughly in a lab environment similar to your organization.
- **Create Collections** Deploy Windows 2000 in phases by creating a set of collections and subcollections to accommodate a phased, balanced distribution of the package. For example, you could create distribution collections based on subnets.

Distributing MSI Applications with SMS

MSI Applications are programs built on the Microsoft Windows Installer Service technology. With MSI, Microsoft has created a whole new way of managing the installation of applications by including features for autorepair, system and shared file integrity, and install-on-demand. Microsoft Office 2000 was the first application to introduce this new technology.

Keeping the Windows Installer Service Current

The Windows Installer Service comes included with Windows 2000 because this installation method has been adopted as the Microsoft standard. For Windows 95, 98, and Windows NT, the Windows Installer Service is generally installed or updated during the specific application setup. This can cause a problem when distributing MSI installations via SMS because the computer may need to be rebooted after the Windows Installer components are updated and before the actual application installation can continue. If the computer is rebooted before the entire package is complete, SMS still returns a success status, but only the Windows Installer components have been updated.

When the MSI application installation is started, the Windows Installer components are checked to verify they are the required version for the application. As long as the components meet or beat the requirement, the Windows Installer Service installation is skipped. For this reason, you should always keep the client's Windows Installer version up-to-date. The redistributable Windows Installer components (instMSI.exe) for Windows 95, 98, and Windows NT can be found at http://www.microsoft.com/msdownload/platformsdk/instmsi.htm. You should monitor Microsoft's Web site for updates to the technology and distribute the new versions as they become available.

NOTE: instMSI.exe requires administrative rights to install on the client computer.

Administrative Installation

In addition to keeping the Windows Installer client components at the most current revision level, a requirement is that the SMS package be created based on the source directory containing an Administrative Installation of the application's source files.

In the past, application setup files were comprised of an executable program with an .exe extension. Windows Installer-based installation files are identified with the extension .msi, and that file kicks off the application's installation.

When you create an Administrative Installation of an application, you must initiate the Windows 2000 MSIEXEC tool in Administrative mode and use the application's setup .msi file. For example, the command line to begin the Administrative Installation of MS Office 2000 is MSIEXEC /a setup.msi.

This Administrative Installation enables you to create a complete software installation with all the specific software features tailored to the needs of the organization. The Administrative Installation also expands the installation files to a network location, which the SMS package uses as its source directory.

Creating the SMS Package

The command line for the SMS package properties uses **msiexec** to initiate the program installation. Msiexec interprets the .msi file and installs products. In addition to providing the Administrative Installation, MSIEXEC offers the installation options shown in Table 5-7.

In addition to creating the proper command line in the SMS Program Properties, you must modify the SMS Run Mode option to Run with Administrative Rights on the Environment tab in the Program Properties dialog box.

MSIEXEC Option	Description
/i	Installs the product.
/x	Uninstalls the application.
/m *MIFFile*	Creates a SMS 2.0 status MIF file (ISMIF32.dll must be present on the target system).

Table 5-7. MSIEXEC Command Line Options for Installations

Other Important MSIEXEC Options

The following additional Msiexec options can be used to improve the MSI Installation process. These aren't necessary, but they can be used to accommodate distribution preferences.

- **Currently Logged-on User** MSIEXEC.exe /i mypackage.msi ALLUSERS=""
- **All Users** MSIEXEC.exe /i mypackage.msi ALLUSERS="1"
- **Silent Mode Installation** MSIEXEC.exe /i mypackage.msi /q
- **Silent Mode Uninstallation** MSIEXEC.exe /x mypackage.msi /q

Distributing Internet Explorer with SMS

Trying to deploy Internet Explorer through SMS is an exercise in frustration—a serious problem is that the computer requires three reboots during the process. Fortunately, you can take advantage of some tools designed to help you accomplish this difficult task.

Start by downloading the following files:

- Ie5deploy.IPF, available at http://www.swynk.com/trent/Articles/ie5deploy.asp. This is a SMS Installer script that prepares the computer for the Installation process and forces the reboots.
- Shutdown.exe, available at http://www.microsoft.com/technet/download/indexfiles/SMS/Shutdown.exe, which the Installer script uses to perform reboots.
- Internet Explorer Administration Kit (IEAK), available at http://www.microsoft.com/windows/ieak/en/default.asp. The IEAK provides instructions for creating a customized version of IE and uses a wizard to prepare the installation.

Here's an overview of the tasks you face, none of which is terribly onerous, thanks to the tools at your disposal:

1. Use the IEAK to create your custom installation package and store the package on a network share.
2. Create a domain account (and password) with administrator privileges. This account is automatically logged on as the computer restarts. (You can delete the account when the Installation process is complete.)

3. Customize the SMS IPF script to match your organization's specific information: enter the domain administrator account you created; the account's password; and the domain name. Then compile the file using SMS Installer.
4. Copy the compiled executable and Shutdown.exe to the network share where your custom IE installation is located.
5. Create the SMS package for Internet Explorer in the same way you would create any SMS package, except observe the following specific configuration parameters:

- **Command Line** Point to the compiled SMS Installer file for the package's command line.
- **Source Directory** Select the directory where the IEAK custom files reside for the source directory of the package.
- **Environment Tab** On the package's Environment Tab, clear the User Input Required check box.
- **Administrative Rights** Also, on the Environment Tab, in the Run Mode section, select the Run With Administrative Rights option.
- **Access Account** Remove the Guests and Users accounts in the Access Account option of the package, and add the domain account you created earlier.

Now you can distribute the software. When you create the advertisement, consider the same issues discussed in the previous section on deploying Windows 2000. Make sure the distribution points have enough hard disk space, take care to test the package thoroughly, and phase-in the deployment to a limited number of users at a time.

TIP: Notify the target user base. Users won't be able to work because the installation process continually restarts the computer.

Registry Reference for Software Distribution

You can use scripts to adjust the registry to make software distribution automatic, without risking user interference.

Disable Keyboard and Mouse Action

If you are concerned that the end user has the ability to cancel installations, you can modify the computer's registry to disable the mouse and keyboard. The registry information in this section gives you the information to perform this action. You must also script a method to reenable the mouse and keyboard.

To perform this procedure correctly, create a script that follows these steps:

1. Modify the registry to disable the mouse and keyboard.
2. Restart the computer.
3. Perform some function when the computer restarts.
4. Modify the registry to reenable the mouse and keyboard.
5. Restart the computer again.

To disable/enable the keyboard, go to HKEY_LOCAL_MACHINE\SYSTEM\CurrentControlSet\Services\Kbdclass

Value Name = Start: Off = 4; On = 1

To disable/enable the mouse, go to HKEY_LOCAL_MACHINE\SYSTEM\CurrentControlSet\Services\Mouclass

Value Name = Start: Off = 4; On = 1

Enable Automatic Logon

When disabling the mouse and keyboard, you might want to consider using the AutoAdminLogon function (in the next section) when the computer restarts.

The AutoAdminLogon feature causes the computer to log in automatically upon boot. You can force the computer to log on with an administrative account and password, giving full access to the computer for software installations that require it.

NOTE: All of the following registry modifications must be made for the AutoAdminLogon function to work.

- HKEY_LOCAL_MACHINE\SOFTWARE\Microsoft\Windows NT\CurrentVersion\Winlogon. Value Name = AutoAdminLogon: On = 1; Off = 0
- HKEY_LOCAL_MACHINE\SOFTWARE\Microsoft\Windows NT\CurrentVersion\Winlogon. Value Name = DefaultUserName: On = [Enter the Administrator-equivalent account name]; Off = [Leave the field blank]
- HKEY_LOCAL_MACHINE\SOFTWARE\Microsoft\Windows NT\CurrentVersion\Winlogon. Value Name = DefaultPassword: On = [Enter the Administrator-equivalent password]: Off = [Leave the field blank]
- HKEY_LOCAL_MACHINE\SOFTWARE\Microsoft\Windows NT\CurrentVersion\Winlogon. Value Name=DontDisplayLastUserName: On = 0; Off = 1

RunOnce Registry Keys

The RunOnce registry keys can be modified to run a program after the computer is rebooted. Enter the name of the program to run on startup; you can opt to run the program as a computer setting or as a setting for the logged-on user.

- HKEY_LOCAL_MACHINE\SOFTWARE\Microsoft\Windows\CurrentVersion\RunOnce
- HKEY_CURRENT_USER\SOFTWARE\Microsoft\Windows\CurrentVersion\RunOnce

Chapter 6

Remote Control Tools

SMS provides a wealth of tools to enable remote administration and troubleshooting. You can manage remote computers through a LAN or WAN environment, as well as through a RAS dial-up connection (though, the dial-up connection is much slower). Note that: the minimum connection speed for Remote Tools and RAS computers is 28.8 Kbps.

The Remote Control Tools

Understanding the full spectrum of Remote Tools helps you administer and troubleshoot your enterprise. The following tools are part of the remote suite:

- **Remote Control** The Remote Control tool provides complete control over the target computer. The target computer's screens display in a window on the controlling computer. All mouse and keyboard movements on the controlling computer are passed to the target computer. You can establish up to four simultaneous sessions of Remote Tools.
- **Remote Reboot** The Remote Reboot feature allows the controlling computer to shut down and restart the target computer.
- **Remote Chat** The Remote Chat component creates a communication box on both the controlling and target computers for quick text messages back and forth. This feature is particularly helpful when communication through telephone is not an option.
- **File Transfer** File Transfer gives you the ability to copy files from the controlling computer to the target computer. You can use this feature to transfer critical files that could be corrupt or missing on the remote computer, as well as general files such as data files.
- **Remote Execute** The Remote Execute tool allows you to execute programs on the target computer. You can use this feature to run installations, initiate fixes, or install patches.

The Windows/Windows 2000/Windows NT Diagnostics suite is comprised of tools designed to determine possible computer hardware problems remotely. The following applications are included:

- **Windows Memory** The Windows Memory tool provides the following information about the remote computer:
  - Memory allocation
  - Free memory, as well as memory that is locked and unlocked

    - The size of the swap file
    - The percentage of used memory in the GDI and USER heaps
- **Windows Modules** This shows the files and system libraries that are in use on the remote computer.
- **Windows Tasks** This displays the currently running tasks on the remote computer.
- **Windows Classes** This displays the Windows-based classes that are in use on the remote computer.
- **Windows Heap Walk** This displays the address and size of each memory object on the remote computer.
- **GDI Heap Walk** This shows the memory that is allocated when applications open new windows.
- **CMOS Information** This displays CMOS information on Intel-based AT-class or better computers.
- **Device Drivers** This shows the currently loaded device drivers on the remote computer.
- **Interrupt Vectors** This shows the remote computer's IRQ information for hardware devices and software components.
- **ROM Information** This displays information contained in the computer's ROM.
- **DOS Memory Map** This shows the programs running in the computer's conventional (first 640Kb) and upper memory (up to 1,024Kb).
- **PING Test** The PING test helps determine possible network problems on the client computer. It sends network packets to the remote computer to determine, first, if there is connectivity. If a connection is received, it then sends additional packets to the computer for four seconds to determine the maximum number of packets per second, the average number of packets per second, and any errors that result from the packet delivery.

Client Agent Installation

When the Remote Tools feature is enabled in the SMS site hierarchy, the client installation process initiates the installation by running the \SMS\Inboxes\Clicomp.src\<platform>\Remctrl.exe (Remc16.exe for 16-bit clients) program from the SMS site server.

Table 6-1 describes the files and directories installed by Remctrl.exe.

File	Description
%WINDIR%\MS\SMS\Clicomp\RemCtrl_wchat32.dll	DLL file used by the Remote Chat program (Wchat32.exe).
%WINDIR%\MS\SMS\Clicomp\RemCtrl_wslav32.dll	DLL file used by the File Transfer program (Wslave32.exe).
%WINDIR%\MS\SMS\Clicomp\RemCtrl_wuser32.dll	DLL file used by Remote Tools Agent (Wuser32.exe).
%WINDIR%\MS\SMS\Clicomp\RemCtrl\Install.log	Log file that includes all the information from the Remote Tools installation.
%WINDIR%\MS\SMS\Clicomp\RemCtrl\kbstuff.sys	Wuser32 Keyboard Stuffer file. This is the driver for both the Virtual keyboard and mouse support.
%WINDIR%\MS\SMS\Clicomp\RemCtrl\multprot.dll	The DLL file that provides multiprotocol support.
%WINDIR%\MS\SMS\Clicomp\RemCtrl\queuebuf.dll	The DLL file used to enable buffering between the target and administrative computers to provide better connection performance.
%WINDIR%\MS\SMS\Clicomp\RemCtrl\rcclicfg.exe	Security Munger.
%WINDIR%\MS\SMS\Clicomp\RemCtrl\rchwcfg.exe	Hardware Munger.
%WINDIR%\MS\SMS\Clicomp\RemCtrl\rcsvcs.exe	Remote Control Services Manager.
%WINDIR%\MS\SMS\Clicomp\RemCtrl\RCUninst.exe	The Remote Tools uninstallation program.
%WINDIR%\MS\SMS\Clicomp\RemCtrl\Wchat32.exe	Remote Chat program.
%WINDIR%\MS\SMS\Clicomp\RemCtrl\Wslave32.exe	Remote File Transfer program.
%WINDIR%\MS\SMS\Clicomp\RemCtrl\Wuser32.exe	Remote Tools Agent.
%WINDIR%\MS\SMS\Clicomp\RemCtrl\wusermsg.dll	The DLL file that provides the interactive messages.
%WINDIR%\MS\SMS\Clicomp\RemCtrl\Help\00000409\	This directory contains the Remote Tools help files that are available to the user.

Table 6-1. Files and Directories installed by the Remctrl.exe Package

File	Description
%WINDIR%\MS\SMS\Clicomp\RemCtrl\Kbstuff\kbs-kbd.inf	The installation information file for the SMS Virtual Keyboard Device adapter.
%WINDIR%\MS\SMS\Clicomp\RemCtrl\Kbstuff\kbs-mou.inf	The installation information file for the SMS Virtual Mouse adapter.
%WINDIR%\MS\SMS\Clicomp\RemCtrl\Kbstuff\kbstuf5i.cat	The catalog file for the installation of the SMS Virtual Keyboard and Mouse adapters.
%WINDIR%\MS\SMS\Clicomp\RemCtrl\Kbstuff\kbstuf5i.cdf	The driver files for the Virtual adapter installation.
%WINDIR%\SYSTEM32\SMSrc.cpl	The SMS Remote Tools Control Panel Applet.
%WINDIR%\SYSTEM32\IDISNTKM.DLL	Screen Acceleration driver for 32-bit computers.

Table 6-1. Files and Directories installed by the Remctrl.exe Package *(continued)*

NOTE: For Windows NT computers, the computer must be restarted after the Remote Tools Agent installation.

Shutting Down the Remote Control Agent

Before you install the Remote Control Agent, be sure to shut down the Remote Control service to ensure that files can be overwritten (files in use cannot be overwritten).

On Windows 2000 and Windows NT clients, this is merely a matter of shutting down the Wuser32 service. To perform this task manually, you would need to give users access to the Component Services tool in Windows 2000, or the Service Control Panel applet in Windows NT. Therefore, it's preferable to perform this function with an SMS Installer script. The following SMS Installer script uses the Start/Stop Service script action to shut down the Windows 2000/Windows NT Wuser32 service:

```
--Begin Script

item: Start/Stop Service

  Service Name=wuser32
```

```
  Flags=00000001

end

--End Script
```

The SMS Installer script option can be run at the computer or distributed through the SMS software distribution system.

TAKE COMMAND

You can also use the command line to stop the Remote Control service:

- On Windows 2000/Windows NT, enter: **net stop wuser32**.
- On Windows 9*x*, enter: **%WINDIR%\MS\SMS\Clicomp\RemCtrl\WUSER32.EXE /X**.

Again, SMS Installer can be used to automate this process, or else the end user may have to type in the command manually. The following SMS Installer script uses the Execute Program script action to stop the Wuser32 service on Windows 95 and Windows 98 computers:

```
--Begin Script

item: Execute Program

  Pathname=%WINDIR%\MS\SMS\Clicomp\RemCtrl\WUSER32.EXE

  Command Line=/X

  Flags=00000110

End

--End Script
```

TIP: You can also use these shutdown methods when troubleshooting client problems.

Starting the Remote Control Agent

When you've finished troubleshooting, you need to make sure the Remote Control Agent starts again.

NOTE: Some organizations configure the SMS site Properties so that Remote Control does not start automatically when the computer boots. This is due to a company policy based on the "Big Brother" syndrome. Users are not comfortable with Remote Tools running constantly; they fear that individuals who have access to the computer through Remote Control can easily view sensitive data.

To start or restart the Remote Control Agent service on Windows 2000 and Windows NT clients, just restart the Wuser32 service. Again, because of the security of Windows 2000 and Windows NT, SMS Installer is the best way to perform this function. The following SMS Installer script uses the Start/Stop Service script action to start the Wuser32 service on Windows 2000/ NT computers:

```
--Begin Script

item: Start/Stop Service

  Service Name=wuser32

end

--End Script
```

TAKE COMMAND

You can also use the command line to start the service:

- In Windows 2000/Windows NT, enter the following: **net start Wuser32**.

- In Windows 9*x*, enter the following: **%WINDIR%\MS\SMS\Clicomp\RemCtrl\WUSER32.EXE**.

The following SMS Installer script uses the Execute Program script action to employ this command line. It starts or restarts the Wuser32 service on Windows 95 and Windows 98 computers:

```
--Begin Script

item: Execute Program

  Pathname=%WINDIR%\MS\SMS\Clicomp\RemCtrl\WUSER32.EXE

  Flags=00000110

end

--End Script
```

NOTE: For a method that makes the Remote Control Agent easier to enable and disable, see the "Security for Remote Tools" section in this chapter.

CODE BLUE

You may run into some problems due to security issues that exist between the service and the logged-on user in Windows 2000 and Windows NT. The Wuser32 service runs under the system context, which means access may be prohibited to users. You can avoid permissions problems by using the /nosvc switch, which allows Wuser32 to run under the user's context. The syntax is **Wuser32 /nosvc**.

Mungers

Part of the Remote Control Agent setup is the installation of "mungers." A munger is a service that handles the differences between particular settings across multiple sources. There are two types of Mungers included with the Remote Tools: Security and Hardware.

Security Munger

The Security Munger keeps the client security list for Remote Tools in synch with the list on the SMS site server. It is also responsible for updating the client computer with the Remote Tools configuration settings from the SMS site server. This is updated on the standard CCIM maintenance cycle (23 hours). The Security Munger scans the SMS registry keys, and if any changes have been made, it resets the configuration to that of the SMS site. This feature provides automated security on the Remote Tools configuration. If you want to update the security list on the client computer before the maintenance cycle, you can run the Security Munger manually with the following command: **%WINDIR%\MS\SMS\Clicomp\Remctrl\Rcclicfg.exe**.

You should update the security list manually when either of the following conditions exists:

- Remote Tools is not connecting due to a security permission problem.
- The site's Remote Tools configuration has been changed and the changes are critical to a specific individual client computer for remote access.

CODE BLUE

After the Remote Tools Agent has been installed on the client, changes made to the Advanced tab of the Remote Tools Client Agent properties are not to be propagated to the client computers. To push the changes to the client, you must disable Remote Tools in the SMS Administrator console. When the next CCIM cycle has completed, re-enable Remote Tools to reinstall the component with the new settings.

The Security Munger is specifically responsible for maintaining the Remote Control configuration registry settings on the client computer. Changes that are made through the Control Panel applet for Remote Control are immediate. If you don't permit user access to the Remote Control settings, you need a way to modify the client's remote settings in order to administer or troubleshoot the feature. You can only accomplish this by modifying the client computer registry.

Table 6-2 describes the pertinent Remote Tools registry values you can modify to accommodate quick changes in the remote configuration on the client computer. These data items are contained in HKEY_LOCAL_MACHINE\SOFTWARE\Microsoft\SMS\Client Components\Remote Control.

Registry Value	Options	Description
Allow Chat	0 = Off 1 = On	Turns on and off the Chat component.
Allow File Transfer	0 = Off 1 = On	Turns on and off the ability to transfer files between the target and administrative computers.
Allow Ping Test	0 = Off 1 = On	Turns on and off the ability to PING the client computer and test for network connectivity.
Allow Reboot	0 = Off 1 = On	Turns on and off the ability to reboot the remote computer.
Allow Remote Execute	0 = Off 1 = On	Turns on and off the ability for programs to be executed remotely.
Allow Takeover	0 = Off 1 = On	Turns on and off the ability for the administrative computer to take over the mouse and keyboard functions of the client computer.
Audible Signal	0 = No audible signal 1 = Repeated audible signal 2 = Audible signal only at the beginning and end of remote session	This registry value modifies the way the audible signal is heard on the client computer.
Control Level	0 = No control 1 = Limited control 2 = Full control	This registry value determines the level of control the administrator has on the computer. This information is the same as the level of Remote Access Allowed on the Policy tab of the Remote Tools Client Agent properties.

Table 6-2. Remote Tools Registry Information Controlled by the Security Munger

Registry Value	Options	Description
Indicator Type	0 = System Tray icon 1 = High security indicator	Determines the type of Remote Control indicator that will be displayed on the client computer.
Permission Required	0 = Off 1 = On	Turns on and off the end-user notification to grant permission for the computer to be controlled.
Permitted Viewers		This registry value reflects the list of users or groups with rights to control the computer.
Visible Signal	0 = Off 1 = On	Turns on and off the indicator that runs when the computer is being controlled.

Table 6-2. Remote Tools Registry Information Controlled by the Security Munger *(continued)*

NOTE: Changes to the computer's registry are immediate on Windows 2000 and Windows NT computers. For Windows 95 and Windows 98 computers, the Wuser32 service must be stopped and restarted. In essence, the Windows 95 or Windows 98 computer needs to be rebooted after the registry modification in order for the changes to take effect.

At the next CCIM cycle, the Security Munger attempts to reset the options to match the SMS site's configuration. You can exclude certain computers from the Security Munger process by following the instructions in the following section.

Excluding a Computer from the Security Munger Cycle

You can use the SMS Administrator console to set Remote Tools security to run under a user context or a system context. You find this option in the Access Permission section of the Policy tab in the Remote Tools Client Agent properties.

Setting the access permission to run under the user context across the site means the user is prompted for permission before the computer can be remote-controlled. This can cause a problem for a target computer that does not generally have a user logged on. (For example, Windows 2000 and Windows NT servers with locked consoles generally do not have logged-on users).

You can modify the computer's registry to enable the system context, and exclude the computer from the Security Munger update during the CCIM cycle.

To disable the Security Munger operation on the computer, go to HKEY_LOCAL_MACHINE\SOFTWARE\Microsoft\SMS\Client\Client Components\Remote Control. Create an additional REG_DWORD value named **UpdateEnabled** and set the data value to No.

To disable the Display a Message to Ask for Permission policy, go to HKEY_LOCAL_MACHINE\SOFTWARE\Microsoft\SMS\Client\Client Components\Remote Control and change the value of the following data items to 0:

- Audible Signal
- Permission Required
- Visible Signal

Hardware Munger

The Hardware Munger runs during the Remote Tools installation process, or when the Remote Tools have been selected for repair. The Hardware Munger determines the default network protocol for connection, the compression type for the client, and the video acceleration configuration.

If you have altered the hardware settings in the SMS site configuration, the Hardware Munger needs to run in order to reflect the changes on the client computer. For example, if you have adjusted the default protocol for the site from IPX to TCP/IP, the Hardware Munger amends the client to match the site configuration.

To run the Hardware Munger, disable Remote Tools for the entire site and wait for the CCIM cycle to complete (which de-installs Remote Tools on all clients). Then create the desired Remote Tools hardware settings, and re-enable Remote Tools for the site. During the next CCIM cycle, the Remote Tools Agent is reinstalled with the new settings.

TAKE COMMAND

If you need to make a critical change to a specific client immediately, you can run the Hardware Munger manually using the following command: **%WINDIR%\MS\SMS\Clicomp\Remctrl\Rchwcfg.exe install**

Table 6-3 shows the Remote Control registry information that is controlled and updated by the Hardware Munger.

Virtual Keyboard and Mouse Drivers

Because Windows 2000 and Windows NT provide a direct link to the hardware subsystem, SMS includes virtual keyboard and mouse drivers. Without these drivers, Remote Control functions could not perform any tasks beyond viewing the remote screen. The drivers also enable "Gold Key," which provides the functions of the CTRL-ALT-DEL combination in the Remote Control window.

CODE BLUE

During the installation of Remote Tools on Windows 2000 client, the user might see a warning and a request for user input. This warning informs the user that the Remote Tools installation is installing the SMS Virtual Mouse Device and the SMS Virtual Keyboard Device, and it's possible for the user to stop the installation by choosing No. If a warning message is appearing to your Windows 2000 clients, do a repair of Remote Tools from the Systems Management Control Panel applet, and choose Yes to allow the installation of the devices without user input.

Registry Value	Options	Description
CommandLine	-IP -TCP -IPX -Lx	Determines the protocol switch that is used when Remote.exe is executed.
CompressionType	0 = RLE 1 = LZ 2 = Auto	Determines the compression type used when connecting to the computer.
Use IDIS	0 = Off 1 = On	This turns on and off the video acceleration feature.

Table 6-3. Remote Control Registry Settings Controlled by the Hardware Munger

Remote Control Logging

As with the other SMS Client Agents, Remote Tools includes a log file for troubleshooting. The log file is located in %WINDIR%>\MS\SMS\Logs\Remctrl.log.

By default, logging for Remote Control is enabled on the client, but it is not very dynamic. You can enable a more robust Remote Tools log file by adding a registry value on the client computer. This new log file is better suited for troubleshooting Remote Control problems.

To enable a different log file, go to HKEY_LOCAL_MACHINE\Software\Microsoft\SMS\Client\Client Components\Remote Control and create a new REG_DWORD item named **LogToFile** and set the value to 1.

Wuser32.exe, which is the file that runs on the client computer for Remote Control, runs as a Windows 2000/NT service. Therefore, the registry change takes place automatically. On Windows 95 and 98 machines, the client computer must be rebooted for the change to take effect.

After making this change, you can view the more verbose information in the new log file, %WINDIR%>\MS\SMS\Logs\Wuser32.log.

In addition to log files, Remote Control Agent writes to the Windows 2000/NT Security log, and you can view any entries in the Event Viewer. You may see some of the following codes in the security log:

- Event ID 1 = A remote reboot was performed.
- Event ID 2 = A remote chat session was initiated.
- Event ID 3 = A remote File Transfer was started.
- Event ID 4 = A file was remotely executed.
- Event ID 5 = A Remote Control session started.
- Event ID 6 = A Remote Control session ended.
- Event ID 7 = The local user granted permission to be remote-controlled.
- Event ID 8 = The local user denied permission to be remote-controlled.

Connecting with Remote Tools

To identify any issues that may arise when using the MMC to connect to the client's remote agent, it helps to understand how the SMS Administrator console contacts the client.

Remote Tools connects in three phases:

1. **SMS Administrator console (local computer)** Remote Tools is initiated on the local computer that is running the SMS Administrator console.
2. **SMS site server** The MMC queries the SMS site database.
3. **Remote client** Functions are passed on to the SMS Client Agent.

Remote Connection Detail Checklist

When Remote Tools is selected to run on the resource from the SMS Administrator console, the MMC first queries the SMS Provider for the client's resource ID. Using the resource ID, the MMC runs the Remote.exe command with the following command line:

```
Remote.exe 0 <Resource ID> [\\<Site Server Name>\]
```

NOTE: The MMC runs Remote.exe from the SMS\i386\Bin directory on the SMS site server. Alternatively, you can run Remote Tools outside of the SMS Administrator console. This is discussed in the next section. The 0 in the command line indicates that Remote.exe attempts to connect on all allowed protocols.

If the currently logged-on administrator does not have the proper security access rights for Collections-Use Remote Tools, the remote connection process stops.

CHECKPOINT: If the remote connection ends at this point, verify that the administrator has the proper security access rights for the Collection that the selected client computer belongs to. Also, double-check that the administrator has the Use Remote Tools access permission in the SMS hierarchy.

- Remote.exe now connects to the SMS site database and uses the SMS Provider to query for the Resource ID.
- When the Resource ID query is successful, Remote.exe retrieves the IP addresses, NetBIOS name, and IPX addresses inventoried for the client.
- The connection information is passed to the ldwmnt.dll file.
- Remote.exe tries to connect to the client computer in the following order:
    1. Queries the client computer across the network using the computer's network name.

2. Queries client computer across the network using NetBIOS name resolution. The NetBIOS name resolution is provided through DNS, WINS, or an LMHosts file.
3. Queries the client computer across the network using the connection information stored in the memory resident ldwmnt.dll file.

CHECKPOINT: If all connection points fail, you first need to identify that both the client computer and the local workstation running the SMS Administrator console have a valid network connection. The client computer may not be logged in or may be experiencing a general network error. Also, verify that the client computer has the Remote Agent running.

- When a valid connection is identified for the client computer, the client's Wuser32.exe (or Wuser.exe for 16-bit clients) creates the remote link using the default network protocol.
- Remote.exe passes the permitted viewers list to Wuser32.exe. If the client computer is assigned to a different domain, a credential box will display allowing the administrator to enter his or her user name, domain name, and password.
- Remote.exe uses Wuser32.exe to determine the specific Remote Tools that are available for the client computer and then displays the Remote Tools user interface for the administrator.
- When the specific tool is selected in the Remote Tools user interface, and the option for prompting the user is selected, the dialog box will display.

Connecting with Remote Tools Outside the SMS Administrator Console

Remote Tools can be run outside of the SMS Administrator console, forfeiting the MMC interface altogether. The files needed to use Remote Tools can be copied to a directory on the local computer and run from there with a Windows shortcut.

The files needed to run Remote Tools are located in the SMS\i386\Bin directory on the SMS site server. For this method to work, the following files must be copied to the local computer from the \Bin directory: ldftrans.dll, ldwmnt.dll, mmcpgres.dll, msvcpso.dll, multprot.dll, sms_nmgr.dll, sms_nwbm.dll, sms_rmgr.dll, sms_rwbm.dll, uitlures.dll, uitoolsu.dll, and remote.exe.

Running Remote Tools outside of the SMS Administrator console is helpful for two reasons:

- You can give Remote Tools access to help desk personnel without giving them access to the MMC SMS interface.
- Copying the files locally causes Remote Tools to load faster.

TAKE COMMAND

Optionally, you can use the command Remote.exe <*Address Type*> <*Address*> [*SiteServerName*\] where *Address Type* is:

- 1 = IPX
- 2 = IP
- 3 = LM or NetBIOS name

Address is any valid IPX, IP, or NetBIOS name or address.
SiteServerName is the name of the computer acting as the site server.

NOTE: The user account must have the appropriate rights to run Remote Tools.

Security for Remote Tools

Remote Tools provides two different levels of security: the Collection-level security and the Permitted Viewers list.

Collection-Level Security

Collection-level security for Remote Tools allows very stringent security settings against the computer collections in the SMS site hierarchy. Based on the same class and instance security of the other SMS components, remote access to client computers can be limited to specific collections. Collection-level security is the first level of protection for Remote Tools.

Table 6-4 outlines the minimum security rights needed to enable Remote Tools access to an administrator or help desk individual.

Using Table 6-4 as a reference, Figure 6-1 displays the class and instance model required for access to a specific Collection. Once the proper Collection-level security has been configured for the individual, you must configure the Permitted Viewers list.

Permitted Viewers–Level Security

The Permitted Viewers list is the secondary level of Remote Tools security. When Remote Tools run, and the Collection security passes, the Permitted Viewers list is referenced in

SMS Object	Security Permissions
Collections (class)	Read, Read Resource
Collection (instance)	Use Remote Control
Status	Read
Queries	Read

Table 6-4. Minimum Collection-Level Security to Use Remote Tools

order to complete the transaction. The Permitted Viewers list is accessed on the Security tab of the Remote Tools Client Agent properties in the SMS Administrator console. The Security Munger keeps the list of permitted viewers current on the client computer, based on its 23-hour CCIM cycle.

NOTE: The Permitted Viewers list is kept in the registry on the client computer at HKEY_LOCAL_MACHINE\SOFTWARE\Microsoft\SMS\Client Components\Remote Control\PermittedViewers.

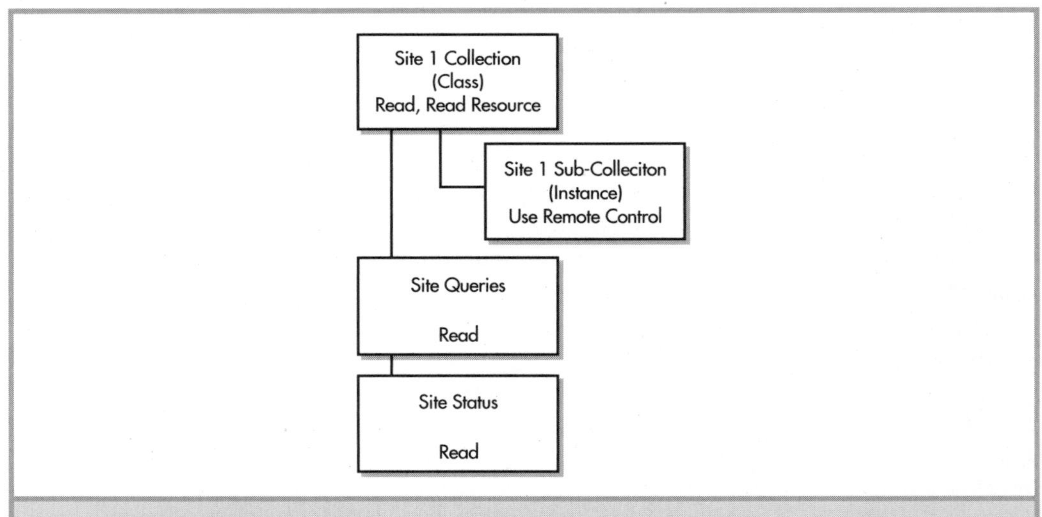

Figure 6-1. Graphical representation of the Remote Tools security model

TIP: This is another instance where forcing the Security Munger to initiate a cycle is beneficial. If you have just modified the Permitted Viewers list, this makes the new entry available on the client computer.

This list of permitted viewers allows entry of any valid Windows 2000/Windows NT user or group account. As long as the account has the proper Collection security clearance, and is part of the Permitted Viewers list, the appropriate remote access to the client computer is available. Local administrator rights are not required to use Remote Tools, as long as the Collection and Permitted Viewer security is correct.

CODE BLUE

The Permitted Viewers list is limited to 512 characters. If the list exceeds this character count, you will not be able to perform any Remote Control functions on Windows 2000 or Windows NT computers. In fact, Remote Control will not even start.

Also, the user name convention in the Permitted Viewers list is important. If a space is contained in a name or group, that individual or group of individuals will be unable to Remote Control Windows 95 and Windows 98 computers.

Accessing Client Tools in Locked-Down Environments

Some organizations prefer not to load the Remote Tools Agent when the computer is started. This causes a small problem for locked-down environments that disable access to the Control Panel. There are probably several different workarounds for this issue, including having the end user manually start the Remote Control session by running a command. However, for the user to be able to run the command, he or she would need access to the entire %WINDIR% directory.

One quick and completely secure method is to add a couple of options into the Windows right-click menu. This menu addition, shown in the next illustration, allows quick access for the end-user to initiate a Remote Control session. It also makes the user feel more in control over the computer. When the user right-clicks anywhere in Windows Explorer or on the My Computer icon, the option is available.

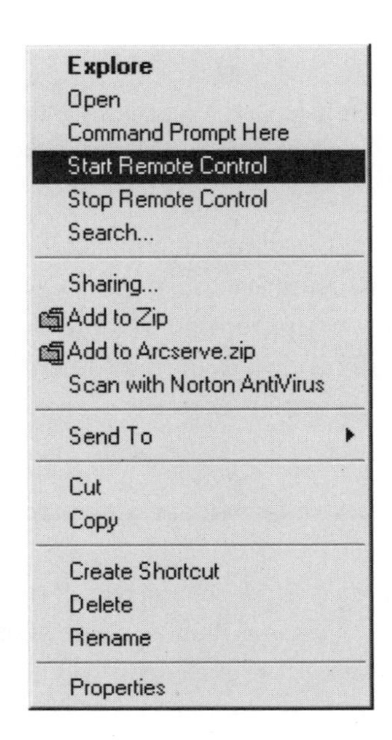

To add these menu options, follow these steps:

1. Open a registry editor and navigate to HKEY_CLASSES_ROOT\Folder\Shell.
2. Add a new key that represents the name that will appear on the right-click menu. In this example, I'm using Start Remote Control and Stop Remote Control.
3. Under the new key, add a new REG_SZ (string) item named **Command**.
4. Double-click on Command and add the value that represents the drive letter, path, and executable of the command that is executed when the user selects this right-click menu command.

The commands for Remote Control differ between Windows 2000/NT and Windows 9*x*. For Windows 2000 and Windows NT, use the following commands:

- For Start Remote Control, enter: **net start wuser32**.
- For Stop Remote Control, enter: **net stop wuser32**.

For Windows 9*x*, use the following commands:

- For Start Remote Control, enter: **C:\WINDOWS\MS\SMS\Clicomp\Remctrl\Wuser32.exe**.

- For Stop Remote Control, enter: **C:\WINDOWS\MS\SMS\Clicomp\Remctrl\Wuser32.exe /x**.

To automate the process, you can use SMS Installer to create a SMS package to install this feature on the client computer. (For Windows 2000/NT computers, you can use the Start/Stop SMS Installer script action to install the functions). The following scripts install this feature to the respective platforms.

SMS Installer script for Windows 95 and Windows 98 computers:

```
--Begin Script

item: Edit Registry

  Total Keys=2

  item: Key

    Key=Folder\Shell\Start Remote Control\command

    New Value=%WINDIR%MS\SMS\Clicomp\Remctrl\Wuser32.exe

  end

  item: Key

    Key=Folder\Shell\Stop Remote Control\command

    New Value=%WINDIR%MS\SMS\Clicomp\Remctrl\Wuser32.exe /x

  end

end

--End Script
```

SMS Installer script for Windows 2000 and Windows NT computers:

```
--Begin Script
```

```
item: Edit Registry
  Total Keys=2
  item: Key
    Key=Folder\Shell\Start Remote Control\command
    New Value=NET START WUSER32
  end
  item: Key
    Key=Folder\Shell\Stop Remote Control\command
    New Value=NET STOP WUSER32
  end
end
--End Script
```

Remote Control Performance Tips

Remote Control is the most widely used of the SMS Remote Tools collection, and thus it is critical that this component works properly. Remote Control relies on several core computer fundamentals for uninterrupted operation: dependable data compression, fast screen acceleration, and compatible video interfaces. For each of these components, SMS provides configurable options to help improve performance and reliability. To optimize Remote Control, you need to understand the options that the Remote Tools configuration provides.

Remote Control Performance and the Data Compression Type

To provide improved performance for data distribution, SMS allows different data compression configurations. Remote Tools includes two different data compression types: RLE (Run Length Encoding) and LZ (Lempel-Ziv). RLE is considered low compression and LZ is the high-compression type.

There are three different options for the client's compression type: RLE, LZ, and Automatically Select. Automatically Select is the default setting for the SMS site installation. When Automatically Select is set as the default for the SMS site, and the Hardware Munger has determined that the computer's processor is a Pentium 150 or better, LZ (high) compression will be used. But, if the computer is not completely compatible with high data compression, performance can suffer.

RLE is generally the best compression type for the majority of computers, because it provides sustained performance, and because all computers can use this compression type. The higher the client's screen resolution, the more CPU Remote Control uses. For incompatible video components, when screen acceleration is enabled and compression is set at high (LZ), the CPU utilization creeps up and stays around the 90-percent to 100-percent range. When screen acceleration is enabled and you set the compression at low (RLE), CPU usage stays around the 50-percent to 70-percent range.

When you enable high compression for the SMS site's computers and the compression is incompatible with the computer's components, if the CPU is being severely taxed the Remote Control performance will slowly degrade until it is virtually unusable or the computer will lock up.

To enable the proper compression type for your organization, test each compression type on the different models of computers in your company to determine the optimum setting. You modify the CompressionType Remote Tools registry value to test each compression method. While testing each type, watch the CPU utiliziation to establish which method should be used.

Remote Control Performance and Screen Acceleration

SMS 2.0 includes video acceleration for use with Remote Control on the Windows 2000 and NT client computer. Video acceleration speeds up the video transfer between the administrative and the remote computers, creating an optimum Remote Control environment. The use of video acceleration is determined by the following factors:

- Whether or not video acceleration is enabled at the 2.0 site
- Whether the Remote Tools Agent video driver can be resolved closely enough to match the client computer's installed video adapter

CODE BLUE

As of this writing, video acceleration for Windows 2000 clients is not available. Due to public demand for this feature, Microsoft is working on a HotFix, so check the Microsoft Web site for information. Because video acceleration must be enabled before compression works, Remote Control performance on Windows 2000 clients is very poor. When video acceleration is enabled on the Windows 2000 client, Remote Control performance is slower than if it were completely disabled. To disable Remote Control acceleration on specific computers, see "Disabling Remote Control Acceleration on Individual Computers," later in this section.

The video acceleration properties are accessed by going to the Remote Tools Client Agent properties in the Client Agents Class of the site settings.

The default list should provide enough compatible options to successfully run video acceleration. The list of default drivers installed by SMS 2.0 includes ART, CIRRUS, FRAMEBUF, MGA, QV, S3, TGA, TRIDENT, VGA, VGA256, VGA64K, W32, and XGA. As long as the computer's video driver is compatible with one of the items in the list, Remote Control should function correctly and performance should be optimum. You can add drivers to the default list by clicking the Add button and entering the name of the driver that you would like SMS 2.0 to resolve.

NOTE: Even though the SMS list of video options is labeled "drivers," these are actually the names of the specific chipsets that reside on the video card interface. When adding new drivers to the list, enter the chipset name.

During the Remote Tools Agent installation, the Hardware Munger determines the appropriate video driver that should be installed on the Windows 2000 and Windows NT client computer. The selected driver is installed in the %WINDIR%\System32 directory with the filename IDISNTKM.DLL. Hardware Munger stores the list of default drivers in the client computer's registry at the following location:

HKEY_LOCAL_MACHINE\SOFTWARE\Microsoft\SMS\Client\Sites\System\<Sitecode>\ Client Components\Remote Control\Video Drivers

CAUTION: It is a smart idea to thoroughly test the driver on one client before adding it and implementing it enterprise-wide. Adding a driver name that is not completely compatible can cause the remote PC to blue screen, because video on Windows 2000 and Windows NT has hooks into the OS kernel itself.

To help troubleshoot video acceleration problems, you can disable screen acceleration by modifying the client computer's USE IDIS registry value.

Disabling Remote Control Screen Acceleration on Individual Computers

Due to possible video hardware incompatibilities, you may need to disable video screen acceleration on specific computers. You can do this by adding a value to the client computer's registry.

NOTE: The following registry change must be accomplished prior to the Remote Tools Agent installation on the client computer. If Remote Tools is already installed, remove it and then perform the following operation.

1. Open Regedt32 and navigate to HKEY_LOCAL_MACHINE\SOFTWARE\Microsoft\ SMS\Client\Client Components\Remote Control\Hardware Settings.
2. Open the REG_DWORD data item: Install Video Driver.
3. Change the value to 0.
4. Install the Remote Tools Agent.

NOTE: The Install Video Driver accepts the following options: 0=Never install the accelerated driver; 1=Install the accelerated driver only if it exists in the driver list; 2=Always install the accelerated driver, even if it does not exist in the list.

Screen Acceleration and Active Desktop

Client computers with Active Desktop components enabled do not update during a Remote Control session. The Active Desktop update component constantly polls the item sources for updates. This means the Remote Control Agent would need to constantly refresh in order to pick up the screen changes when the Active Desktop updates. This seriously impacts the ability of the Remote Control Agent, causing sluggish Remote Control performance; and any screen acceleration tweaks you configure would be futile.

Because of this, when the Remote Control session is started on the client computer, the client's Active Desktop is automatically and silently disabled by the Remote Control Agent. When the Remote Control session is shut down, the Active Desktop is automatically and silently reenabled.

Screen Acceleration and High-Performance Video Cards

High-performance video cards can cause issues with Remote Tools. Evidence of a problem with a high-performance video card can include the following:

1. When the Remote Control Agent is installed (but not in an active Remote Control session), the computer locks up when you drag and drop files to the floppy drive.
2. When a Remote Control session is active, the computer locks up.

This would seem like a problem because of the Remote Control Agent, but this is actually a conflict between the high-performance video card installed in the computer and the computer's BIOS.

To troubleshoot high-performance video card problems, you can add a Windows 2000 and Windows NT registry key that allows you to temporarily disable the high-performance video card.

1. Go to HKEY_LOCAL_MACHINE\SYSTEM\CurrentControlSet\Control\GraphicsDrivers.
2. Add a new key named **DisableUSWC**.
3. Do not add any data items to the new key; the presence of the key is enough.
4. Restart the computer and retry the operations that failed.

To re-enable the high-performance video card, just delete the DisableUSWC key and reboot the computer.

TIP: If you determine that the high-performance video card is causing the problem, check with the video card's manufacturer for updated drivers, or replace the video card.

Permitted Viewers List

When Remote Tools connects to the client computer, the Permitted Viewers list is verified on both the remote computer and the list configured at the SMS site server. When the list is verified, each name in the list is enumerated. If this list gets large, enumeration can take a long time. To increase the connection performance level, keep the list small by consolidating user accounts into group accounts.

Sixteen-Color Viewing

When the target computer is being controlled, the speed of the Remote Control Client Viewer screen can seem slow. You can get better performance out of the Remote Control session by enabling the 16-color viewing option. Computers that display colors above 256 can cause performance problems for the Remote Control Client Viewer. Enabling the 16-color viewing option speeds the Remote Control session by limiting the number of colors displayed in the Remote Control window. You enable the 16-color view by clicking on the top-left corner of the Remote Control window and choosing the 16-color viewing option.

Wallpaper Suppression

Another option built into the Remote Control Client Viewer allows you to temporarily suppress the target computer's wallpaper. This will increase the overall speed of the Remote Control session when the target computer has a high-resolution, elaborate background image.

Remote Tools Gotchas

The following Remote Tools issues can help identify any difficulties before you experience them. Make a special note of these items to alleviate problems before they become critical.

Video Driver Compatibility

Across the industry, it seems that video card compatibility is an issue that causes problems with software applications and hardware components. SMS Remote Control is no exception. Before adding new video drivers to the inclusion list in the Remote Tools Client Agent properties, or before installing a new video card in a computer, verify that the new equipment is completely compatible with the Remote Control Agent. Test the new equipment with the Remote Control Agent on one computer before rolling it out to the organization.

Mouse Driver Compatibility

Mouse hardware manufacturers include drivers that provide specific features and functions. The functions built into these drivers can cause problems with the Remote Control component of SMS. If you are experiencing mouse control problems in Remote Control, such as sluggish performance or the inability to control mouse functions on the target computer, you should remove the specific driver and install a Microsoft-compatible driver.

Two specific manufacturer's drivers that can cause problems are from Logitech and Toshiba, so be wary of these.

RAS and Remote Control

When the client computer dials-in using RAS, Remote Control may not work. This is due to the RAS server assigning IP addresses when the client dials in. Remote Control is designed to work with the current IP address, and when this is changed by the RAS server, the Remote Control Agent cannot connect.

To work around this issue, shut down the Wuser32 service after dialing-in and receiving the new IP address. Then restart the Wuser32 service. When the service is restarted, the new IP address is initialized and a Remote Control session can be started.

TIP: As indicated previously in this chapter, SMS Installer can be used to deploy the stopping and starting functionality to the Wuser32 service.

Third-Party Remote Control Applications

Try to avoid using additional Remote Control applications on a computer that has the SMS Remote Control Agent installed. Remote Control applications generally use the same memory addresses and interrupts to control the video portion. Look for any of the following as an indication of this problem:

- Loss of some Remote Control functionality
- General protection faults (GPFs) in the Administrator console during a Remote Control session
- Abrupt ending of the Remote Control session

When the Remote Tools Agent is scheduled to install, it first checks to see if any identified third-party Remote Control applications are installed. If any are installed, the

Remote Tools Agent is cancelled and the Systems Management Control Panel applet indicates that the Remote Control status is "unavailable."

NOTE: The Remote Tools Agent can be forced to try a reinstallation by choosing Repair in the Remote Control –Control Panel applet. When the repair initiates, the Remote Control Agent retries the installation. If no incompatibilities are found, it will install. Though this method forces the installation of the Remote Tools Agent, it is not recommended. A better option is to uninstall the third-party agent. During the next CCIM cycle, the installation function notices that the third-party agent is gone and the Remote Tools Agent installs automatically.

Remote Control Agent is Uninstalled on Windows 2000/NT Clients

When the Remote Control Agent service is reinstalled or repaired, the service is uninstalled before it is reinstalled. Before the uninstallation, the Component Services Manager attempts to shut down the Remote Control Agent service. If the service cannot be shut down, the Remote Control Agent is marked for deletion when the server is restarted.

The reason the service is unable to shut down is generally due to Wuser32 attempting to validate the permitted viewers against the list on the SMS site server. If user or group names listed in the Permitted Viewers list are not defined in the current domain, Wuser32 may never complete the verification.

To alleviate this problem, make sure that the Permitted Viewers list contains valid domain user and group accounts. This list needs to be maintained as accounts are deleted from the Windows 2000/NT domain.

You can identify this issue by viewing the RemCtrl.log file. Look for the following line: RCSvcs – WUSER32 service stopped, return code 1. The return code 1 indicates that there was a problem stopping the Wuser32 service.

Computers with Multiple Network Cards

The Remote Control Agent can only listen on one address for the remote connection. Many Windows 2000/NT servers have multiple network cards installed to provide better performance through connection teaming, and to provide fault tolerance. When the Remote Tools Client Agent runs, it binds to the first network card that it identifies. This network card may not be the preferred option.

You can use the Multinic.exe utility from the BackOffice Resource Kit to allow the Remote Tools Agent to bind to a specific network card. The syntax is: Multinic.exe s=<*subnet*> m=<*subnet mask*>.

The basic purpose of the Multinic.exe utility is to add information to the client computer's registry. If you don't have access to the Multinic.exe utility, you can make the modification manually or through a SMS Installer script. Here are the details:

- Open Regedt32 and navigate to the following location: HKEY_LOCAL_MACHINE\SOFTWARE\Microsoft\SMS\Client\Client Components\Remote Control.
- Create a REG_SZ (string value in Regedit) data item named **subnet**. Enter the IP subnet as its value.
- Create a REG_SZ (string value in Regedit) data item named **subnet mask**. Enter the IP subnet mask as its value.

Upgrading SMS Administrator Console

If you have SMS 2.0 Service Pack 2 applied to your site, make sure to upgrade the SMS Administrator consoles throughout the organization if you plan on using Remote Tools. SP2 introduced the first change to the network ports that are utilized for Remote Tools since SMS 1.2. Tables 6-5 and 6-6 list the network port differences.

Tool	TCP/IP Port
Rights Verification	1761
Remote Control	1762
Remote Reboot	1761
Remote Chat	1763
File Transfer	1764
Remote Execute	1761

Table 6-5. SMS 1.2 – SMS 2.0 SP1 Remote Control Network Ports

Tool	Port	Protocol
RCINFO	2701	TCP
RCINFO	2701	UDP
File Transfer	2702	TCP
File Transfer	2702	UDP
Chat	2703	TCP
Chat	2703	UDP
Remote Control	2704	TCP
Remote Control	2704	UDP

Table 6-6. SMS 2.0 SP2 Remote Control Network Ports

NOTE: When a Remote Control session is started, the title bar of the RC window will display the computer name and the network port number that it is connecting with. After applying SP2 (which uses port number 2701) and updating the SMS Administrator console, the port number value on the title bar still indicates it is connecting on port 1761 (the SMS 1.2 – SMS 2.0 SP1 value). For Remote Control sessions connected to pre-SP2 client computers, the port number that is used is still 1761, but when connecting to a SP2 client the value does not change. This is an error in the title bar only. With SP2 installed on the client computer, Remote Control really is connecting on port 2701.

Remote Control File Transfer and Windows 2000

When using the File Transfer utility of Remote Tools to copy files to a Windows 2000 client computer, files and directories that are encrypted and compressed do not show up in the File Transfer interface. To work around this issue, use Remote Control to copy the files to a network location for retrieval.

911

Chapter 7

Software Metering

In the last few years, software companies have become aggressive about tracking down companies that have unlicensed (illegal) copies of applications. Some large companies have been targeted and fined for software piracy in the corporate workplace. Because of the legal implications of allowing pirated software on company computers, organizations need a way to track and manage software licenses.

Systems Management Server's Software Metering provides several ways to manage the installed software in the organization and to ease the burden of administering license management. It saves money, time, and manual administration in the areas of tracking, distributing, and accounting for the use of applications. Software Metering provides software license tracking in two areas:

- **Software license management** This allows the administrator to track the company's software by providing information regarding when an application is used, how long the application is used, and who exactly has used the application.
- **Application management** This lets you control the use of software by placing restrictions on its use. An administrator can limit the number of licenses available for an application, prevent specific applications from being executed, and place time and specific user constraints on the application.

SMS Software Metering works both for client computers that are connected to the network and client computers that are disconnected or mobile.

Installing Software Metering

Employing Software Metering in your organization can provide great benefits. But, before execution, you must put together a clear plan on how it will be implemented. There are a few factors to consider for providing an optimum Software Metering environment.

Server Software Metering Communication Properties

To improve performance for the Software Metering services, you should modify the schedules for the Local and Intersite communications. You access these configuration settings by opening the Software Metering Properties in the Component Configuration of the SMS Administrator console.

NOTE: The Software Metering console itself is accessed through the SMS Administrator console in the Tools section, but it can also be executed as an external program. The Software Metering console program is the Licadmin.exe file stored in the \SMS\Bin\i386 directory on the SMS site server. The Software Metering console is used to configure the metered software, maintain the user and computer permissions, monitor the real-time usage of the programs, and maintain the Excluded Programs list.

Local Communications

To tune system performance on the local Software Metering server, you must test and modify the following areas for best performance:

- **License balancing** License balancing determines the schedule for license transfers to be balanced between the Software Metering servers. The default is four hours.
- **Site management** Site management determines the schedule for the site server to update the Software Metering servers with the latest program information. The default is once per hour.
- **Data collation** Data collation refers to the frequency that the license metering service updates the Software Metering database with the most recent usage information.

Intersite Communications

The intersite communications settings allow licenses to be managed across the multiple Software Metering sites. If the Real-Time License Verification option (described in the next section) is enabled for the site, you will also want to enable the Intersite License Management schedule. Modify the schedule according to what is logical for your organization, ensuring optimum performance.

NOTE: Testing of the communication configuration settings cannot be performed in a lab environment because it lacks an adequate number of client computers. There are several factors that will help you decide the optimum settings for your environment, such as network speeds, server processing power, and so on. You will need to test these in your live environment to determine the most favorable settings.

Client Software Metering Methods

Depending on the method of license verification that you configure for the site, Software Metering can be a server-intensive process. The software also puts increased demands on the network infrastructure. You should highly consider designating a server specifically for Software Metering.

By default, the Software Metering Agent is installed in *offline* mode. Offline mode is a passive method of tracking application license usage. In offline mode, the Software Metering Agent contacts the Software Metering server only periodically to retrieve any updates on software exclusions. Also, when the offline method is used for the SMS site, license balancing is not performed across the License Servers.

NOTE: On a network with high traffic, or one that performs slowly, or is designed poorly, Windows 95 and Windows 98 clients utilizing offline mode can hang for 20 to 30 seconds at a time when the License Server is contacted. Making a registry edit on the client computer can rectify this issue. Navigate to HKEY_LOCAL_MACHINE\SOFTWARE\Microsoft\ SMS\Client\Client Components\LICENSE_METERING\Properties, create a new DWORD key called GoOfflineAfterFailure, and assign a value of 1 to the key value.

If you select the Force Real-Time License Verification option in the Software Metering Client Agent properties of the SMS Administrator, application license tracking becomes dynamic. Anytime an application is run on a client computer, the Software Metering Agent contacts the License Server for verification that the application is authorized. The Agent also confirms that there are active licenses available (if the application has been configured with limits). The real-time method also enables license balancing within the SMS site.

You need to determine the license tracking method that best suits your organization. Doing so will also help you ascertain the server and network hardware needed to accomplish the task. The real-time license verification method allows you to actively manage license usage in your organization, but it also increases License Server processing and network bandwidth utilization. If you select this method, you will definitely need to assign the role of Software Metering to a separate server. If network bandwidth increases dramatically, you will want to add another Software Metering server to the infrastructure.

NOTE: In addition to using a separate server for Software Metering you will want to plan your Software Metering implementation on the following specs:

- The default installation of a single Software Metering server can support up to approximately 500 users. With the appropriate SMS hotfixes in place, a single Software Metering server can support up to 1,250 users.
- Software Metering in online mode needs high availability. It is recommended that at least two Software Metering servers be installed per site. This allows for at least one server to provide license processing should the other server be unavailable for a time.

Real-time licensing also adds processing overhead to the client computer. Instead of contacting the License Metering server periodically, as in offline mode, the client is in constant contact with the License Metering server in order to obtain licenses for the managed applications.

When real-time licensing is enabled, the client computer contacts the License Metering server each time an application is run. You can reduce the communication frequency between the client computer and the Software Metering server by excluding programs that do not need to be managed.

To determine which method of license verification is required in your organization, keep these two points in mind:

- If you want to implement application usage monitoring, use offline metering. You can generally use the same SMS site server for License Metering.
- If you want to enforce license management, use real-time Software Metering, and plan to implement License Metering on its own server.

NOTE: Software Metering configuration settings are site-wide. You cannot configure Software Metering on a per-client or per-computer basis.

Client Polling Intervals

To provide better network bandwidth performance and improved computer processing, the Software Metering Client Agent polling intervals can be limited.

Configuration Polling

In both real-time and offline modes, the client computer polls the License Server for updated configuration information on a fixed time frame. The default is 240 minutes.

NOTE: This configuration information is also passed to the client computer each time it is logged into the network.

If you have a slow network, you may want to increase this setting. It is modified through the Software Metering Client Agent properties on the Timings tab (shown in Figure 7-1).

Client Time-Out Settings

By default, the Software Metering Client Agent communicates with the License Server every 30 minutes to indicate that the client computer is active. To improve network bandwidth utilization, and also to increase reserve-processing power on the client computer, you should increase this value (refer to Figure 7-1).

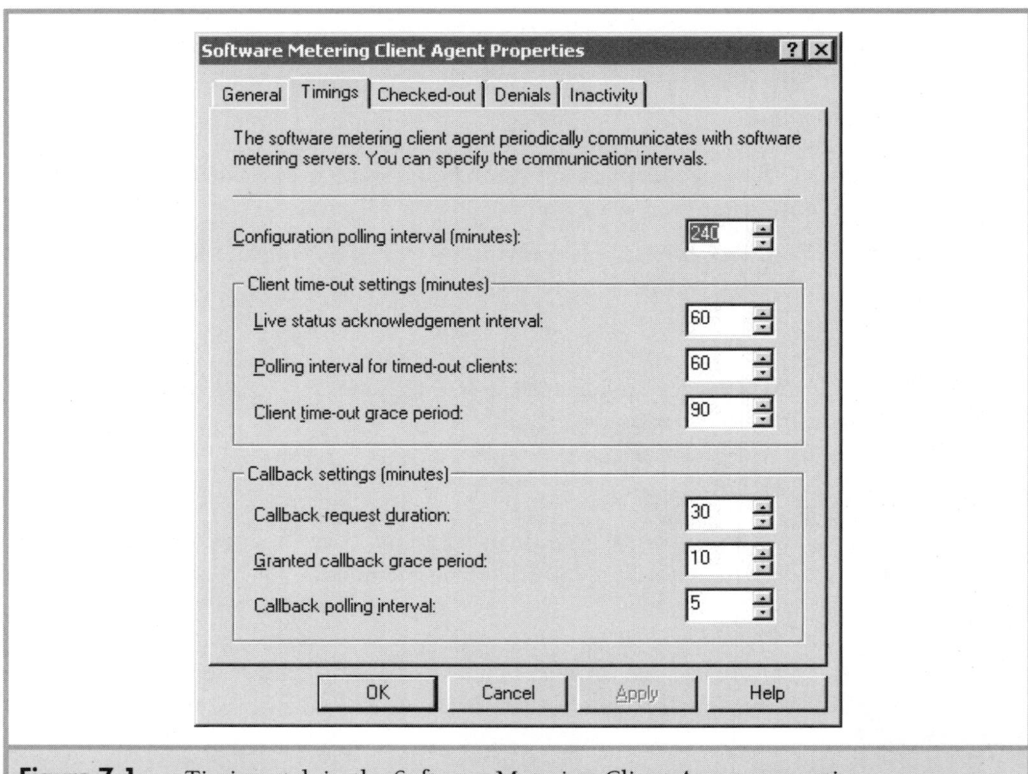

Figure 7-1. Timings tab in the Software Metering Client Agent properties

Service Pack Requirements

SMS 2.0 Service Pack 1 included numerous patches for Software Metering. It is recommended that you install Software Metering from at least this service pack. SMS 2.0 Service Pack 2 includes all the fixes from SP1, all the between-SP HotFixes, as well as interoperability with Windows 2000. If you plan on installing Software Metering on a Windows 2000 server and/or have Windows 2000 workstations in your organization, you must install Software Metering from the Service Pack 2 image.

Client Installation

The Software Metering Agent is installed on the client computer with the other SMS 2.0 client components when Software Metering is installed as part of the initial SMS site installation and configuration. Because Software Metering can be added to the SMS site at a later time, the Software Metering Agent is installed as part of the CCIM cycle.

There are only a few files installed as part of the Software Metering Agent. The entire file set is installed into the %WINDIR%\MS\SMS\Clicomp\Licmtr\i386 directory on the client computer. The bulk of the files are .dll files, which are used to provide the library of functions to the Software Metering Agent. In addition, the following files are installed:

- **Check32.exe** This runs when the client requests a license check for an application. If you see this program listed in the Running Tasks list, you know that the Agent is requesting a license.
- **Licclnt.exe** and **Liccl95.exe** These are the Software Metering Agents (Licclnt.exe for Windows 2000/ NT computers, and Liccli95.exe for Windows 95 and Windows 98 computers).

CODE BLUE

When Software Metering is running on the client computer, Licclnt.exe or Liccl95.exe should be present in the list of running tasks. If you do not see the file in the Running Tasks list, a problem may have prevented the automatic launching of the Software Metering Agent.

Try executing the appropriate file manually. To do so, enter the following command at a command prompt: ***%windir%*\ms\sms\clicomp\licmtr\i386\licclixx.exe**

NOTE: You must run the program from the %WINDIR%\MS\SMS\Core\Bin directory because Licclxx.exe is reliant on the .dll files that reside there.

- **Prof32.exe** The Prof32.exe program loads specific Software Metering profiles (*.lic) on the client computer. The Software Metering profiles are created at the SMS site and then distributed to the client computer. The *.lic file will always contain the current License Metering software configuration.
- **Unsetup.exe** The Unsetup.exe file is the program that performs the Software Metering Agent's uninstall.

CODE BLUE

Software Metering does not support OS/2, DOS, and Windows 3.*x* clients. Additionally, any 16-bit application that is started by the virtual MS-DOS thread (NTVMD.exe on Windows 2000 and Windows NT computers) or Wowexec.exe is not supported. To determine if Software Metering can manage the 16-bit application on a Windows 2000 or Windows NT computer, open Task Manager and click the Processes tab. Run the program. If the program file shows up in the listed processes, the Software Metering process can track it.

Manual Installation

If problems arise with the installed Software Metering Agent, or you do not wish to wait for the CCIM cycle to perform a mass installation, you can install the component manually. There is an installation file for each operating system located in the Clicomp.box\Licmtr\<platform> directory on the CAP. For Windows 95 and Windows 98 computers, the installation file is setup95.exe. For Windows 2000 and Windows NT computers, the installation file is setupnt.exe.

Software Metering Logs

As shown in the previous chapters, the SMS system does a first-rate job at recording all the information for each process, thread, and component. Software Metering is no exception.

Everything is monitored and all information is recorded—from the installation on the server, to the granting, revoking, and management of licenses. Both the server and the client computer retain logs for retrieving information on both success and failure of the processes.

Server Logs

All the server information (success and failure) is stored in the log files shown in Table 7-1.

In addition, you should enable the SMS_License_Server Service log, which can help troubleshoot grants and denials of software applications to the client computer. This log is not enabled by default when the Software Metering server is installed. To enable this log, the Remodbc.ini file must be modified on both the SMS site server and the Software Metering server(s). The Remodbc.ini file is located in the SMS\<platform>\bin directory.

Open the Remodbc.ini file in any text editor, locate the Logging section, and modify it to match the following:

```
[Logging]
Logon=1
FileName=Remodbc.log
BackupName=Remodbc.lo_
MaxSize=200000
```

Component	Log File	Process
SMS Administrator	SMS\Logs\SMSprov.log	Server installation
Site Control Manager	SMS\Logs\Sitectrl.log	Server installation
License Server Manager	SMS\Logs\Licsvcfg.log	Server installation, license granting, license return, callback processing
Inbox Manager	SMS\Logs\Inboxmgr.log	Server installation
License Metering	SMS\Logs\Licsrvc.log	Server installation, license balancing, license granting, license return, callback processing

Table 7-1. Software Metering Server Log Files

Client Logs

As the Software Metering Agent is installed on the client, a specific client log file is created. The log file for Software Metering is located at %WINDIR%\MS\SMS\Logs\Licclixx.log (Liccli95.log for Windows 95/98 computers and LiccliNT.log for Windows 2000/NT computers). It records information on the following functions:

- Granting a license
- License return
- Callback processing

When there are problems with Software Metering, the client log file should be used in conjunction with the server log files. You cannot pinpoint Software Metering issues by looking in one log location and not the other. This is because the Software Licensing Agent on the client computer initiates the whole license request process by executing an application. The Software Metering server then tries to fulfill the request.

Enabling Debug Mode

The client logging provides verbose information about the Software Metering/Licensing process, but it does not provide real-time information. In order to troubleshoot Software Metering Agent problems on the client in real time, you should enable the Software Metering "Spy" window, shown in Figure 7-2.

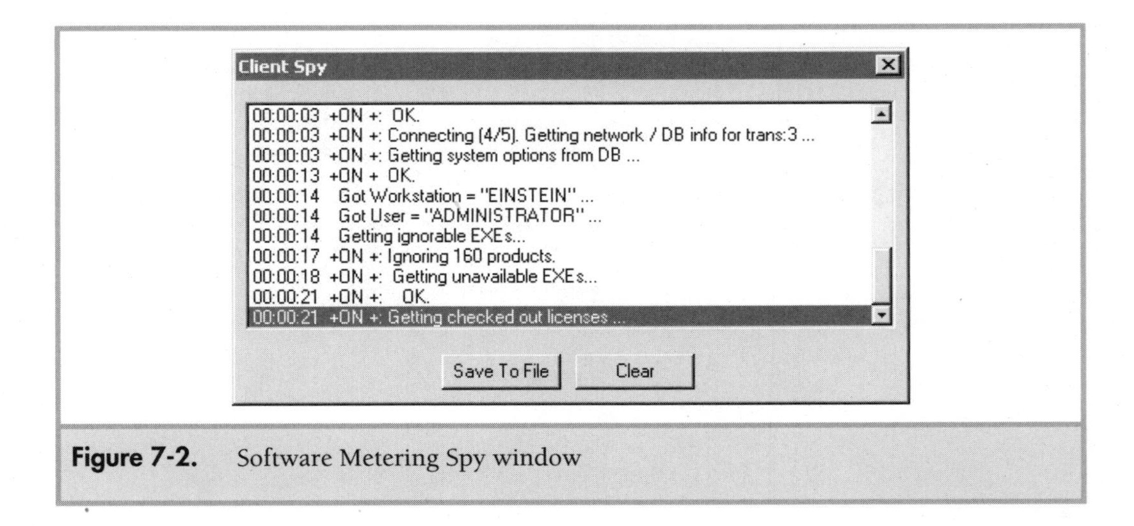

Figure 7-2. Software Metering Spy window

The Software Metering Spy window provides instantaneous monitoring of the execution of applications. The Spy window allows you to watch each step of the Software Metering Agent's processes. The information can be viewed in the Spy window or saved to a file for later review or printing. To enable the Spy window, perform the following steps:

1. Open a registry editor.
2. Go to HKEY_LOCAL_MACHINE\SOFTWARE\Microsoft\SMS\Client\Client Components\License Metering.
3. Add a new REG_SZ data item named **Spy** and make the value Yes.
4. Close the registry editor.
5. Restart the computer.

NOTE: The Software Metering Spy window is a very intensive process. When the tool is no longer needed, disable it by removing the registry value.

Software Metering Checklists

The Checklists in this section outline the installation of the Software Metering server, and the different tasks performed by the License Metering process.

Server Installation

The server installation begins by installing the Software Metering server software. It can be set up at the time the initial SMS site is installed or later on. It can be installed by either running the SMS setup from the server's Programs menu or by rerunning the setup from the SMS CD and adding the component.

NOTE: The version of the Software Metering installation that is required is the one that comes with SMS 2.0 SP1. Service Pack 1 provided several patches for Software Metering. If you are installing License Metering on Windows 2000 servers, you must install Service Pack 2. Service Pack 2 includes all of the Service Pack 1 fixes and the HotFixes between service packs, and adds interoperability between SMS and Windows 2000.

The following checklist assumes that the setup has already been initiated through one of the previously mentioned methods:

- License Server Manager starts the License Server Connection Agent.

- License Server Manager starts the SMS_License_Server_Manager thread.
- License Server Manager verifies the administrative rights on the target server.

CHECKPOINT: If the License Server Manager does not have administrative rights on the server targeted as the Software Metering server, the installation will fail. License Server Manager needs the administrative rights to create the services and registry entries. Verify that there is not a lockout listed in the security log of the target server. Looking in Licsvcfg.log will also pinpoint a lack of security rights. License Server Manager must also have connectivity to the target server. Use the PING command to test the connectivity using the NetBIOS name. If the PING is successful, attempt to connect with the C$, D$, and Admin$ shares using a domain administrator account.

- License Server Manager creates the \SWMTR directory on the target server and drive specified.
- License Server Manager creates a Windows 2000/NT share of the \SWMTR directory and names it \\Licmtr on the target server.

CHECKPOINT: Verify that the \SWMTR directory was created and that the License Server Manager was able to generate the \\Licmtr share. If these are not evident within 10 minutes, check the network connection. Also, confirm that the NetBIOS name resolution is able to contact the server name.

- If the directory and share were created successfully, the License Server Manager installs the data storage files (Visual FoxPro files with a .dbf extension) and the Remodbc.exe and Remodbc.ini files to the \\Licmtr share.
- License Server Manager creates a Software Metering user account in the domain called SWMAccount.

NOTE: The SWMAccount is given the Logon as a Service right and added to the target computer's local Administrators group.

CHECKPOINT: View the user Account list to determine if the Software Metering account was created. Also, verify that the proper rights have been granted. If the account has not been created, confirm again that the License Server Manager has administrative rights on the target server.

- License Server Manager installs the ODBC Installation service (Inodbcsv.exe) and then starts the service. The service's display name is Install_ODBC.
- Install_ODBC's only function is to install the ODBC 3.51 driver on the target server. Once the installation is complete, Install_ODBC is removed as a service.

CHECKPOINT: The installation of ODBC 3.51 is relatively quick; therefore, the only way to determine if the installation is experiencing problems is if the Install_ODBC service remains in the Service window. Processes running on the target server can hang the ODBC installation. Determine which processes are hindering the installation by removing them one at a time.

NOTE: The License service will not proceed with the Software Metering server installation unless the ODBC drivers on the server are version 2.52 or newer.

- License Server Manager creates the Software Metering directory structure in the \\Licmtr share and installs the component's files.
- License Server Manager configures the local Software Metering server data cache.
- License Server Manager creates the ODBC data source name.

CHECKPOINT: Verify that the directory structure has been created in the \\Licmtr directory and that the data cache exists. The data cache is also a Visual FoxPro format, but with a .cdx file extension. Also, check to see that the ODBC data source name is present on the target server. To confirm the ODBC data source name has been generated, open the ODBC data source administrator on the target server, click on the System DSN tab, and verify that the License Server local DSN data source exists

NOTE: On Windows 9x and Windows NT computers, the ODBC data source administrator can be executed from the Control Panel. On Windows 2000 computers, the icon for this program no longer exists in the Control Panel by default, due to a specific registry setting. To run the program on Windows 2000 computers, execute the C:\WINNT\SYSTEM32\ODBCAD32.EXE file. Or, to allow the ODBC applet to be displayed in the Control Panel, navigate to HKEY_CURRENT_USER\Control Panel\don't load, locate the odbccp32.cpl value, and delete it, and then restart the computer.

- Inbox manager creates the Software Metering Inboxes directory in the \SWMTR directory.
- License Server Manager creates the inbox directory structure (\Alert and \Offline).

- License Server Manager performs the first license balancing process.
- License Server Manager installs the SMS_License server service on the Software Metering Server and starts the service.

CHECKPOINT: After verifying that the inbox directory structure is in place, look in the Service list of the target server to confirm that the SMS_License Server service is installed and running. If the service does not start for a long time, try starting the service manually. If the service will not start manually, make sure that the License Server Manager has completed the service installation by viewing the Licsvcfg.log file. You can also check that the server has been correctly assigned the role of License Server by looking in the \Clicomp.box\Licmtr.cfg file on the CAP. This file contains the list of License Servers assigned to the SMS site. The following is an example of the information that is found in the Licmtr.cfg file:

```
[Component Configuration]
  LastUpdate=29358089, 982804768
  Name=LICENSE METERING
  KeyFlags=0
  Site Version=2.00.1493.2000
  (REG_DWORD)ContinuousOffline=0
  (REG_DWORD)Flags=0
  (REG_DWORD)GoOnlineInt=14400
  (REG_SZ)LicenseServers=EINSTEIN
  (REG_DWORD)TriesBeforeOffline=5

[EINSTEIN]
  (REG_SZ)Name=EINSTEIN
  (REG_DWORD)Platform=3
  (REG_SZ)UncDbPath=\\EINSTEIN\LicMtr

[IDENT]
  TYPE=Base Config File Type
```

License Granting

The client Software Metering Agent initiates the license granting process. Every time a new application is executed, the Software Metering Agent polls the License Metering server for a free license. The license granting process is performed in two phases: the client phase and the Software Metering Server phase.

Client Phase

The following steps are part of the client phase of license granting:

- Depending on the installed operating system, the specific Software License Agent (Liccli95.exe for Windows 9*x* and LiccliNT.exe for Windows 2000 and Windows NT) identifies that a new application has been started.
- The Software License Agent retrieves the License Server's name that was last accessed for the application from the client computer's registry.
- The Software License Agent contacts the server name that was retrieved from the registry and requests a license for the application.

Software Metering Server Phase

The following steps and checkpoints help you troubleshoot the server phase:

- The License Server receives the license request from the client computer and checks the local Software Metering data cache to see if the application is a registered product. If it is not a registered product, License Server writes the application's usage information to the data cache and the process stops.
- If the application is a registered product, is defined for active metering, and has a license available, the following steps complete the process:
  - The License Server writes the license use to the data cache and decrements the license count.
  - The License Server grants the application license to the client and the process is complete.

CHECKPOINT: When the license is granted, the permission information is written to the SMS\Logs\Licclixx.log (Liccli95.log for Windows 9x, and LiccliNT.log for Windows 2000 and Windows NT) file on the client computer. If the application is a registered product and is defined for active metering, but does not have a license available, the following steps complete the process:

- The License Server sends a denial message to the client computer.
- The Software License Agent on the client computer receives the message and then displays it to the user.
- The License Server stops the application from running on the client computer and displays the callback option message (see the callback processing checklist). The license granting process is complete.

CHECKPOINT: If the user agrees to the callback notification, the License Metering thread connects (every 15 minutes) to each Software Metering server, waiting for a free license that can be balanced to the local server. When a license becomes available on any License Server in the hierarchy, it is moved (balanced) to the local Software Metering server. When the license is moved, it is then granted to the user that accepted the callback request, and the application is executed.

License Return

When the client computer is finished with the application license (the program is closed), the Software License Agent frees the acquired license and gives it back to the License Server. The license return is performed in two phases: client phase and License Server phase.

NOTE: The client will only send a release notification to the local Software Metering server, when the Force Real Time License Verification option has been enabled for the SMS site.

Client Phase

Depending on the installed operating system, the specific Software License Agent (Liccli95.exe for Windows 9*x*, and LiccliNT.exe for Windows 2000 and Windows NT) detects that the application has been shut down.

The Software License Agent notifies the local Software Metering server that the software license has been released.

CHECKPOINT: The client Software License Agent has released the license. The processing of the license now takes place at the License Server.

License Server Phase

The License Server updates the data cache with the released license information.

CHECKPOINT: If there are any callback requests identified, the License Server writes the information to the data cache. The client computer that placed the callback request checks the data cache for the available license (described next).

License Callback

The license callback process causes the client computer to continually poll the local License Metering server's data cache until a license becomes available. The following short checklist identifies the steps involved in the process. Each time the Software License Agent polls the License Metering server, an entry is recorded into the Liccli95.log or LiccliNT.log file.

- Depending on the installed operating system, the specific Software License Agent (Liccli95.exe for Windows 9*x*, and LiccliNT.exe for Windows 2000 and Windows NT) checks the Software Metering server every five minutes to see if the callback request has been fulfilled.
- When the callback request has been granted, the Software License Agent displays the callback message to the user.
- The user initiates the execution of the application.

CHECKPOINT: If the application fails to execute even when a license becomes available, make sure that the client computer still has connectivity with the network. The Liccli95.log or LiccliNT.log file on the client computer will contain information concerning any errors on connectivity and also on callback status.

Troubleshooting Software Metering

Primary focus on Software Metering is scheduled for the next service pack, and HotFixes will be released along the way. For now, there are a number of specific items noted in this section that you should pay special attention to.

Unavailable Software Metering Server

When Software Metering is installed on a Windows 95 or Windows 98 computer, the client computer is configured to connect to a specific Software Metering server until the CCIM cycle occurs. If the specific Software Metering server becomes unavailable, the Windows 95 and Windows 98 computer continually try to connect to that server. This can cause the client computer to slow and the Liccli95.log to fill up with errors. Rebooting the computer resolves the errors and performance problems, and once the CCIM cycle occurs, the client computer receives the list of available Software Metering servers.

NOTE: It is recommended that you have at least two Software Metering servers per site to provide failover and availability.

SP2 Upgrade Can Hang

The SMS_License_Server service may hang the Service Pack 2 upgrade if it is not shut down correctly. If a site system is running as a Software Metering server, the SMS_License_Server may not be able to be stopped remotely. If this scenario happens, the SP2 upgrade will have to be initiated again. You must stop the service manually before the SP2 upgrade to make sure the installation runs successfully.

Prohibiting License Workaround Tricks

A useful feature of Software Metering is the ability to restrict applications even if they are renamed. Some end users who realize that Software Metering is in force may try renaming files in an attempt to run them. If Software Metering is configured correctly, even this technique will be futile.

In order for Software Metering to correctly prohibit access to renamed applications, it must be configured to read the header information of the files instead of just the application's display name. To do this, open the Software Metering properties by navigating to the Component Configuration under Site Settings in the SMS Administrator console. As shown in Figure 7-3, change the "Program name policy" to the second setting: "Original. Use the program name stored in the header information of the program's executable file."

Applications Start Before the Software Metering Agent

The Software Metering Agent loads as part of the SMS 2.0 client process when the computer boots. Applications may be configured to start before the Software Metering Agent. When this happens, the Software Metering Agent will not monitor those applications. Most applications allow you to change the order in which they are loaded. There are some applications where this scenario cannot be remedied.

Enabling Software Metering

Keep in mind that after Software Metering is installed, enabling Software Metering for the SMS site is actually a three-step process. You must first configure the Software Metering properties in the Component Configuration section of the site settings. Then, you must enable and configure the Software Metering Client Agent. When those tasks are complete, you must assign the role of Software Metering to a specific server.

If the Software Metering Client Agent is installed on the client computers before a server has been assigned to the role of Software Metering, the client records registry errors in the

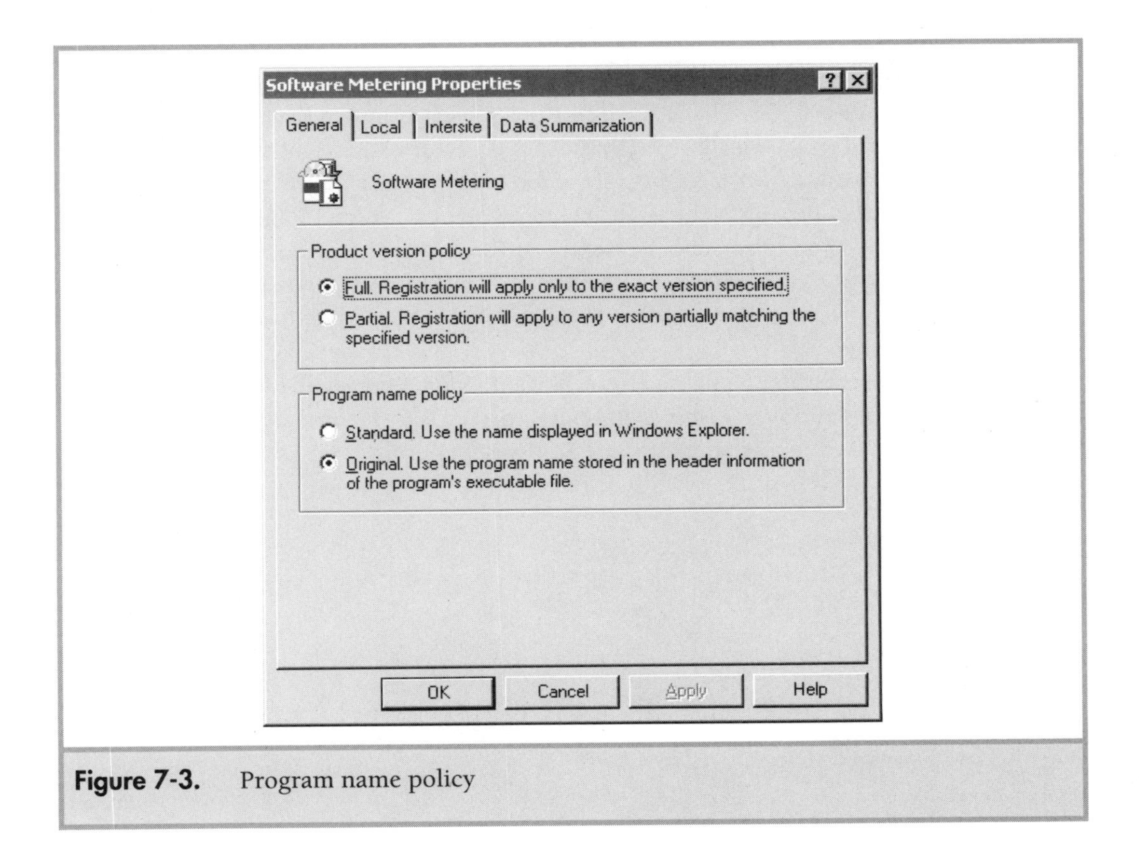

Figure 7-3. Program name policy

Licclixx.log file. The log file indicates that registry entries are either corrupt or missing and the Agent cannot continue. When the Software Metering server is added and accessible, the client computer resolves the errors and functions properly.

Registering with the Parent Site

Application license information must be registered at the parent site for License Metering to work. SMS's Software Metering only transfers application license information from the parent site to the child site. If an application is installed on the child site, usage information for the application will only be reported to that child site. The parent site will not be able to manage the licenses, nor will the intersite license balancing take place. Always install the application at the parent site first.

Monitor the Offline Directory

When using the offline mode of license verification, closely monitor the SWMTR\Inboxes\Offline directory. If data in this directory builds up before the files can be processed, the server will become saturated. When this saturation point is reached, the Software Metering server will stop processing the files and the client computers will no longer be able to contact the server for license requests.

The Software Metering server can process the offline log files at a rate of about 2.5MB per hour. Based on this rate, the saturation point will be reached when the \Offline directory contains 10–15MB of data.

If this happens on a consistent basis, you will want to first upgrade the server's processor and RAM to see if the problem resolves. If upgrading the server does not resolve the data build-up, you will need to add an additional Software Metering server to the hierarchy.

Chapter 8

Site-to-Site Communications

If you have the budget to upgrade the network infrastructure in an SMS setup that contains numerous remote sites, you'll see a performance improvement. However, most of us must settle for understanding (and have realistic expectations for) site-to-site communications within the SMS infrastructure.

Overview of Site Traffic

If you have a multiple-site hierarchy (more than one SMS server) with child and secondary sites, SMS data could be flowing across the network constantly. When you consider all the SMS functions that require a network connection, you realize how important network performance is to SMS. The following list of SMS processes will help you comprehend the scope of data transfer that is processing in the background and to understand that network performance is key for optimizing the SMS site. Each of these processes performs its functions by distributing data files across the network connection.

- CAP processing
- CCIM cycle
- Child site installation
- Client installation
- Copying, moving, and mirroring files
- DDR processing
- File collection
- License callback processing
- License load balancing
- License granting
- License return
- Hardware inventory reporting
- Hardware inventory resynchs
- Parent site changes
- Remote Tools
- Replication
- Secondary site installation

- Senders
- Site assignment changes
- Site boundary changes
- Site verification
- Software distribution
- Software inventory reporting
- Software Metering server installation
- Software inventory resynchs
- Status messages (success and failure for every function, thread, process, and component)

These processes perform their functions by distributing specific data files throughout the site hierarchy, as shown in Table 8-1.

NOTE: The file types listed in Table 8-1 do not include all the file types used within the SMS system. This table notes only those files that use network bandwidth.

File Extension	Description
.adc	The .adc file contains additions to the Collection Evaluator before the Collection list is replicated throughout the hierarchy.
.ccr	Client configuration request file.
.cmn	Offer Manager uses this collection membership update file to distribute collection changes.
.ct0	Master site control file.
.ct1	Hierarchy manager creates the *.ct1 file. This file represents changes in the site hierarchy.
.ct3	The *.ct3 file represents proposed site modifications from the SMS site services.
.dat	The .dat file is the inventory data file that is replicated to the parent site.

Table 8-1. SMS File Types that Cause Network Traffic

File Extension	Description
.dc	The .dc file contains the collection information that will be deleted from the Collection Evaluator before the changes are distributed throughout the hierarchy.
.ddr	The .ddr file is the Discovery Data Record that must be collected from all discovered resources.
.ins	This instruction file contains information for designating which advertisements are tied to which collection.
.ist	This instruction file determines which component a package file belongs to. The .ist file is received from another site in the hierarchy.
.lkp	The lookup file is used to determine which recipients should receive a specific instruction file.
.mif	The management information format file is used to pass inventory information from the client to the SMS site server.
.mof	The managed object format file, such as the SMS_DEF.MOF file, is used to transfer specific inventory information.
.nhm	The no history MIF file is used to pass data inventory from the clients to the SMS site server.
.ofr	The offer file contains the offer data that is read by the offer manager.
.p*	This package file is copied between sites, allowing the package to exist on the distribution servers in the hierarchy.
.pck	The package file is the file that contains the compressed files that are replicated throughout the hierarchy to the distribution servers.
.pkg	This package file contains the instructions for the distributed package.
.rpt	The .rpt file is the replication file that is processed through the transaction system.
.sca	The site control addition file contains the instructions for adding modifications to the site.
.scd	The site control deletion file contains the instructions for deleting site information.
.scu	The site configuration update file is sent through the hierarchy to update each site with the configuration changes.
.sha	The site hierarchy addition file is distributed throughout the hierarchy when adding site systems.

Table 8-1. SMS File Types that Cause Network Traffic *(continued)*

File Extension	Description
.sic	The software inventory complete file is forwarded from the client to the SMS site upon the initial software inventory process.
.sid	The software inventory delta file, forwarded to the SMS site from the client, contains only the changes in software inventory.
.svf	The .svf file is the status system file that is replicated throughout the hierarchy to report on the overall SMS system status.

Table 8-1. SMS File Types that Cause Network Traffic *(continued)*

Data Transmission Times for Software Distribution

SMS software distribution can be one of the most demanding stresses on the network infrastructure. When sending large or small packages to the computer-base, it is helpful to understand what to expect from a network transmission standpoint.

When users request a package, they usually expect it immediately. However, this isn't feasible if the package has never been copied to the distribution points. Using Tables 8-2 and 8-3, which describe the amount of time needed for packages to move across the network,

	Fast Ethernet	Token Ring	Ethernet	128 Kbps	56 Kbps	28 Kbps
1MB	< sec	1 sec	1 sec	1 min	2 min	5 min
5MB	< sec	2 sec	4 sec	5 min	10 min	20 min
10MB	1 sec	5 sec	8 sec	10 min	25 min	45 min
20MB	2 sec	10 sec	16 sec	20 min	45 min	90 min
100MB	8 sec	50 sec	90 sec	90 min	> 4 hrs	> 8 hrs

Table 8-2. Network Transmission Time (10 clients to 1 distribution server)

	Fast Ethernet	Token Ring	Ethernet	128 Kbps	56 Kbps
1MB	10 sec	30 sec	30 sec	30 min	90 min
5MB	15 sec	1 min	2 min	3 hrs	6 hrs
10MB	20 sec	2 min	4 min	5 hrs	12 hrs
20MB	40 sec	4 min	7 min	10 hrs	24 hrs
100MB	3 min	20 min	35 min	50 hrs	5 days

Table 8-3. Network Transmission Times (Site to Site)

you can better manage the end user's (and your) expectations. These times are approximate and depend upon the current load on the network.

Managing Network Bandwidth with Sender Addresses

To help manage the amount of network bandwidth that is utilized by SMS, you can modify the specific sender address per destination. Each sender address can be configured to allow you to control the network load by modifying the availability schedule and the percentage of bandwidth used.

The sender addresses are accessed from the SMS Administrator console by navigating to the Site Database | Site Hierarchy | Site | Site Settings. For each SMS site where you want to modify the sender settings, you should create a separate sender address. Sender addresses can be created for the following senders:

- Standard sender address
- Asynchronous RAS sender address
- ISDN RAS sender address
- X25 RAS sender address
- SNA RAS sender address
- Courier sender address

NOTE: You cannot modify schedule and rate limits for the courier sender address.

The following two sections describe the schedule and rate limit settings that can improve the overall performance of the network during peak times. You should review these settings and compare them with the needs of your organization. The way the organization is structured—that is, how it does business—will determine how they should be configured.

For example, if your company's business hours are strictly between 8:00 A.M. and 5:00 P.M. Monday through Friday, the peak hours of operation are on a standard working level. Many individuals in numerous companies work around the clock, or do not have a set schedule as long as the work gets done. These factors may prohibit certain configurations on the sender address. For a better representation of the daily and weekly traffic cycle on your network, use the Network Monitor utility, described in the "Tools" section of this chapter.

Schedule

The sender address schedule offers features that let you modify the days and times when SMS can send its data. This allows you to control the priority of the send request, plus specify when it can be sent. The schedule setting gives you the ability to be specific by providing entries for the 7-day week, shown in Figure 8-1.

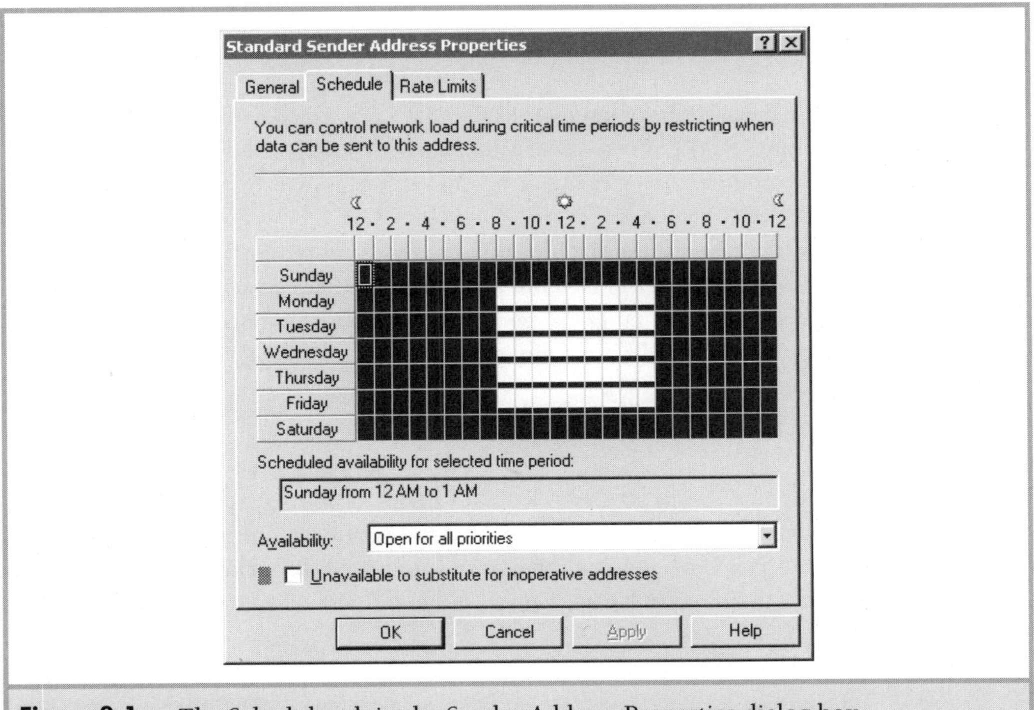

Figure 8-1. The Schedule tab in the Sender Address Properties dialog box

To use the interface, either click in a specific block and modify the Availability option (telling SMS how to handle the selected date and time), or drag to select a number of days and times, and then change the Availability option.

The list of Availability options is the key to controlling the bandwidth schedule. The following options are available:

- **Open for all priorities** Use this option to give SMS full access to the network bandwidth. You may consider allowing this option only for weekends and after business hours. Keep in mind if you have a network backup scheduled for after hours, this will also need network bandwidth. Opening the bandwidth up to SMS could cause your network backups to take longer.
- **Allow medium and high priority** Use this option to prohibit SMS from sending data unless it is marked with a medium or high priority.
- **Allow high priority only** Use this option to allow SMS to send data only if the process has been marked with a high priority.
- **Close** Use this option to prohibit SMS from sending any data during the specified period of time.

Rate Limits

You should also limit the amount of bandwidth that SMS can use. The rate limits configuration (see Figure 8-2) is a per-day setting and works with schedule configuration. Making changes here modifies the percentage of allowable bandwidth for the sender addresses for the same time each day.

Using the same technique as described for the schedule information, you can click a specific time of the day, or multiselect a combination of times and set each rate to a different setting. When you select the time period, modify the "Limit (% of connection bandwidth)" setting. The drop-down box includes the following percentages: 10, 25, 50, 75, 90, and, of course, 100 (Unlimited).

Tools

Microsoft has provided some network bandwidth and utilization monitoring tools as part of the SMS installation. These tools help you diagnose network performance problems, as well as help you plan for network capacity upgrades.

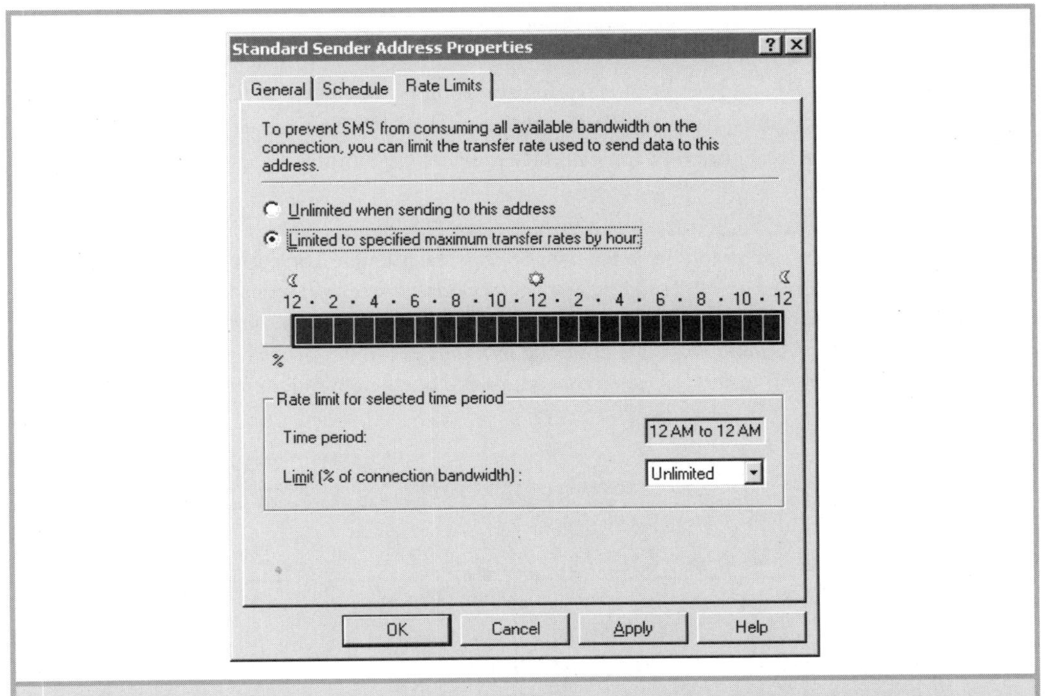

Figure 8-2. Rate Limits tab in the Sender Address Properties dialog box

Network Monitor

Probably the best tool for determining network performance for SMS is the Network Monitor tool. Network Monitor is available as an option during the SMS installation and can be accessed from within the SMS Administrator console under the Tools section.

NOTE: Network Monitor can also be installed manually from the \NMEXT\<platform> directory on the SMS CD. The installation is contained within a single Setup.exe file, which can be installed from the local computer or distributed through the SMS software distribution system. In fact, you should use the software distribution method to install and start Network Monitor on computers that you wish to monitor remotely.

Network Monitor is a highly misunderstood tool that can provide immense benefits for SMS site configuration. Not only does Network Monitor allow you to gather network utilization information, but it is also a great tool for troubleshooting network resources, such as faulty or chattering network adapters, network routers that are flooded with data, or network routers that have failed. As shown in Figure 8-3, the interface is relatively simple.

NOTE: Another, similar tool included with SMS, is the Monitor Control tool. This tool is excellent for troubleshooting failed network components because it scans the network in real time and reports on specific conditions or events. While this is a very useful tool, it is not covered in this section because it is designed more for providing proactive management of network components instead of determining network bandwidth requirements.

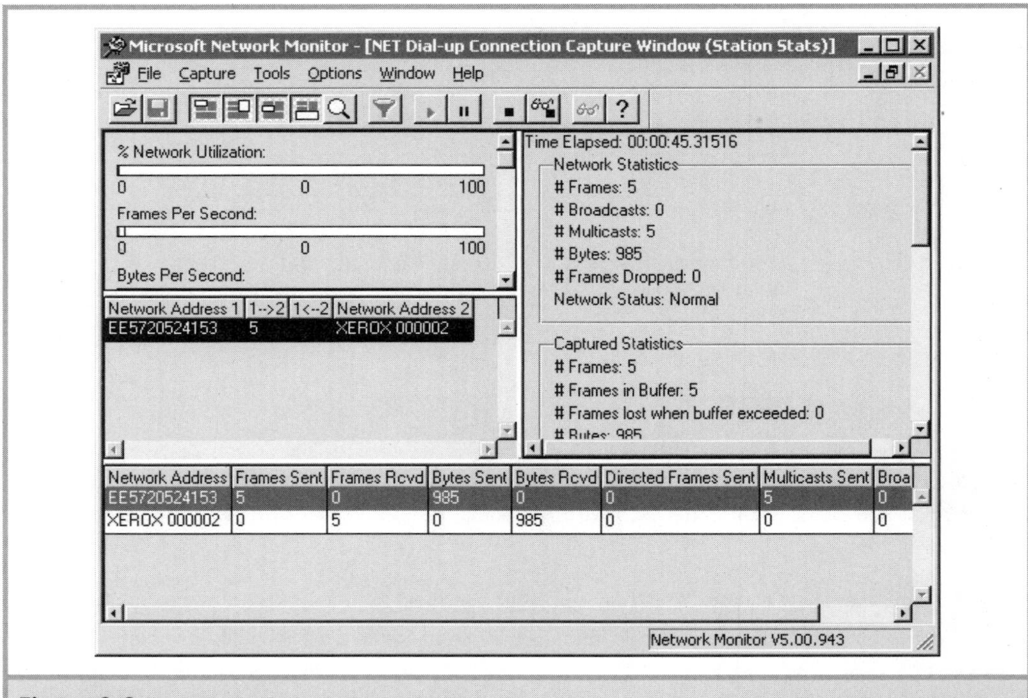

Figure 8-3. Network Monitor interface

Windows Network Monitor

A version of Network Monitor comes with Windows 2000 and Windows NT, but it is not as full-featured as the one available with SMS. Some of the features the SMS version provides over the Windows 2000/NT version are as follows:

1. The ability to perform a remote capture to retrieve data from a separate subnet and network segment.
2. The ability to determine the heaviest user of network resources.
3. The ability to determine which protocol is using the most bandwidth.
4. The resolution of a NetBIOS name to a MAC address.
5. The capability to find routers.

The interface is divided into four sections, or panes: Graph (top left), Total Statistics (top right), Session Statistics (directly underneath the Graph pane), and Station Statistics (the frame at the bottom of the window).

The Graph pane displays the current network activity in a thermometer-type graphic. It shows network activity in percentage of utilization, frames per second, bytes per second, broadcasts per second, and multicasts per second. The thermometer changes as the network activity increases and decreases, and a small stationary bar indicates the maximum result.

The Total Statistics pane displays the total network activity that has been detected since the capture process began. These captured frames represent the data that has been trapped for investigation.

The Session Statistics pane indicates the current connection (or session) between two network addresses. Network address 1 and network address 2 have established a session for packet capturing and utilization monitoring.

The Station Statistics pane displays the network activity for specific nodes on the network. This pane allows you to quickly determine specific nodes that may be utilizing more network bandwidth than they should.

The first time you use Network Monitor, create a baseline for future network performance profiling. This enables you to determine if the network may cause a bottleneck for your SMS implementation, and also offers data to suggest which changes should be made.

To set up a baseline, you must run Network Monitor at the three different phases of the day: high activity, medium activity, and low activity. Gathering data during each of these periods will give you an idea of how much traffic traverses across your network, and also provide you with data to compare with future monitoring reports.

Low activity for the network is generally after business hours when most employees are out of the office. Medium activity is any time during the day, except for the high-activity period. The high-activity period for most companies is when employees arrive at work and log into the network. In most organizations, this high-activity period occurs at the same time every day and lasts for about 1.5 hours.

Using all the accumulated data, you can intelligently set the sender address schedules and rate limits.

NOTE: The Network Monitor tool can also be used to continuously monitor the network. You can set up a computer dedicated to monitoring traffic on the particular subnet and have Network Monitor running at all times. This will allow a more detailed view of your network performance and will also help you to proactively identify any pending issues. If you decide to do this, make sure to set the capture buffer setting to a small value by clicking on Capture-Buffer Settings on the File menu. The smallest value you can select is 0.5MB. Setting the buffer to a lower value will allow Network Monitor to run continuously without running out of available computer memory.

Network Monitor Requirements

The following are the requirements for running Network Monitor:

- Windows 2000 or Windows NT 4.0 w/SP4 or better.
- You must be logged in as a user with administrator rights on the computer that is running Network Monitor.
- Microsoft Internet Explorer 4.01 w/SP1 or later. Internet Explorer is used to access the program's help files and to configure the monitors.
- The computer running Network Monitor must have a network adapter that supports promiscuous mode. Promiscuous mode (or p-mode) interacts with a drive driver to allow the data that is captured to be stored in a temporary capture file on the local hard drive.
- The most current version of WMI must be installed. This can be installed using the Wbemsdk.exe file from the \SMSSetup\Bin\<platform> directory on the SMS CD.

- To use Network Monitor to capture frames on a remote computer, Network Monitor must be installed and running on both computers. Earlier versions of Network Monitor installed a Network Monitor Agent that ran as a Windows NT service. The latest version of Network Monitor included with SMS 2.0 starts the Agent with the Network Monitor program.
- The individual who is running Network Monitor must have administrative privileges both on the local computer and the remote computer, if capturing remote data.

Important Installation Notes for Network Monitor

The installation directory path that you specify must contain less than 100 characters. If the path exceeds this number, installation will fail.

Token-ring adapter cards are not recommended, as there are issues with capturing all the network activity data.

Installation will not continue if an instance of the Microsoft Management Console and/or Network Monitor is running. Before attempting the installation, exit these applications.

CODE BLUE

Before installing Network Monitor, uninstall any previous versions. If this is not practical, and a newer version is installed, the Performance Monitor counters could be duplicated. To remedy this problem, open a command prompt window and type in the following command: **lodctr.exe nmctrs.ini**. Lodctr.exe is a Windows 2000/NT command that is used for loading Performance Monitor counters. It is located in the %SYS32% directory.

Capturing and Reviewing Data

To start capturing data in Network Monitor, use any of these actions:

- Click the Run button on the Tool menu.
- Choose Capture | Start.
- Press F10.

During the capture process, Network Monitor receives data about the network traffic that is passing through the computer on the local subnet. You can watch the real-time statistics, but when you want to view the data, take one of these actions:

- Click the Stop and View Capture button on the toolbar.
- Choose Capture | Display Captured Data.
- Press F12.

Displaying the captured data stops the frame capture, and opens the Network Monitor viewer, shown in Figure 8-4.

If you want to retrieve data and monitor the network traffic on a remote computer, you must first install and then start Network Monitor on the remote computer. Then choose Capture | Networks, type the remote computer's NetBIOS name or IP address, and click OK

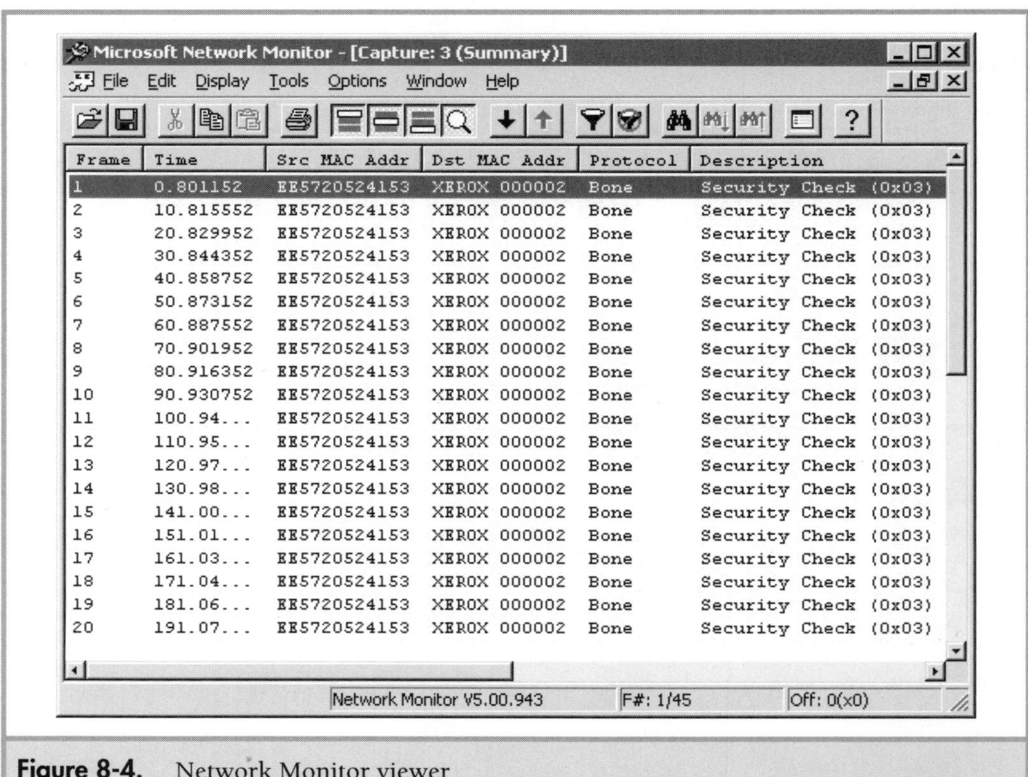

Figure 8-4. Network Monitor viewer

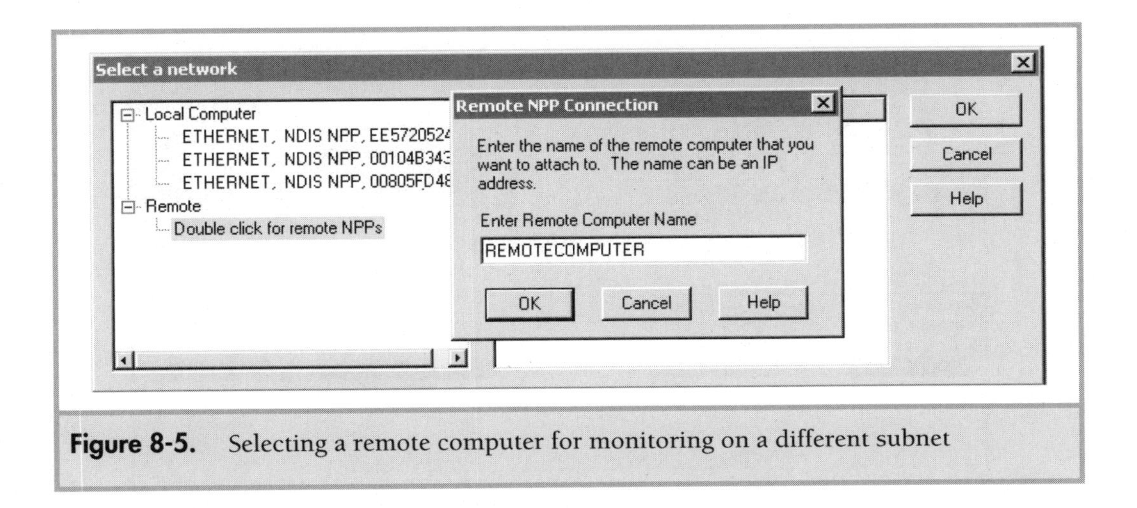

Figure 8-5. Selecting a remote computer for monitoring on a different subnet

(see Figure 8-5). After Network Monitor resolves the remote computer's name or IP address, the computer is available for capturing network data. This function is particularly useful for monitoring the network traffic on a different subnet.

NOTE: During the monitoring process on a remote computer, the captured data is stored in a temporary location on the remote computer's hard drive. When the monitoring session is stopped, the capture file is stored on the remote computer's hard disk.

The Network Monitor viewer screen displays all of the frames that have been captured, along with their stats. Double-clicking one of the frames splits the view into three panes, shown in Figure 8-6. These three panes are the Summary pane (top), the Detail pane (middle), and the Hex pane (bottom). The information provided in the separate panes shows the protocols that were detected in the frame, as well as the actual data contained within the frame.

- The Summary pane displays the following: the captured frames, the elapsed capture time, source and destination MAC addresses, the protocol being employed, and a text description of the frame.
- The Detail pane shows more recorded information about the selected data frame. It shows the exact content of the frame and the different protocols that are within the frame. This information allows you to perform detailed packet analysis using the OSI model for reference.
- The Hex pane displays the specific data contained within the frame in ASCII text format, allowing you to peruse the information that is being passed through the network.

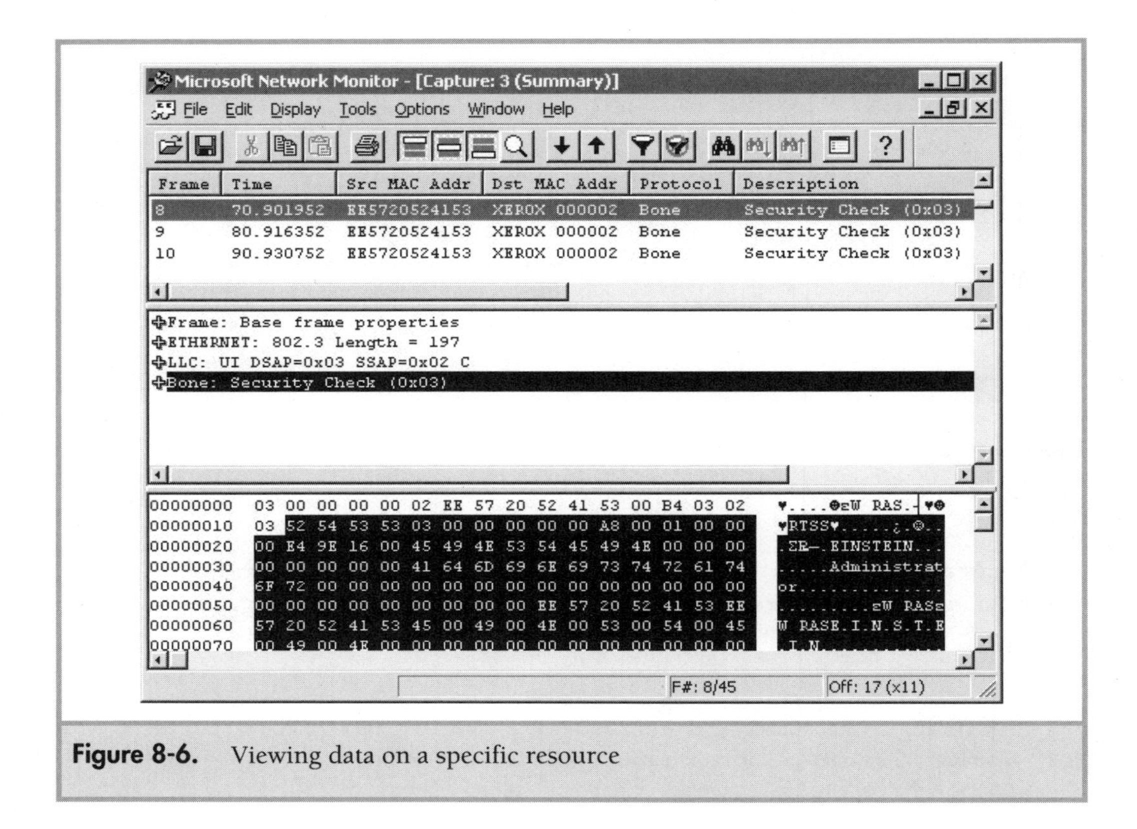

Figure 8-6. Viewing data on a specific resource

The data in the Network Monitor viewer can be saved to a capture file for later review, and also to compare it to future data captures. To make more sense of the data, you should insert some comment frames. To accomplish this, choose Tools | Insert Comment Frame. The Comment properties allow you to input specific text as a note or a bookmark. Later, when you open the saved capture file, the comments will help locate any issues you have identified. And, if the capture file has been forwarded on to another individual or group for review, they will also be able to see your notes.

NOTE: When saving capture files from the Display Capture Data option, be sure to turn off the Read Only option. Otherwise, the capture file may fail to open.

It's very important to be aware of these guidelines for capturing:

- If you change the default temporary capture directory, do not select a network or floppy drive. The temporary capture directory must be on a local, nonremovable drive. Also, when monitoring a remote computer, the temporary capture directory must be local to that computer.
- The maximum size for the capture buffer is 1MB. When this limit is reached, Network Monitor will still capture data (although some frames may be dropped due to storage availability), but when the capture is complete, there may not be enough free memory to display the results. Always save the capture results before trying to view them.
- When starting a new capture, Network Monitor prompts you to save the current data. You could receive an error message: "The file cannot be overwritten because access is denied." This is because Network Monitor cannot capture any frames, either because there is no network traffic or because you have strict filters in place in the current session. Just click No.
- If you use the Microsoft IntelliMouse, the mouse scroll wheel does not work in the Graph pane.

Filtering and Searching Data

In addition to being able to view and save data, you can filter the way the data is viewed and you can also perform context searches.

While in the Network Monitor viewer, click the Display Filter icon on the toolbar to open the Display Filter dialog box shown in Figure 8-7. By using the filter function, you can build a complete capture filter expression (similar to the way the SMS queries work). You can stipulate filtering on specific protocols, address pairs, and data patterns. You can choose to either include or exclude the information from the Capture window.

You can use the Find function on the toolbar to perform comprehensive searches of the collected data, based on the address, protocol, and specific property. The Find feature uses common operators to create the inclusive searches. These common operators include equal to (=), greater than (>), less than (<), greater than or equal to (>=), and less than or equal to (<=). Some less common operators that are included as part of the search are: contains, exists, and includes. Using these operators, you can quickly find specific data within the frames.

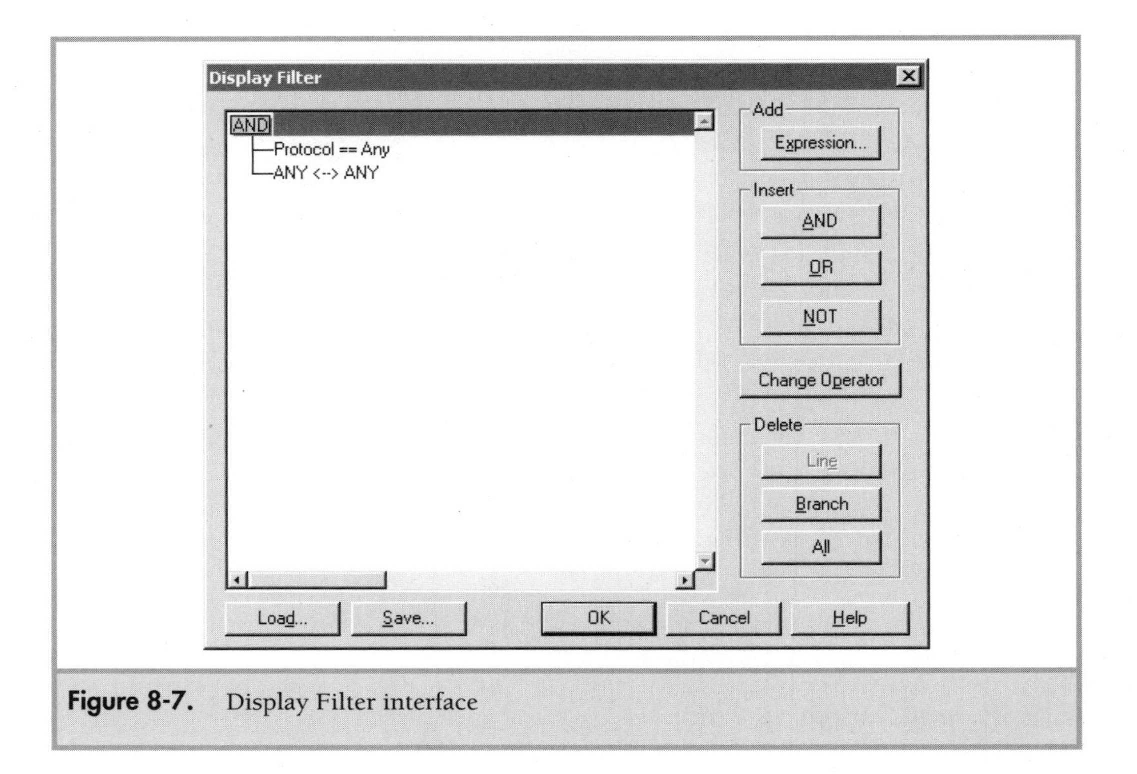

Figure 8-7. Display Filter interface

Network Monitor Experts

Another feature of the Network Monitor tool is the ability to run Experts, which are predefined queries you can run against the collected data. Choose Tools | Experts to access the Experts. Shown in Figure 8-8, the specific Experts that will help identify the network bandwidth for the SMS hierarchy are as follows:

- Average server response time
- TCP retransmit
- Top users

To use the Experts, you highlight the ones you require (you can select as many as you need) in the list on the left, click on the Add to Run List button, and then click the Run Experts button at the bottom right. The Expert(s) run and separate the collected data based on the built-in criteria.

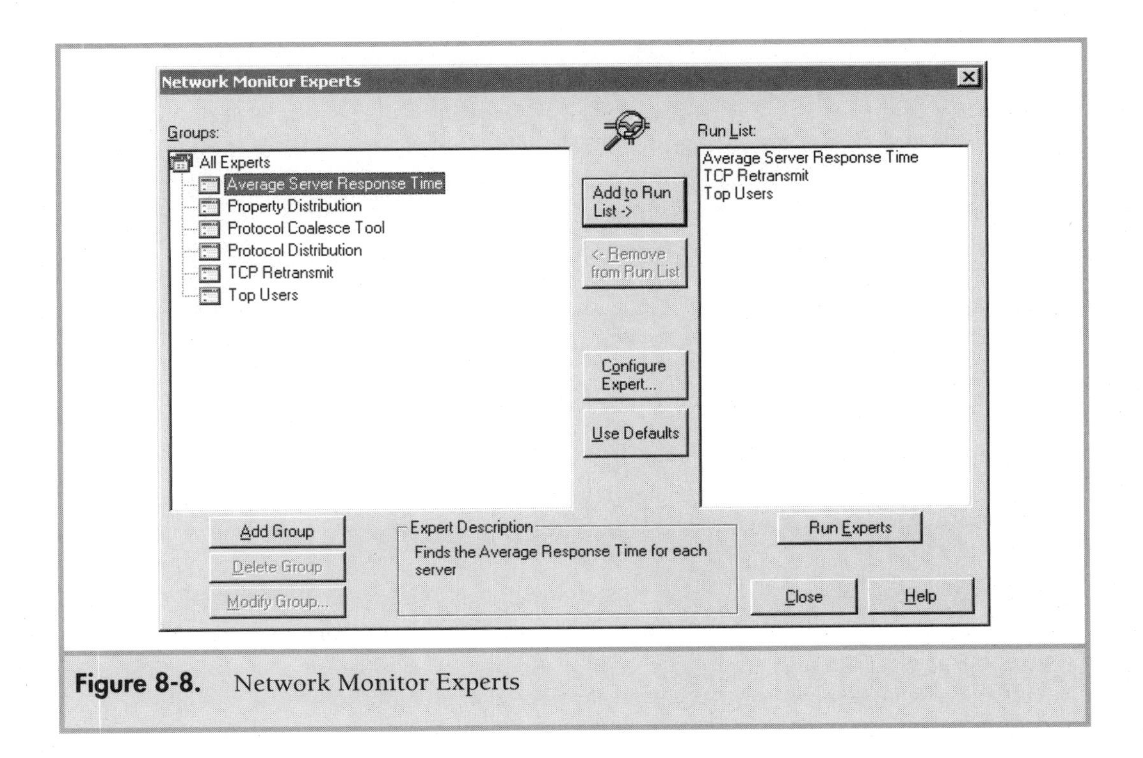

Figure 8-8. Network Monitor Experts

Distributing Network Monitor

To use network monitoring on a remote computer, you need to distribute the Network Monitor tool to the remote computer. When you create the distribution package, you must be aware of the following issue.

The Network Monitor's Setup.exe installation file has a hard-coded reference to the License.txt file in the \SMSSETUP directory on the SMS CD. To create a successful distribution of the Network Monitor installation, you must emulate the same directory structure contained on the SMS CD. In your package source directory, create both the \SMSSETUP and \NMEXT\<platform> directories. Copy the Network Monitor Setup.exe from the SMS CD into the newly created \NMEXT\<platform> directory. Then, copy the License.txt file from the SMS CD to the \SMSSETUP directory you created in the package's source directory. When you create the SMS package for Network Monitor, point to Setup.exe as the package's source executable. When SMS creates and stores the Network Monitor distribution package, it will compress and distribute the entire subdirectory structure.

CODE BLUE

You may experience a problem when trying to connect to the Network Monitor Agent on a remote Windows 2000 computer. The problem results in the error message: "Connection Failure Unknown. Error 0x80004002." This situation can be corrected by reregistering the Network Monitor Agent on the Windows 2000 computer. In a command prompt window, enter **regsvr32 psnppagn.dll.**

Network Trace

The Network Trace tool, installed as part of the SMS Administrator console, is another underutilized tool for determining network metrics. The Network Trace tool is accessed in the SMS Administrator console by navigating to the site systems section in the site settings node. When you right-click any of the listed site systems, you can choose Start Network Trace from the All Tasks menu.

When Network Trace starts, it polls the connections to the selected server and creates a graphical representation (shown in Figure 8-9) of the underlying network supplying connections to the SMS infrastructure.

Network Trace displays the following information in a graphical format:

- All servers found along the selected computer's route
- The SMS roles assigned to each server
- Network devices along the route (i.e., routers, hubs, switches, etc.)
- Subnets
- IP addresses

The information you gather from the Network Trace tool, along with the data you collect with Network Monitor, saves you time when you need to improve the network infrastructure for your SMS implementation. There is currently no option to save the Network Trace diagram, but you do have the option of printing it for review.

Network Trace can also be used as a diagnostic tool for the SMS hierarchy. If an SMS server or a network route is down, you can refresh the Network Trace display to determine when the failed connection is restored. Network Trace also lets you verify that all of the SMS servers are available. Network Trace sends an Internet Control Message Protocol (ICMP)

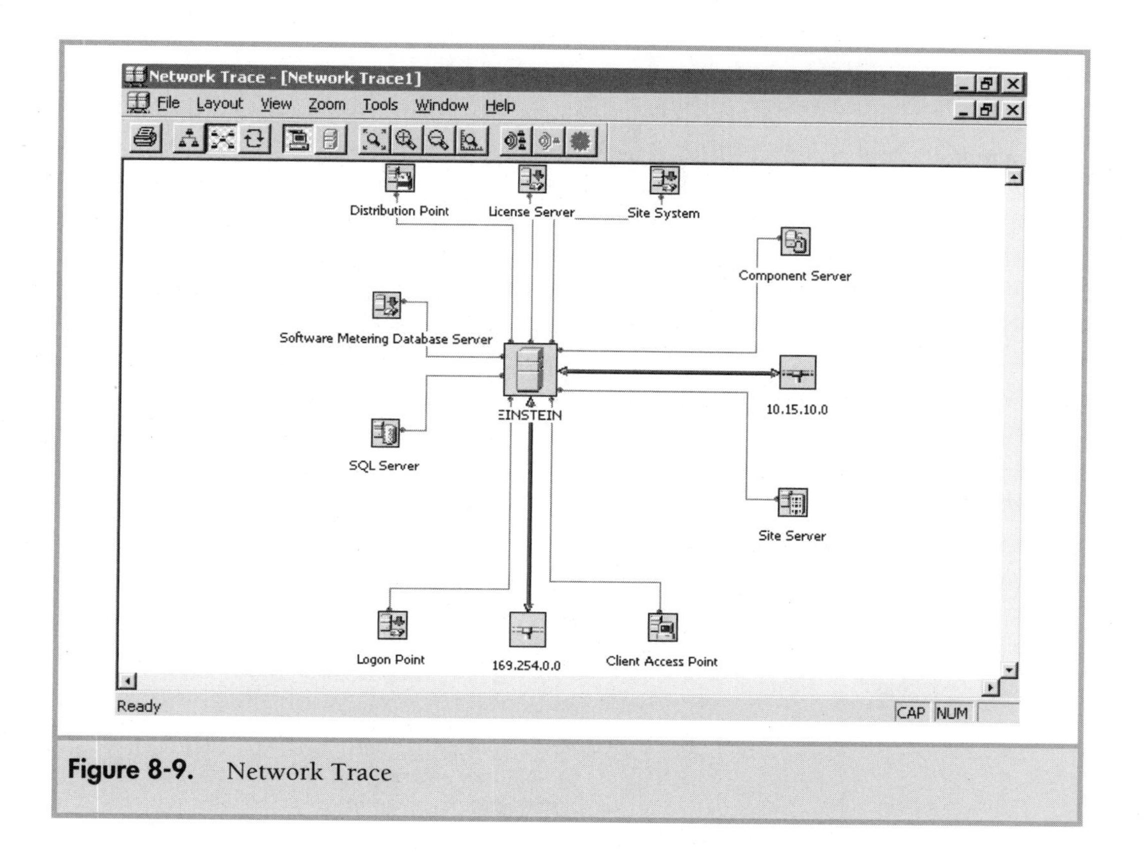

Figure 8-9. Network Trace

echo request along the route of the known SMS resources. If a resource does not return the echo, Network Trace determines that the SMS resource is unavailable and displays a Cloud icon where the resource should be in the diagram.

Another feature of Network Trace is the ability to poll the SMS components of a selected server and display the component status. This allows you to quickly determine if a component is failing.

NOTE: If Network Discovery is not enabled for the site, or has not been run at least once on all the subnets, Network Trace will only display information on the local subnet. Also, Network Trace will only diagram IP subnets.

Windows 2000/NT Performance Monitor

The Windows 2000/NT Performance Monitor provides one of the best tools for determining general network performance statistics. The object counters in Table 8-4 help you determine if your network is actually creating a bottleneck for the SMS infrastructure, and also help you conclude which network component(s) should be branded for problem resolution.

NOTE: If you are unsure whether a performance issue is network related, check the SMS log files first for more information. Hung SMS services and sluggish Client Agent processing can easily be mistaken for a slow network.

The Performance Monitor data can be viewed in real time by watching the graph, but this does not provide a long-term outlook of the network traffic. You should use Performance Monitor and the listed object counters to profile your network, much like you

Object	Counter	Information
Network Segment	%Utilization	A network utilization value of 80 percent or above indicates a network bottleneck.
Processor	Interrupts/sec	If this counter value increases radically, without a noticeable increase in server activity, it could indicate a hardware problem with the installed network adapter(s).
Server	Bytes Total/sec	You will want to consider segmenting your network if the bytes total/sec is close to or equal to the maximum transfer rate of the network.
Network Segment	%Network Utilization	The value from this counter will indicate when the network is at full capacity. If the value is 30-40 percent, you can expect data collisions.
Network Segment	Total frames received/sec	Use this counter to determine when networking bridges and routers are flooded with data.

Table 8-4. Performance Counters for Network Specific Troubleshooting and Planning

did with Network Monitor earlier in this chapter. To determine whether the network is causing a bottleneck for your SMS data, follow the same method described for Network Monitor: run Performance Monitor during low-traffic, medium-traffic, and high-traffic periods. The best way to accomplish this is to use the logging feature of the Performance Monitor. To create logs with Performance Monitor, follow these steps:

1. Choose View | Log.
2. Choose Edit | Add to Log.
3. In the Add to Log dialog box, select the computer (local or remote) for which you want to gather data into a log file.
4. In the Objects section, add the network object counters listed previously.
5. Under Options, select Log.
6. Under File Name, give the Log file a name that is descriptive of the data that is being logged.
7. Find the Update Time option at the bottom of the window and set this to 1 minute.
8. Click the Start Log button.

NOTE: When running Performance Monitor for an extended period of time, it is important to set the Update Time interval. If you run Performance Monitor for an hour or less, the default 15-second update interval should suffice. When using Performance Monitor to profile the network traffic, it should be allowed to run for a longer period, so, this update interval should be increased.

It's important to keep the following guidelines in mind:

- If the computer that is running Performance Monitor goes down, you can restart the logging and append the data to the original log file.
- If the user logs off the computer during logging, Performance Monitor stops. Performance Monitor can be installed as a Windows 2000/NT service.

When you are ready to review the log file, stop the logging and then open the log file. Keep in mind that unless you add the original objects and counters that were used during logging, the log file data will not be viewable.

General Network Performance Tips

Network bandwidth is one of the most common server bottlenecks. Using the Windows 2000/NT Performance Monitor and the SMS Network Monitor utility, you can determine the amount of traffic on your network. If the data you gather indicates that the level of traffic is close to its maximum and there are still CPU resources available, the network is the performance bottleneck.

You can improve overall network performance by reviewing and applying the following performance tips:

- **Increase the MTU window size** The network adapter should be configurable to change the MTU window size. The larger the MTU window size, the fewer packets are required to transfer data. See your network adapter's documentation for specific values and relative information.
- **Modify the TCP window size** The TCP window size determines the number of bytes that the sender can transmit without receiving an acknowledgement. For large, high-capacity networks, a larger window size will dramatically improve performance.

The TCP window size is modified through the server's registry. Add a REG_DWORD item named **TcpWindowSize** to HKEY_LOCAL_MACHINE\CurrentControlSet\Services\Tcpip\Parameters. Enter a value that represents the number of bytes (in Hex) for the window size (you need to verify the network adapter's values in the vendor's documentation).

CAUTION: If your network is generally unreliable, changing the TCP window size value could actually degrade network performance because the data needs to be retransmitted until it is received.

- **Add additional network adapters** Adding additional network adapters to the server helps balance the data received from the network with the data sent from the server.
- **Distribute access to data across multiple network segments** If you add additional network adapters, make sure to balance the network to take advantage of the extra

connection (similar to Figure 8-10). This is accomplished by segmenting the network across the available network adapters. Modern network switches also provide extra manageability for data routing. If you have used the SMS Network Trace utility, you should be able to quickly determine where the network should be segmented using the graphic diagram.

- **Unbind network adapters that are not being utilized** When multiple network adapters are installed in a server, but are not being used, the server's network services must still manage the inactive adapter and periodically check its status. Unbinding the network adapter will free the service processes to concentrate only on the active network adapter(s).
- **Remove unneeded network protocols** If your network does not use network protocols such as IPX or NetBIOS, remove these from the list of protocols. When these network protocols remain, they are bound to the installed network adapter and cause specific data packets to be transmitted over the network.
- **Reorganize the network access order** If your network environment includes a number of different network types, make sure the network access order is optimized to provide SMS with the fastest access.
- **Set the network adapter receive buffers for optimal performance** Modifying the network adapter's receive buffers allows a larger quantity of data to be received by queuing data to be acted upon.
- **Separate the network adapter from the other adapters** For servers with multiple PCI buses, install the network adapter in its own bus. It is generally a wise practice to completely separate the RAID controller from the network adapter, since the RAID controller utilizes a lot of server I/O.
- **Upgrade to Windows 2000** Windows 2000 provides much better data throughput management than earlier versions of Windows NT. There are specific technologies—such as TCP checksum offloading, advanced offloading features using smart network adapters, and Ipv6—that add to overall network performance gains.

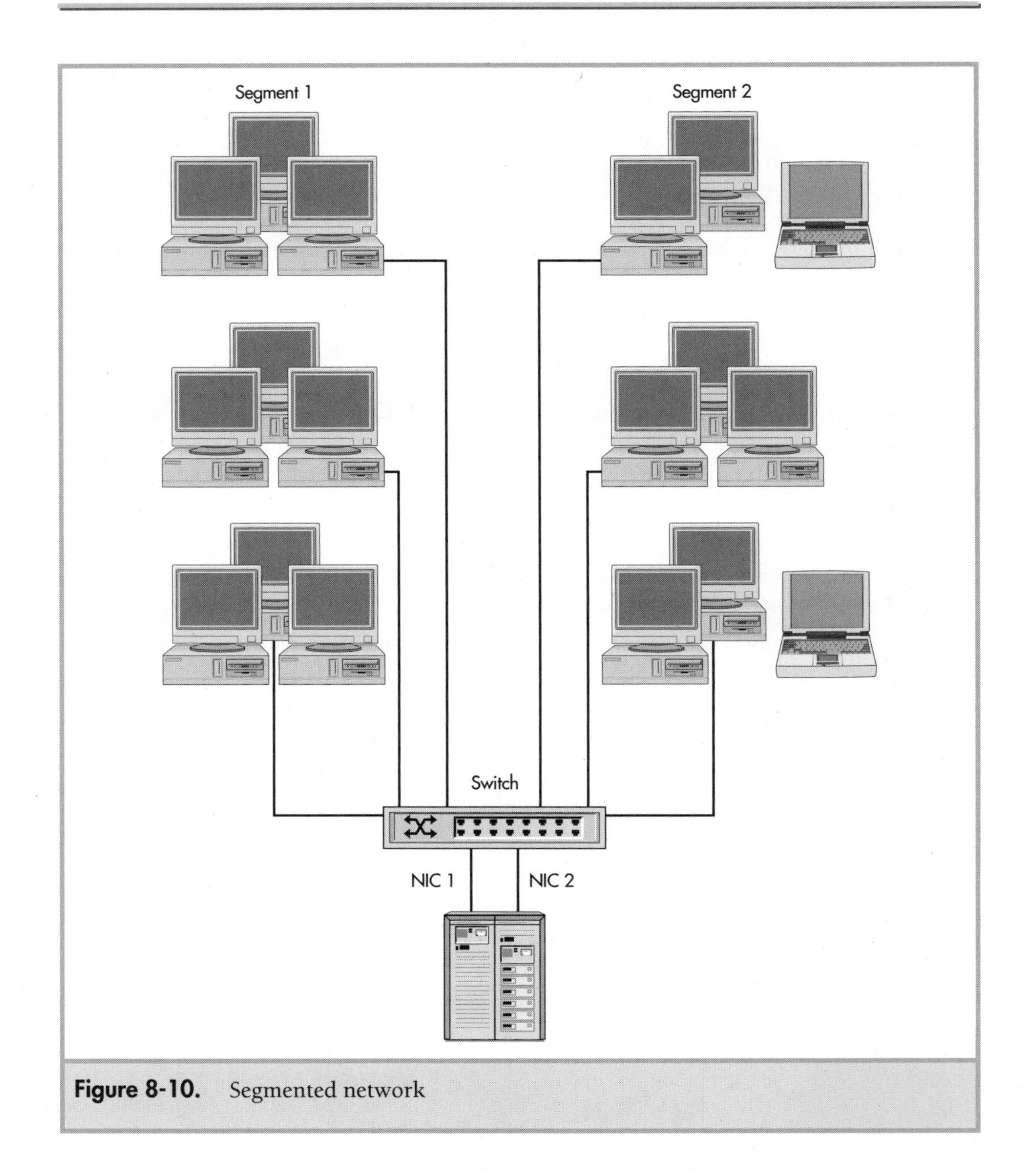

Figure 8-10. Segmented network

Chapter 9

Site Status

SMS contains a sophisticated mechanism that supplies a central location from which to monitor, review, and pinpoint troubles. Called the status system, it is the cornerstone of SMS troubleshooting. It provides tools to help you examine the SMS site status and to identify specific problem areas. The system status node in the SMS Administrator console should be your first stop for troubleshooting. The SMS status system is actually comprised of several different components: the individual service component logs, the individual thread components logs, the status filter rules, the status summarizers, the status message viewer, and the SMS query system.

Elements of Status Information

To make the information that is gleaned by the status system readily available, SMS provides several methods for obtaining both quick status information and comprehensive status reports.

Status Icons

To provide "at-a-glance" site status and component information, Microsoft formatted the SMS Administrator console to use graphical icons to indicate site condition. When you open system status in the SMS Administrator console, you see the Site Status icon. Expanding this below the site level, as shown in the next illustration, you can quickly identify any issues that the SMS site may be experiencing. Based on the illustration, it is clear that the SMS components need attention because of the Warning icon; and when delving into the Component Status window, it becomes evident that the SMS_LICENSE_SERVER_MANAGER is having problems.

NOTE: The status icons are only used to report component status and site system status. They are not used for package status and advertisement status.

Understanding the status icons can help determine whether you need to take immediate action to repair a problem with the SMS site, or if you can wait to see if the SMS components resolve the issue through their own self-repair mechanisms.

Error (critical) messages The Error Message icon (shown in the next illustration) indicates that a severe error has occurred that requires immediate attention. This means that the SMS site has stopped processing and will not continue to function until the issue is resolved.

The following are examples of problems that produce error messages:

- A server is down or unavailable.
- A hard disk or database has reached its capacity.
- Security problems.
- Critical SMS system files are missing.
- Data is corrupted.
- An operation has retried enough times to warrant an error message.

Warning messages The Warning icon (shown in the following illustration) indicates an error has occurred that can normally be resolved by the SMS system. The warning indicator means that this item should be flagged as a potential problem if the warning doesn't clear itself.

The following are examples of problems that produce warning messages:

- A hard disk or database is close to reaching its capacity.
- A noncritical file, such as a MIF file or DDR from a client, has been corrupted.
- A specific operation is taking a long time to complete processing.
- The SMS configuration is invalid.
- An operation has failed, but will be retried to resolve the problem.

Site Status OK The Site Status OK icon (shown in the following illustration) indicates the SMS site is functioning properly and has either experienced no errors or all errors have been resolved.

Status Filter Rules

The status filter rules, accessed in the site settings node of the SMS Administrator console, provide a way to help manage the amount of information that flows through the SMS site. During the initial SMS installation, several stock filters are included to manage the data flow, but you should review what is there and add any requirements for your site. The common reasons for creating additional status filter rules are to provide more functionality in the way that the status messages are handled, and to optimize the performance of the status message system. For example, your site may be flooded with many informative messages that you really don't care to see. You can use a status filter rule to keep a specific informational message ID from being stored in the status system. Not only does this keep the message from showing up, it also helps to increase the SMS server performance by filtering out unneeded messages that could take more processing power.

NOTE: Do not modify the default status filter rules. Not only are these extremely useful, but they are required for proper operation of the site. Become very familiar with the status filter rules before creating additional ones. If you are not careful, you could create a filter that makes the status system completely unusable as a troubleshooting tool.

The status filter rules allow you to filter the types of messages that are acted upon in the SMS site. These filters use the *FilterType* options described later in this chapter in the "Status Message Viewer" section. The filters also allow you to select the way the messages are handled by entering an action based on the component's threshold being reached. On the Actions tab of a specific status filter rule, SMS provides the following actions:

- **Write to the SMS database** Choosing this option writes the status message to the SMS SQL database so the data can be queried and manipulated. This option also allows you to select the number of days that the status message is retained before it is purged from the SMS database.
- **Report to the Windows NT event log** Selecting this option causes the component to write additional status message information to the Windows 2000 or Windows NT Application event log.

- **Replicated to the parent site** Setting this option forces the status message to replicate to the SMS parent site. This option also allows you to set the replication priority (Low, Medium, High).
- **Run a program** Based on the threshold for the component being reached, you can cause a specific program to be run. One example, shown in the next section, uses the NET SEND command to use a proactive alerting mechanism. Other examples include sending an e-mail alert, stopping or starting the specific service controlling a failing thread, or using a paging program to send an alert.
- **Do not forward to the status summarizers** Selecting this option causes the status message not to be included in status summarization.
- **Do not process lower-priority status filter rules** If this option is selected, the status message will prevent the lower-priority rules from being processed. The list of status filter rules in the SMS Administrator console is sorted by priority, with the most critical at the top.

Proactive Monitoring with Customized Status Programs

From time to time, after logging directly onto the SMS server, you may notice a pop-up window on the display indicating that a component is failing or has experienced a problem. These messages are queued and only displayed when someone logs onto the server console. A status filter rule initiates these messages. SMS can use an alerting process based on the "Run a program" setting in a status filter rule. The alert shown in the following illustration is the result of the LICENSE_SERVER_MANAGER having problems, and the status filter rule is configured to display an alert message.

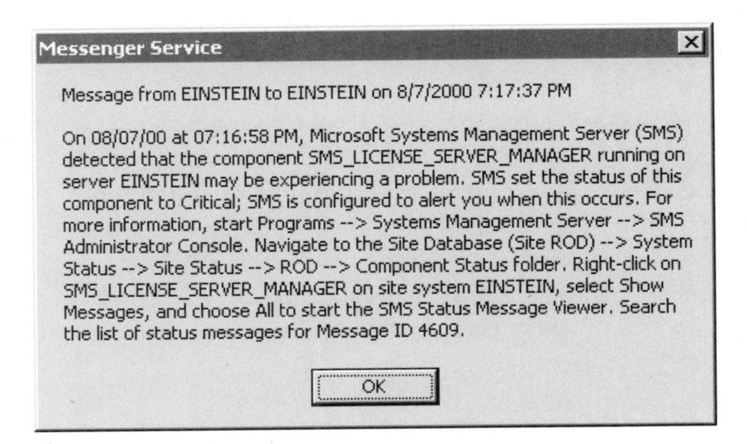

This "Messenger Service" is actually the NET SEND command configured to run when a threshold is reached. The NET SEND command is configured to give comprehensive information on the specific error, the component that produced the error, the server that is experiencing the error, and further steps on using the SMS Status Message Viewer to review the specific message ID number; in this case, message ID number: 4609.

The command that created the pop-up message in Figure 9-5 is as follows:

```
C:\WINNT\System32\net.exe send %sitesvr "On %msgltm/%msgltd/%msglty at
%msgltI:%msgltM:%msgltS %msgltp, Microsoft Systems Management Server (SMS)
detected that the component %msgis01 running on server %msgis02 may be
experiencing a problem. SMS set the status of this component to Critical; SMS is
configured to alert you when this occurs. For more information, start Programs -->
Systems Management Server --> SMS Administrator Console. Navigate to the Site
Database (Site %sc) --> System Status --> Site Status --> %msgsc --> Component
Status folder. Right-click on %msgis01 on site system %msgis02, select Show
Messages, and choose All to start the SMS Status Message Viewer. Search the list
of status messages for Message ID 4609."
```

NOTE: Shown in this NET SEND command, the status filter rule alert is configured to only display on the server that is experiencing the component errors. To view these alerts, you must be logged into the server and have access to the server's display (either sitting in front of it or using Remote Control) to see the messages. If you want to have the alerts sent to your specific computer, create a new status filter rule with the same command and replace the %sitesvr value with the NetBIOS name of your computer.

The NET SEND command is just one of many programs you can run as part of proactively monitoring the SMS site. For example, using the "Run a command" option in the status filter rules, you can receive an e-mail or pager alert when SMS_EXECUTIVE has problems, or when a package has been successfully delivered to all client computers. The ideas for using this option are endless, and they can help make the SMS system run smoothly and keep you well informed of any problems.

CODE BLUE

The "Run a command" option of the status filter rules can cause problems if you don't use it carefully. Call a program that exits gracefully, that is compatible with the SMS server applications, and that executes quickly. When the command runs, Status Manager processing pauses until the command exits. If the command fails, causes a problem with an SMS thread or component, or takes too long to exit, status messages aren't processed.

When you use a command with the status filter rules, you can tap into the status filter rules escape sequences. These escape sequences provide the ability to send alerts that include very comprehensive information on the site or component. Appendix F of the *SMS Administrator's Guide* contains the entire list of valid escape sequences to allow you to customize the information that is included with the alerts. For example, the command line:

```
net send rtrent "Hey, Rod! %msgcomp reported a %msgid error code. This indicates
that the %msgcomp service could not write to %msgsys's registry. This is a very
critical error and needs to be diagnosed immediately!"
```

sends the following message to my computer screen:

"Hey, Rod! SMS_EXECUTIVE reported a 579 error code. This indicates that the SMS_EXECUTIVE service could not write to EINSTEIN's registry. This is a very critical error and needs to be diagnosed immediately!"

%msgcomp is the escape code that represents the name of the service; %msgid is the escape code that represents the ID of the status message; and, %msgsys is the escape code that represents the name of the computer that reported the status message.

Status Summarizers

The status summarizers (accessed under the site Properties node of the SMS Administrator console) provide different levels of detail on the SMS Status Messages. Status summarizers provide real-time data on the overall health of the SMS sites and site hierarchies. They provide almost a "snapshot" of the hierarchy status as they recap the data into readable information. SMS provides four specific status summaries: component status, site system status, advertisement status, and package status.

The status summarizers use the following elements to summarize the SMS status message data:

- **Counts** The status summarizers use the counts to keep a record of the number of events that occur over a specific period of time. These counts are exhibited when you right-click on one of the status options under System Status and choose the Display Interval. They are also used to provide the query information available in the Status Message Viewer. Using the counts, the Status Message Viewer can filter status messages on any range of date and time.
- **States** The status summarizers use the states to record the last known condition of a component. This enables the SMS site to retain history information.

- **Display intervals** The display intervals are the set queries contained within the Display Interval option on the right-click menu of the status components. The status summarizers organize the data to fall within these set categories.
- **Status indicators** These status indicators, described earlier as the status icons, provide a quick look at the overall health of the site.
- **Thresholds** The status summarizers use thresholds to determine when to change the status of a component from just a Warning to Critical. If you look at the Thresholds tab in the properties of a status summarizer, you will see that these thresholds can be modified. In the components status summarizer, you can specify the number of error, warning, or informational messages that are received before the component's status is upgraded. In the site system status summarizer, you can change the data thresholds for databases and hard disks. The storage objects that SMS will add by default are the SMS database, the SMS transaction log, the License Metering database, and the License Metering database log. You can add any type of storage object, such as the E: drive of the server, and then set the Warning and Critical thresholds based on the free space that you determine should always be available. Used with the status filter rules, you can receive an alert when disk space is low on the server.

NOTE: Advertisement status and package status do not use thresholds.

Status Message Viewer

Shown in Figure 9-1, the SMS Status Message Viewer is the SMS central location for the reviewing of the SMS status messages retrieved by the system. The tool is generally accessed through the SMS Administrator console by right-clicking on a specific component (that has failed or exhibits a warning message) within the System Status node. When you right-click, a context menu allows you to swiftly query for all messages for the specific component, only the error messages, only the warning messages, or only the info messages. This quick context menu from the SMS Administrator console helps you rapidly pinpoint a trouble area and view verbose information to help resolve the problem. Looking at Figure 9-1, you can see the very detailed information that was made available for the SMS_NDS_LOGON_SERVER_MANAGER component. The Status Message Viewer allows you to immediately understand the situation by giving a specific problem description and offering a possible solution.

When the Status Message Viewer is opened, you are not limited to the information on the specific component you selected in the SMS Administrator console. The Status Message

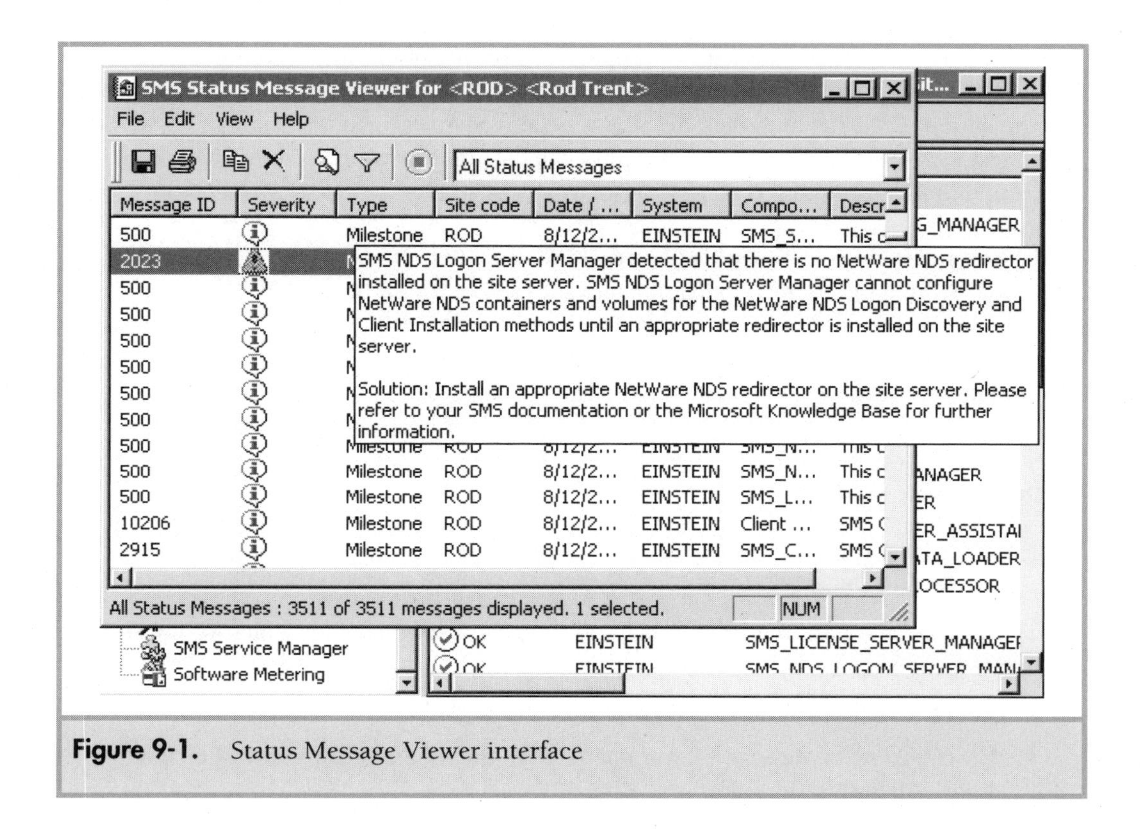

Figure 9-1. Status Message Viewer interface

Viewer is completely reliant on the SMS query system. When you look inside the System Status node and then at the status message queries, you find a wealth of queries that SMS included by default during its initial installation. These same queries are available by expanding the drop-down box on the toolbar of the Status Message Viewer.

To provide even more functionality, the Status Message Viewer offers very specific filtering options. These options are described in more detail later in this section. This provides a way to run the Status Message Viewer external to the SMS Administrator console. The command-line query options include all of the filtering options that are available within the Status Message Viewer.

The Status Message Viewer also allows you to customize the way the data is displayed, such as the specific column headings, the number of messages displayed at one time, how often the query is refreshed to retrieve new messages, font type and size, and export settings.

While the Status Message Viewer does provide printing of the status messages and saving to text files for later review, you must always have an initial connection to the SMS site in order to access the status messages. There is a better way to review the messages (described in the next section) that will allow you to take the data with you and examine it without a connection to the SMS site server.

Analyzing Status Messages with Microsoft Excel

The Status Message Viewer provides an excellent view of the status of the SMS system, but you may want to get an overall picture of the health of your SMS site in a way the Status Message Viewer cannot provide. You can export the status messages to a Microsoft Excel format that will allow you to review them offline. Using Microsoft Excel, you can get a comprehensive view of the SMS site and its child sites, and manipulate the data using Excel's built-in features and functions. To export the status message into Microsoft Excel, use the following steps:

1. In the SMS Administrator console, navigate to the Site Status node by expanding the system status node.
2. Open the site status and right-click on the specific site name for which you want to review the status messages.
3. From the right-click menu, choose Show Messages-All.
4. When the Status Message Viewer opens, click the toolbar's drop-down box and choose All Status Messages.
5. When prompted to specify the date and time range for the query, filter the Status Message Viewer on your specific requirements and click OK.
6. Once the query is complete and the status messages show in the window, choose File | Save As.
7. Name the file you are saving with an .xls extension, leaving the type of file as Tab Delimited.
8. After you save the file, you are prompted with the Export options. In the Exported Details section, choose All Possible Columns. In the Export Selection area, choose All Messages.
9. Click OK to finish the file save procedure.
10. Open the saved file in Microsoft Excel.

As shown in Figure 9-2, Microsoft Excel offers a comprehensive way to peruse the exported status messages. If you are familiar with Microsoft Excel and its features, you can now manipulate the data in any way you want and take it with you for a leisurely review.

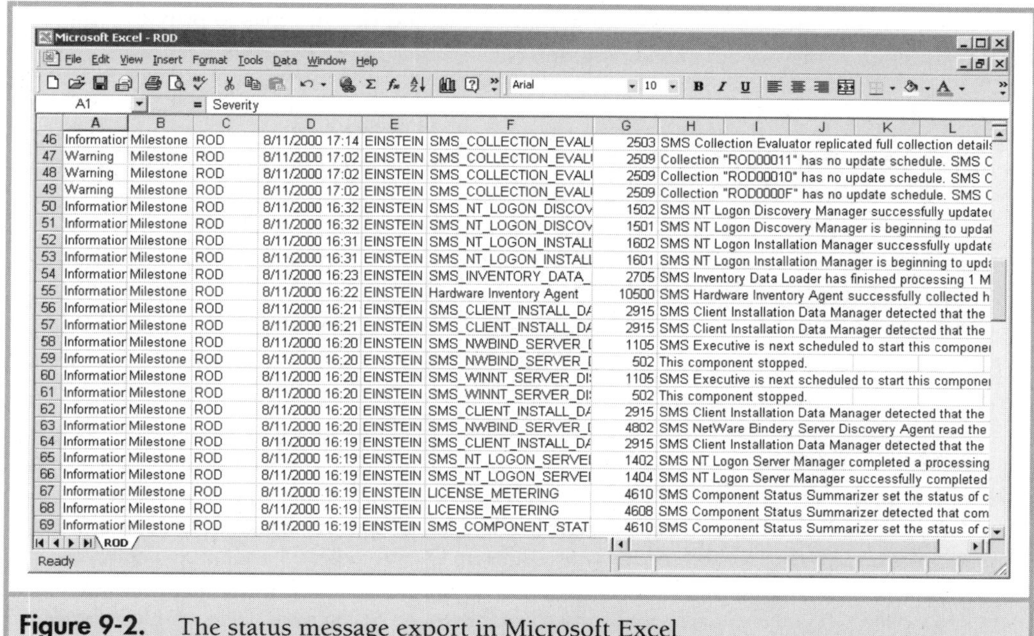

	A	B	C	D	E	F	G	H
46	Informatior	Milestone	ROD	8/11/2000 17:14	EINSTEIN	SMS_COLLECTION_EVALI	2503	SMS Collection Evaluator replicated full collection detail:
47	Warning	Milestone	ROD	8/11/2000 17:02	EINSTEIN	SMS_COLLECTION_EVALI	2509	Collection "ROD00011" has no update schedule. SMS C
48	Warning	Milestone	ROD	8/11/2000 17:02	EINSTEIN	SMS_COLLECTION_EVALI	2509	Collection "ROD00010" has no update schedule. SMS C
49	Warning	Milestone	ROD	8/11/2000 17:02	EINSTEIN	SMS_COLLECTION_EVALI	2509	Collection "ROD0000F" has no update schedule. SMS C
50	Informatior	Milestone	ROD	8/11/2000 16:32	EINSTEIN	SMS_NT_LOGON_DISCOV	1502	SMS NT Logon Discovery Manager successfully update
51	Informatior	Milestone	ROD	8/11/2000 16:32	EINSTEIN	SMS_NT_LOGON_DISCOV	1501	SMS NT Logon Discovery Manager is beginning to updat
52	Informatior	Milestone	ROD	8/11/2000 16:31	EINSTEIN	SMS_NT_LOGON_INSTALI	1602	SMS NT Logon Installation Manager successfully update
53	Informatior	Milestone	ROD	8/11/2000 16:31	EINSTEIN	SMS_NT_LOGON_INSTALI	1601	SMS NT Logon Installation Manager is beginning to upd
54	Informatior	Milestone	ROD	8/11/2000 16:23	EINSTEIN	SMS_INVENTORY_DATA_	2705	SMS Inventory Data Loader has finished processing 1 M
55	Informatior	Milestone	ROD	8/11/2000 16:22	EINSTEIN	Hardware Inventory Agent	10500	SMS Hardware Inventory Agent successfully collected h
56	Informatior	Milestone	ROD	8/11/2000 16:21	EINSTEIN	SMS_CLIENT_INSTALL_DA	2915	SMS Client Installation Data Manager detected that the
57	Informatior	Milestone	ROD	8/11/2000 16:21	EINSTEIN	SMS_CLIENT_INSTALL_DA	2915	SMS Client Installation Data Manager detected that the
58	Informatior	Milestone	ROD	8/11/2000 16:20	EINSTEIN	SMS_NWBIND_SERVER_I	1105	SMS Executive is next scheduled to start this compone
59	Informatior	Milestone	ROD	8/11/2000 16:20	EINSTEIN	SMS_NWBIND_SERVER_I	502	This component stopped.
60	Informatior	Milestone	ROD	8/11/2000 16:20	EINSTEIN	SMS_WINNT_SERVER_DI:	1105	SMS Executive is next scheduled to start this compone
61	Informatior	Milestone	ROD	8/11/2000 16:20	EINSTEIN	SMS_WINNT_SERVER_DI:	502	This component stopped.
62	Informatior	Milestone	ROD	8/11/2000 16:20	EINSTEIN	SMS_CLIENT_INSTALL_DA	2915	SMS Client Installation Data Manager detected that the
63	Informatior	Milestone	ROD	8/11/2000 16:20	EINSTEIN	SMS_NWBIND_SERVER_I	4802	SMS NetWare Bindery Server Discovery Agent read the
64	Informatior	Milestone	ROD	8/11/2000 16:19	EINSTEIN	SMS_CLIENT_INSTALL_DA	2915	SMS Client Installation Data Manager detected that the
65	Informatior	Milestone	ROD	8/11/2000 16:19	EINSTEIN	SMS_NT_LOGON_SERVEI	1402	SMS NT Logon Server Manager completed a processing
66	Informatior	Milestone	ROD	8/11/2000 16:19	EINSTEIN	SMS_NT_LOGON_SERVEI	1404	SMS NT Logon Server Manager successfully completed
67	Informatior	Milestone	ROD	8/11/2000 16:19	EINSTEIN	LICENSE_METERING	4610	SMS Component Status Summarizer set the status of c
68	Informatior	Milestone	ROD	8/11/2000 16:19	EINSTEIN	LICENSE_METERING	4608	SMS Component Status Summarizer detected that com
69	Informatior	Milestone	ROD	8/11/2000 16:19	EINSTEIN	SMS_COMPONENT_STAT	4610	SMS Component Status Summarizer set the status of c

Figure 9-2. The status message export in Microsoft Excel

Running Status Message Viewer Externally

For convenience, the Status Message Viewer can be run outside of the SMS Administrator console. The StatView.exe file is the executable that runs the Status Message Viewer application. When the Status Message Viewer is run from with the SMS Administrator console, a specific query is performed in the background based on the component or service and the message type you choose. This query can be run with the StatView.exe file to create a shortcut that will open the Status Message Viewer in a format that you use most often. The StatView.exe command is located in the <*Driveletter*>:\SMSAdmin\Bin\<*platform*> directory of the computer that has the SMS Administrator console installed on it.

CAUTION: StatView.exe must be run from the <driveletter>:\SMSAdmin\Bin\<platform> directory because it is dependent on a horde of DLL files that already exist in this directory and were registered with the operating system during the installation of the SMS Administrator console.

The command line for running the Status Message Viewer external to the SMS Administrator console is:

statview [options] *@optionfile1 @optionfile2*

The command-line options are separated into several different types to provide simple startup parameters or very advanced parameters.

- **Basic Query Options**
  - **/SMS:DisplayQuery=<QueryID>** (Launches the viewer and displays the status viewer with the specified query ID.)
- **Advanced Command Line Options**
  - /SMS:<QueryType>=<QueryValue>
  - /SMS:<FilterType>=<FilterValue>
  - /SMS:<FilterType>=<Partial FilterValue>

NOTE: Multiple QueryTypes can be on the same command line or loaded via the ASCII text file option OPTIONFILE. @OPTIONFILE will always include the path to the file or it will be assumed that the file is in this directory when executed. There are no spaces around the "=" and a single space is an indicator between option types. Different QueryTypes on the same command line implies AND between them, while the same QueryType indicates OR. There are no spaces around the "=" and a single space is an indicator between option types. Different QueryTypes on the same command line implies AND between them, while the same QueryType indicates OR.

- **QueryType Options**
  - **SITE=<SITE STR>** (The SITE STR is the specific site code.)
  - **SYSTEM=<SYSTEM STR>** (The SYSTEM STR is a Windows 2000 or Windows NT computer name.)
  - **SOURCE=<SOURCE MOD STR>** (The SOURCE MOD STR indicates a specific module name such as "SMS SERVER" or "SMS CLIENT.")
  - **COMPONENT=<COMP STR>** (The COMP STR is the specific SMS component name.)
  - **SEVERITY=<SEV STR>** (The SEV STR is the specific severity message. The valid values are INFO, WARNING, or ERROR.)
  - **MESSAGETYPE=<TYPE>** (The TYPE is the status message type. The valid values are MILESTONE, DETAIL, or AUDIT.)
  - **MSGID=<MSGID>** (The MSGID is the specific message ID.)

- **PROPERTY=<ID>** (This value accepts the specific property of the status message.)
- **PROPERTY=<ID>,<STR VALUE>** (This option retrieves the specific property of the status message that is set to the specified string value.)
- **STARTTIME=<TIME STR>** | Prompt (Includes only messages at or after this time. The Prompt option specifies that the viewer should prompt you for a start date and time before running the query. <TIME STR> must be formatted as [year][month][day][military time].[microseconds(three digits)].)
- **ENDTIME=<TIME STR>** | Prompt (Includes only messages at or before this time. The Prompt option specifies that the viewer should prompt you for an end date and time before running the query. <TIME STR> must be formatted as [year][month][day][military time].[microseconds(three digits)].)

- **Advanced Query Options**
  - **PID=<PID>** (Retrieves the 32-bit process ID.)
  - **TID=<TID>** (Retrieves the 32-bit thread ID.)
  - **PERCLIENT=<Boolean>** (The Boolean value (TRUE or FALSE) indicates whether or not you want to retrieve messages generated on a per client basis. TRUE = yes; FALSE = no.)
  - **WIN32ERR=<ERROR INT>** (The specific 32-bit error code.)
  - **INSSTR<X>=<VALUE>** (This retrieves the value of the specific insertion string.)
- **FilterType Options**
  - **FSITE=<SITE STR>** (The SITE STR is the specific site code.)
  - **FSYSTEM=<SYSTEM STR>** (The SYSTEM STR is the Windows 2000 or Windows NT computer name as would be displayed using the NET VIEW command. You can use partial strings.)
  - **FSOURCE=<SOURCE MOD STR>** (Filters on the specific module name. Examples of valid values are "SMS SERVER," "SMS CLIENT," or "THIRD PARTY." Partial strings cannot be used.)
  - **FCOMPONENT=<COMP STR>** (The COMP STR indicates the specific SMS component name as it would appear in the Status Message Viewer. You can use partial string values.)

- **FSEVERITY=<SEV STR>** (The SEV STR is the specific severity message. The valid values are INFO, WARNING, or ERROR.)
- **FMESSAGETYPE=<TYPE>** (The TYPE is the status message type. The valid values are MILESTONE, DETAIL, or AUDIT.)
- **FMSGID=<MSGID>** (The MSGID is the specific message ID.)
- **FPROPERTY=<ID>** (This value accepts the specific property of the status message.)
- **FPROPERTY=<ID>,<STR VALUE>** (This value accepts the specific property of the status message.)
- **FDESCRIPT="<String to Match>"** (Filters on the description of a message ID. You can use partial string values.)
- **FPID=<PID>** (Filters on the 32-bit process ID.)
- **FTID=<TID>** (Filters on the 32-bit thread ID.)
- **FSTARTTIME=<TIME STR>** (Filters on messages at or after this time. <TIME STR> must be formatted as [year][month][day][military time].[microseconds (three digits)].)
- **FENDTIME=<TIME STR>** (Filters on messages at or before this time. <TIME STR> must be formatted as [year][month][day][military time].[microseconds(three digits)].)

- **Remote Connection Options**
  - **Server=\\servername** (The servername is the name of the remote server you want to connect to when the Status Message Viewer starts.)
  - **Path=namespace** (The namespace relates to the specific WBEM namespace you want to connect to when the Status Message Viewer starts. For example: Root\SMS\SiteCode.)

Status Message Log Files

The SMS log files must be used in conjunction with the status messages to fully troubleshoot the SMS site. The log files in Table 9-1 indicate the SMS site components that the SMS status message system uses to report the overall status of the site and its individual processes. The log files in Table 9-2 list the log files associated with Client Agent status processing.

Component	Log file
Status Manager Service	SMS\Logs\Statmgr.log
Client Configuration Manager	SMS\Logs\Ccm.log
Client Install Data Manager	SMS\Logs\Colleval.log
Collection Evaluator	SMS\Logs\Colleval.log
Component Status Summarizer	SMS\Logs\Compsumm.log
Courier Sender Confirmation	SMS\Logs\Cscnfsvc.log
Despooler	SMS\Logs\Despool.log
Discovery Data Manager	SMS\Logs\Ddm.log
Distribution Manager	SMS\Logs\Distmgr.log
Hierarchy Manager	SMS\Logs\Hman.log
Inbox Manager	SMS\Logs\Inboxmgr.log
Inbox Manager Assistant	SMS\Logs\Inboxast.log
Inventory Data Loader	SMS\Logs\Dataldr.log
Inventory Processor	SMS\Logs\Invproc.log
LAN Sender	SMS\Logs\Sender.log
License Metering	SMS\Logs\Licrsvc.log
License Server Manager	SMS\Logs\Licsvcfg.log
Network Discovery	SMS\Logs\Netdisc.log
Windows NT Logon Discovery Agent	SMS\Logs\Ntlgdsca.log
Windows NT Logon Discovery Manager	SMS\Logs\Ntlgdscm.log
Windows NT Logon Server Manager	SMS\Logs\NT_logon.log
Offer Manager	SMS\Logs\Offermgr.log
Offer Status Summarizer	SMS\Logs\Offersum.log
Replication Manager	SMS\Logs\Replmgr.log
Scheduler	SMS\Logs\Sched.log
Site Component Manager	SMS\Logs\Sitecomp.log
Site Control Manager	SMS\Logs\Sitectrl.log
Site System Status Summarizer	SMS\Logs\Sitestat.log
Software Inventory Processor	SMS\Logs\Sinvproc.log
SMS Executive	SMS\Logs\SMSexec.log
SMS SQL Monitor	SMS\Logs\SMSdbmon.log
Windows NT Server Discovery Agent	SMS\Logs\Ntsvrdis.log

Table 9-1. Status Message Server Components and Associated Log Files

Client Agent	Log File
Status Manager Service	%WINDIR%\MS\SMS\Logs\Statmgr.log
Copy Queue Manager	%WINDIR%\MS\SMS\Logs\Cqmgr32.log (32-bit client)
	%WINDIR%\MS\SMS\Logs\Clearque.log (16-bit client)
SMS Client Agent	The specific Client Agent log files in the %WINDIR%\MS\SMS\Logs directory on the client computer.

Table 9-2. Status Message Client Agents and Associated Log Files

Enabling Logging

By default, logging is not enabled for all components. The primary reason for this is that logging adds an additional 10–20 percent to the processor utilization of the server. But, the benefits definitely outweigh the increase in processor consumption. Without logging, it is nearly impossible to troubleshoot SMS issues.

Each specific component and service can be set to report status information to its log file. There are several ways to do this, and they are discussed in the following sections.

Enabling Component Logging Through SMS Service Manager

The primary way to enable logging is to run the SMS Service Manager and enable the log for each component individually. You perform this function in the SMS Service Manager by right-clicking the mouse cursor on a specific component and choosing the Logging option, as shown in Figure 9-3. Once the Component Logging Control dialog box displays, you can click the check box to enable the logging for the component, modify the path and filename of the log file, and change the maximum log file size (1MB is the default).

The SMS Service Manager provides a central location to manage the SMS services, threads, and components. It allows you to do this by providing quick queries for each component, along with the ability to stop, pause, start, and restart the SMS services.

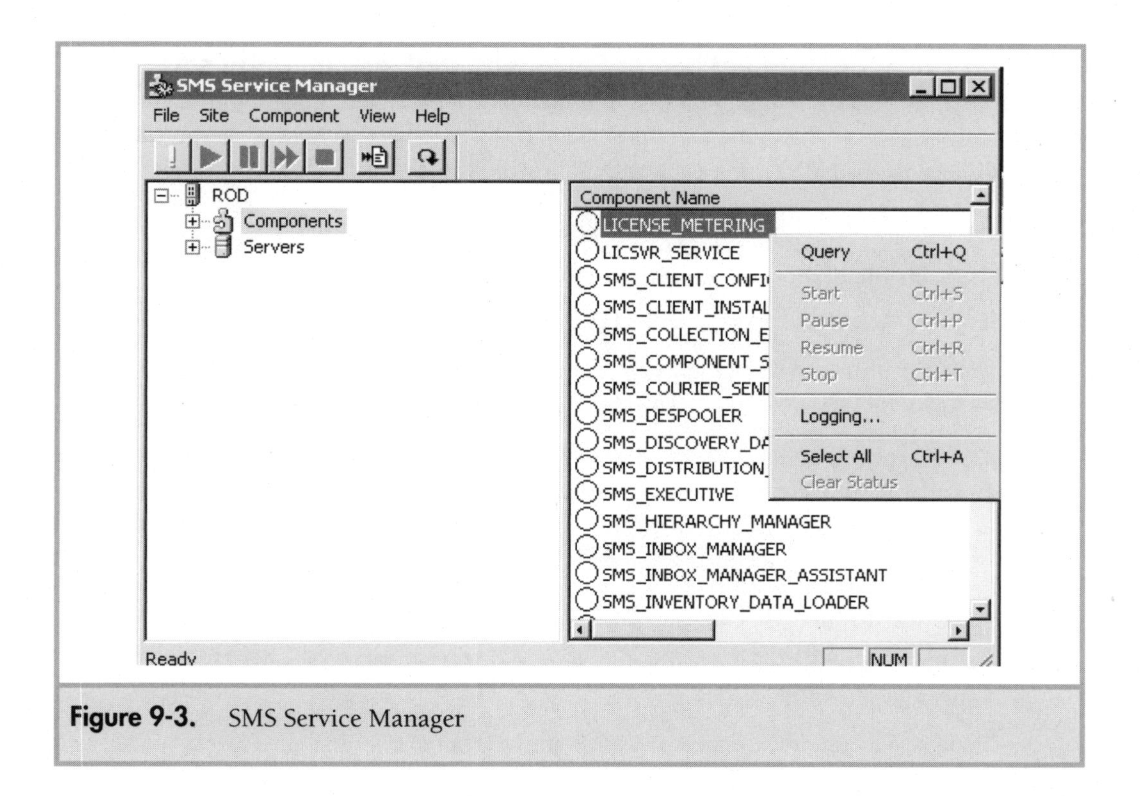

Figure 9-3. SMS Service Manager

NOTE: You can run SMS Service Manager outside of the SMS Administrator console by creating a shortcut to the Compmgr.exe file on the local computer. For any computer that has the SMS Administrator console installed, the Compmgr.exe file is located in the <driveletter>:\SMSAdmin\Bin\<platform> directory (Compmgr.exe is also located on the SMS site server in the \SMS\Bin\<platform> directory). Also note that you can create a shortcut that opens SMS Service Manager and automatically connects to a specific SMS server by using the following command line: **Compmgr.exe <Servername>**. This will allow you to set up a different program shortcut for servers that you normally connect with in order to manage the SMS services. A program that will set up these different shortcuts for you can be found at http://www.swynk.com/trent/servmanq.asp.

Enabling Every Component Log at Once with dial_me_in_baby.sms

As indicated, by default, logging for all components is not enabled. Logging for each component must be enabled one at a time through the SMS Service Manager. You can enable all logs on the SMS server at once by following these steps:

1. Use Notepad to create a blank file called **dial_me_in_baby.sms**.
2. Place this file in the root of the SMS server's C: drive.
3. Stop and Restart the SMS_EXECUTIVE service using the SMS Service Manager.
4. Using the SMS Service Manager, stop and restart the SITE_COMPONENT_MANAGER service.

Remember, turning on logging for all components requires more processing power from the server. Turn off this feature when it is not needed. Deleting the file and then stopping and restarting the services does not turn this feature off. You must use the following steps to set the logging back to the default:

1. Delete the dial_me_in_baby.sms file.
2. Run Regedit, and navigate to the following key: HKEY_LOCAL_MACHINE\Software\Microsoft\SMS\Tracing.
3. Change the data of the enabled value from 1 (Hex) to 0.
4. Using SMS Service Manager, stop and restart the SMS_EXECUTIVE service.
5. Stop and restart the SITE_COMPONENT_MANAGER service using the SMS Service Manager.

Enabling Single Component Logs Using the Registry

While you are reviewing the SMS Tracing registry key (HKEY_LOCAL_MACHINE\Software\Microsoft\SMS\Tracing), notice the list of components, each in its own subkey. These relate to each SMS component for which logging can be enabled. Contained within each subkey are the following values:

- **Enabled** A data value of 1 (REG_DWORD; Hex) enables logging for the component, and a data value of 0 disables logging.
- **MaxFileSize** This data value (REG_DWORD; Hex) can be modified to change the allowable size of the log file once it is enabled. The default is 1MB.
- **TraceFilename** This data value (REG_SZ) contains the path and file name to the component's log file.

Enabling Component Logging Using SMS Installer

You can easily create an SMS Installer script to make these modifications for you. The following script example turns on logging for the SMS_DISTRIBUTION_MANAGER. Similarly, you can use an SMS Installer script to modify the maximum log size and change the location and name of the specific log file using the value and data value information from the previous section:

```
--Begin Script
item: Edit Registry
  Total Keys=1
Key=HKEY_LOCAL_MACHINE\Software\Microsoft\SMS\Tracing\SMS_DISTRIBUTION_MANAGER
  New Value=1
  Value Name=Enabled
  Root=2
  Data Type=3
end
--End Script
```

To provide even more functionality, you could create an SMS Installer script that prompts with a dialog screen that has each component listed, as well as radio button options for turning the specific component log on or off. SMS Installer is an excellent tool to automate this process. To create this utility, you just need to modify the particular registry values in the following keys:

- HKEY_LOCAL_MACHINE\SOFTWARE\Microsoft\SMS\Tracing\LICENSE_METERING
- HKEY_LOCAL_MACHINE\SOFTWARE\Microsoft\SMS\Tracing\SMS_CLIENT_CONFIG_MANAGER
- HKEY_LOCAL_MACHINE\SOFTWARE\Microsoft\SMS\Tracing\SMS_CLIENT_INSTALL_DATA_MGR
- HKEY_LOCAL_MACHINE\SOFTWARE\Microsoft\SMS\Tracing\SMS_COLLECTION_EVALUATOR
- HKEY_LOCAL_MACHINE\SOFTWARE\Microsoft\SMS\Tracing\SMS_COMPONENT_STATUS_SUMMARIZER
- HKEY_LOCAL_MACHINE\SOFTWARE\Microsoft\SMS\Tracing\SMS_COURIER_SENDER_CONFIRMATION
- HKEY_LOCAL_MACHINE\SOFTWARE\Microsoft\SMS\Tracing\SMS_DESPOOLER

- HKEY_LOCAL_MACHINE\SOFTWARE\Microsoft\SMS\Tracing\SMS_DISCOVERY_DATA_MANAGER
- HKEY_LOCAL_MACHINE\SOFTWARE\Microsoft\SMS\Tracing\SMS_DISTRIBUTION_MANAGER
- HKEY_LOCAL_MACHINE\SOFTWARE\Microsoft\SMS\Tracing\SMS_EXECUTIVE
- HKEY_LOCAL_MACHINE\SOFTWARE\Microsoft\SMS\Tracing\SMS_HIERARCHY_MANAGER
- HKEY_LOCAL_MACHINE\SOFTWARE\Microsoft\SMS\Tracing\SMS_INBOX_MANAGER
- HKEY_LOCAL_MACHINE\SOFTWARE\Microsoft\SMS\Tracing\SMS_INBOX_MANAGER_ASSISTANT
- HKEY_LOCAL_MACHINE\SOFTWARE\Microsoft\SMS\Tracing\SMS_INVENTORY_DATA_LOADER
- HKEY_LOCAL_MACHINE\SOFTWARE\Microsoft\SMS\Tracing\SMS_INVENTORY_PROCESSOR
- HKEY_LOCAL_MACHINE\SOFTWARE\Microsoft\SMS\Tracing\SMS_LAN_SENDER
- HKEY_LOCAL_MACHINE\SOFTWARE\Microsoft\SMS\Tracing\SMS_LICENSE_SERVER_MANAGER
- HKEY_LOCAL_MACHINE\SOFTWARE\Microsoft\SMS\Tracing\SMS_NDS_LOGON_SERVER_MANAGER
- HKEY_LOCAL_MACHINE\SOFTWARE\Microsoft\SMS\Tracing\SMS_NETWORK_DISCOVERY
- HKEY_LOCAL_MACHINE\SOFTWARE\Microsoft\SMS\Tracing\SMS_NT_LOGON_DISCOVERY_AGENT
- HKEY_LOCAL_MACHINE\SOFTWARE\Microsoft\SMS\Tracing\SMS_NT_LOGON_DISCOVERY_MANAGER
- HKEY_LOCAL_MACHINE\SOFTWARE\Microsoft\SMS\Tracing\SMS_NT_LOGON_INSTALLATION_MANAGER
- HKEY_LOCAL_MACHINE\SOFTWARE\Microsoft\SMS\Tracing\SMS_NT_LOGON_SERVER_MANAGER

- HKEY_LOCAL_MACHINE\SOFTWARE\Microsoft\SMS\Tracing\SMS_NT_USER_DISCOVERY_AGENT
- HKEY_LOCAL_MACHINE\SOFTWARE\Microsoft\SMS\Tracing\SMS_NT_USER_GROUP_DISCOVERY_AGENT
- HKEY_LOCAL_MACHINE\SOFTWARE\Microsoft\SMS\Tracing\SMS_NW_LOGON_SERVER_MANAGER
- HKEY_LOCAL_MACHINE\SOFTWARE\Microsoft\SMS\Tracing\SMS_NWBIND_SERVER_DISCOVERY_AGENT
- HKEY_LOCAL_MACHINE\SOFTWARE\Microsoft\SMS\Tracing\SMS_OFFER_MANAGER
- HKEY_LOCAL_MACHINE\SOFTWARE\Microsoft\SMS\Tracing\SMS_OFFER_STATUS_SUMMARIZER
- HKEY_LOCAL_MACHINE\SOFTWARE\Microsoft\SMS\Tracing\SMS_REPLICATION_MANAGER
- HKEY_LOCAL_MACHINE\SOFTWARE\Microsoft\SMS\Tracing\SMS_SCHEDULER
- HKEY_LOCAL_MACHINE\SOFTWARE\Microsoft\SMS\Tracing\SMS_SITE_BACKUP
- HKEY_LOCAL_MACHINE\SOFTWARE\Microsoft\SMS\Tracing\SMS_SITE_COMPONENT_MANAGER
- HKEY_LOCAL_MACHINE\SOFTWARE\Microsoft\SMS\Tracing\SMS_SITE_CONTROL_MANAGER
- HKEY_LOCAL_MACHINE\SOFTWARE\Microsoft\SMS\Tracing\SMS_SITE_SYSTEM_STATUS_SUMMARIZER
- HKEY_LOCAL_MACHINE\SOFTWARE\Microsoft\SMS\Tracing\SMS_SOFTWARE_INVENTORY_PROCESSOR
- HKEY_LOCAL_MACHINE\SOFTWARE\Microsoft\SMS\Tracing\SMS_SQL_MONITOR
- HKEY_LOCAL_MACHINE\SOFTWARE\Microsoft\SMS\Tracing\SMS_STATUS_MANAGER
- HKEY_LOCAL_MACHINE\SOFTWARE\Microsoft\SMS\Tracing\SMS_WINNT_SERVER_DISCOVERY_AGENT

Reviewing the Log Files

Using the Service and Thread Component list covered in this chapter, you can identify the specific log files. You can open the log files in any program that can read ASCII text files, but this does not provide a perfect way for searching specific data for troubleshooting. Also, depending on the log configuration, the log files can become too large to sift through with a standard text file reader. To provide more functionality for searching the log files, you need to use a separate program. Two very useful programs, described in the next sections, will help you make sense of the data that is contained in the log files.

Real-Time Monitoring with SMS Trace

Included in the Microsoft Systems Management Server 2.0 Resource Guide is the SMS Trace utility (shown in Figure 9-4). SMS Trace provides detailed, real-time monitoring of the service and component log files. Multiple log files may be opened simultaneously to monitor the operation of several SMS components at once.

In addition to allowing you to review the SMS logs in real time, SMS Trace also provides options to maximize the viewing experience. SMS Trace contains the following features:

- You can browse the network to quickly connect to a specific SMS server in the organization.
- SMS Trace automatically starts in the \SMS\Logs directory on the connected SMS server.
- You can pause the real-time log monitoring to review the data.
- You can filter the log files by specific text, component, or thread, or date and time.
- You can highlight specific log entries based on a custom text string.
- You can search the open log file for specific text.
- SMS Trace can be configured to become the default viewer for any log file (.log extension).
- You can change the interval at which the log file is updated (the default is 500 milliseconds).
- SMS Trace includes full save functions.
- SMS Trace includes full printing functions.

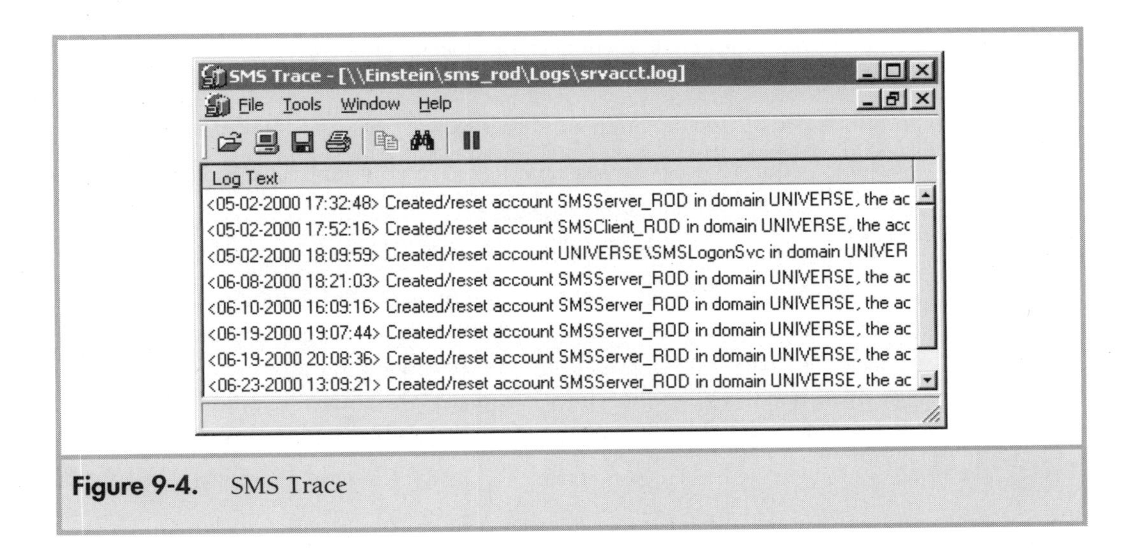

Figure 9-4. SMS Trace

NOTE: SMS Trace requires the smsmfc.dll, base.dll, trace.reg, and tracer.dll files.

Comprehensive Searching with "Search"

One of the hardest things to accomplish when searching the log files is to quickly pinpoint a specific error message or text string that indicates a problem. While SMS Tracer does a great job of reviewing the log files in real time, it does not offer a comprehensive search facility.

SadMan Software has a free utility, downloadable from http://www.simes.clara.net/programs/search.htm. You must register the program, but the registration is free, and the Web site provides a mailto: link so you can easily send the registration request. I received registration information back within an hour after sending the e-mail.

Search offers the following features:

- It allows you to search for logical combinations of up to two search strings.
- Logical combinations can be AND, OR, or AND NOT.
- You can optionally see the lines from the files that matched the search criteria.

- You can find all files that match a wildcard file specification by omitting the search strings.
  - It can optionally recurse through subdirectories.
  - It remembers your 12 previous search criteria, so you don't have to keep reentering information that you use frequently.
  - You can easily edit a file from the result list, using the text editor of your choice.

The interface is clean and easy to use, and the program is powerful enough to search through all the SMS log files for all instances of a specific error message. The example shown in Figure 9-5 allowed me to search the \Logs directory for any log files that contained the strings "thread" and "stopped." When the utility completed the search, I could review the results, which allowed me to quickly identify the SMS threads that had been stopped due to a processing error.

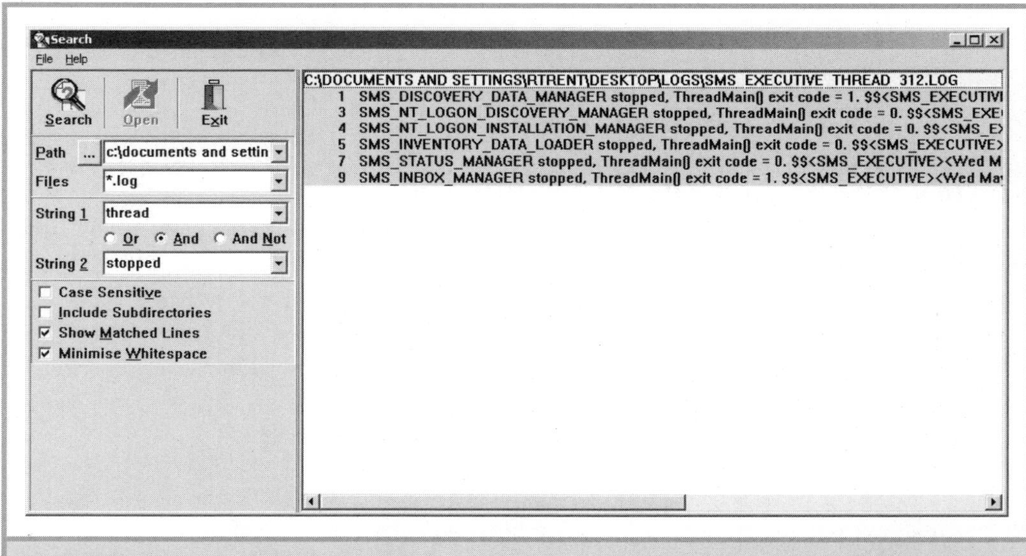

Figure 9-5. Search by SadMan Software

CAUTION: When you perform the search, copy the log files to another location first before running the utility against the files. If you run the utility on files that are open by an SMS process, the search will fail. This actually provides a perfect opportunity to copy the log files to your local hard disk and take them with you to review later.

Status Flow Checklists

The status system receives messages from both the SMS service components and the SMS thread components. While both component types can be configured to write to the Windows NT Application Event log file, there is a slight difference in the way they pass the status message to the Status Manager. The SMS service components write a physical file (*.svf) to the SMS\Inboxes\Statmgr.box\Statmsgs directory on the site server. The SMS thread components write the status message information to the in-memory queue of the Status Manager.

NOTE: Because the SMS service components write a physical file to be retrieved by the Status Manager, this file could become corrupt or the service component may have trouble writing to the \Statmsgs directory. If this happens, the SMS server component writes the status message to a temporary storage directory (%WINDIR%\SYSTEM32). You can find all files that match a wildcard file specification by omitting the search strings (i.e., \SMSmsgs\<ServiceComponentName>\ *.svf), and retrying the operation until it is successful.

Again, keep in mind that if allowed to, the SMS service components and the SMS thread components create status messages for everything: informational, errors, and warnings. Allowing all status messages to be written to the SMS database can increase the processing requirements of the server, the bandwidth requirements of the network, and the disk space requirements for the SQL database.

If you have logging enabled for several site components, you should use the status filter rules (accessed through the SMS Administrator console by going through site settings) to filter the types of status messages that are written to the SQL database. SMS includes several stock status filters to help minimize the status information, but you may need to add your own. For example, you may not wish to review information SMS Provider messages. By creating a new status filter rule, you can prevent this information from passing through the status system.

The status filter rules allow you to filter on the status source (SMS client, SMS Provider, and SMS server), a site code, a specific system, any of the SMS components, a message type (milestone, detail, or audit), the severity of the status message (information, warning, or error), and a specific status message ID.

Primary Site Flow

Here is an overview of the behavior of status messages on the primary site:

- If the status message originated from the service component, the message is read from the in-memory queue. If the status message stems from the thread component, the Status Manager reads the oldest status message from the SMS\Inboxes\Statmgr.box\Statmsgs directory on the SMS site server. The status messages have a *.svf extension.
- Status Manager uses the status filter rules to determine how the status message should be handled.
- If the status filter rules indicate that the status message should be written to the SMS site database, and this is the primary site, Status Manager writes the status message to the database. Also, if the status filter rules are configured to write the status message to the Windows NT Application Event log, Status Manager writes the status message to the log file.

NOTE: If the status filter rules are configured not to write the status message to the site database or the Windows NT Application Event log, the above item is skipped. The status message may have already been written to the log file if the status reporting settings have been configured to allow the thread or service component to make the write. This option is configured on the Actions tab of the Status Filter Rule Properties dialog box.

- If the status filter rules indicate that the status message should be reported to the status summarizers, Status Manager passes the status message to the summarizer's in-memory queue.

NOTE: The status filter rules can also be configured to pass the status message to a program that is executed. If the status filter rules have been configured this way, the external program is run at this point and the Status Manager process stops.

Child Site Flow

Here is an overview of the behavior of status messages on the child site:

NOTE: When a child site is first connected to the hierarchy, only new status messages (from the time of the connection) are forwarded to the SMS site server.

- If the status message has come from the service component, the message is read from the in-memory queue. If the status message has come from the thread component, the Status Manager reads the oldest status message from the SMS\Inboxes\Statmgr.box\Statmsgs directory on the SMS site server. The status messages have a *.svf extension.
- Status Manager uses the status filter rules to determine how the status message should be handled.
- If the status filter rules indicate that the status message should be written to the SMS site database, and this is the child site, Status Manager writes the status message to a *.svf file and places it in the \\<Servername>\SMS_<SiteCode>\Inboxes\Statmgr.box\Outgoing directory.
- Replication Manager forwards the *.svf file to the \\<Servername>\SMS_<SiteCode>\Inboxes\Statmgr.box\Statmsgs.box directory on the parent site.

NOTE: Also, if the status filter rules are configured to write the status message to the Windows NT Application Event log, Status Manager writes the status message to the log file. The status message may already have been written to the log file if the status reporting settings are configured to allow the service or thread component to write the information. This option is configured on the Actions tab of the Status Filter Rule Properties dialog box.

- If the status filter rules indicate that the status message should be reported to the status summarizers, Status Manager passes the status message to the summarizer's in-memory queue.

NOTE: The status filter rules can also be configured to pass the status message to a program that is executed. If the status filter rules have been configured this way, the external program is run at this point and the Status Manager process stops. The primary site has the *.svf file and will begin processing the status message.

Client Component Flow

In addition to providing the status information on the SMS site's services and components, the SMS status system also receives information from the client computer processes. The following flow indicates the steps that the client computer takes in order to pass the status information to the SMS site server for inclusion into the reporting scheme:

- The specific SMS client components generate a status message.
- A status message is written to the Application Event log if the client computer is running Windows 2000 or Windows NT, and the site's status reporting settings are configured to do so. If the site's status reporting settings are not configured to write to the Application Event log, or the client computer is running Windows 95 or Windows 98, this step is skipped.
- The specific SMS client component writes the status message to either the %WIN%, %TEMP%, or %TMP% directory on the client computer. This file is identified by a filename of svf????.tmp.
- Copy Queue moves the file to the CAP into the \Statmsgs.box directory.
- Copy Queue then renames the svf????.tmp file to *.svf.
- The Inbox Manager Assistant moves the *.svf file to the SMS site server into the \Inboxes\Statmgr.box\Statmsgs directory.
- Inbox Manager renames the *.svf to a new filename with the same .svf extension.
- The Status Manager reads the status message and starts the primary site flow process listed in the previous section.

Failed Components and Fatal Exceptions

Like other applications that run on the server, SMS services and threads can raise exceptions with the operating system. These exceptions are normally exhibited by the famous Dr. Watson debugger (drwtsn32.exe), and are caused by conflicts between the specific service and corrupt areas of memory, mismatched DLL files, or incompatible programs. By default, Dr. Watson is the debugger configured for Windows 2000 and Windows NT computers, but you can modify the operating system to use a different debugging tool in place of Dr. Watson. To determine the debugger that is configured for the server, navigate in the computer's registry to HKEY_LOCAL_MACHINE\SOFTWARE\Microsoft\Windows NT\CurrentVersion\AeDebug. The Debugger value lists the specific debugging tool command that is used by the computer when exceptions occur.

When an SMS service or thread raises an exception, it performs the following actions:

1. A status message (ID 669) is reported for the specific component.
2. A YYYYMMDD_HHMMSS_ServiceName folder is created in the SMS\Logs\CrashDumps directory on the SMS server. As an example, if the SMSEXEC service raised an exception, the new folder name could be 20000503_193515_smsexec where 2000 is the year, 05 is the month, 03 is the day, 19 is the hour, 35 is the minute, 15 is the second, and smsexec is the service name.
3. If logging for the service is turned on, all of the log files are copied into the new folder. If logging is not turned on, SMS still dumps the last 10 log messages in memory from every thread of the service into the folder.
4. In addition to the log files, a Crash.txt file is also created in the folder. The Crash file contains valuable information to aid in pinpointing the problem, as shown in the example following this numbered list.
5. The service quietly stops and then Site Component Manager attempts to restart the service in an hour.

```
EXCEPTION INFORMATION
Time = 05/03/2000 19:35:15
Service name = SMS_EXECUTIVE
Thread name = SMS_COMPONENT_STATUS_SUMMARIZER
Executable = F:\SMS\bin\i386\smsexec.exe
Process ID = 104
Thread ID = 404
Instruction address = 0x77F1D479
Exception = 0xEEEEFFFF (EXCEPTION_SMS_FATAL_ERROR)
Description = "Attempting to release a connection with a pending transaction!!!"
Raised inside CService mutex = No
CService mutex description = ""
```

This process continues until the exception is identified and rectified. When an exception is raised with the operating system, the only way to identify the source of the problem is to use a debugger to determine what conflicts exist within the server subsystem. By default, the debugger does not receive the information and you have no way of visibly knowing that there is a problem. You can enable the debugger to receive the exception by following these steps:

1. Use Notepad to create a blank file called die_evil_bug_die.sms.
2. Stop the SMS_EXECUTIVE service.
3. Place the die_evil_bug_die.sms file in the root of the server's C: drive.
4. Start the SMS_EXECUTIVE service.

With the die_evil_bug_die.sms file in place, the exception is handled in the same way as described earlier except now a debugger window will also display a pop-up message on the server's monitor.

NOTE: The pop-up message will only be displayed if the Auto value in the HKEY_LOCAL_MACHINE\SOFTWARE\Microsoft\Windows NT\CurrentVersion\AeDebug key is set to 0. If this value is set to 1, the next configured debug operation will be performed and the pop-up window will not be displayed.

Status System Gotchas

The SMS status system provides a wealth of information to help troubleshoot SMS site problems. To maximize the status system and to use it to its fullest potential, take special note of the items in this section.

Losing Status Messages During Server Shutdown

Status Manager gathers status messages for bulk processing, instead of committing them to the SMS database one at a time. This allows for better database efficiency and scalability. If you need to shut down the SMS server before these status messages have been written to the SMS database, these status messages could be lost. Status message IDs are stored in the server's registry. This ID is used as a primary key and is incremented for each status message that is written to the database. If Status Manager is not able to get the next ID because the security subsystem has already closed due to the system shutdown, the messages are discarded.

Since status messages are crucial to the SMS troubleshooting process, losing any messages could be disastrous. To keep from losing these messages, make sure to shut down the SMS_EXECUTIVE services before shutting down the server. When SMS_EXECUTIVE is shut down prior to the server shutdown, the security subsystem is still available and still able to pass the IDs required to write the messages to the SMS database.

Incorrect SQL Status Messages

SQL Server errors are handled the same way as the other SMS components. When a SQL error occurs, SMS records a status message with an ID range of 615–620, and displays it as an informational message. This is incorrect. The status messages should be displayed as follows:

- 615–618 = Informational
- 616–619 = Warning
- 617–620 = Error

SQL 6.5 and Status Messages

If you use Microsoft SQL Server version 6.5 to run the SMS 2.0 database, you may experience a scenario where not all status messages are displayed. This is due to using the default installation of SQL Server 6.5. When the default configuration is installed, SQL Server's system memory is set to 16MB (8,192 pages). This small size setting is insufficient for running certain SMS stored procedures. If you are able, you should upgrade SQL Server to 7.0. SQL Server 7.0 automatically sizes memory based on the workload. If you have other application's databases on the same server as SMS, and these require SQL Server 6.5, increase the SQL Server memory value.

Changing the SQL Database Size

The site System Status pane displays the SMS database and transaction log size. When SMS 2.0 is installed on a Windows 2000 server, and you manually change the SQL database size, the site System Status pane is not updated to reflect the changes. Stop and restart the SMS_EXECUTIVE service and then refresh the site System Status pane to register the change.

Disabling Component Status Summarizer Thresholds

The online help associated with the component status summarizer informs you that if you set the warning or critical threshold for any component to 0, this will disable the threshold. This feature does not work.

Assigning Nonexistent NetWare NDS Servers as a CAP

SMS 2.0 inadvertently allows you to assign a nonexisting NetWare NDS the role of client access point. SMS does not verify that the server exists, and since the server is not available, the status system will report an error ID 4711, which indicates that the server has 0 bytes free of available hard disk space. To fix the error, remove the nonexistent NetWare NDS server from the list of CAPs. Before assigning a NetWare NDS server to the role of CAP, make sure to manually verify that it exists.

Delete Status Messages Task Reports 0 Records Deleted

The Status Message Deletion Task runs to clean the SQL database of old status messages. When this is run, the SMS_SQL_MONITOR services always report a status message that indicates 0 records have been deleted, when, in fact, status messages have been deleted. To determine the exact number of status messages that have been deleted by the task, you must use the SMS_SQL_MONITOR log file. This means you must enable logging for SMS_SQL_MONITOR. After the log has been enabled and the task runs again, open the log and search for the DeleteDiscoveryItems line. This line will indicate the actual number of status messages that have been successfully deleted.

Chapter 10

Data Access and Manipulation

As the SMS services perform their processes, data is collected and forwarded to the site's SQL database. This central repository contains all the hardware and software inventory data, site status, site hierarchy properties, and package and advertisement information. Most of the management personnel who ask for data can't use SMS to extract the information they need, so your ability to present data in an easy-to-read format helps them understand the significance of the information you're collecting. For example, if the purchasing agent of the company needs to know how many computers need a RAM upgrade, you can extract the data and produce a nice-looking report, which is both appealing and descriptive. To accomplish this, you need the proper tools.

NOTE: You can access the SMS database through Microsoft SQL, but Microsoft doesn't support or recommend modifying the SMS data directly. When data is retrieved and manipulated, SMS provides the data joins and relationships for the data tables on the fly. Few relationships are between tables in the SMS SQL database. These are done on the fly as the data is queried.

Data Access Tools

SMS provides several tools that allow access to the data stored in the SMS SQL database, and other tools can be obtained from the SMS Resource Guide and from third-party vendors. The following sections outline the data access methods provided by Microsoft. These different solutions provide a plethora of ways to retrieve information from the SMS database. Mastering them all can expand your data-retrieval capabilities and enable you to choose the exact tool you need for any situation.

If you find the tools described in the following sections don't provide what you need for every scenario, check out these third-party vendors products for alternate solutions:

- **WebReports** from Computing Edge at http://www.computingedge.com
- **SnapReports for SMS** from Aelita Software at http://www.aelita.com/products/Snapreports.htm

NOTE: A Web-reporting tool (SMS Web Reporting) from Microsoft is currently under development. For a first look at this product, visit the following Web location: http://www.swynk.com/trent/Articles/SMSWebReports.asp.

MMC

The SMS Administrator Console, which is built around the *Microsoft Management Console (MMC)*, is the primary means of accessing the data in the SMS database. The console is a special MMC snap-in. Opening the SMS Admin Console reveals all the data stored in the SMS site database. Each Site Property, Collection, Query, and so on has a record tucked away in the SMS SQL database. When new information is added, such as a Collection, this information is inserted into the SQL repository, so it is centrally stored and can be centrally accessed and managed. When SMS Site information is modified, the changes are written to this central database.

CODE BLUE

For the MMC to connect with the SMS site database, SQL Server Named Pipes network support is required. If the SQL Server network support is configured incorrectly, the SMS utilities and services won't connect. In addition, if Named Pipes isn't enabled on the server when SMS is initially installed, the installation will fail. If the SQL Server Named Pipes network support isn't enabled or has been changed, follow these steps to correct the problem:

1. Run the SQL Client Configuration utility on the server.
2. Select the Net Library tab.
3. Select Named Pipes in the Default Network drop-down box.
4. Click Done.
5. Run the SQL Server Setup and click Continue twice.
6. Select the network protocol(s) you want SQL Server to use. In this case, choose Named Pipes.
7. Click OK.
8. When the Named Pipe name dialog box appears, click Continue.
9. Click the Exit to Windows button.

Exporting from the MMC

In addition to providing a direct window into the SMS site data, the MMC offers an export feature that enables you to save the information quickly that you see directly in the SMS Administrator Console. Most of the specific nodes in the SMS Administrator Console support this export feature. Exporting the information from the SMS Site Hierarchy node produces the example information shown in the following table.

Name	Type	Version	Build Number	State	
CIN-Cincinnati	OH Site Server	Primary	2.00.1444.200.0	1444	Active

To export SMS data from the MMC, highlight the node containing the data you want, and then choose Action | Export List. When the Save As dialog box displays, you have four file type options: Text (tab delimited), Text (comma delimited), Unicode Text (tab delimited), and Unicode Text (comma delimited). If you only want to view the data in a standard text format, you can choose one of the tab-delimited options. But, if you want to be able to view, modify, and manipulate the data, you should choose the Text (comma delimited) option. This file type format saves the file with a .CSV extension, which is easily imported into Microsoft Excel. (The preceding table was created with Microsoft Excel using this method).

NOTE: The Export function is only available with MMC version 1.2 or later of the MMC. If you need an upgraded version of the MMC, it can be obtained from http://download.microsoft.com/download/platformsdk/Utility/1.2/W9X2K/EN-US/IMMC.EXE.

MMC Options

Running the SMS Administrator Console from the shortcut created by its installation, runs the SMS MMC snap-in and allows access to the wealth of data the SMS agents have collected. But, using a few command line parameters, you can customize the way the SMS Administrator runs.

For example, you can open just the Resource Explorer by providing a specific command line. The Resource Explorer can be used to view the hardware and software inventory data collected for a specific SMS client.

To open only the Resource Explorer, use the following command line (the command should be typed as one continuous line):

```
mmc <driveletter>:\sms\bin\i386\explore.msc -s
SMS:ResExplrQuery="select * from sms_r_system where Name='<clientname>'
-SMS:Connection=\\<servername>\root\sms\site_<sitecode>
```

If you intend to use this method of opening Resource Explorer frequently, you can create a shortcut using the specific command line. The command must be modified with the following information:

- <driveletter> = The drive letter mapped to the SMS site server
- <clientname> = The client computer NetBIOS name
- <servername> = The SMS site server to which you are connecting
- <Sitecode> = The three-letter site code of the SMS site

If you know the actual Resource ID of the client computer, you can enter a shorter command line:

```
mmc <driveletter>:\sms\bin\i386\explore.msc -s SMS:ResourceID=<IDNumber>
-SMS:Connection=\\<servername>\root\sms\site_<sitecode>
```

Using the NodeInfo switch for the SMS Administrator Console identifies the Resource ID of the client computer. In addition to targeting only Resource Explorer to run, the SMS Administrator Console offers other command-line options that provide you with more functionality in the way the SMS site data is accessed or viewed. The command-line options, shown in Table 10-1, are primarily for those individuals who develop add-on solutions for SMS or who want to extend the SMS Administrator Console. Some of these options, such as the NodeInfo selection, can be extremely useful when you are trying to pinpoint specific data and data types for Queries and Collections. The command line syntax for the options in Table 10-1 is:

```
<driveletter>:\SMSADMIN\bin\i386\sms.msc /<option>
```

Command-Line Option	Description
/SMS:BuildMSC=1	Creates an .msc file without persisting the connection information in the file. The /SMS:Connection command-line option is ignored when you use the /SMS:BuildMSC option.
/SMS:Connection= <namespace path>	Connects to the given Windows Management Instrumentation (WMI) namespace.
/SMS:DeleteConfirmation=0	Disables the Delete Confirmation dialog box.

Table 10-1. SMS Administrator MMC Commands

Command-Line Option	Description
/SMS:NodeInfo=1	Adds a property sheet that contains node information (such as the GUID, WMI instance data, and the named values associated with the node) to a node's property page. You access the node information sheet by selecting the Node Information tab. Setting NodeInfo to 1 places the Node Information sheet last on the property page.
/SMS:NodeInfo=2	Adds a property sheet that contains node information (such as the GUID, WMI instance data, and the named values associated with the node) to a node's property page. You access the Node Information sheet by selecting the Node Information tab. Setting NodeInfo to 2 places the Node Information sheet first on the property page.
/SMS:ProviderLocale=<LocaleID>	Changes the code page the provider uses.
/MMF:DebugAll=n	A value of 1 is the same as using the /MMF:TraceEnabled, /MMF:DebugTrace, and /MMF:DisplayErrors command-line options. A value of 2 increases the verbosity of some of the debug statements.
/MMF:DebugErrors=1	Displays errors caught by the trace facility. Property sheet errors handled in a normal manner are also displayed.
/MMF:DebugTrace=1	Provides route tracing by calling the OutputDebugString API.
/MMF:TraceEnabled=1	Trace information is collected during the run-time operations of the framework.
/SMS:DebugPutInstance=n	A value of 1 enables the trace information to be written to the OutputDebugString API in debug builds only. A value of 2 displays a dialog box that contains the object text of the WMI object.
/SMS:DebugRoot=1	Adds the SMS Debug menu item to the context menu for the root node. This menu item gives you the option of dumping the central mediator. The central mediator is an internal SMS Administrator Console object.
/SMS:EE=238	Displays the names of those who worked on the SMS product. This option adds the Credits... menu item to the Action menu. Selecting the Credits... menu item displays the credits of those who worked on the SMS product. The credits scroll continuously until you press the Close button.
/SMS:ShowCmdLine=1	Causes the Status Message Viewer to display the parsed command line in a dialog box.
/SMS: Status MessageViewer="<name of executable file>"	Lets you specify the path and name of the Status Message Viewer.

Table 10-1. SMS Administrator MMC Commands *(continued)*

Crystal Info

As part of the SMS installation, Microsoft includes the Seagate Crystal Info reporting utility, from Seagate Software. Because Crystal Info is a MMC snap-in (located in the \SMS\Cinfo\SnapIn directory on the SMS site server, as Cisnapin.dll), it's available directly within the SMS Administrator Console. Located in the Tools node of the SMS Administrator Console, Crystal Info provides full-featured reporting. Crystal Info contains a subset of features also found in the full Crystal Reports product from Seagate Software, but this subset is optimized for use with the SMS data structure.

NOTE: Microsoft provides limited support for the Crystal Info snap-in. For the best support, use Seagate Software's Support Knowledge Base at http://support.seagatesoftware.com/library/kbase.asp.

Using the Crystal Info reporting tool is straightforward. You schedule the report to run and specify the domain account with which the report should be run.

You can schedule the report to run immediately or on a set recurrence schedule, such as once a day, once a week, every *n*th day of the month, and so on. The custom schedule allows the data in the report to be refreshed and available when it's needed.

Because the reporting tool is straightforward in its use, working with and modifying the reports isn't covered in this section. For more information on working with the Crystal Info product, look into purchasing a book on using Crystal Reports from Seagate Software. This section concentrates on the specific items identified as common issues when using the Crystal Info SMS snap-in.

Adding a Report from an External Source

When you create reports in the Crystal Info program, these reports are saved to the server's hard disk. This is the location from which the SMS Administrator Console retrieves the reports when they are selected to run. These saved reports can also be distributed to different sites in the hierarchy. Custom reports can take a long time to create and test, so having the capability to share the reports throughout the SMS hierarchy, instead of requiring each site to create their own reports is an advantage.

Crystal Info report files are identified with a .rpt file extension. The reports installed as part of the Crystal Info selection (the reports shown in the SMS Administrator Console) are located in the \SMS\Cinfo\Samples\SMS directory. Each type of report has its own folder name underneath this directory structure. The built-in reports exist in the following subdirectories:

- \Config
- \Hardware

- \ProdComp
- \Queries
- \Status

Adding a Crystal Info report to a SMS site isn't a quick process. The following three steps are involved:

1. Copy the report to the SMS site server that will use the report. Once the report is received, it can be installed anywhere on the network, as long as the SMS site server has the proper access rights. For better organization, though, you should plan to copy the report to the directory structure the SMS has already established. Create a directory under the \SMS\Cinfo\Samples\SMS directory and place the report file there.
2. Import the report. To import the report into the SMS site, the SetLocation.exe utility must be run from the \SMS\Cinfo\Winnt directory on the server.

NOTE: The SetLocation utility must be run on the SMS site server. Set Location cannot be run from another computer or workstation. To run the program successfully, you must either be physically at the server's console or connected through a Remote Control connection.

As shown in the following illustration, enter the Site Code, SMS server name, and an account that has the proper rights to add the new report. Once the information is entered, click the Update Report button. If the import succeeds, a dialog box displays, indicating the report was imported successfully. If the report import fails, verify the information you entered into the SetLocation utility fields, specifically the Account field.

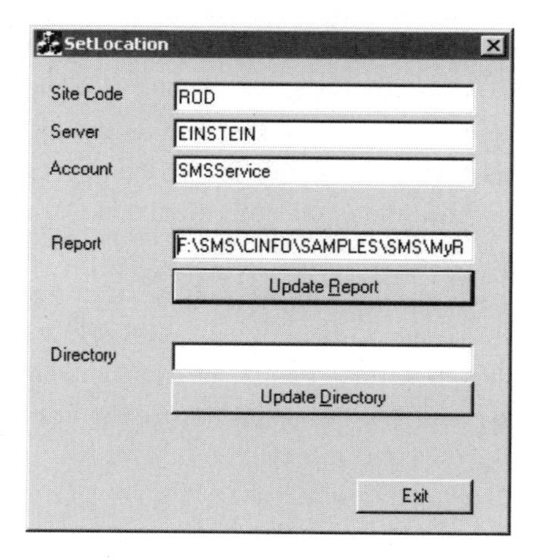

3. Add the report to the SMS Administrator Console. Open the SMS Administrator Console and go to the Reports section in the console tree by expanding the Tools node. If you want the new report to be placed into an existing Report folder, right-click the folder and choose New | Report Object.

NOTE: If you haven't already created a custom Report folder, you can create one by right-clicking the Reports node and choosing New | Folder. Give the new folder a name that's descriptive of the type of reports it will hold. Once the new folder is created, right-click the folder and choose New | Report Object.

When the New Report Object window displays (see the next illustration), enter the Report File Location (as a complete UNC path), the Title, and the Description. Once you click the OK button, the report is ready to be run and is available for the specific SMS Site until the report is removed.

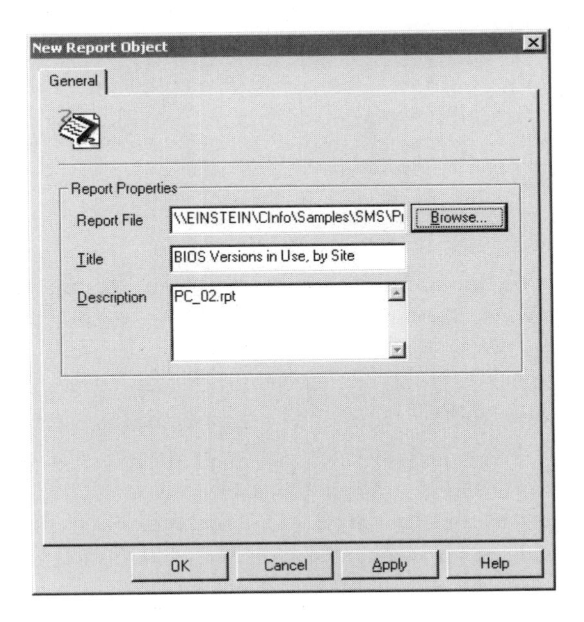

Crystal Info Best Practices

The Crystal Info SMS snap-in is an excellent tool for creating reports based on the database stored in the SMS database. Because of poor performance, however, Microsoft recommends that Crystal Info shouldn't be installed on a SMS server with more than 500 clients. A SMS server with more than 500 clients reporting to it increases the demands on the server's processing time. This can cause Crystal Info's performance to degrade as reports are scheduled and run.

To work around this issue, you should dedicate a server to house the Crystal Info component. This Reporting server functions as a central-report processing mechanism for the entire SMS site. The server performs no other SMS functions; it only provides reporting services to the site. To create a Reporting server, follow these steps:

1. Build a Windows NT or Windows 2000 server that is part of the domain in which the SMS site resides. This server should be a stand-alone member server in the domain and not a DC.
2. Start the SMS installation on the server and use the Custom Setup option.
3. When selecting the installation components, select only the Crystal Info option. Don't select any other SMS components from the list.
4. Follow the steps to complete the installation.

The Reporting server should be configured as the central site in your SMS hierarchy, with the other SMS servers in the hierarchy configured as child sites reporting to this server.

Crystal Info Gotchas

The SMS Crystal Info snap-in is a powerful tool that produces great looking reports. Crystal Info has been a problematic tool in the past, forcing companies to look elsewhere for reporting tools. Most of the problems were because of little documentation and public perception. To make Crystal Info work well in your organization, take special note of the issues covered here.

Crystal Info and Windows 2000 During the upgrade from Windows NT 4.0 to Windows 2000, the WMI ODBC driver is removed. This prevents Crystal Info from working. The WMI ODBC driver should be restored from the SMS 2.0 SP 2 compact disc rather than from the Windows 2000 compact disc because SMS 2.0 SP 2 includes a newer version.

Install the WMI ODBC driver using Wbemsdk.exe, which is in the \SMS\bin\i386 directory on the site server and in the \SMSSetup\bin\i386 directory on the SMS 2.0 SP 2 compact disc. From the command line, type

```
wbemsdk /s /server
```

The /s option must precede the /server option. This option configures the program to run silently.

NOTE: At press time, there's a newer release of the WMI Core and WMI SDK (version 1.5). They can be obtained from http://msdn.microsoft.com/downloads/sdks/wmi/default.asp. Previous versions of the WMI Core and WMI SDK could be overwritten with earlier offerings, but the latest upgrade has been developed with safeguards to make sure it cannot be overwritten with older versions. This means, if the newer version is installed on the computer, the WMI Core components from SMS 2.0 RTM, SP 1 and SP 2 won't overwrite the newer version, which would cause conflicting data between clients using the different versions. Also note, WBEMPERM (the executable included with the WMI Core components used to grant WBEM permissions to users and groups) is no longer available if this newer version is installed.

In addition, when you upgrade the SMS server from Windows NT 4.0 Service Pack 4 to Windows 2000, the Crystal Reports services (Info Agent, Info APS, and Info Sentinel) are all installed as local system accounts. This causes the Crystal Reports services to fail on startup. After the upgrade to Windows 2000, open the Services Control Panel applet and change the Crystal Reports services to use the SMS Service account.

CODE BLUE

The Services Control Panel applet isn't available through a default installation of Windows 2000. After Windows 2000 is installed (or upgraded), you must be logged in with an administrator equivalent account and follow these steps:

1. Choose Start | Settings | Taskbar & Start Menu.
2. Click the Advanced tab.
3. In the Start Menu Settings window, check the box next to Display Administrative Tools, and then click OK.

When the Administrative Tools are enabled, choose Start | Settings | Control Panel | Administrative Tools, and then choose the Services applet from the submenu.

Crystal Info and the SMS Service Account The Seagate Info Windows 2000/NT services: Info Agent, Info APS, and Info Sentinel, run under the default SMS service account (SMSService or whatever the account was named when SMS was installed). If the name of the service account or its password is changed, these Seagate Info services are unable to communicate until their properties are modified to use the new account or new account password. To modify the properties of the Seagate Info NT service, follow these steps:

For Windows 2000:

1. In the Windows 2000 Control Panel, open the Administrative Tools submenu and click the Services applet.
2. Double-click the Seagate Info service whose properties need to be modified.
3. In the Log On As group box, change the account under which these services are to be run, its password, or both. However, don't select the System Account.

For Windows NT:

1. In Control Panel, double-click the Services icon.
2. Double-click the Seagate Info service whose properties need to be modified.
3. In the Log On As group box, change the account under which these services are to be run, its password, or both. However, don't select the System Account.

NOTE: Don't change the account Seagate Info services runs under to a system account. The Info Agent, Info APS, and Info Sentinel must run as a user account that has the same rights as the SMS Service account.

Verify the ODBC Driver If the ODBC driver file on the SMS server isn't dated 1998 or later, you could experience Crystal Info reports that don't sort and group properly. The ODBC driver file is located in the \%SystemRoot%\System 32 directory on the SMS server. The file name is Wbemdr32.dll.

Simultaneous Access The Crystal Info reporting tool doesn't allow the same report to be open simultaneously in two different windows or by two different SMS Administrator Consoles. Only one person can access a specific report at a time. When this situation occurs, the only error message Crystal Info will report is "An Error Occurred Communicating With APS." This issue also presents itself if you created a new report and you try to add the report to a folder before the Info Report Designer is closed.

Verify the Info APS Service Has Started When you install the SMS Administrator Console on a Windows 2000 or Windows NT 4.0 computer while logged in as a domain administrator, the Info APS service doesn't start automatically. The Info APS service must be started for the Reports node to be accessible. Open the Services Control Panel applet and modify the Startup Type to Automatic for the Info APS service.

The Reporting User Account The primary cause of Crystal Info reports not running is the result of a problem with the specifics of the domain user account being used. When setting up an account for running reports, follow these guidelines:

1. The account must have the appropriate NTFS access permissions to the Crystal Report .RPT file. The account used must have at least Read (R), Write (W), and Execute (E) rights to the \SMS\CInfo directory.
2. Add the account to the SMS Administrator's user group.
3. The account must have the Act As A Part Of The Operating System advanced user right on the SMS site server.

NOTE: If you have to change the advanced user right on the account running the report, you must first stop the Crystal Info services (Info Agent, Info APS, and Info Sentinel), and then restart them.

SMS20Info

The SMS20Info utility is new to SMS 2.0 with the release of Service Pack 2 and is installed (along with many other support utilities) using the Support.exe installation file in the \Support directory on the service pack CD. After installation, SMS20Info.exe is located in the \Site Maintenance Tools\ subdirectory of the \SMS 2.0 Support Tools\ directory.

SMS20Info gathers more information from SMS clients or servers than you would probably want to see, but the information can be useful when determining processes that are running on a computer, loaded modules, specific BIOS information, active documents, and so forth.

Double-clicking the SMS20Info.exe file starts the program, and you are prompted for specific information concerning the SMS client or server, as shown in the following illustration.

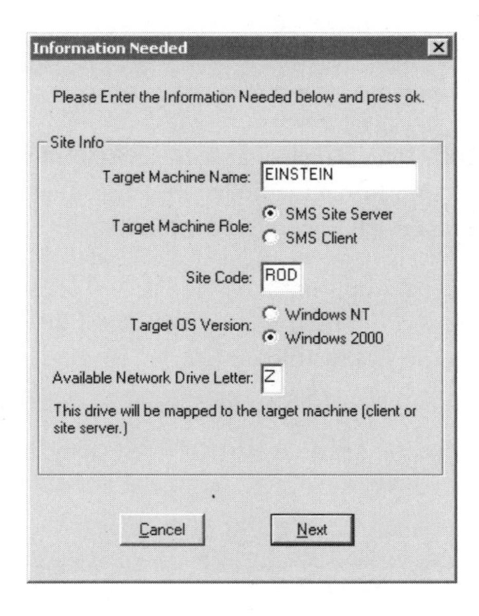

After you enter the requested information, SMS20Info performs the following steps:

- Creates SMSINFO_<Target> dir on C:
- Creates WinMSD report for site server
- Dumps SMS registry key
- Creates SMS\Inboxes directory summary
- Creates SMS\Bin\ directory summary
- Copies all logs from \SMS\Logs
- Stops and starts WMI on Site Server

CAUTION: Because of the differences in the WinMSD program between Windows NT and Windows 2000, if the SMS20Info program is run from a Windows NT computer, it won't produce a WinMSD report for a Windows 2000 computer.

SMS20Info takes a while to run, specifically as the registry dump is being performed, but the data retrieved is well worth perusing. You'll be surprised by both the amount and the type of information collected.

NOTE: You must have administrative rights on the targeted Site Server when running this utility. Additionally, you must have write access to the location from which this utility is run.

Windows Script Host

You can use Windows Script Host to retrieve information from the SMS database, either local or remote to the SMS server. When accessing the SMS site through a WSH script, the following WSH line is used in all instances to connect to the SMS server:

winmgmt1 = "winmgmts:{impersonationLevel=impersonate}!//*Server*\root\sms\site_*XXX*"

where

Server is the SMS Server NetBIOS name

XXX is the three-letter site code

Once you establish the connection to the SMS server in your WSH script, you can insert the specific SMS query that retrieves the data you are requesting. The following example can be used to connect to the SMS server and to retrieve software product information.

```
-- Begin Script

'This will build your WMI connection to SMS. Replace SERVER with the specific SMS
Server name.
'Replace XXX with the SMS 3-letter site code.

winmgmt1 = "winmgmts:{impersonationLevel=impersonate}!//SERVER\root\sms\site_XXX"

'Echo the connection and then get the object.
WScript.ECho winmgmt1
Set SystemSet = GetObject( winmgmt1 )

'Next, the query is run.  The query lists Machine Name, Product, and Product
Version.
'Then the query is run and displays all recorded instances.
strQuery = "select
SMS_R_System.Name,SMS_G_System_SoftwareProduct.ProductName,SMS_G_System_Software
Product.ProductVersion from SMS_R_System inner join SMS_G_System_SoftwareProduct
on SMS_G_System_SoftwareProduct.ResourceID = SMS_R_System.ResourceId"
Set objEnumerator = SystemSet.ExecQuery(strQuery)
for each instance in objEnumerator
WScript.Echo "-> " & instance.SMS_R_System.Name & " " &
instance.SMS_G_System_SoftwareProduct.ProductName & " " &
instance.SMS_G_System_SoftwareProduct.ProductVersion
Next

-- End Script
```

If you aren't familiar with the SMS query language—WQL—you can generate the queries in the SMS Administrator Console first, and then copy them into your WSH scripts. WQL is explained briefly in the next section.

Queries

The *SMS Query mechanism* is the means by which stored SMS data is manipulated. Using this mechanism, data can be retrieved, parsed, and filtered. When you use different tools to access the SMS data, including the Query node in the SMS Administrator Console, you are actually creating small WQL statements.

SMS supports a superset of the *Windows Management Instrumentation (WMI) Query Language (WQL)* known as Extended WQL. Both WQL and Extended WQL are retrieval-only languages used to create queries. Neither language can be used to create, modify, or delete classes or instances.

WQL and Extended WQL are based on the *American National Standards Institute Structured Query Language (ANSI SQL)* standard. They differ from standard SQL because they retrieve from classes rather than from tables, and they return instances rather than rows.

Extended WQL includes a much broader range of operations than WQL. The following SELECT clauses are supported by Extended WQL:

- DISTINCT
- COUNT
- JOIN
- WHERE
- ORDER BY
- UPPER, LOWER, and DATEPART functions

SMS 2.0 provides Query functionality from the *Microsoft Management Console (MMC)* SMS Administrator Console. The SMS WMI Query language supports the following value operators:

- IN ([value1], [value2], [value . . .])
- IN (subselect)
- BETWEEN ([value1] AND [value2])
- NOT IN ([value1], [value2], [value . . .])

- NOT IN (subselect)
- UPPER ([expr])
- LOWER ([expr])
- NULL ([expr] is NULL)
- NOT NULL ([expr] is not NULL)
- DATEPART ([part], [date 1]) (part = “mm”,”dd”,”yy”,”hour”,”minute”,”second”,”ms”) = (equal) < > or != (not equal) < (greater than) > (less than)

With SMS 2.0 Service Pack 2 or later, Extended WQL supports fully case-insensitive statements. Extended WQL supports the standard comparison operators, including LIKE and IN, and also subqueries.

WQL supports three types of queries:

- **Data queries**—Data queries are WMI WQL statements that request instances of classes.
- **Event queries**——Temporary event consumers, permanent event consumers, and event providers use Event queries. Event consumers use event queries to specify the events they're interested in, and event providers use them to specify the events they provide.
- **Schema queries**—Schema queries are WMIWQL statements that request class definitions and information about schema associations.

The SMS Administrator Console makes the creation of these WQL statements simple by providing a graphical interface that keeps the WQL statements in the background. These statements can still be viewed by clicking the Show Query Language button in a specific Query's property.

As an example, the following sample WQL statement enables you to query the SMS site to identify all the computers assigned to the site.

```
--Begin Query

select Name, SMSAssignedSites, IPAddresses, IPSubnets,
OperatingSystemNameandVersion, ResourceDomainORWorkgroup, LastLogonUserDomain,
LastLogonUserName, SMSUniqueIdentifier, ResourceId, ResourceType, NetbiosName from
sms_r_system where Client = 1

--End Query
```

Help for Learning WQL

WQL can be tough to learn because of the extent of the query language. A great resource to help learn the WQL objects and statements is at Microsoft's MSDN site. Go to http://msdn.microsoft.com/downloads/sdks/platform/platform.asp and download the SMS SDK.

This site offers the Platform SDK that includes tools, headers, libraries, and sample code for building Win32 applications. The Platform SDK download includes information on all Microsoft's applications, but you can choose to install only those items pertaining to SMS by choosing the following items during a custom installation:

1. Documentation / Management Services / Microsoft Management Console
2. Documentation / Management Services / Systems Management Server
3. Documentation / Management Services / Windows Management Instrumentation
4. Documentation / Networking/ Network Monitor
5. Build Environment / Systems Management Server Headers and Libs
6. Build Environment / WMI Headers and Libs
7. Tools / Systems Management Server Tools
8. Sample Code -> Management Samples / Systems Management Server samples
9. Sample Code -> Management Samples / WMI samples

This query was created using the graphical interface of the SMS Query tool, and then it was copied from the Query Statement Window. Based on the WQL statement, the information in Table 10-2 is displayed in the SMS Administrator Console (the specific Attribute Class associated with the display name is included).

As identified in the WQL statement, creating a query uses a specific syntax. WQL starts with the 'select' statement, followed by the 'from' statement, and ends with the 'where' statement. In a nutshell, WQL enables you to 'select' a specific instance (or instances) 'from' a specific attribute class (Object Type), based on a required operator ('where').

SMS provides WQL with the specific Object Types shown in Table 10-3.

NOTE: The SMS SDK provides a complete list of the WQL statements and the SMS data Attributes, Attribute Classes, and Object Types. In addition to the SMS SDK, Appendices B and C of the *Systems Management Server 2.0 Resource Guide* contain information on the object properties and the hardware inventory classes.

Displayed Field	Associated Attribute
Computer Name	Name
SMS Assigned Sites	SMSAssignedSites
IP Address	IPAddresses
IP Subnet	IPSubnets
Installed Operating System Name	OperatingSystemNameandVersion
Resource Domain or Workgroup Name	ResourceDomainORWorkgroup
Last Logon User Domain	LastLogonUserDomain
Last Logon User Name	LastLogonUserName
SMS Unique Identifier	SMSUniqueIdentifier
Resource ID	ResourceID
Resource Type	ResourceType
NetBIOS Name	NetbiosName

Table 10-2. Display Query Field and the Associated WQL Attribute Class Name

Queries are used to extract data and to output it in a specific manner. Within the SMS system, the queries are used by the Status Message system for creating reports and for creating Collections. Collections enable you to organize the discovered devices into folders within the SMS Administrator Console. A Collection created by using a specific query helps separate the client computers into manageable objects. For example, your organization may have both Windows NT and Windows 2000 computers in use by the user population. When

Attribute Class	Specific Attribute	Description
Advertisement	SMS_Advertisement	Queries on the site's specific Advertisement information.
IP Network Resource	N/A	No Attributes are associated with the IP Network Resource. Also, the IP Network Resource Attribute only supports direct editing of WQL. There's no option for using the SMS Query editing mechanism.

Table 10-3. Default Attribute Classes for Queries

Attribute Class	Specific Attribute	Description
Package	SMS_Package	Queries on the site's specific Package information.
Program	SMS_Program	Queries on the specific package's program details.
Site	SMS_Site	Queries on the SMS site itself.
Software Product Compliance	SMS_SoftwareProduct Compliance	Queries on the Software Compliance information (Y2K).
System Resource	The specific attributes for the System Resource depend on the SMS Site's settings for hardware and software inventory and collection gathering.	The System Resource contains all the Attribute Classes and Associated Attributes for the computers in the SMS site. Everything you see in Resource Explorer is available for the System Resource.
User Group Resources	SMS_R_UserGroup and SMS_G_UserGroup	The SMS_R_UserGroup WMI class consists of a single attribute class representing discovery data for user-group objects. This is a predefined class that is dynamically generated. The SMS_G_UserGroup WMI class is an abstract with no properties, which is currently unused.
User Resource	SMS_R_User and SMS_G_User	The SMS_R_User WMI class is also a Windows Management Instrumentation (WMI) resource class. It consists of a single attribute class representing the discovery data for User objects. This object type represents users in an SMS site hierarchy. The SMS_G_User WMI class is an abstract class with no properties, which is currently unused.

Table 10-3. Default Attribute Classes for Queries *(continued)*

distributing applications to the computer base, instances may occur where the distributed application will only run on Windows NT, and you don't want the Windows 2000 computers to receive the package. By using queries, SMS automatically fills your Collections with the proper computers.

Microsoft provides some stock Collections with the installation of SMS. These default Collections are installed for example only and, in most cases, don't meet the needs of an organization (although some might). Collections are similar to the directory structure on a computer, with the root folder at the top, and subdirectories (subcollections) underneath in a hierarchal fashion. When planning your Collections structure, you should consider creating Collections based on the composition of your company. For example, if you work in a large environment that encompasses different countries, you should create a Collections structure similar to the example in Figure 10-1. Each subcollection builds on the query from the previous one in the hierarchy.

You create a Collection from a query by following these steps:

1. Right-click the Collections folder, and choose New | Collection.
2. Type a name for the Collection.
3. On the Membership Rules tab, click Query Rules Property to add a query to the membership rules.
4. In the Query Rule Properties dialog box, click Browse, and then select the query for which you want to get a count.
5. Click OK three times to complete creation of the new Collection.

Query Tips

This section is dedicated to specific tips that you can use to perform your queries quickly. These tips can aid you in creating queries that can minimize the time spent extracting SMS data.

Site Object Types

When creating queries to retrieve SMS Site information, one Site Object type is the Site Status. Five values exist:

- Active = 1
- Pending = 2
- Failed = 3
- Deleted = 4
- Upgrade = 5

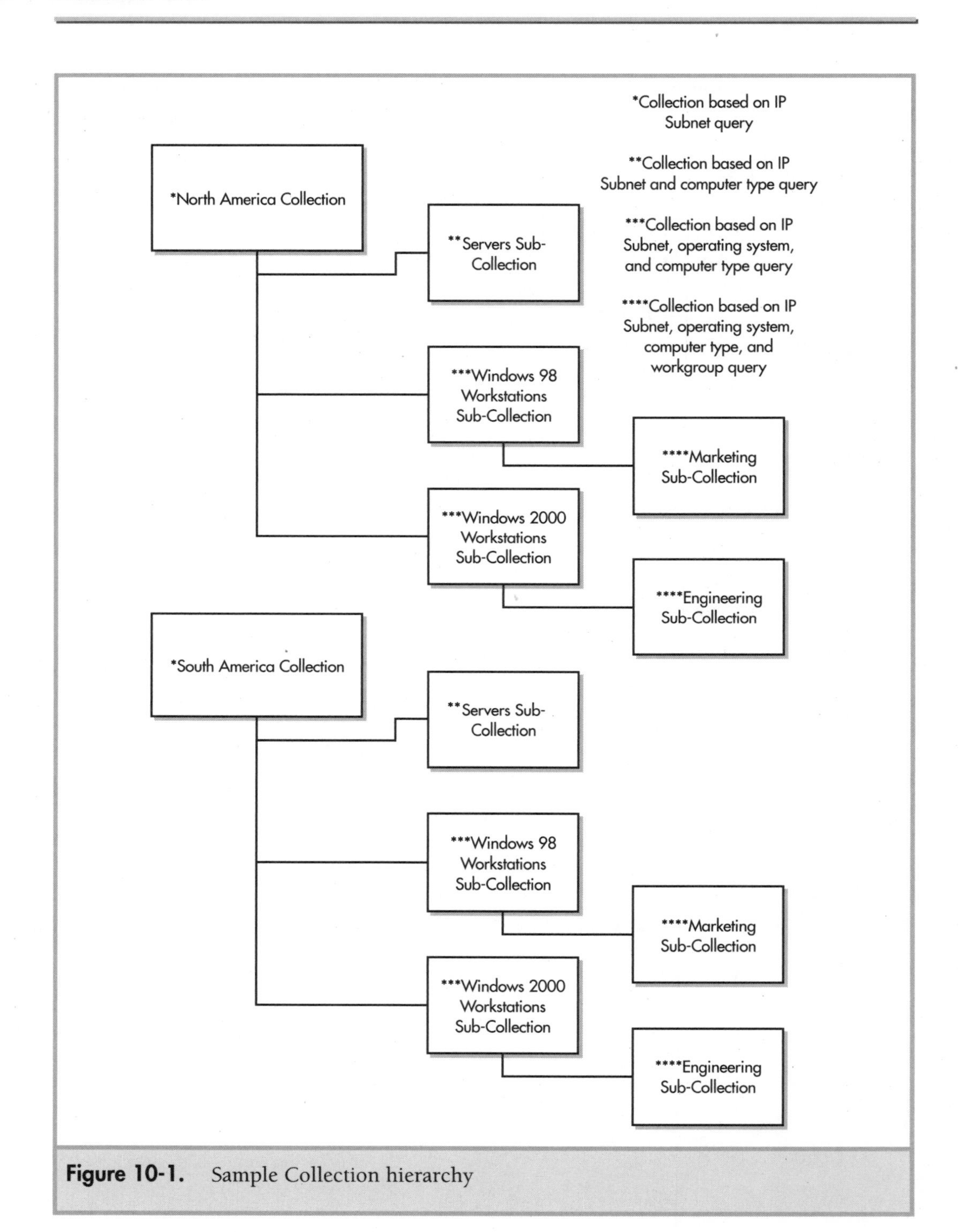

Figure 10-1. Sample Collection hierarchy

Also, to query on the different site types, use the following two values:

- Secondary Site = 1
- Primary Site = 2

The SMS_G_System Classes

When SMS 2.0 inventories the client computers on the network, the data is placed into specific SMS_G_System Resource Classes. These classes are listed with their descriptions in Table 10-4 to let you identify quickly the specific class that holds the information you want to retrieve. When you're creating queries through the SMS Administrator Console tool by coding a WQL statement or using Windows Script Host, these SMS_G_System classes can be used to retrieve specific hardware (and, in some cases, software) information.

Excluding the SMS Client Connection Account from Queries

When creating queries that target user names, you should exclude the SMSCliTknAcct& (SMS Client Connection Account) so it doesn't show up in your queries or in reports based on queries. On the Criteria tab in the Query Properties, add a Criterion based on the following information:

- Criterion Type: Simple Value
- Where: Computer System—User Name
- Operator: Is not equal to
- Value: SMSCliTknAcct&

Class	Description
SMS_G_System	Represents the current state specific object. When you update an object, the previous instance becomes a member of an SMS_GH_System history class. An SMS_GEH_System (extended history) class includes both the historical instances and the current instance of the object. Not every SMS_G_System attribute class has history and extended history classes.
SMS_G_System_CollectedFile	Contains information about files collected from clients.
SMS_G_System_Current	Is the parent of all hardware inventory classes representing the current state of the system, at the time of the last inventory. These classes have the prefix "SMS_G_System_" followed by all capital letters, such as SMS_G_System_ACCOUNT.

Table 10-4. The SMS_G_System Classes

Class	Description
SMS_G_System_ExtHistory	Derives hardware inventory class objects. It works the same way as the SMS_G_System_History class, except you must initiate a query to find an instance of an inventory class. These classes have the prefix "SMS_GEH_System_" followed by all capital letters, such as SMS_GEH_System_ACCOUNT classes.
SMS_G_System_History	Is the parent of all hardware inventory classes that contain history information on all systems.
SMS_G_System_LastSoftwareScan	Contains information about the most recent software inventory scan. It is an attribute class of SMS_G_System. It isn't a software inventory class controlled by sms_def.mof.
SMS_G_System_SoftwareFile	Contains information about software files found on the client computers that have a valid ProductId.
SMS_G_System_SoftwareProduct	Contains information about software inventoried on the client computer. This information is grouped by software company name.
SMS_G_System_UnknownFile	Lists resources by file name, if their *.exe and *.dll files don't have informational details embedded in them that can be extracted for the SMS software inventory.
SMS_G_System_ACCOUNT	Contains information about a user or group account.
SMS_G_System_BASE_SERVICE	Represents any service or process.
SMS_G_System_BOOT_ CONFIGURATION	Represents information required to restart a client computer.
SMS_G_System_CDROM	Represents the client CD-ROM drive information, such as manufacturer, media type, and availability.
SMS_G_System_COMPUTER_ SYSTEM	Represents the information about the client computer, such as the status, manufacturer, system role, and the computer name.
SMS_G_System_DESKTOP	Contains client computer desktop information, such as the wallpaper and icon spacing.
SMS_G_System_DEVICE_MEMORY _ADDRESS	Contains information about a *device memory address (DMA)*.
SMS_G_System_Directory	Represents the actual directories on the disk.
SMS_G_System_DISK	Represents physical disk drive information, such as the manufacturer, partitions, and the total number of sectors.
SMS_G_System_DISPLAY_ CONFIGURATION	Represents client display driver information, such as display frequency.
SMS_G_System_DISPLAY_ CONTROLLER_CONFIGURATION	Provides video adapter configuration information, such as bits per pixel and resolution.
SMS_G_System_DMA_CHANNEL	Contains information about a specific DMA channel on a client computer. This class is not enabled by default in the SMS_DEF.MOF file.
SMS_G_System_DRIVER_VXD	Identifies a virtual device driver.
SMS_G_System_ENVIRONMENT	Represents an environment or system variable on the client computer.

Table 10-4. The SMS_G_System Classes *(continued)*

Class	Description
SMS_G_System_GROUP	Contains information for user groups.
SMS_G_System_IRQ	Represents an interrupt request (IRQ) number, such as IRQ 11.
SMS_G_System_KEYBOARD_ DEVICE	Describes a client computer's keyboard specific information.
SMS_G_System_LOAD_ORDER_ GROUP	Represents a grouping of system services that define execution order dependencies.
SMS_G_System_LOGICAL_DISK	Represents information about a logical disk drive on a client computer, such as the volume name and file system.
SMS_G_System_MODEM_DEVICE	Represents data on the client computer's modem hardware.
SMS_G_System_MOTHERBOARD_ DEVICE	Represents client computer motherboard information.
SMS_G_System_NETWORK_ ADAPTER	Represents client computer network adapter information.
SMS_G_System_NETWORK_ ADAPTER_CONFIGURATION	Represents the configuration information of a network adapter.
SMS_G_System_NETWORK_CLIENT	Represents a client computer on a network.
SMS_G_System_NETWORK_ CONNECTION	Contains data pertaining to the client computer's network connection.
SMS_G_System_NETWORK_LOGIN _PROFILE	Contains the network login information of a specific user.
SMS_G_System_NT_EVENTLOG_ FILE	Contains information about a Windows 2000/NT log file on a client computer.
SMS_G_System_NT_LOG_EVENT	Contains events taken from Windows 2000/NT log files.
SMS_G_System_OPERATING_ SYSTEM	Represents any 32-bit Microsoft operating system.
SMS_G_System_OS_RECOVERY_ CONFIGURATION	Contains information about how a client computer's operating system is configured to perform during a failure.
SMS_G_System_PAGE_FILE	Contains information about a client computer's paging file.
SMS_G_System_PARALLEL PORT	Represents information about a parallel port on a client computer.
SMS_G_System_PARTITION	Represents an area of a physical disk on a Win32 system.
SMS_G_System_PC_ANALYSER	Contains information on products that were found by the Y2K PC analyzer.
SMS_G_System_PC_BIOS	Contains information about the BIOS of a client computer.
SMS_G_System_POINTING_DEVICE	Represents the client computer's pointing device.
SMS_G_System_PORT	Contains information about a specific port on a client computer system.
SMS_G_System_POWER_SUPPLY	Contains information on the *uninterruptable power supply* (*UPS*).
SMS_G_System__PRINTER_ CONFIGURATION	Represents printer configuration information.

Table 10-4. The SMS_G_System Classes *(continued)*

Class	Description
SMS_G_System_PRINTER_DEVICE	Represents information about the capabilities and status of a printer.
SMS_G_System_PRINT_JOB	Contains information about print jobs pending on a client printer.
SMS_G_System_PROCESS	Represents information about a process running on a client machine.
SMS_G_System_PROCESSOR	Represents client processor information, including the family, manufacturer, and version number.
SMS_G_System_PROGRAM_GROUP	Contains Windows program group information.
SMS_G_System_PROTOCOL	Represents information about a network protocol installed on a client computer.
SMS_G_System_REGISTRY	Contains information about the client computer's registry.
SMS_G_System_SCSI_CONTROLLER	Represents a SCSI controller on a client computer.
SMS_G_System_SERIAL_PORT	Represents client computer serial port information.
SMS_G_System_SERIAL_PORT_CONFIGURATION	Represents information about the serial port configuration on the client computer.
SMS_G_System_SERVICE	Represents a service running on a client computer.
SMS_G_System_SHARE	Represents a directory on the client computer that has been configured to be shareable.
SMS_G_System_SOUND_DEVICE	Contains information about sound devices installed in the client computer.
SMS_G_System_SYSTEM	Contains information about a client computer's system.
SMS_G_System_SYSTEM_ACCOUNT	Contains information about the client computer system.
SMS_G_System_SYSTEM_DRIVER	Represents the system driver for a hardware service.
SMS_G_System_SYSTEM_MEMORY_RESOURCE	Represents system memory location information.
SMS_G_System_TAPE_DRIVE	Represents a tape drive attached to a client computer.
SMS_G_System_TIME_ZONE	Represents the time zone set for a client computer.
SMS_G_System_USER	Contains information about an individual user account.
SMS_G_System_VIDEO	Represents information about a client video subsystem.
SMS_G_System_WORKSTATION_STATUS	Contains information about when inventory was last collected on a client computer.
SMS_G_System_X86_PC_MEMORY	Represents client memory configuration information, such as page file space and virtual memory.

Table 10-4. The SMS_G_System Classes *(continued)*

Querying for NULL Values

If you want to find computers that have a NULL value for instance, the SMS query will error-out during setup of the query. You can still query collections for a NULL value by typing a space in the field (press the keyboard space bar once). The space acts the same as a NULL entry.

The Subselect (NOT) Query

In SMS 1.2, when you wanted to create a query based on a piece of software that didn't exist on the SMS clients or a piece of hardware that wasn't installed, you could click the NOT button, the query was created, and then it was run. The "NOT" query was a particularly useful method of identifying computers that needed to have a piece of software installed during a rollout. For example, you could quickly identify the SMS site's entire client computer base that didn't have the latest virus update installed. This aspect is still available in SMS 2.0, but the process has changed.

The following example demonstrates how the new process is used to create a query to list computers that don't have Microsoft Excel installed. In SMS 2.0, you must create two queries to produce the same result as you achieved with SMS 1.2. The first query gives you a list of all SMS clients *with* the software installed. The second query returns a list of all SMS clients who *don't have* the software installed, but it relies on the first query to obtain the information.

Query 1 Create the first query like this:

1. Right-click Queries and choose New | Query.
2. Give your query a name similar to All Systems with Microsoft Excel.
3. Click Edit Query Statement.
4. On the General tab, click the add button.
5. On the Result Properties dialog box, click the Select button.
6. Select System under Attribute Class, and then select the Name attribute.
7. Click OK.
8. Click OK again to close the Result Properties dialog box.
9. Next, select the Criteria tab, and then click the Add button.
10. On the Criterion Properties dialog box, click the Select button.

11. On the Select Attribute dialog box, select the Attribute class Software Files and choose File Name as the Attribute.
12. Click OK.
13. On the Criterion Properties dialog box, leave the Operator set to *is equal to* and type **excel.exe** in the Value field.
14. Click OK to close the Criterion Properties dialog box.

Now you have designed the query that finds systems with the software. You can use this query in your subselected query to find systems that don't have this software.

Query 2 To create the subselected query:

1. Right-click Queries and choose New | Query.
2. Give your query a name similar to All Systems w/out Microsoft Excel.
3. Click Edit Query Statement.
4. On the General tab, click the Add button.
5. On the Result Properties dialog box, click the Select button.
6. Select System under Attribute Class, and then select the Name attribute.
7. Click OK.
8. Click OK again to close the Result Properties dialog box.
9. Next, select the Criteria tab, and then click the Add button.
10. Use the Criterion Type pull-down list to select Subselected values as your Criterion Type.
11. Click the Select button.
12. On the Select Attribute dialog box, select the Attribute class System and choose Name as the Attribute.

NOTE: You used System.Name as the results for your first query.

13. Click OK.
14. On Criterion Properties, set the Operator to *is not in*.
15. Click Browse, under Subselect.
16. On the Browse Query dialog box, select the All Systems with Microsoft Excel query that you created previously.

17. Click OK.
18. Notice the WQL statement query from your first query is pulled into your subselect statement for this query. Click OK.
19. Click OK again, and then click OK one last time to save the subselect new query.

The second query uses the WQL statement resulting query. You now have a query that uses the results of another query (the subselected values) to create its own data result set.

Query Gotchas

The Query function of SMS is a critical tool for creating Collections, viewing System Status information, and for extracting data. To use the SMS Queries, the following information should be noted to allow for uninterrupted access.

SMS_R_System vs. SMS_G_System

The SMS_R_System class is an array based on several SQL tables. In the SMS Administrator Console Query Builder, SMS_R_System is listed as the System Resource class. If you use the SMS_R_System class in a query that uses joins, you may receive inaccurate results that lists duplicate information, even though the Omit Duplicate Rows option is checked.

Instead of using SMS_R_System, use the SMS_G_System class in your queries. SMS_G_System is the Computer System class in the SMS Administrator Console Query Builder.

WQL Date Format

Several WQL references indicate the Datetime format for retrieving time information should be yyyymmddHHMMSS.mmmmmmsUUU. If you create a SMS query based on this format, you will receive a Generic Failure error message. Instead of using the Datetime format, use the Datepart operator. For example, the following Datetime format will fail:

```
select * from sms_statusmessage where time="20000404000000.000000+000"
```

The following Datepart operator works fine:

```
select * from sms_statusmessage where datepart (mm, time) = 04 and datepart (dd,
time) = 4 and datepart (yy, time) = 2000
```

BUG ALERT: If you create a query that has a join to an array column, you receive the following error message when the query is run: **Out of Virtual Memory**. When you press OK to continue past the Out of Virtual Memory error, you receive another error message: **The thread %lu (0x%x) completely used up its stack and raised an exception_stack_overflow exception**. This is a confirmed bug in SMS 2.0, even with Service Pack 2 applied.

911

Index

References to figures and illustrations are in italics.

C

D

E

F

G

H

I

K

L

M

R

S

T

U

V

W

Z